Basics and Applications of Sociology

James W. Grimm
Amy C. Krull
D. Clayton Smith
Western Kentucky University

KENDALL/HUNT PUBLISHING COMPANY
4050 Westmark Drive Dubuque, Iowa 52002

Contents

Unit 4

Unit 5

Unit 6

Preface to Instructors and Students

Our teaching philosophy for introductory sociology textbooks includes the following points: First, reading material should illustrate sociological theory and concepts, including terms frequently used in our field. Second students need to see how sociology can come alive by reading short essays and articles that illustrate specific sociological concepts. Third, students at the introductory level need checks on their reading comprehension by taking quizzes over material. Finally, students more fully grasp the sociological imagination when they complete exercises or applications in which they must apply sociological concepts to themselves and in their everyday lives.

Current options to meet these needs are limited. One can choose a standard, hardcover, edition. These usually come with a variety of supplements-study guide books, CDs, interactive websites, etc.- although usually at increased cost to the student. One can also choose a compilation of sociological readings. To remain faithful to our teaching philosophy, we would have to require the student to buy a variety of these texts, each of which would not fully be covered during the semester, as only parts of each would likely be used, and resulting at a significant cost to our students.

The creation of this text was the solution to our dilemma. It combines the basic concepts of sociology, quizzes, readings and exercises in one comprehensive, low-cost text. We feel it is an excellent solution and can serve a variety of instruction needs. It is useful as a stand-alone text, during any semester, giving the instructor freedom to incorporate a large range of lecture material. It might be especially useful during compact semesters such as summer sessions. It is cost-effective enough, so additional books of the instructor's choosing could also be required reading. We also see it as a supplement to brief editions, where it could be used to reiterate and expand concepts and to increase exercises and applications.

Introductory courses in sociology can be quite challenging, especially to the incoming first-year students, who are most of our introductory sociology students. Introductory sociology courses include an unusually diverse and broad ranging curriculum: from parenting to global political interrelationships, from attitudes toward sex roles to theories about crime rates, from differing theoretical perspectives on human behavior to the presentation and discussion of statistical information in the tables, charts, and graphs. The material to be covered and the limited time in which to do so demand fast-paced learning, which adds to the challenge for introductory sociology teachers and their students. To this end, a variety of educational resources can help in learning.

This volume is the outcome of our continuing efforts to adapt our introductory courses, texts, and class presentations to the changing needs of our students. Student comments and reactions to our introductory courses have led us to the conclusion that a volume like ours -with condensed text, expanded topics, and applied exercises- serves both the academic and economic needs of our students. Students in our courses consistently have enjoyed the sorts of brief introductions and exercises included here, many of which concern topics and applications we have developed because they are unavailable in other texts. Moreover, students enjoy exercises related to students' campus and hometown experiences, allowing them to see sociology as a part of their everyday lives.

Beyond simply being an economical and efficient way of learning, we feel that there are other very useful benefits to our text. First, we are convinced that new ways of assessing student performance in introductory sociology are needed. Because of their test anxiety, many students respond poorly to the midterm and final examination format, especially if only multiple-choice questions are used. Such exams serve the professor's schedule more than the student's learning. Furthermore, poor student performance is not sufficiently improved by altering the content of an essential text that is still 500 pages or by providing aids. We believe students, if given the choice, perform better when they are given more exercises and written work. These changes allow introductory sociology students to appreciate material better and perform better overall if they have shorter text material and more applications. Second, since the costs of comprehensive sociology texts and their supplements are already quite high, we believe that using a shorter text is much more economical. We ourselves typically use a paperback version of a comprehensive text and a supplement. Consequently, we have worked very hard to produce a text that is both economical and still covers a broad range of sociological topics. Third, the student reactions to and performances on applied exercises have convinced us that students learn more by completing assignments and application exercises that are understandable through their own lives. We have carefully developed material, and exercises, and carefully selected the readings in this volume so that they relate to student experiences.

We have used various forms of the material that we include here in our introductory classes. Students have enjoyed and benefited from completing a series of independent exercises either as a supplement to exam scores or substitute for a low exam score. We have also found that the material helps students prepare for exams, especially for essay questions. Writing about sociological terms and issues is very good test practice. We have also used the material to represent the essay portions of tests.

While we have developed our book, in part, as a supplement for comprehensive texts, we believe that our text may be used as a primary text. For example, we have especially felt the need to move away from a lengthy and costly comprehensive introductory text when teaching shorter courses, such as the three-week May term and the five-week summer sessions. We hope that others who teach such courses or want a book that covers material broadly, but in less depth, will find our book very useful. Moreover, on-line courses, evening, and weekend courses may find our combination of shorter expositions and more critical thinking exercises suitable for their instructional needs. In longer semester classes, using our text as the primary learning instrument supplemented by use of many excellent readers now available is possible. We strongly believe that sociology becomes more accessible from short chapters, readings that present the research and viewpoints of working sociologists, and exercises than from a lengthy compendium of comprehensive text chapters.

While we believe that students in all types of class settings and in various types of institutional settings would benefit by using our book, we have attempted to focus our text and our exercises to comprehensive universities in less urban environments. Often examples in modern textbooks are inaccessible to our students because they are not in a world city with a subway or a bus system.

In sum, our fifty years of collective experience in teaching introductory sociology have been at six different universities, varying in both size and type. We believe that we have developed a text that will appeal to and be appropriate for students in the wide variety of classroom situations. Primarily, we hope it either can be used as a standalone text or combined with a reader. We welcome reactions to our volume and hope that it can continue to serve others' needs as well as it does our own, as we all continue to improve our introductory sociology courses and student performance in them.

Jim Grimm
Amy Krull
D. Clayton Smith

Acknowledgments

We gratefully acknowledge these people's help in developing the book: Jay Dougherty for his cover art work; Judith Grimm for her help in selecting films for the exercises, Stephen Groce, Tamela Maxwell, and Eric Mielants for their editorial service and Joan Krenzin for assistance in identifying potential adopters of this textbook.

UNIT

ONE

Sociologists study people in their social settings. Individuals are important, but society is more than the sum of individuals. To think sociologically, imagine the symbolic and sociological meaning of the marriage candle that is both larger and higher on the candelabra than the candles representing the two people getting married. The patterns of social activity in social settings—from spouses in their marriage to workers in their workplace to citizens in their native countries—have a reality more important and complex than the sum of the people involved.

In this first unit, we cover important theoretical viewpoints and concepts sociologists use to study how people are influenced in social settings. These main theories in sociology are presented as different approaches to social life. Similarly, we review the major research approaches sociologists use to study different social settings, depending both on the objective of the study and the types of settings.

We have included a chapter in this unit to show how sociologists conduct research. We do so to introduce the techniques that comprise the research skills important to the private sector and areas of government like schools and criminal justice. Such skills have very marketable value in the many jobs for sociologically trained people who strive to understand social life in order to retain aspects that work and to identify and improve what can be improved.

Sociological Theories

Sociological theories are interrelated sets of explanatory statements about social life. Theories develop in several ways. Inductive theories develop through investigations and interpretations of the patterns observable in the information available on people in social settings. Emile Durkheim's classic explanations of suicide rates among different groups emerged from his extensive scrutiny of death certificates (Durkheim 1966). George Herbert Mead and Charles Horton Cooley developed influential theories of childhood maturation based upon observations of their own and others' children (Cooley 1964; Mead 1962). Deductive theories develop by means of researchers formulating predictive statements and then testing them with evidence from social settings (Babbie 2002). Theoretical predictions about the lifelong advantages of educational attainment for mobilizing economic resources and for maintaining health have been supported by the results of studies of national samples of adults (Mirowsky and Ross 1998; Ross and Mirowsky 2000).

A sociological theory develops not as a complete explanation of all facets of social reality, but as a logical and relevant explanation of selective aspects of the social world. Conflict theory focuses upon explanations of the contentious aspects of social life like competition, argument and debate, conflicts of interests, the ways powerful groups dominate weaker ones, and the ways ideas of wealthy and powerful people influence the social order. Functional theory, in contrast, develops explanations of the mechanisms that unify the participants in groups and organizations and the ways that groups change to adapt to their social environments. How a restaurant staff adapts to customers' needs at rush hours or how a manufacturing firm adapts to competition and changing consumer tastes illustrates the uses of functionalist theory. Symbolic interactionism provides explanations of the ways in which commonly understood and accepted meanings for words, behaviors, objects, and gestures enables meaningful interrelationships among people in social settings. Appropriate and diverse behavior reflecting such common understandings for action in church services, parties, job interviews, and family reunions illustrate the application of symbolic interactionism. In their entirety sociological theories complement each other in focusing upon diverse aspects of social life. No one theory is a complete explanation, nor is any one theory intended to be (Ritzer 2000).

Theories also vary depending upon the social entities upon which their explanations are focused. Micro-theories provide explanations of small social contexts such as families, married couples, work teams, committees, boards of directors, and so on. Macro-theories deal with explanatory ideas relevant for understanding whole societies, major geographical areas such as large metropolitan areas, social class systems, and societal institutions like economies and types of government. Meso-theories, or so-called middle-range theories, develop explanatory ideas for middle-size social entities such as organizations, public agencies, political parties, and interest groups like unions. Increasingly, American sociologists have developed multilevel theories that interrelate explanations of micro and macro levels, such as George Ritzer's multilevel explanation of individuals' credit card debt and societal level problems in overextended credit and bankruptcies (Ritzer 1995). (See Chapter 15.)

Sociological theories vary greatly in terms of the specific concepts and the social process upon which they focus. This diversity of ideas can be illustrated by brief references to the three sociologists who have been recognized by the National Academy of Sciences' MacArthur Awards, or the so-called genius awards: Gary Becker, Robert Merton, and William Julius Wilson. Becker's theories deal with the social factors in the creation and reward processes of resource allocation and markets. His concept of human capital refers to aspects of social advantage in seeking employment such as higher skills, greater education, and successful employment experiences. He has analyzed the degree to which people's salaries are commensurate with their human capital (Becker 1971). Robert Merton has been recognized for his theoretical ideas about the consequences of social actions (or functions), especially unintended consequences (or latent functions). He has analyzed diverse social arenas to illustrate his theoretical ideas including scientific research that often unintentionally discovers technologies that were not the focus of the research (Merton 1968). William Julius Wilson received his award to recognize his ideas in explaining an underclass, or permanently poor people in various urban or rural areas. His and others' studies of job availability have confirmed his idea that long-term unemployment is the primary cause of the social problems experienced by permanently poor people. The absence of employment opportunity explains their lack of economic resources and not their ethnic background or moral deficiencies (Wilson 1996).

Generalizability refers to the range of applicability a theory has in a society. A theory of juvenile delinquency called social control theory has been widely verified in studies of youth in different cities in the United States and elsewhere. As the theory predicts, youth with fewer close social ties (or bonds) with community groups like youth centers and churches and who spend less time with coaches and teachers are more likely to become or remain delinquents (Hirschi 1969). (See Chapter 5.) Isomorphism is the idea that a theory's explanatory principles are relevant for and have application at more than one level of analysis: the micro and meso levels, for example. The principles of social exchange theory have been widely verified at the micro and meso levels. Individuals in small groups as well as organizations like banks, insurance companies, and larger manufacturing firms establish and maintain social relationships by exchanging different and valuable social commodities such as love, capital funds, trust, and so on (Carruthers and Babb 2000; Wellman and Frank 2001). (See Chapter 14.)

Hermeneutical contexts refer to the idea that theoretical principles reflect the viewpoints and experiences of the theorists. Such contexts are used to explain how the focal issues and explanatory ideas of a theory are delimited by the types of social experiences of people applying the theory as an explanation. Several important theoretical perspectives in sociology stress hermeneutics. One such perspective is ethnomethodology that seeks explanations of the everyday meanings people accept without questioning them, such as polite behavior or the rules for conversation. Feminist theory focuses upon theoretical explanations of aspects of the social world such as family life and paid employment from the viewpoint of women's traditional experiences. The increasing emphasis in sociological theories upon the diverse meanings that different types of people have for social life, such as "love" or "fairness," and how those meanings develop and change in various social settings is called post modernism. The general process such an emphasis is trying to explain is called the social construction of reality, or the social processes that create and change the diverse meanings of ideas and actions in social settings in postmodern society. Contemporary society is characterized by many diverse subcultures and social categories with different meanings for ideas and actions in church, at home and elsewhere (Ritzer 2000).

Sociological theories are updated and adapted through replication and verification. Replication occurs when existent theories are retested, often in new settings, new locations, and with different types of people. For example, theoretical explanations of supportive parental involvement in schools developed in schools with whites and African American children could be retested by studies of such ideas in schools with many non-English speaking Hispanic parents. Or, theories of successful organizational operations in the manufacturing sector could be replicated among firms in the financial sector like large insurance companies. All sociological theories should be replicated to take into consideration the continuing changes of social life. Theories of family life and employment, for example, must be replicated to reflect the rapid increase and present predominance of dual-employed parent couples, including same-sex couples (Hochschild and Manchung 1989). (See Chapter 11.)

Verification is the extent to which existent theoretical ideas and principles are confirmed or denied in replication. The results of replication may confirm the entire theory, parts of it, or little of it. Or, in replication it may be found that the theory applies to workers in some industries but not others, to boys but not girls, or to some types of organizations such as for-profit firms but not to governmental agencies or nonprofit hospitals. Sociologists gain as much understanding from partial verification as they do from complete verification, since partial verification yields a means of understanding the limitations to theoretical explanation. For example, the theoretical principles behind early prison release programs may be verified among men who have access to employment but not among men with few skills and no job prospects. Or, theoretical principles that explain effective health care delivery in suburban areas may not work in certain areas of the inner city or in rural areas. Knowing when theories do not work enables sociologists to develop new and more relevant explanatory models. This is especially true in multilevel explanations of such issues as health care resources that show that health insurance is not always adequate for all household health needs (Smith, Grimm and Brewster 2002).

Naturally, with the increasing diversity of the U.S. population and the increasing multicultural composition to American life, including the increasing proportion of Americans who are active and healthy into their 80s, sociological theories will be in need of updating and alterations in the decades ahead. (See Chapters 13 and 14.)

Name: ______________________________

Quiz Questions: Sociological Theories

1. Developing a theory of consumer behavior by watching people shop would illustrate a deductive theory. (True or False?)

2. A sociological theory usually is a complete explanation of all facets of social reality. (True or False?)

3. Which of these sociological theories provides explanations for commonly understood meanings in social life?

   a. conflict theory
   b. symbolic interactionism
   c. functionalist theory
   d. feminist theory

4. A theory of how hospitals operate most effectively would be which of these types of theory?

   a. macrotheory
   b. mesotheory
   c. microtheory
   d. none of the above

5. Unintended consequences of social action were stressed by which of these sociologists?

   a. Charles Horton Cooley
   b. William Julius Wilson
   c. Gary Becker
   d. Robert Merton

6. The idea that theoretical ideas reflect the social experiences of the theorists who develop theories is which of these ideas?

   a. isomorphism
   b. hermeneutical contexts
   c. generalizability
   d. none of the above

7. Finding out that an existent theory's ideas apply in a current study in urban areas but not in rural areas primarily illustrates replication. (True or False?)

8. It is unlikely that most present sociological theories will need to be verified in the next 25 years. (True or False?)

9. Wilson's theory of the underclass stresses how traits of people's character, such as work motivation explain permanent poverty. (True or False?)

10. Which of these theorists stressed the idea of "human capital"?

    a. George Herbert Mead
    b. Robert Merton
    c. Gary Becker
    d. William Julius Wilson

Name: ____________________________

Exercise: Sociological Theories

1. In the space provided, illustrate some examples of social processes on your campus that conflict theory could be used to explain.

Name: ______________________________

Exercise: Sociological Theories

2. In the space provided, discuss how a campus group you are a member of—sorority, drama club, and so on—would be studied by one of the theories discussed in this chapter.

Name: ______________________________

Exercise: Sociological Theories

3. Think about a recent shopping trip you made to a mall. In the space provided, discuss how the trip illustrated *any two* of these ideas: symbolic interactionism, functions, social exchange theory, micro-theories, and ethnomethodology.

Name: ______________________________

Exercise: Sociological Theories

4. Think about a recent social event on campus (a dance, sports event, or club meeting, for example) and in the space provided, discuss how the event you were a part of illustrated symbolic interactionism, functions, social exchange theory, micro-theory, and macro-theory.

Name: ______________________________

Exercise: Sociological Theories

5. Watch the science fiction movie classic, *The Day the Earth Stood Still*. In the space provided, discuss how the movie illustrated *any two* of these ideas: <u>conflict theory</u>, <u>functionalism</u>, <u>symbolic interactionism</u>, <u>ethnomethodology</u>, <u>micro-theory</u>, and <u>macro theory</u>.

Name: ______________________________

Exercise: Sociological Theories

6. Watch any of the science fiction series *Star Wars* movies and in the space provided, discuss how the movie illustrated *any two* of these ideas: conflict theory, functionalism, symbolic interactionism, ethnomethodology, micro-theory, and macro theory.

Name: ______________________________

Exercise: Sociological Theories

7. Go to the campus library or online and select a sociology article in a recent issue of the sociological journal *Social Problems*. Select any one article, read it, and in the space provided, describe how the article illustrated each of the following: a theory, level of analysis, generalizability, and verification.

Name: ____________________

Exercise: Sociological Theories

8. Go to the campus library or online and select an article from a recent issue of the sociological journal *Marriage and Family*. Select any one article, read it, and in the space provided, describe how the article illustrated each of the following: a theory, level of analysis, generalizability and verification.

Name: ________________________________

Exercise: Sociological Theories

9. Think about recent Internet communication you have had with friends and family. In the space provided discuss how the email exchanges illustrated *any two* of these ideas: conflict theory, functionalism, symbolic interactionism, ethno-methodology, micro-theories, and social exchange theory.

Name: ______________________________

Exercise: Sociological Theories

10. Go to the web site of any major U.S. firm, like Ford Motor Company. Look at the web page, and in the space provided, discuss how the web page illustrates *any two* of these ideas: symbolic interactionism, functionalism, social exchange theory, and meso theories.

Research Methods

Sociologists do research to understand social settings and their effects upon people. Research that focuses upon a single social setting such as one factory, or one daycare center, is called a case study. The goal of case studies is to gain an idiographic explanation of the particular forms and meanings of social experiences in the focal setting. Discovering why workers in a plant are alienated or what the specific problems in cooperation are among children in a daycare center illustrate idiographic explanation. In contrast, nomothetic explanation is exemplified by finding how the major patterns of plant supervision in plants in general—closer versus less close—are related to workers' alienation or how types of play activity in daycare centers generally—structured versus unstructured—are associated with children's cooperation. As these examples illustrate, idiographic explanation involves more detailed explanation, while nomothetic explanation provides a less detailed but more generalized understanding (Babbie 2002).

The appropriateness of a particular research method—case studies versus others like research using documents, taking observations, or doing surveys by asking questions—depends upon researchers' explanatory goals. The details sought in case studies often require examining records and documents, taking observations of how a setting operates, and asking questions (Ragin and Becker 1992). Case studies can be and are done on specific communities, some of which, like Middletown (or Muncie, Indiana), have been studied over many years (Caplow, Bahr, Chadwick, Hill and Williamson 1982). Research involving studying a representative sample of people or social settings often uses a method called survey research. Such research involves sampling and questioning people who make up a representation of all the people or settings of interest (Bradburn and Sudman 1988). All major manufacturing plants in a region might be sampled, for example, to complete a survey of productivity and profit sharing, by asking plant officials to answer questions about output and worker benefits. The alumni of a university could be studied by means of a survey asking a representative sample of graduates questions about their feelings about their educational experiences. A survey of a representative sample of hospitals might be completed by asking hospital officials information about the cost and length of hospitalized time required for various types of operations.

Sociologists who do research using observational techniques employ various approaches (Marshall and Rossman 1995). One is to spend a long time observing activity in one setting, like a particular factory or store or neighborhood. Often such researchers use a diary in which they record daily observations of activities. Another approach is to use a more structured means of observing such as periodically (every fifteen minutes) recording the major forms of activities. In settings in which there are continuous activities such as in a store or at a stop sign, researchers can systematically record aspects of every fifth transaction or every tenth vehicle that approaches the stop sign. No matter what forms of observational techniques are used, researchers are usually not able to study as many different settings as they can when records are used or surveys are conducted. Observational techniques are usually more appropriate for the richness of detail sought by case studies (Babbie 2002).

Records and documents can be studied in a variety of ways. Usually, the volume of records or documents is so large that information must be sampled. Taking samples of patients and obtaining their medical records illustrates one way to do records-based research. Another technique, called content analysis, is useful when studying the content of newspapers, books, magazines, or Internet correspondence (Weber 1990). Essentially, content analysis involves taking a representative sampling of issues or volumes or instances of communication and carefully counting the major types of meanings in the content. For example, editorials in a representative sample of newspaper issues might be characterized by types of political positions or topics. Or, a representative sample of textbooks could be selected and their content sampled to illustrate how ideas are exemplified. Since the scope of research using records and documents is usually quite broad, content analysis and other techniques for studying records are more appropriate for survey studies of informational content.

Ethical principles must be followed when completing sociological research (Lee 1993). These moral guidelines in doing research are just as important as the care taken to complete the technical aspects of research. Most studies done by government agencies, schools and universities, and by organizations such as hospitals and business firms are carefully monitored for compliance with a professional code of ethics. Most agencies and organizations use an institutional review board (IRB) consisting of a group responsible for ensuring that ethical guidelines are followed. Such boards have been known to deny permission for a particular project or to deny funding it, until proper ethical procedures are developed and used. During and at the end of research projects, researchers send reports to IRB's that make clear how ethical guidelines have been maintained. Several ethical principles are of major concern to IRB's and to researchers. Informed consent means that researchers must inform people involved in research what the purposes and procedures and the risks involved in the study are. Potential participants must have understood the explanations asking for their consent (for example, verbal explanations must be required for people who cannot read, or translations provided for non-English readers or speakers). People being studied have the right to stop participating or to refuse ever to participate. Participants must be carefully informed of the potential risks, and their agreement to participate must depend on their understanding potential risks. Overall, however, risks are avoided by procedures that protect the physical well-being of participants (using sterilized medical equipment, for example) as well as their emotional well-being (using non-offensive and nonjudgmental questions, for example). Another ethical guideline is the right to privacy, which means that the individuals studied, or the settings studied, cannot be identified or become identifiable. Finally, honesty in reporting means that researchers never lie about or alter the information they have collected (Hoyle, Harris, and Judd 2002).

Sociological research varies as to the way time plays into data collection. Studies done to understand the nature of people and social settings at a particular point in time are called cross-sectional research. How workers feel about the benefits their employer provides or how alumni feel about their university at any particular time would exemplify such research. When researchers study changes in people or social settings over time, they conduct longitudinal research (Menard 1991). How employers' benefits have changed over a ten-year period or how workers' opinions about them have changed during this period, or how alumni views of a university change over a decade illustrate such research. Longitudinal studies must collect data at least two or more times. How many data collections to use and how much time to have between them depend upon the particular research topics and research questions. People such as those in studies of alumni, workers in studies of careers, and patients in longer-term medical studies are often studied every five to ten years. Other research such as that on incomes or on cost-of-living raises involves collecting information yearly. These longer-term studies that involve yearly information illustrate time series research. Usually, sociological researchers conduct studies with five to ten years elapsed time between data collections. Two major types of such research are cohort studies and trend studies. Cohort studies collect information from a group of people born at about the same time (a cohort), such as people born during the same decade (1980's). Studying them every ten years by drawing random samples of the group each time is a good way to study how the group changes as it ages, and such changes are called maturation. How people's incomes or their political views change as they age would illustrate maturation. Trend studies collect information from successive random samples of entire populations. General health surveys and research on perceived community problems illustrate trend research, and temporal changes in the general population's health or perceived community problems illustrate history. Maturation and history must carefully be distinguished, as when maturation refers to illnesses people get as they age, while history refers to diseases that anyone can get and that vaccinations prevent. Historical trends can and do affect all people simultaneously.

While doing research, sociologists follow various technical procedures to help ensure high quality results (Babbie 2002). One such procedure involves reliability. Reliability is defined as evidence that the information gathered on people or settings (such as age or output) has been collected in a consistent and accurate way. With judgments (about how completely drivers stop at a traffic light, or how pleasant a salesperson was to a particular customer), multiple judges' (or observers') judgments or evaluations are compared. Usually, at least 90 percent consistency in comparing judgments on each instance or transaction is required to establish the reliability of the information. In surveys, two similar questions may be asked at different points in the questioning (total years of education and highest diploma, for example) to assess reliability (again, a high level of consistency is desirable). After data have been gathered and reliability has been assessed favorably, researchers must also test for the validity of their results. Validity is evidence that the research results do in fact appear to have measured what the study was intended to measure. To assess validity, researchers often use comparative evidence other than the information that was the focus of research, but is still related to the topic of the study. Such information is referred to as the validity criterion. For example, researchers completing a survey of workers' alienation may find that workers with higher alienation scores (on a ten-point alienation scale) produce less per work day than workers with lower alienation scores. As a test of validity, the researchers also obtained records of workers' absences and found that the higher scorers also had missed more days of work. Remembering that validity testing provides support for research results being valid is important. Validity tests are not, nor are they intended to be, absolute proof of validity (Babbie 2002).

Sociologists must complete research carefully to find information that will provide meaningful understanding of the social world and appropriate means of improving social life. Only by following the technical and ethical guidelines for doing research can researchers avoid the common prejudices behind, and the errors in, many people's everyday decisions.

Name: ______________________________

Quiz Questions: Research Methods

1. Studying the history of one church congregation would illustrate a case study. (True or False?)
2. Studying whether workers in small companies are more alienated than workers in large companies illustrates the goal of idiographic research. (True or False?)
3. Videotaping a football game in order to judge the percentage of successfully executed plays by each lineman would illustrate which of these methods?

   a. longer term observation
   b. survey research
   c. content analysis of official documents
   d. structured observation

4. Studying the meanings of men's and women's actions in advertisements in magazines would illustrate which of these methods?

   a. longer term observation
   b. survey research
   c. content analysis of official documents
   d. structured observation

5. Allowing a person who is feeling uncomfortable to stop answering the questions during an interview would best illustrate which of these ethical guidelines?

   a. informed consent
   b. right to privacy
   c. honesty in reporting
   d. avoidance of risks

6. Being able to identify a research location from a research report is still a possible violation of the ethical principle of the right of privacy. (True or False?)
7. Studying how people's income changes before and after they retire would best be done with which of these types of research?

   a. trend study
   b. cohort study
   c. cross-section survey
   d. structured observation

8. Studying how much healthier the general population in a community is now as compared to ten years ago would best be done with which of these types of research?

   a. trend study
   b. cohort study
   c. cross-section study
   d. structured observation

9. Comparing people's individual answers to two similar questions on an interview would be a test of validity. (True or False?)
10. Comparing results showing that better-educated people report being in better health to clinical information that they are healthier would be a test of reliability. (True or False?)

Name: ______________________________

Exercise: Research Methods

1. In the space provided, mention the types of information you could use to complete an idiographic or a nomothetic explanation of activity in all your classes this semester.

Name: ______________________

Exercise: Research Methods

2. In doing a survey of alumni attitudes toward a university, in the space provided, discuss how you would test for reliability of the survey information.

Name: ______________________________

Exercise: Research Methods

3. Watch one-half hour of news programming on any TV network with your wristwatch or other clock handy, and a sheet of paper. Time and identify news segments, so the length of time in minutes and the news topic is known. In the space provided, present and briefly discuss your results.

Name: ______________________________

Exercise: Research Methods

4. Observe how students are seated in any three locations on campus: classrooms, cafeteria, student union, the library, and so on. Observe and make notes on any patterns you see in where people sit. You might take account of students' gender, race, and the size of groups seated near or with another. In the space provided, briefly describe the patterns of seating you observed.

Name: ______________________________

Exercise: Research Methods

5. Watch the classic science fiction movie, *Them*, and in the space provided, discuss how the movie illustrated observational techniques, case studies, ethical guidelines in reporting, and reliability.

Name: ______________________

Exercise: Research Methods

6. Watch the science fiction movie, *Bats*, and in the space provided, discuss how the movie illustrated observational techniques, ethical principles in research, longitudinal studies, and case studies.

Name: ___________________________

Exercise: Research Methods

7. Go to the campus library or online and select a sociology article in a recent issue of the sociological journal, *Social Problems*. Select an article by quickly skimming it in order to see if it deals with the following topics. If so, read and in the space provided, discuss how it illustrated nomothetic explanation, ethical principles, a timeframe for research (i.e. cross-sectional or longitudinal), and survey research.

Name: ______________________________

Exercise: Research Methods

8. Go to the campus library or online to select a sociology article in a recent issue of the sociological journal, *Marriage and Family*. Select an article by skimming it quickly to see if it deals with the following topics. If so, read it, and in the space provided, discuss how it illustrated nomothetic explanation, ethical principles, a timeframe for research (i.e. cross-sectional or longitudinal), and survey research.

Name: ______________________________

Exercise: Research Methods

9. Go to the various websites of social science departments or natural science department websites on your campus that deal with research done on people. On the websites search for, find, and describe in the space provided, a research project in progress or a report on one that has been completed. The research must involve people. In the space provided, describe the project in terms of type of research, being nomothetic or idiographic, the timeframe for research (i.e. cross-sectional or longitudinal), and ethics.

Name: ______________________________

Exercise: Research Methods

10. Go to the website of the popular magazine on consumer product quality, *Consumer Reports*. Select a product evaluation of your choice from information on the website (cars, TVs, appliances, skateboards, etc.). After reading the results of product testing, in the space provided, discuss these aspects of the quality testing: methods, timeframe, reliability, and validity.

3

Analyzing and Presenting Research Results

Sociologists must analyze appropriately the evidence that they gather during research, and they must report their findings and conclusions in understandable ways. Sociological research results often appear as research notes, or as articles in journals, or as chapters in books. Sociology journals include general coverage publications like the *American Journal of Sociology* and specialty journals such as *Crime and Delinquency*. Sociological articles and chapters in books are usually fifteen to twenty pages long with these sections: Introduction, Background, Methods, Results, Discussion and Conclusion. The focus of the research is in the Introduction, a summary of previous related research in Background, procedures in Methods, findings in Results, implications of the findings in Discussion, and general concerns for future research in (a short) Conclusion. Research notes are shorter versions of articles, usually without Background and Discussion.

Lengthier sociological communication includes research reports, monographs, and books. Reports are from sixty to one hundred pages long and are prepared for Institutional Review Boards (IRBs) (see Chapter 2) and funding agents. Such documents inform the boards and agencies of research procedures and results, doing so in ways that verify proper usage of funding and the use of ethical standards. Reports usually include more tables, charts, graphs, and figures, and more extensive discussions of results than do articles or book chapters. Research monographs are like research reports, except that the university, agency, or organization that sponsored the study distributes them widely. Research-oriented books have two formats: one is a series of chapters, each of which is like an article and deals with a separate study, and the other is an in-depth treatment of a single study that has chapters corresponding to the sections of an article and may have multiple chapters dealing with different aspects of findings and their meaning (Schott 1999).

Sociologists use several techniques to analyze and present their research results. Which techniques they will use depend upon their research topic and method(s), as well as who their audiences will be. Technical details will be more prominent in reporting to sponsors or other sociologists, while practical implications will be stressed more to sponsoring organizations and to the public.

The techniques used to analyze and to report the findings of case studies that involve diary records of observation and lengthy (often recorded) interviews are called ethnographic procedures (Lofland and Lofland 1995). Such techniques include the use of frameworks and typologies for classifying and interpreting the meaning of events and other aspects of social settings. Transcribing, sorting, and interpreting the meanings of notes and recorded interviews usually involves painstaking ethnographic efforts. Researchers are careful to triangulate ethnographic sources by demonstrating similarity of conclusions drawn from different data sources. Further complicating ethnographic procedure is the fact that different people often give very different meanings to, and have very different understandings of, the same events, such as the diverse meanings doctors and patients give to social interaction during office visits. Discourse Analysis focuses on deriving and explaining the differences in meanings people have for events and actions (Brennan 1997).

Various forms of research, including some case studies and content analyses of media material (See Chapter 2), involve techniques useful for analyzing and reporting the analysis of information in records, files, minutes of meetings, operations records, and so on (Berg 1989). Content analysis is not only a way to obtain a representative sample of written or pictorial records, it is also a means of using typologies to classify and interpret themes, viewpoints, and symbolic meanings in the content. Content analysis involves a distinction between manifest content and latent content. The former refers to themes or viewpoints apparent in the content such as being for or against certain ideas or policies. The latter refers to the political or philosophical viewpoints, or the other rationales such as cost considerations or other constraints, that are behind thematic positions. Newspaper editorials may oppose tax increases based upon political viewpoints, because of difficult economic circumstances in communities, or on other grounds. Latent content refers to the reasoning behind positions (Berg 1989).

Many sociological studies that take a broader approach to studies of how social settings change use historiography. Such procedures have been used to study social movements and political change such as the Temperance Movement that led to the Prohibition Era in the U.S. from 1920 until 1933 (Gusfield 1963). (See Chapter 17.) Historiographic methods involve using historical information and analyses to characterize the nature and meaning (and particularly the symbolic meaning) of social changes. Agencies, organizations (like the Temperance Union), universities, political parties, and all other forms of social entities can be studied with historiographic approach. Like ethnographic procedures, sociological historiographers sift through historical records and extract the important patterns of meanings for drawing conclusions about how and why social entities and social settings change. Often such changes can be mapped and their meanings drawn from use of critical events analysis. Very important events such as movement leaders being imprisoned or devastating occurrences such as the tragedies of 9/11 often provide the means of demarcating and understanding social change. (See Chapters 16 and 17.)

Statistical documents like education and employment statistics in government publications and statistical data obtained through content analysis or numerical analysis of survey research data are all analyzed and presented in several important ways with the use of descriptive statistics, correlational techniques, contingency or percentage tables, and multivariate analyses (Lewis-Beck 1995). Descriptive statistics are useful for analyzing and communicating numerical meanings concerning one sociological variable, such as the age distribution of the people being studied. A variable is the numerical scheme used to measure and record information on a single issue, such as people's age at their last birthday, their incomes in actual dollars, or their attitudes indicated by the Likert format of strongly agree = 5, agree = 4, unsure = 3, disagree = 2, and strongly disagree = 1.

Several types of descriptive statistics are used in sociological reports. The mean or average is a number that represents the typical central value in a distribution of values (or a ranking of ages or incomes from highest to lowest). A mean of 4.6 on a Likert-type measure means that people in the study agree with that issue. An average income of $160,000 indicates that people being studied tend to be quite wealthy. The standard deviation is a number representing the average amount of variation in values (of incomes or ages ranked from highest to lowest) above and below the mean. For example, if the mean age of people in a study was 41 years and the standard deviation was 17 years, most of those studied ranged in age from 24 (17 less than 41) to 58 (17 more than 41). Percentages are numbers that refer to what proportion of all cases in a study is in a particular category or type. That proportion is then multiplied by 100. For example, if 20 of 100 people strongly agree, that is 20/100, or .20 of all cases, and .20 x 100 = 20 percent. Descriptive statistics help audiences understand statistical results without reference to all of the details of the data.

Correlational techniques are like descriptive statistics except that they represent relationships between two variables, such as that between education and income. A correlation, most often Pearson's "r," is a proportion-like measure that can vary from .01 through .99. The larger it is, the stronger the relationship is between two variables. A correlation of .7 between education and income indicates a strong relationship, while a correlation of .2 between age and IQ scores shows a very weak one. The coefficient of determination is obtained by squaring the value of r, or multiplying the r value by itself. This measure indicates the proportion of total relationship possible that was actually found. For example, a correlation of .7 between education and income when squared (.7 x .7 = .49) means that there is a 49 percent of a total association or a complete relationship between the two.

A contingency or percentage table is a chart representing the relationship between two categorized variables. A categorized variable is usually a measure with three or four divisions as in types of religious affiliation (Protestant, Catholic, Jewish, other) or levels of social class (upper, middle, working, and lower). The columns of contingency tables are the categories of the (independent) variable presumed to influence the other (dependent) variable, whose categories make up the rows. Thus, contingency tables like the one below show how the percentages vary by comparing results across the row of the table (in a two-row table only the top row percentages need to be compared since those in the bottom row are mirror images of those in the top row):

Table 1. Percentage of Respondents with Higher versus Lower Income by Their Level of Education (Less Than High School, High School or GED, Some College, College or More)

		Level of Education				
		Less Than High School	**High School**	**Some College**	**College or More**	**Total**
Income Level	Higher ($40,000 or more)	17%	36%	49%	78%	45%
	Lower (less than $40,000)	83%	64%	51%	22%	55%
		100% (100)	100% (100)	100% (100)	100% (100)	100% (400)

This table presents the percent of people with each income level in each (increasing) educational level left to right. Since education was presumed to influence income, the levels of education made the columns and the income levels became the rows. The table shows that the percent of people with higher income increases over four times in value (78/17 = 4.6), from the less than high school column to the college or more column. People's education clearly makes a very large difference with respect to income levels.

Three general rules should be followed when making and presenting contingency tables. First, to avoid making tables hard to follow, do not have more than four columns and/or three rows. Second, to avoid confusion remember that while percentages total downward, those in the same row must be compared across. Third, to avoid a mathematical error, remember that a difference between two percentages is a difference of percentage points, and not a percent difference. Seventy-eight percent is 61 percentage points more than 17 percent, not 61 percent greater.

Multivariate analyses are like correlational analyses, except that they involve several (usually six to ten) independent variables in relation to one dependent variable. Age, being white, being male, having 20 or more years of work experience, and education, could all be combined in an analysis of income differences (Newton and Rudestan 1999). Multiple regression, a popular approach, yields a correlation-like measure for each independent variable called a beta. The larger the value of beta (from .001 through .999), the stronger the relationship is between that independent variable (education) and the dependent variable (income). A beta shows net relationships, or relationships that exclude the influence of all other independent variables. Multiple regression methods also assess the effect of a successive combination of independent variables. R squared, or the multiple coefficient of determination, like its counterpart r squared, shows the percent of variation in the dependent variable (income) explained as successive independent variables are added into the explanation. This is called stepwise regression. When all independent variables have been included, an $R^2 = .67$ would mean that 67 percent of the total variation in income has been explained by all of the independent variables acting together. The effect of each successive independent variable is measurable by subtracting the R^2 value of any stage of the analysis (except the first) from the R^2 of the previous step.

Name: ______________________________

Quiz Questions: Analyzing and Presenting Research Results

1. An article is usually the lengthiest type of sociological report. (True or False?)
2. Monographs and articles usually reach larger audiences than research reports do. (True or False?)
3. Triangulation and discourse analysis are techniques primarily used in historiography. (True or False?)
4. Analyzing diaries of observations and long, recorded interviews is most related to which of the following methods?
   a. descriptive statistics
   b. historiography
   c. ethnographic procedures
   d. content analyses
5. Latent content is to content analysis as critical event analysis is to historiography. (True or False?)
6. Which of these types of statistics is used primarily to analyze numerical values concerning one sociological issue or variable?
   a. multivariate analyses
   b. contingency tables
   c. correlational techniques
   d. descriptive statistics
7. The standard deviation is a measure showing a typical or central value. (True or False?)
8. The correlation value, r, shows the percentage of total relationship between two variables. (True or False?)
9. The columns of a contingency table are the categories of the independent variable. (True or False?)
10. A beta shows how much variation in a dependent variable is explained by several independent variables acting together. (True or False?)

Name: ______________________________

Exercise: Analyzing and Presenting Research Results

1. In the space provided, discuss the three "critical events" that took place during one semester of your classes.

Name: ______________________

Exercise: Analyzing and Presenting Research Results

2. In the space provided, briefly discuss the manifest and latent content of one day's worth of notes in one of your classes.

Name: ______________________________

Exercise: Analyzing and Presenting Research Results

3. Select a two variable percentage or contingency table from any of your current texts other than this one. Study the table and information in it. Then, in the space provided, describe the basic parts of the table including categories of the independent and dependent variables, and what the pattern of percentage points of difference across the table shows.

Name: ______________________________

Exercise: Analyzing and Presenting Research Results

4. Look in recent issues of your campus or local newspaper for a two variable percentage or contingency table. Study the table and the information in it. Then, in the space provided, describe the basic parts of the table including categories of the independent and dependent variables, and what the pattern of percentage points differences across the table shows.

Name: ______________________

Exercise: Analyzing and Presenting Research Results

5. Watch the classic Western movie, *Shane*, and in the space provided, discuss how the movie illustrated historiography, critical events analysis, symbolic meanings of social change, and discourse analysis.

Name: ______________________

Exercise: Analyzing and Presenting Research Results

6. Watch the western movie, *Tombstone*, then in the space provided, discuss how the movie illustrated historiography, critical events analysis, symbolic meanings of social change, and discourse analysis.

Name: ________________________________

Exercise: Analyzing and Presenting Research Results

7. Go to the campus library or online to select an article from a recent issue of the sociology journal *Social Forces*. Select an article that involved multiple regression and in the space provided, discuss how the author(s) used <u>multiple regression</u>, <u>betas</u>, and the <u>multiple coefficient of determination</u>.

Name: ________________________________

Exercise: Analyzing and Presenting Research Results

8. Go to the campus library or online to select a recent article from the sociological journal *The American Journal of Sociology*. Select an article that involved multiple regression and in the space provided, discuss how the author(s) used multiple regression, betas, and the multiple coefficient of determination.

Name: ______________________________

Exercise: Analyzing and Presenting Research Results

9. Think about recent Internet communication that you have had with friends and family. In the space provided, discuss how the e-mail communication illustrates latent content, discourse analysis, critical events analysis, and manifest content.

Name: ______________________________

Exercise: Analyzing and Presenting Research Results

10. Go to the webpage of your university, and study the content. In the space provided, discuss how the webpage illustrates manifest content, latent content, critical events analysis, and any descriptive statistics.

Damned Lies and Statistics

Untangling Numbers from the Media, Politicians, and Activists

Joel Best

The Importance of Social Statistics

Nineteenth-century Americans worried about prostitution; reformers called it "*the* social evil" and warned that many women prostituted themselves. How many? For New York City alone, there were dozens of estimates: in 1833, for instance, reformers published a report declaring that there were "not less than 10,000" prostitutes in New York (equivalent to about 10 percent of the city's female population): in 1866, New York's Methodist bishop claimed there were more prostitutes (11,000 to 12,000) than Methodists in the city; other estimates for the period ranged as high as 50,000. These reformers hoped that their reports of widespread prostitution would prod the authorities to act, but city officials' most common response was to challenge the reformers' numbers. Various investigations by the police and grand juries produced their own, much lower estimates; for instance, one 1872 police report counted only 1,223 prostitutes (by that time, New York's population included nearly half a million females). Historians see a clear pattern in these cycles of competing statistics: ministers and reformers "tended to inflate statistics"; while "police officials tended to underestimate prostitution."

Antiprostitution reformers tried to use big numbers to arouse public outrage. Big numbers meant there was a big problem: if New York had tens of thousands of prostitutes, something ought to be done. In response, the police countered that there were relatively few prostitutes—an indication that they were doing a good job. These dueling statistics resemble other, more recent debates. During Ronald Reagan's presidency, for example, activists claimed that three million Americans were homeless, while the Reagan administration insisted that the actual number of homeless people was closer to 300,000, one-tenth what the activists claimed. In other words, homeless activists argued that homelessness was a big problem that demanded additional government social programs, while the administration argued new programs were not needed to deal with what was actually a much smaller, more manageable problem. Each side presented statistics that justified its policy recommendations, and each criticized the other's numbers. The activists ridiculed the administration's figures as an attempt to cover up a large, visible problem, while the administration insisted that the activists' numbers were unrealistic exaggerations.

Statistics, then, can become weapons in political struggles over social problems and social policy. Advocates of different positions use numbers to make their points ("It's a big problem!" "No, it's not!"). And, as the example of nineteenth-century estimates of prostitution reminds us, statistics have been used as weapons for some time.

Creating Social Problems

We tend to think of social problems as harsh realities, like gravity or earthquakes, that exist completely independent of human action. But the very term reveals that this is incorrect: *social* problems are products of what people do.

This is true in two senses. First, we picture social problems as snarls or flaws in the social fabric. Social problems have their causes in society's arrangements; when some women turn to prostitution or some individuals have no homes, we assume that society has failed (although we may disagree over whether that failure involves not providing enough jobs, or not giving children proper moral instruction, or something else). Most people understand that social problems are social in this sense.

But there is a second reason social problems are social. Someone has to bring these problems to our attention, to give them names, describe their causes and characteristics, and so on. Sociologists speak of social problems being "constructed"—that is, created or assembled through the actions of activists, officials, the news media, and other people who draw attention to particular problems. "Social problem" is a label we give to some social conditions, and it is that label that turns a condition we take for granted into something we consider troubling. This means that the processes of identifying and publicizing social problems are important. When we start thinking of prostitution or homelessness as a social problem, we are responding to campaigns by reformers who seek to arouse our concern about the issue.

The creation of a new social problem can been seen as a sort of public drama, a play featuring a fairly standard cast of characters. Often, the leading roles are played by *social activists*—individuals dedicated to promoting a cause, to making others aware of the problem. Activists draw attention to new social problems by holding protest demonstrations, attracting media coverage, recruiting new members to their cause, lobbying officials to do something about the situation, and so on. They are the most obvious, the most visible participants in creating awareness of social problems.

Successful activists attract support from others. The *mass media*—including both the press (reporters for newspapers or television news programs) and entertainment media (such as television talk shows)—relay activists' claims to the general public. Reporters often find it easy to turn those claims into interesting news stories; after all, a new social problem is a fresh topic, and it may affect lots of people, pose dramatic threats, and lead to proposals to change the lives of those involved. Media coverage, especially sympathetic coverage, can make millions of people aware of and concerned about a social problem. Activists need the media to provide that coverage, just as the media depend on activists and other sources for news to report.

Often activists also enlist the support of *experts*—doctors, scientists, economists, and so on—who presumably have special qualifications to talk about the causes and consequences of some social problem. Experts may have done research on the problem and can report their findings. Activists use experts to make claims about social problems seem authoritative, and the mass media often rely on experts' testimonies to make news stories about a new problem seem more convincing. In turn, experts enjoy the respectful attention they receive from activists and the media.

Not all social problems are promoted by struggling, independent activists; creating new social problems is sometimes the work of powerful organizations and institutions. *Government officials* who promote problems range from prominent politicians trying to arouse concern in order to create election campaign issues, to anonymous bureaucrats proposing that their agencies' programs be expanded to solve some social problem. And *businesses, foundations, and other private organizations* sometimes have their own reasons to promote particular social issues. Public and private organizations usually command the resources needed to organize effective campaigns to create social problems. They can afford to hire experts to conduct research, to sponsor and encourage activists, and to publicize their causes in ways that attract media attention.

In other words, when we become aware of—and start to worry about—some new social problem, our concern is usually the result of efforts by some combination of *problem promoters*—activists, reporters, experts, officials, or private organizations—who have worked to create the sense that this is an important problem, one that deserves our attention. In this sense, people deliberately construct social problems.

Efforts to create or promote social problems, particularly when they begin to attract attention, may inspire opposition. Sometimes this involves officials responding to critics by defending existing policies as adequate. Recall that New York police minimized the number of prostitutes in the city, just as the Reagan administration argued that activists exaggerated the number of homeless persons. In other cases, opposition comes from private interests; for example, the Tobacco Institute (funded by the tobacco industry) became notorious for, over decades, challenging every research finding that smoking was harmful.

Statistics play an important role in campaigns to create—or defuse claims about—new social problems. Most often, such statistics describe the problem's size: there are 10,000 prostitutes in New York City, or three million homeless people. When social problems first come to our attention, perhaps in a televised news report, we're usually given an example or two (perhaps video footage of homeless individuals living on city streets) and then a statistical estimate (of the number of homeless people). Typically this is a big number. Big numbers warn us that the problem is a common one, compelling our attention, concern, and action. The media like to report statistics because numbers seem to be "hard facts"—little nuggets of indisputable truth. Activists trying to draw media attention to a new social problem often find that the press demands statistics: reporters insist on getting estimates of the problem's size—how many people are affected, how much it costs, and so on. Experts, officials, and private organizations commonly report having studied the problem, and they present statistics based on their research. Thus, the key players in creating new social problems all have reason to present statistics.

In virtually every case, promoters use statistics as ammunition; they choose numbers that will draw attention to or away from a problem, arouse or defuse public concern. People use statistics to support their point of view, to bring others around to their way of thinking. Activists trying to gain recognition for what they believe is a big problem will offer statistics that seem to prove that the problem is indeed a big one (and they may choose to downplay, ignore, or dispute any statistics that might make it seem smaller). The media favor disturbing statistics about big problems because big problems make more interesting, more compelling news, just as experts' research (and the experts themselves) seem more important if their subject is a big, important problem. These concerns lead people to present statistics that support their position, their cause, their interests. There is an old expression that captures this tendency: "Figures may not lie, but liars figure." Certainly we need to understand that people debating social problems choose statistics selectively and present them to support their points of view. Gun-control advocates will be more likely to report the number of children killed by guns, while opponents of gun control will prefer to count citizens who use guns to defend themselves from attack. Both numbers may be correct, but most people debating gun control present only the statistic that bolsters their position.

Guessing

Activists hoping to draw attention to a new social problem often find that there are no good statistics available.* When a troublesome social condition has been ignored, there usually are no accurate records about the condition to serve as the basis for good statistics. Therefore, when reporters ask activists for facts and figures ("Exactly how big is this problem?"), the activists cannot produce official, authoritative numbers.

What activists do have is their own sense that the problem is widespread and getting worse. After all, they believe it is an important problem,

*While activists are particularly likely to face this problem (because they often are the first to try to bring a problem to public attention), anyone trying to promote a new social problem—including experts, officials, and those representing the media or other institution—may have the same difficulties. Just as I sometimes use the general terms "advocates" or "promoters" to refer to all the sorts of people who help create social problems, I use "activists" to suggest that they are the ones especially—but not uniquely—likely to handle statistics in particular ways.

and they spend much of their time learning more about it and talking to other people who share their concerns. A hothouse atmosphere develops in which everyone agrees this is a big, important problem. People tell one another stories about the problem and, if no one has been keeping careful records, activists soon realize that many cases of the problem—maybe the vast majority—go unreported and leave no records.

Criminologists use the expression "the dark figure" to refer to the proportion of crimes that don't appear in crime statistics. In theory, citizens report crimes to the police, the police keep records of those reports, and those records become the basis for calculating crime rates. But some crimes are not reported (because people are too afraid or too busy to call the police, or because they doubt the police will be able to do anything useful), and the police may not keep records of all the reports they receive, so the crime rate inevitably underestimates the actual amount of crime. The difference between the number of officially recorded crimes and the true number of crimes is the dark figure.

Every social problem has a dark figure because some instances (of crime, child abuse, poverty, or whatever) inevitably go unrecorded. How big is the dark figure? When we first learn about a problem that has never before received attention, when no one has any idea how common the problem actually is, we might think of the dark figure as being the entire problem. In other cases where recordkeeping is very thorough, the dark figure may be relatively small (for example, criminologists believe that the vast majority of homicides are recorded, simply because dead bodies usually come to police attention).

So, when reporters or officials ask activists about the size of a newly created social problem, the activists usually have to guess about the problem's dark figure. They offer estimates, educated guesses, guesstimates, ballpark figures, or stabs in the dark. When *Nightline*'s Ted Koppel asked Mitch Snyder, a leading activist for the homeless in the early 1980s, for the source of the estimate that there were two to three million homeless persons, Snyder explained: "Everybody demanded it. Everybody said we want a number. . . . We got on the phone, we made a lot of calls, we talked to a lot of people, and we said, 'Okay, here are some numbers.' They have no meaning, no value." Because activists sincerely believe that the new problem is big and important, and because they suspect that there is a very large dark figure of unreported or unrecorded cases, the *activists' estimates tend to be high*, to err on the side of exaggeration. Their guesses are far more likely to overestimate than underestimate a problem's size. (Activists also favor round numbers. It is remarkable how often their estimates peg the frequency of some social problem at one [or two or more] million cases per year.)

Being little more than guesses—and probably guesses that are too high—usually will not discredit activists' estimates. After all, the media ask activists for estimates precisely because they can't find more accurate statistics. Reporters want to report facts, activists' numbers look like facts, and it may be difficult, even impossible to find other numbers, so the media tend to report the activists' figures. (Scott Adams, the cartoonist who draws *Dilbert*, explains the process: "Reporters are faced with the daily choice of painstakingly researching stories or writing whatever people tell them. Both approaches pay the same.")

Once a number appears in one news report, that report is a potential source for everyone who becomes interested in the social problem; officials, experts, activists, and other reporters routinely repeat figures that appear in press reports. *The number takes on a life of its own, and it goes through "number laundering."* Its origins as someone's best guess are now forgotten and, through repetition, it comes to be treated as a straightforward fact—accurate and authoritative. Soon the trail becomes muddy. People lose track of the estimate's original source, but they assume the number must be correct because it appears everywhere—in news reports, politicians' speeches, articles in scholarly journals and law reviews, and so on. Over time, as people repeat the number, they may begin to change its meaning, to embellish the statistic.

Consider early estimates for the crime of stalking. Concern about stalking spread very rapidly in the early 1990s; the media publicized the problem, and most state legislatures passed anti-stalking laws. At that time, no official agencies were keeping track of stalking cases, and no studies of the extent of stalking had been done, so there was no way anyone could know how often stalking occurred. After a newsmagazine story reported "researchers suggest that up to 200,000 people exhibit a stalker's traits," other news reports picked up the "suggested" figure and confidently repeated that there were 200,000 people being stalked. Soon, the media began to improve the statistic. The host of a television talk show declared, "There are an estimated 200,000 stalkers in the United States, and those are only the ones that we have track of." An article in *Cosmopolitan* warned: "Some two hundred thousand people in the U.S. pursue the famous. No one knows how many people stalk the rest of us, but the figure is probably higher." Thus, the original guess became a foundation for other, even bigger guesses.

Measuring

Any statistic based on more than a guess requires some sort of counting. Definitions specify what will be counted. Measuring involves deciding how to go about counting. We cannot begin counting until we decide how we will identify and count instances of a social problem.*

To understand the significance of measurement, let's begin by considering one of the most common ways social scientists measure social concern—survey research. Surveys (or polls) involve asking people questions, counting their answers, and drawing general conclusions based on the results. (Choosing which people to survey presents special problems that we'll consider in the next section, on sampling.) For example, we might ask 1,000 people whether they favor or oppose a new law; if we discover that 500 of the people asked favor the law and 500 oppose it, we might generalize from those findings and conclude that public opinion is about evenly split.

Although the media sometimes report survey results as though public issues involve clear-cut splits in opinions—implying that people either favor or oppose gun control, that they're either pro-choice or pro-life—this is an oversimplification. *Public attitudes toward most social issues are too complex to be classified in simple pros and cons*, or to be measured by a single survey question. For example, surveys find that about 90 percent of Americans agree that legal abortions should be available to women whose health would be endangered by continuing their pregnancies (see Table 1). Pro-choice advocates sometimes interpret such results as evidence that most Americans support legalized abortion. However, surveys also find that only about 45 percent of Americans support abortion regardless of the woman's reason for wanting it, and pro-life advocates sometimes view this as evidence that most Americans oppose abortion on demand. Combining the responses to these questions (as well as others measuring attitudes toward abortion under various circumstances) reveals a more complex pattern of public opinion: there is a small, hard-core antiabortion faction (roughly 10 percent of the population) that opposes abortion under any circumstances; a larger minority (roughly 45 percent) that accepts women's right to choose abortion under almost any circumstances; and another large minority (roughly 45 percent) that occupies a territory between these extremes, that approves of abortion for "good" reasons but does not approve of all abortions, regardless of the circumstances. Attitudes toward abortion are too complicated to

Table 1. Percentages of Americans Favoring Legal Abortions under Different Circumstances, 1996

If the woman's own health is seriously endangered by the pregnancy	92
If she became pregnant as a result of rape	84
If there is a strong chance of serious defect in the baby	82
If she is married and does not want any more children	47
If the family has a very low income and cannot afford any more children	47
If she is not married and does not want to marry the man	45
If the woman wants it for any reason	45

SOURCE: Data from the 1996 General Social Survey, the "The American Survey—Release 1997" (CD-ROM; Bellevue, Wash.: Micro-Case, 1997).

*In fact, researchers recognize that what I'm calling measurement actually is a type of definition. They refer to *operational definitions*, that is, the operations one goes through to identify an instance of whatever is being defined.

be measured by a single survey question or to be described in terms of simple pro/con categories. Obviously, then, measurement makes a difference. The choice of questions used to measure abortion attitudes affects what public opinion surveys discover.

Survey researchers know that *how questions are worded affects results*. Advocates who can afford to sponsor their own surveys can shape the results; usually they try to demonstrate widespread public support for their position. (This is sometimes called *advocacy research*.) Advocates word questions so as to encourage people to respond in the desired way. For example, surveys by gun-control advocates may ask: "Do you favor cracking down against illegal gun sales?" Most people can be counted on to oppose illegal acts, and such questions routinely find that (according to the gun-control activists' interpretations of the results) more than three-quarters of Americans favor gun control. On the other hand, the National Rifle Association opposes gun control, and it sponsors surveys that word questions very differently, such as: "Would you favor or oppose a law giving police the power to decide who may or may not own a firearm?" Not unexpectedly, most people answer that they oppose giving the police so much power, and the NRA can report that most Americans (roughly three-quarters) oppose gun control. As in the example of abortion discussed above, public opinion seems to divide into minorities at the two extremes (some favoring a ban on all guns; others opposed to any gun control), and a large middle mass that, presumably, favors keeping guns out of the hands of "bad" people while letting "good" people have guns. However, the complexity of public opinion can be hard to recognize when our information comes from surveys sponsored by advocates who word questions to produce the results they desire.*

In addition to wording questions to encourage some responses, *advocates who conduct their own surveys can decide how to interpret the results*. A few years ago, the press reported that a national survey estimated that 2 percent of adult Americans (nearly four million people) had been abducted by UFOs. How did the researchers arrive at this figure? Did they ask: "Have you ever been abducted by a UFO?" No. The researchers argued that such a straightforward question would be a poor measure because many UFO abductees do not realize they've been abducted (or are unwilling to talk about the experience); therefore they could not (or would not) answer a direct question accurately. (Note that this is another instance of advocates trying to avoid false negatives; in this case, they did not want to measure abduction in a way that might exclude some cases they felt ought to be included.) Instead, the researchers devised a very different measure: they identified five indicators or symptoms that often figured in the accounts of people who say they've been abducted, and then asked whether respondents had experienced these more innocuous symptoms, for example: "Waking up paralyzed with a sense of a strange person or presence or something else in the room?" They then concluded that anyone who reported four or more symptoms probably had been abducted. Two percent of the survey respondents fell into this group, leading to the researchers' conclusion that 2 percent of the population had been abducted.

This example illustrates the importance of measurement decisions. Measurement involves choices. Had the UFO researchers decided that only one or two symptoms indicated abduction, they would have found more abductees. Had they decided to insist that respondents report all five symptoms, they would have found fewer. (And, of course, had they decided to only count people who reported having been abducted, they presumably would have found fewer yet.) Such choices shape the results of many surveys. Based on affirmative answers to such questions as "Have you had sexual intercourse when you didn't want to because a man gave you alcohol or drugs?" one survey concluded that roughly a quarter of female college students had been raped. Critics challenged this finding; they argued that the questions were ambiguous, and noted that nearly three-quarters of the respondents identified as rape victims indicated they did not consider the incident a rape. But, as these examples demonstrate, it is the advocates conducting the surveys—not the respondents—

*Although I have chosen to focus on question wording, there are many other ways researchers can design surveys to encourage particular responses. For example, the order in which questions are asked can make a difference in how people respond.

who create the measurements and interpret the results, who identify the victims of UFO abduction or rape.

Characteristics of Good Statistics

This chapter's focus has been the production of bad statistics through guessing, dubious definitions, questionable measurement, and poor sampling. At this point, you may be wondering whether all statistics are bad, nothing more than "damned lies." Are there any good statistics? How can we tell the good numbers from the bad?

The problems identified in this chapter suggest some standards that good statistics meet. First, *good statistics are based on more than guessing*. The most basic question about any statistic is: How did someone arrive at this number? All statistics are imperfect, but some flaws are worse than others. Obviously, we should not place too much confidence in guesses (even educated guesses). Watch for the danger signs of guessing: Do the people offering the statistic have a bias—do they want to show that the problem is common (or rare)? Is the statistic a big, round number? Does the statistic describe an unfamiliar, hidden social problem that probably has a large dark figure (if so, how did the advocates manage to come up with their numbers)?

Second, *good statistics are based on clear, reasonable definitions*. Remember, every statistic has to define its subject. Those definitions ought to be clear and made public. An example—particularly a dramatic, disturbing example, a horror story, a worse case—is not a definition. Anyone presenting a statistic describing a social problem should be able and willing to explain the definition used to create the statistic. Definitions usually are broad: they encompass kinds of cases very different from (and usually less serious than) the examples. We need to ask: How broad? What does the definition include? Again, ask yourself whether the people offering the statistic favor broad (or narrow) definitions, and why. Consider whether their definition might exclude too many false negatives or include too many false positives.

Third, *good statistics are based on clear, reasonable measures*. Again, every statistic involves some sort of measurement; while all measures are imperfect, not all flaws are equally serious. People offering a statistic should be able and willing to explain how they measured the social problem, and their choices should seem reasonable. If the people offering the statistic have some sort of bias (in favor of big—or small—numbers), that bias may be reflected in the way they've measured the problem. For example, they may have worded survey questions to encourage certain responses, or they may interpret responses in peculiar ways. Be suspicious of statistics based on hidden measurements, and consider how measurement choices might shape statistics.

Finally, *good statistics are based on good samples*. Clear, reasonable definitions and clear, reasonable measurements are not enough. Almost all statistics generalize from a sample of cases to a larger population, and the methods of selecting that sample should be explained. Good samples are representative of that larger population; ideally, this means the sample has been selected at random. Watch out for statistics based on small, nonrandom, convenience samples; such samples are easier and cheaper to study, but they are a poor basis for sweeping generalizations. Ask yourself how the sample chosen might skew the resulting statistics.

One sign of good statistics is that we're given more than a number; we're told something about the definitions, measurement, and sampling behind the figure—about how the number emerged. When that information remains concealed, we have every reason to be skeptical.

UNIT TWO

Each of us is a unique human animal, but the process by which we developed as a unique human being, with desires and capabilities and interests, reflects our socialization experiences. In this unit we address the social influences upon human development represented in socialization. We also examine the traits and organization of social groups that are so important in influencing people's development and in shaping their ongoing lives. In addition, a discussion of social networks, an increasingly popular focus of sociological research, is also included. It shows that social life is not a mass of unorganized or alienating random associations among strangers. Social network analyses show that modern social life is an intricately interconnected series of interpersonal linkages, some direct and others only indirect. Some people hold key positions that indirectly link large clusters of people together as shown in the excerpts from the popular book by Malcolm Gladwell, *The Tipping Point.* The various forms of interpersonal connections in social networks explain the pathways by which we interpersonally share communication, emotional support and aid, information, and other forms of social capital.

People are not robotic clones like those in many science fiction stories and films. All social settings pattern behavior, but people vary in their expression of what social settings encourage. Families differ in their favorite forms of fun, workgroups approach work tasks in different ways, professors and students teach and learn using different strategies, and so on. Moreover, social settings allow some leeway concerning expected behaviors, but too much nonconformity results in negative and punitive social reactions called deviance. In this unit we discuss various forms of punitive reactions by dealing with types of crime and various types of rule breakers, including those who receive almost no punishment as shown in the Chambliss reading on gangs.

In this unit we also introduce the most fundamental social unit that people collectively depend upon and thrive within: a community. Surprisingly, this important sociological entity is difficult to define. The several perspectives on community that we include will show that communities are fragile and not always enduring. They, like all other forms of important social enterprise, require continuing collective commitments from and cooperation among their members.

4

Socialization and the Self

Socialization is the lifelong process by which social settings and experiences in them influence people's development. Sociologists study the ways social experiences in families, schools, in workplaces, during leisure activities, in health care facilities including hospices, and so on influence how people act and think at various times in their lives. These effects upon people's actions and thoughts and how such experiences influence the way people feel about themselves as individuals are called the social self. Self-identity refers to our awareness of who we are in relation to important others (or significant others) in social settings like the family, school, work, and church (Mead 1934). Self-esteem refers to people's evaluations of how well they are doing in these relationships. To sociologists, life course socialization refers to the major stages of life in which different social influences or agents of socialization influence people's development and in broad patterns shape the different stages of life most people experience, as well as their self-identity and self esteem.

Several important concepts are used by sociologists who study life course socialization. Primary socialization refers to the first and extremely important social influences upon development found in families. Young human beings are very dependent upon the responses of caring others for their proper development. A broad range of studies has demonstrated the importance of the comfort and security principle, or the importance of loving care and social bonding between parents or other significant others and children. Such attention and support are vital for the development of basic orientations such as trust, basic skills such as playing games, and mature ways of thinking including George H. Mead's concept of the ability to role take, or to consider the views of others when we act (Shepard 2002). Family and especially parents provide important sources of moral values and basic life orientations like occupational interests (Hodson and Sullivan 2002). Same-sex parents and older siblings provide important role models for children's gender identity formation. Family socializers also are socialized by infants, if in no other way than the need to adapt their schedules to those of the newborn. This process is called reciprocal socialization and occurs later in other forms as children's interests in sports and school activities shape those of their parents. Processes by which families cooperate to accomplish daily household activities also provide advanced knowledge and skill for adult roles, as a part of anticipatory socialization.

Peer socialization involves the influence of same-age others, or people in the same social status, or those who enter a social setting together (new army recruits or new hires in a firm). Most studies of adolescent peer socialization show that youthful peers have strong but temporary influences upon people, especially with respect to personal appearance including clothing styles and tastes in entertainment, especially music (Macionis 2002). In contrast, parents and family and early teachers are much more influential in shaping longer-term interests such as schooling and occupational activity (Lewis, Mirowsky, and Ross 2001). Children in the U.S. spend as much time watching TV as they do in activities with peers and families. George Herbert Mead (1934) used the term referent other to refer to the influence of characters in books and film or famous entertainers or athletes upon people's development. Studies of children's television viewing have established a correlation between TV viewing and video game usage and aggressive behaviors (Robinson, Wilde, Navracroz, Haydel, and Varady 2001). Children's TV viewing also is related to their more traditional views of gender roles, since males and females in children's programming continue to be portrayed in traditional ways (Thompson and Zerbinos 1995).

Young adulthood in the U.S. (usually referring to people in their late twenties and thirties) is increasingly characterized by multiple role demands. This concept refers to the increasing number of young adults in the U.S. who have careers, families, and other community-related responsibilities, such as church activities. Nearly two-thirds of the wives in the U.S. with preschool children also are employed in the labor force. A variety of arrangements among couples have evolved to deal with these multiple roles. Many spouses work different shifts and block scheduling is the idea that a parent will work two long days such as on weekends to be with children during the week (or to pick them up after school) (Hodson and Sullivan 2002). Grandparents in the U.S. are increasingly involved in caring for preschool children as well as adolescents. Although multiple roles require much effort and planning, sociologists have found that couples who share responsibilities for family income, child care, and household duties experience less depression and have higher emotional well-being than those who do not share multiple roles (Mirowsky 1985). Sociologists also have found that multiple roles among working-age adults contributes to the self-enhancing experiences that promote physical and mental health (Ross and Wu 1995). Multiple roles are therefore thought to improve the quality of life of American adults. (See Chapters 8, 9, and 10.)

The major changes in the social experiences related to the socialization of older Americans stem from their longer lives. Most older people including retired people in the U.S. live independently and engage in more activities over a longer time. Most elderly people in the U.S. do not have major physical or mental impairments until they are in their eighties. The generally good health that most elderly people in the U.S. report is verified by the actual measures of their health that are available (Mirowsky 1999). Increasingly, American communities and firms are using older Americans who can provide extremely valuable services (even in part-time positions) as volunteers, mentors, and caregivers. Employers in particular are taking better advantage of the skills and abilities of older employees by offering them retirement in gradual stages (Gardyn 2000). With the additional activities and activeness with which elders in the U.S. pursue their own multiple roles, the general health of older Americans is expected to remain relatively high. (See Chapters 15 and 16.)

Older Americans with health problems including those suffering from dementia and other brain impairments including various stages of Alzheimer's disease are treated by home care. Most disabled elders in the U.S. are still living in their own homes or living with relatives; they are not in nursing homes. The costs of nursing homes and the limits of Medicare in providing for such care make that option a very unrealistic one for most American families. Often very old Americans who survive until they have disabilities still do not require hospitalization or other forms of institutional living. Consequently, providing home care for older people will be an increasing issue for hospitals, health care providers, and families to arrange and coordinate. Family members in particular must share the responsibilities and duties of home health care giving to provide better care and to benefit from the sharing of multiple roles. Studies show that if particular members of the family are the primary caregivers to chronically ill family members, the stress of caregiving can cause more serious problems for caregivers (Chumbler, Grimm, Beck, and Gray 2002). Whole families will benefit from sharing multiple roles, just as couples do.

The focus of hospices in the U.S. is to give palliative care to terminally ill patients. Usually given in the patients' home or in a homelike setting, such care is intended to keep patients emotionally and physically comfortable, and as pain free as is possible while they wait to die. Hospices provide more comfortable and homelike surroundings for patients and their loved ones to experience the social process of death. Medicare provides some benefits for hospice services and hospitals increasingly cooperate to provide more humane and considerate social environments for those who are dying (Burns 1995).

Name: ______________________________

Exercise: Socialization and the Self

2. In the space provided, discuss some examples of multiple role-sharing among couples you know.

Name: ______________________________

Exercise: Socialization and the Self

3. Think about recent adult activity toward young children you have observed in your family or in social settings like a daycare center, churches, and so on, which you have been in recently. In the space provided discuss how the adults' behavior illustrates primary socialization, reciprocal socialization, and anticipatory socialization.

Name: ______________________________

Exercise: Socialization and the Self

4. Think about the influence of peers and television watching in your own socialization prior to coming to college. In the space provided, discuss how the influences of peers and TV watching in your own development illustrate peer socialization, referent others, and anticipatory socialization.

Name: ______________________________

Exercise: Socialization and the Self

5. Watch the classic movie *Rebel without a Cause*, and in the space provided, discuss how the movie illustrates primary socialization, peer socialization, self-esteem, and role taking.

Name: ______________________

Exercise: Socialization and the Self

6. Watch the movie *Parenthood*, and in the space provided, discuss how the movie illustrates the comfort and security principle, reciprocal socialization, peer socialization, and anticipatory socialization.

Name: ______________________________

Exercise: Socialization and the Self

7. Go to the campus library or online, and select an article from the journal *Symbolic Interaction*. Select any one article, read it, and in the space provided, discuss how the article illustrated life course socialization, agents of socialization, significant others, and multiple role demands of adults.

Name: ______________________

Exercise: Socialization and the Self

8. Go to the campus library or online, and select an article from the sociological journal *Marriage and Family*. Select any one article, read it, and in the space provided, discuss how the article illustrated life course socialization, the social self, agents of socialization, and significant others.

Name: ______________________

Exercise: Socialization and the Self

9. Think about recent Internet or telephone communication you have had with family members. In the space provided, discuss how the communication illustrates agents of socialization, reciprocal socialization, peer socialization, multiple role demands, and self-esteem.

Name: ______________________________

Exercise: Socialization and the Self

10. Go to the website of a major hospital or nursing home in your town. Look at the web page, and in the space provided, discuss how the web page illustrates life course socialization, comfort and security principle, referent others, the independence of elderly people, and palliative care.

5

Social Groups and Social Networks in Modern Life

Sociologists care about people and are committed to improving the social experiences that people have. However, sociologists focus their concerns and efforts on the ways that social settings like inner-city neighborhoods or single-industry towns and groups like Mothers Against Drunk Drivers (MADD) both shape and reflect people's experiences. Sociologists believe that the most effective ways to improve people's social experiences are to improve the nature and operation of the social settings that people are in. Neighborhood gang activity can be reduced, for example, by creating active community crime watch organizations in addition to sports teams, dance companies, choirs, and so on to engage young people in other activities. The morale of many workers can be improved by making the work that they do more challenging and rewarding and by letting workers help decide how things can be done better and with whom they would prefer to work on particular shifts or projects. People's health can be improved by providing them more community public health services and training them for better jobs that provide health insurance (Seccombe and Amey 1995).

In explaining how social settings shape and reflect people's experiences, sociologists use several key concepts. Social structure refers to the general principles behind and the general expectations for social activity in social settings. For example, the general principles behind social activity in church are quiet, respectful worship and expressions of religious conviction like tithing and helping others. The expectations of social action in church—being quiet, helping with the nursery, volunteering to be an usher or a member of the choir—illustrate the idea that social structures separate responsibilities into social positions, or social statuses, with different duties, or social roles. The social structure of a family is made of parent(s), child(ren), and related kin like grandparent(s), uncles and aunts, cousins, and so on. The branches in any family tree divide family members into positions and these different positions involve specific social expectations, as when all the children in the present generation are expected to be the first people in the family to complete college.

Like the changing expectations for successive generations in a family, the social structures of social settings like communities and firms and hospitals do not stay the same. Sociologists focus on key social processes that change social structures. The key social processes that determine how and how much social structures will change are called social forces. Among all types of firms and in all industries, one key social force is the technology that is driving the skills necessary for many jobs upward to include knowledge of computer usage and decisions based upon data analysis. Another key social force in post-industrial society is the increase in the number and variety of jobs involving services, or being paid to do things for others. Another key social force changing marriage and family life is the increasing proportion of mothers with young children who work outside the home. (See Chapter 11.)

Sociologists use the term the sociological imagination to refer to people using information about key social forces to make better decisions in their own lives. Knowing some things about the key social forces that are changing the nature of work and family life, for example, can be used by people to decide how to prepare for careers, whom to marry, how to have better marriages, and how to raise children better. The focus of sociology in providing information about the key social forces of modern social life and the changing social patterns they result in involves social facts. Social facts are the changing patterns of social activity in employment, family life and juvenile delinquency including gang activity, for example, that help sociologists understand the basic social forces behind the patterns of current social experience. Overall, sociologists believe that the key social forces explaining successful marriages or delinquency lie in the reality of the social settings in which people are involved. Obviously, good marriages require love and caring, but marriages are more likely to last among better educated spouses who respect each others' careers and help each other pursue what sociologists call multiple adult roles: success at home, at work, at church, and so on. (See Chapter 4.) Delinquents have personal problems. However, delinquency is less likely when families and neighborhoods hold lawless juveniles accountable for crimes and provide for good education and youth-centered activities at schools, community centers, and so on (Osgood, Wilson, O'Malley, Bachman and Johnston 1996). (See Chapter 6.)

Considerable emphasis in sociological research is given to the study of social groups. Social groups are the social units that people are associated with or are members of. Membership in groups becomes the basis for people having similar beliefs and orientations with others, sharing common goals and bonds with them, arranging social life to associate together regularly, and engaging in certain expected actions in relation to others. Sociologists study many different types of groups and the different social structures and the social forces involved in them. Groups called voluntary associations are studied to see the reasons people have for deciding to affiliate with them. The type of church, the favorite service or charity group people are in, the types of firm workers decide to go to work in, and so on can be studied as both reflecting and influencing the common beliefs and commitments and priorities in life that people share. Voluntary associations—from fan-clubs to places of work to the church people decide to join—help in understanding the patterns of social activity that endure through people's lives. Social groups called reference groups are those social yardsticks that people use to compare and evaluate their progress and accomplishments (Mirowsky 1987). For example, universities often designate a set of "benchmark" universities to which they can compare their academic standards and accomplishments.

Other groups are studied as to their size, composition, and differences in expected behaviors. Among many contrasting features of different groups, two stand out. Some groups, usually smaller groups, are characterized by being emotionally close and intimate, as in love, and they involve relationships that involve long-lasting caring. Sociologists call such groups primary groups. Other groups, usually larger ones (although smaller groups of work-teams and academic committees can be included), are called secondary groups. Such groups are characterized by being task oriented, formal and non-emotional, non-intimate, and existent for task accomplishment and little else. Sociological analysis gets somewhat more complicated when studies show that some degree of closeness and permanency is useful when accomplishing complex projects like making movies or designing and building a new car (Carruthers and Babb 2000). Letting a smaller group of directors, producers, writers, and actors choose with whom they want to make a movie, or letting a smaller group of designers, engineers, and production specialists decide together how to design and construct a new car often results in better products. Letting primary-like groups accomplish large tasks shows how primary groups can emerge or be created in secondary groups. This process is called social embeddedness. Conversely, groups like families often work better when some degree of secondariness is used in dividing household duties, having rules for using common property like the TVs or the cars, and having formal complaint sessions to resolve troublesome issues. This emergent secondariness in primary groups can be called instrumentalism.

Sociologists also emphasize the importance of social networks as mechanisms through which much of the social activity in life takes place. Social networks are not groups, though they are studied like groups, and researchers use many of the same concepts such as embeddedness and instrumentalism. Social networks are the interpersonal ties that link particular people together in repeated and collectively beneficial activity. The collective benefits obtainable through the interpersonal ties that networks involve can be called social capital (Lin, Cook, and Burt 2001). Types of social capital can be illustrated by the interpersonal ties among particular family members, neighbors, and friends who carpool in taking groups of children on school activities and trips. Other types of social capital are illustrated by the interpersonal ties that connect particular executives, bank loan officers, investment bankers, and investment brokers when large amounts of money have to be invested in a business venture (Carruthers and Babb 2000). Both these examples—the continued use of the same network of child caregivers and capital formation specialists—illustrate the benefits of so-called close ties: interpersonal ties that are close and involve a great deal of trust and responsibility.

Some interesting recent sociological research involves networks that are larger in scope and less dependent on close, immediate relationships. These more extensive and less directly connected networks are called weak ties networks. While their ties are more dispersed and weaker, there are several advantages or strengths of weak ties networks. Job searches, for example, are more successful when the person looking for work asks friends to ask their acquaintances about job openings and to pass the request for work to their friends in the interest of the job seeker who started the original request (Granovetter 1974). The most effective searches for jobs, information, and other forms of social capital such as technological expertise take place through indirect ties that involve only one step. A particular person may be a single link between larger clusters of people who do not know each other except through each cluster's linkages to that particular common link. That type of person occupies what sociologists call a bridge position. Bridge positions are crucial in providing significant connections that enable efficient social action (Burt 1992). Overall, sociologists are finding that much of the community-oriented support and donations that people provide are structured through the particular social networks of aid particular people have received from particular health care providers and other social service representatives like members of the Red Cross (Grimm and Brewster 2002). These particular and pervasive clusters of ties that together yield the ways in which community resources are distributed and exchanged has been called networked individualism (Wellman and Frank 2001).

Sociological ideas increasingly are appropriate for understanding the many ways that the social forces in social groups and social networks provide a way of understanding modern social life. On the one hand, people have never been in a better environment concerning the possible groups and networks to be in. On the other hand, sociologists and others including lawyers and policy makers work very hard to increase everyone's access to and participation in groups and networks. We have a good deal more sociological work to do before social groups and social networks are accessible to most people. (See Chapters 7, 8, 13 and 16.)

Name: ______________________________

Quiz Questions: Social Groups and Social Networks in Modern Life

1. In general sociologists work to improve the experiences of particular people or families. (True or False?)
2. The general expectations for social activity in social settings is which of the following?
   a. social roles
   b. social status
   c. social structure
   d. sociological imagination
3. Key social processes that change social settings and their structures are called social roles. (True or False?)
4. Using social facts to make better decisions about personal life is which of the following?
   a. social forces
   b. social embeddedness
   c. instrumentalism
   d. sociological imagination
5. Members of a family at a family reunion would illustrate a secondary group. (True or False?)
6. A manufacturing firm creating a project team of ten people to produce and market a new product would illustrate which of the following?
   a. instrumentalism
   b. social capital
   c. social embeddedness
   d. networked individualism
7. Family life is seldom improved with instrumentalism. (True or False?)
8. Which of these is the usual benefit of successfully operating social networks?
   a. multiple adult roles
   b. sociological imagination
   c. social facts
   d. social capital
9. Job searches are best done through close-ties networks. (True or False?)
10. Community resources are usually developed through which of the following?
    a. instrumentalism
    b. close ties networks
    c. networked individualism
    d. primary groups

Name: ______________________________

Exercise: Social Groups and Social Networks in Modern Life

1. In the space provided, define and briefly describe a situation of social embeddedness you have been in.

Name: ______________________________

Exercise: Social Groups and Social Networks in Modern Life

2. In the space provided, define and briefly describe a bridge position you have been in.

Name: ______________________________

Exercise: Social Groups and Social Networks in Modern Life

3. Consider a primary group that you have been a part of, and in the space provided, discuss its social statuses, social roles, and social structure. Then give some examples of instrumentalism you experienced with others in the group.

Name: ______________________

Exercise: Social Groups and Social Networks in Modern Life

4. Consider a close-ties social network you have been in. Describe the people linked together in the network and the social capital their interconnectedness involved. In the space provided, discuss especially the evidence that trust and responsibility characterized the network.

Name: ______________________________

Exercise: Social Groups and Social Networks in Modern Life

5. Watch the movie *The Longest Yard*, and in the space provided, describe how the movie illustrates social structures, social roles, and social statuses. Explain the social forces that influence the groups. Discuss, in particular, social embeddedness and instrumentalism, as well as any evidence of bridge positions.

Name: ______________________________

Exercise: Social Groups and Social Networks in Modern Life

6. Watch the movie *The Firm*, and in the space provided, describe how the movie illustrates social structures, social roles, and social statuses. Explain the social forces that influence the groups. Discuss, in particular, social embeddedness and instrumentalism, as well as any evidence of bridge positions.

Name: ___________________________

Exercise: Social Groups and Social Networks in Modern Life

7. Go to the campus library or online, and select an article from the sociological journal *Social Forces*. Select an article, read it, and in the space provided, discuss how the article illustrated social structures, social forces, and social facts.

Name: ______________________________

Exercise: Social Groups and Social Networks in Modern Life

8. Go to the campus library or online, and select an article from the social science journal *Administrative Science Quarterly*. Read it, and in the space provided, discuss how the article illustrated social structures, social forces, and social facts.

Name: ______________________________

Exercise: Social Groups and Social Networks in Modern Life

9. Think of the Internet communication between you and your family and friends. Use the communication as an example and in the space below, illustrate a <u>close ties network</u>, <u>social capital</u>, and <u>give evidence of repeated and collectively beneficial activity</u>.

Name: ______________________________

Exercise: Social Groups and Social Networks in Modern Life

10. Consider your recent e-mail communication. Considering the various e-mail messages you have received and sent, in the space provided, discuss any communication links that illustrate weak ties, bridge positions, and networked individualism.

Deviant Behavior and Crime

To sociologists the act of breaking the rules is less important than the social reaction to breaking the rules. Not every instance of rule breaking is met with the same reaction. Sociologists study rule breaking to learn which rule breakers receive public punishments intended to control and prevent particular types of nonconformity. The types of rule breaking that elicit negative responses are called deviance. Those who receive negative reactions from others expressing reactions indicating that their behaviors are illegal or unacceptable or both are deviants. Social reactions to deviance are shaped by the range of tolerance of the social group in a specific place and time (Cavin 1961). For example, the range of tolerable nonconformity can be illustrated by looking at bystander reactions to drivers in 35 mph speed zones. Those drivers whose cars are going 30 to 40 mph would probably be ignored although they would be breaking the formal norm (i.e., the law), while those going slower than 10 mph or faster than 55 mph would receive either curious or frightened public reaction and possibly elicit a formal response from the society in a ticket from police.

Because there are differences in the range of rule breaking social groups will tolerate and/or ignore, thrill-seeking individuals, especially youth, often experiment with rule breaking behavior. For example a high school student might use alcohol or drugs, but continue to be seen as normal. Even if he or she is caught, the experimental behavior does not change the social group's view of him or her or their self-concept—their own view of themselves. This is what sociologists call primary deviance (Clinard 1968). However, in other situations where rule-breaking behavior becomes a pattern such that it receives negative and punitive reactions, the individual can begin thinking of himself or herself as a deviant. When a person adopts a deviant status as part of his or her identity, his or her deviant behavior is called secondary deviance (Lemert 1972). The range of tolerance and other social processes in a setting establish two types of secondary deviance (Cavin 1961): positive deviance refers to unacceptable overconformity, such as the reactions of an instructor and a class to a "know-it-all" student who wants to be the first to answer every question during a semester; negative deviance refers to intolerable underconformity such as a shoplifter who fails to follow the rules of payment for goods and services.

Since both the patterns of tolerance or overlooking rule breaking and the social rules, or social norms, in social settings change, so do deviance and deviants. Cigarette smoking was a symbol of sophistication in the U.S. during the 1940s and many prominent people including characters in movies smoked. Today, smoking is widely banned and those who smoke including characters in movies receive negative reactions such as the negative reactions of moviegoers to filmmakers. Even so, in certain social settings, such as among youth who want to appear mature or baseball player athletes who are around other users, smoking and chewing tobacco are common. Women's smoking increased dramatically in the U.S. as wives increasingly became employed full-time outside the home (Walsh, Sorensen, and Leonard 1995).

Stigma (Goffman 1963) represents a major form of reactions to deviants and refers to negative evaluations of and references to people, especially those referring to basic faults of character like "pimp," "whore," "cheat," and so on. Stigmatization includes the ways in which authorities like police and judges and people in general punish deviants with stigmatizing reactions. These public and widespread references to faults of character and the decisions to avoid people who have received such references are called labels. From whomever labels come, once deviants have received them, labels like "felon" or "convict" or "delinquent" override other aspects of character and other social relationships, like "father" or "employee" or "teammate." Deviant labels are therefore called master statuses. While some labels such as "serial rapist" or "criminally insane" should not be removed, many other deviant labels can and should be removed after the punishment has been completed. Sociologists have found that for many less serious offenders settings other than prison, or alternative sentencing, helps both to rehabilitate offenders and to reestablish normal social relationships (Lanier and Henry 1997).

One important pattern to the reactions rule breaking receives in social settings reflects the status of those who break rules. White-collar crime (Sutherland 1940) refers to the illegal actions of high status people in the courses of their jobs. Sometimes called occupational crime, serious forms of this criminality include the theft of millions of dollars by illegal stockbroking and illegal loans by bankers. Typically, however, such high status criminals as doctors who give patients illegal drug prescriptions and bankers who embezzle other people's savings receive very short prison terms, often in the so-called minimum-security prisons or with probation. While such offenders are made to pay fines, they are often able to do so and return to a more-or-less normal life often as "advisors" to others interested in controlling white-collar crime. The recent instances of illegality in accounting and corporate management have received considerable publicity and caused much anxiety among public investors. However, it remains to be seen if punishments offenders receive are harsher or whether new regulations against such future crimes get enforced. Common criminals including many drug-dependent people who steal to buy drugs receive longer sentences and more stigma than white collar criminals do. Consequently, average offenders have a much harder time reentering society than higher status offenders do. Another important pattern in the reactions to rule violators is victim discounting, or the process by which offenders whose victims were poor or minorities receive less harsh sentences than offenders whose victims were rich and white. A particular form of victim discounting involves the lesser penalties if any given to offenders whose victims are gay, mentally ill, cross-dressers, and others already stigmatized. In fact, it is often supposed that such stigmatized people are themselves responsible for becoming the victims of crime (Berrill 1992).

Sociological theories of deviance and deviants stress the social conditions and social processes in which some people become deviants. Rather than assuming people are "born bad" or have serious faults of character from an early age, sociologists focus upon being around other deviants, having opportunities to become deviant, and the absence of meaningful relationships with non-deviants, such as teachers, coaches, and non-deviant family members. Control theory (Hirschi 1969) explains juvenile delinquency by the number and types of social bonds youth have with positive role models like instructors, coaches, and older youth. Differential association theory (Sutherland and Cressey 1992) explains criminality through the proportion of important relationships people have that involve well-established deviants such as gang members, repeated felons, and major drug dealers. Occupational crime of course focuses upon employment conditions such as electronic access to large accounts and to drugs in explaining deviance, especially when offenders themselves have problems such as gambling debt and drug dependencies. Strain theory (Merton 1968) stresses the absence in certain communities, neighborhoods, and regions of legally successful opportunities like good schooling and good jobs.

Even so, other sociological explanations of deviance like strain theory stress that most people in circumstances that increase the chances of deviance still do not become deviant (Merton 1968).

Crime is the most prevalent form of deviance in the U.S. Crimes are violations of the criminal laws that apply to localities, to states, or throughout the U.S. One important scheme for classifying crimes is used by the Federal Bureau of Investigation (FBI) in regularly publishing *Crime in the United States*. The FBI's crime index is made up of property crimes and violent crimes with four subtypes of each. Property crimes involve these forms of unlawful taking of others' property: burglary (by entering homes or buildings), larceny-theft (by taking property like purses, or things from cars including theft of credit cards), auto theft, and arson (burning property including what is owned for insurance fraud, out of anger, and so on). Violent crimes are unlawful forms of violence against others including murder and manslaughter (killing others), aggravated assault (attacking or intending to attack others to injure them seriously), forcible rape (forcing sexual relations with others), and robbery (taking property from others while using or threatening to use force or violence). Serious crimes among juveniles are these same types of crimes, while status crimes refer to unlawful acts by youth like drinking and truancy from school that are lawful acts among older people. So-called victimless crimes do not have particular victims, but create major problems both for the offenders and people close to them and for society. Main forms of victimless crimes include illegal drug use, prostitution, and illegal gambling. Drug usage is related to many index crimes and prostitution is related to the spread of sexually transmitted diseases including AIDS.

During the 1990s all forms of index crimes and serious crimes committed by youth significantly declined by 10 to 20 percent on average. These declines are unprecedented during the entire time crime records have been kept. More successful imprisonment of serious offenders, better rehabilitation programs for less serious offenders, and the expanding number of good jobs may be related to the decline in crime (Macionis 2002). That the official declines are real rather than artifacts of record keeping is indicated by the comparable declines during the 1990s in the *National Crime Victimization Survey* (NCVS) data. The NCVS is a national survey of households in the U.S. conducted every six months by the Justice Department to compile reports of being victimized by any type of crime. While some crimes are becoming less frequent in the U.S., others such as hate crimes continue to be quite common. Such crimes involve violence and property crime against others simply because of their race, religion, gender, sexual orientation or lifestyles. Given the increasing diversity of the U.S. population, (see Chapters 6 and 8), it will be a challenge to preserve acceptable ways of living in the U.S. that exclude such crimes.

Name: ________________________________

Exercise: Deviant Behavior and Crime

2. In the space provided, discuss three examples of secondary deviance that you are aware of on your campus or nearby campuses.

Name: ______________________________

Exercise: Deviant Behavior and Crime

3. Consider two different classes that you are taking or have taken. Describe the ranges of tolerance for test grades, written assignment length and attendance requirements. In the space provided, briefly explain any differences.

Name: ______________________

Exercise: Deviant Behavior and Crime

4. Think back over the courses you took last semester and/or are taking this semester (if this is your first). In the space provided, briefly discuss examples of positive and negative deviance, and reactions to them.

Name: ______________________________

Exercise: Deviant Behavior and Crime

5. Watch the original movie version of *The Getaway*, starring Ali McGraw and Steve McQueen. In the space provided, discuss how the movie illustrates negative deviance, occupational deviance, differential association theory, and violent crimes.

Name: ______________________________

Exercise: Deviant Behavior and Crime

6. Watch the movie *Sleepers*. In the space provided, discuss how the movie illustrates victim discounting, stigmatization, labels, occupational crime, differential association theory, and so-called victimless crimes.

Name: ______________________________

Exercise: Deviant Behavior and Crime

7. Go to the campus library or online and select an article from the sociological journal, *Deviant Behavior*. Select any one article, read it, and in the space provided, discuss how the article illustrates deviants, master statuses, control theory, and property crimes.

Name: ______________________

Exercise: Deviant Behavior and Crime

8. Go to the campus library or online and select an article from the sociological journal, *Crime and Delinquency*. Select any one article, read it, and in the space provided, discuss how the article illustrates negative deviance, social norms, control theory, and status crimes.

Name: ________________________________

Exercise: Deviant Behavior and Crime

9. Based upon Internet use in your family or your on campus use, in the space provided, discuss the uses of the Internet to illustrate: social norms, positive deviance, negative deviance, and stigma.

Name: ______________________________

Exercise: Deviant Behavior and Crime

10. Go to the Internet and find a website that in your judgement can be discussed in terms of negative deviance, range of tolerance, labels, and victimless crimes. Discuss these items in the space below.

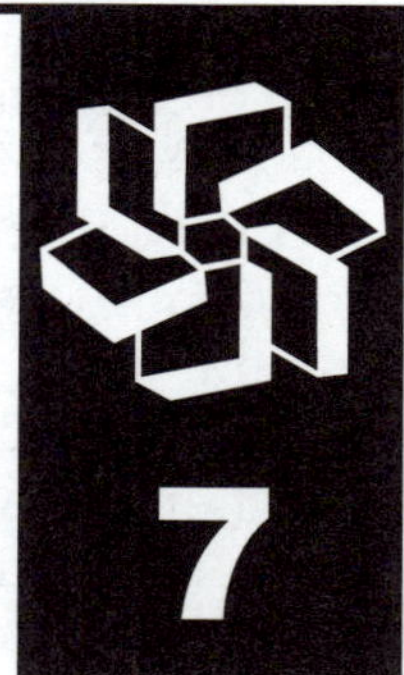

7

Community in Rural and Urban Settings

George Hillery (1955) identified many separate ways sociologists define community and the number of definitions has increased since his time. The common link among these definitions is that they all emphasize various forms of interpersonal ties among people. These ties can be based on shared territory, a shared way of life (i.e., shared norms and goals), collective action and interaction, and/or a shared sense of belonging to the community (Mason 2000, Wilkinson 1991). The concept of community shares all of the characteristics of any other social group. In fact, people often use community to describe their groups or organizations.

Why do people prefer to characterize their group as a community? What makes community so special in comparison to other social groups? First, community is special because it implies honesty and virtuousness among its members. That is, a community is often considered a special group that evokes special feelings of solidarity and fellowship among its members (Mason 2000, Tinder 1980, Wilkinson 1991). Moreover, a sense of trust is evident among group members because community members treat each other fairly (Govier 1997, Wuthnow 1998). No systematic injustice should endure in this special group; the community would not stand for it (Mason 2000). While no real community could ever totally live up to this ideal conceptualization, sociologists have noted that the extent to which individuals develop community ties has profound consequences on personal and societal well being (Banfield 1958, Tinder 1980, Wilkinson 1991, Wuthnow 1998). Second, community is special for sociologists because it is the smallest social unit containing all the social institutions that comprise larger society. Communities are therefore where and how society is experienced (Wilkinson 1991).

Community sociologists have various perspectives on how communities are changing over time (Wellman and Leighton 1979). Some, especially those working with small towns and rural communities, feel that as society has industrialized, people have become more isolated from their neighbors. They argue that cheap and efficient transportation and communication technologies have allowed individuals to be more mobile. People have also felt increased time pressure because mobility and communication technology have blurred the lines between work and leisure (Florida 2002, Hochschild 1989, Robinson and Godbey 1997, Wuthnow 1998). These social forces have encouraged individuals to develop fewer strong, local ties and instead rely more on weaker, more geographically dispersed ties (Granovetter 1973). (See Section 4.) As ties between people have decreased, fewer individuals have been willing to work together to help solve community problems such as crime, drug abuse, homelessness, poverty and lack of quality education for the young. To these community sociologists this lack of interest in civic issues signals the loss of community and has been referred to as the community lost view (Wellman and Leighton 1979). If the sociologists holding the community lost viewpoint are correct and these social forces continue to erode strong, local ties, then our prospects of maintaining a democracy will decline (Wuthnow 1998). A second group of community sociologists is less pessimistic about the continuing existence of local communities. Sociologists, who study urban areas, argue that as society changed, community also changed. Their research documents that people still struggle to develop and maintain communal relationships with kin, co-workers, and neighbors even in the largest cities (Wellman and Leighton 1979). These new forms of communal ties reflect contemporary social life and this perspective is the community saved view (Wuthnow 1998).

One major point of agreement for both the community lost and community saved views is community boundaries. Both viewpoints agree that a community involves some shared territory. C.J. Galpin (1915) was the first sociologist to attempt to define community boundaries. In his study of rural service centers in Wisconsin, he examined ties to local communities by driving out of towns and looking at the ruts in farmers' driveways to see whether they turned toward the town he had just departed. If the ruts turned toward the town, he reasoned that the people living in that homestead were likely to be members of the community of that town. More recently, sociologists of both community lost and community saved camps have argued that community boundaries should be determined by social interaction (Kaufman 1959, Suttles 1972, Wilkinson 1991). Community boundaries extend to the limits of interaction by individuals as they fulfill their daily needs. Researchers within these two traditions have attempted to define community boundaries by using school district boundaries, local newspaper circulation boundaries, and commuting zones (Janowitz 1961; Parisi, Gill and Taquino 2000; Zekeri, Wilkinson and Humphrey 1994).

A third sociological perspective on community is the community liberated view that contends that technological advances in communication technology over the past 25 years allow us to disregard territorial boundaries of community altogether. This view makes the individual, not the place, the center of community (Chaskin 1997). In this view the community has been liberated from its spatial component by the Internet, cell phones, faxes and other related technologies that people use to accomplish their daily activities such as shopping, banking, and communicating information (Wellman and Leighton 1979). The only limit is that imposed by available and affordable communication technology. Individuals, groups, and organizations who can afford the equipment can work and/or socialize with others they interact with online (Wellman et al. 1996). The community liberated viewpoint is controversial because many community sociologists are skeptical that virtual communities are truly communities. Proponents of this view argue that these computer-structured social networks (CSSNs) allow people to make both strong and weak ties to establish the sorts of bonds that define communities. (See Section 5.)

Community sociologists are interested in improving the well-being of communities. Both community lost and community saved sociologists are concerned with removing barriers to interaction at the local level. Community lost scholars are also concerned with the effects of migration on the community. Many small rural communities suffer from the out-migration of intelligent young adult community members who move away to attend college and end up moving to cities. This "brain drain" means that individuals most able to help solve problems have permanently left the community (Voth, Sizer, Farmer 1996; Whiting 1974). On the other hand, community sociologists holding this viewpoint have also been concerned about the effects of rapid in-migration. If a community gets too large too quickly, community institutions are unable to handle the load and social problems such as drug and alcohol abuse and violent crime are likely to increase (Freudenburg and Jones 1991; Hunter, Krannich, Smith 2002; Rodin, Downs, Petterson, and Russell 1997).

Community saved sociologists approach community well-being somewhat differently. Sociologists like Jane Jacobs (1961) argue that comparative studies of urban sub-communities (i.e., neighborhoods) give us clues on how to build cities in ways that foster localized communities. The current movement in this area is called new urbanism and owes much to the work of community and neighborhood sociologists (Duany, Plater-Zyberk, Speck 2000; Lofland 1998). Moreover, community saved sociologists are concerned with making sure that the changing physical structure of the city and social structure of the community are egalitarian. They work on making sure community development equally benefits all members of the community (Wellman and Leighton 1979).

To those sociologists most concerned about liberating the community, a major emphasis is decreasing the digital divide. The digital divide is a metaphor emphasizing that there is structured inequality between those who have access to the Internet and those that do not (Borgida, Sullivan, Oxendine, Jackson, Riedel, Gangl 2002). In the United States, younger, college educated, urban white males are more likely to have and continue to use Internet access (DiMaggio, Hargattai, Neuman, Robinson 2001; Katz, Rice, Aspden 2001). As more information is placed on the Internet, this disparity divides those who can know from those who cannot (Servon and Nelson 2001). While this divide is slowly decreasing domestically, a global digital divide also exists (DiMaggio et al. 2001). It is estimated that just five percent of the world's population has Internet access. (See Chapters 16, 17, 19 and 20.)

Communities reflect the health and state of the larger societies in which they exist. As shown by the many definitions of the term "community" itself, communities are always evolvoing and changing. By focusing on the types of community structures and the changes that are occurring within them, whether from the digital divide or increased mobilization, sociologists can determine issues and challenges facing society today and provide guidance and solutions for the myriad of problems that arise with change. (See Chapters 17,19 and 20.)

Name: ______________________________

Exercise: Community in Rural and Urban Settings

2. In the space provided, discuss the ways in which interaction patterns define the boundaries of your campus.

Name: ______________________________

Exercise: Community in Rural and Urban Settings

3. Consider your hometown or the urban neighborhood that you grew up in. In the space provided, discuss that area with respect to community, community lost view, the community saved view, and the community liberated view.

Name: ______________________________

Exercise: Community in Rural and Urban Settings

4. Think of any campus building that includes members of similar disciplines, like the building for physical sciences, social sciences, or fine arts. In the space provided, discuss the building with respect to community, community saved view, community liberated view, and solidarity.

Name: ______________________________

Exercise: Community in Rural and Urban Settings

5. Watch the movie *Witness*, and in the space provided, discuss how the movie illustrated community solidarity, community saved view, trust and fairness, and community liberated view.

Name: ______________________________

Exercise: Community in Rural and Urban Settings

6. Watch the movie *Thunder Heart*, and in the space provided, discuss how the movie illustrated community, community lost, community saved, and community liberated.

Name: ________________________________

Exercise: Community in Rural and Urban Settings

7. Go to the campus library or online and select an article from the sociological journal, *Rural Sociology*. Select any one article, read it, and in the space provided, discuss how it illustrated community solidarity and trust, community saved view, community liberated view, and migration.

Name: ______________________

Exercise: Community in Rural and Urban Settings

8. Go to the campus library or online and select an article from the *Journal of Urban Affairs*. Select any one article, read it, and in the space provided, discuss how it illustrated community, community saved view, the new urbanism, and community solidarity.

Name: ______________________________

Exercise: Community in Rural and Urban Settings

9. Think of your Internet usage. On the basis of your usage patterns in the space provided, discuss some examples of CSSNs you are in relative to community solidarity, community saved view, solidarity, and community liberated view.

Name: ______________________________

Exercise: Community in Rural and Urban Settings

10. Go to the webpage of any major charity organization in the U.S., such as the Red Cross, or United Way. Look at the webpage information and in the space provided, discuss information related to community, community solidarity, community-liberated view, and CSSNs.

The Tipping Point
How Little Things Can Make a Big Difference

Malcolm Gladwell

1.

In the late 1960s, the psychologist Stanley Milgram conducted an experiment to find an answer to what is known as the small-world problem. The problem is this: how are human beings connected? Do we all belong to separate worlds, operating simultaneously but autonomously, so that the links between any two people, anywhere in the world, are few and distant? Or are we all bound up together in a grand, interlocking web? In a way, Milgram was asking the very same kind of question that began this chapter, namely, how does an idea or a trend or a piece of news—the British are coming!—travel through a population?

Milgram's idea was to test this question with a chain letter. He got the names of 160 people who lived in Omaha, Nebraska, and mailed each of them a packet. In the packet was the name and address of a stockbroker who worked in Boston and lived in Sharon, Massachusetts. Each person was instructed to write his or her name on the packet and send it on to a friend or acquaintance who he or she thought would get the packet closer to the stockbroker. If you lived in Omaha and had a cousin outside of Boston, for example, you might send it to him, on the grounds that—even if your cousin did not himself know the stockbroker—he would be a lot more likely to be able to get to the stockbroker in two or three or four steps. The idea was that when the packet finally arrived at the stockbroker's house, Milgram could look at the list of all those whose hands it went through to get there and establish how closely connected someone chosen at random from one part of the country was to another person in another part of the country. Milgram found that most of the letters reached the stockbroker in five or six steps. This experiment is where we get the concept of six degrees of separation.

That phrase is now so familiar that it is easy to lose sight of how surprising Milgram's findings were. Most of us don't have particularly broad and diverse groups of friends. In one well-known study, a group of psychologists asked people living in the Dyckman public housing project in northern Manhattan to name their closest friend in the project; 88 percent of the friends lived in the same building, and half lived on the same floor. In general, people chose friends of similar age and race. But if the friend lived down the hall, then age and race became a lot less important. Proximity overpowered similarity. Another study, done on students at the University of Utah, found that if you ask someone why he is friendly with someone else, he'll say it is because he and his friend share similar attitudes. But if you actually quiz the two of them on their attitudes, you'll find out that what they actually share is similar activities. We're friends with the people we do things with, as much as we are with the people we resemble. We don't seek out friends, in other words. We associate with the people who occupy the same small, physical spaces that we do. People in Omaha are not, as a rule, friends with people who live halfway across the country in Sharon, Massachusetts. "When I asked an intelligent friend of mine how many steps he thought it would take, he estimated that it would require 100 intermediate persons or more to move from Nebraska to Sharon," Milgram wrote, at the time. "Many people make somewhat similar estimates, and are surprised to learn that only five intermediaries will—on average—suffice. Somehow it does not accord with intuition." How did the packet get to Sharon in just five steps?

The answer is that in the six degrees of separation, not all degrees are equal. When Milgram analyzed his experiment, for example, he found that many of the chains from Omaha to Sharon followed the same asymmetrical pattern. Twenty-four letters reached the stockbroker at his home in Sharon, and of those, sixteen were given to him by the same person, a clothing merchant Milgram calls Mr. Jacobs. The balance of letters came to the stockbroker at his office, and of those the majority came through two other men, whom Milgram calls Mr. Brown and Mr. Jones. In all, half of the responses that came back to the stockbroker were delivered to him by these same three people. Think of it. Dozens of people, chosen at random from a large Midwestern city, send out letters independently. Some go through college acquaintances. Some send their letters to relatives. Some send them to old workmates. Everyone has a different strategy. Yet in the end, when all of those separate and idiosyncratic chains were completed, half of those letters ended up in the hands of Jacobs, Jones, and Brown. Six degrees of separation doesn't mean that everyone is linked to everyone else in just six steps. It means that a very small number of people are linked to everyone else in a few steps, and the rest of us are linked to the world through those special few.

There is an easy way to explore this idea. Suppose that you made a list of the forty people whom you would call your circle of friends (not including family and co-workers) and in each case worked backward until you could identify the person who is ultimately responsible for setting in motion the series of connections that led to that friendship. My oldest friend, Bruce, for example, I met in first grade, so I'm the responsible party. That's easy. I met my friend Nigel because he lived down the hall in college from my friend Tom, whom I met because in freshman year he invited me to play touch football. Tom is responsible for Nigel. Once you've made all of the connections, the strange thing is that you will find the same names coming up again and again. I have a friend named Amy, whom I met when her friend Katie brought her to a restaurant where I was having dinner one night. I know Katie because she is the best friend of my friend Larissa, whom I know because I was told to look her up by a mutual friend of both of ours—Mike A.—whom I know because he went to school with another friend of mine—Mike H.—who used to work at a political weekly with my friend Jacob. No Jacob, no Amy. Similarly, I met my friend Sarah S. at my birthday party a year ago, because she was there with a writer named David who was there at the invitation of his agent, Tina, whom I met through my friend Leslie, whom I know because her sister, Nina, is a friend of my friend Ann's, whom I met through my old roommate Maura, who was my roommate because she worked with a writer named Sarah L., who was a college friend of my friend Jacob's. No Jacob, no Sarah S. In fact, when I go down my list of forty friends, thirty of them, in one way or another, lead back to Jacob. My social circle is, in reality, not a circle. It is a pyramid. And at the top of the pyramid is a single person—Jacob—who is responsible for an overwhelming majority of the relationships that constitute my life. Not only is my social circle not a circle, but it's not "mine" either. It belongs to Jacob. It's more like a club that he invited me to join. These people who link us up with the world, who bridge Omaha and Sharon, who introduce us to our social circles—these people on whom we rely more heavily than we realize—are Connectors, people with a special gift for bringing the world together.

2.

What makes someone a Connector? The first—and most obvious—criterion is that Connectors know lots of people. They are the kinds of people who know everyone. All of us know someone like this. But I don't think that we spend a lot of time thinking about the importance of these kinds of people. I'm not even sure that most of us really believe that the kind of person who knows everyone really knows everyone. But they do. There is a simple way to show this. In the paragraph below is a list of around 250 surnames, all taken at random from the Manhattan phone book. Go down the list and give yourself a point every time you see a surname that is shared by someone you know. (The definition of "know" here is very broad. For example, if you sat down next to that person on a train, you would know their name if they introduced themselves to you and they would know your name.) Multiple names count. If the name is Johnson, in other words, and you know three Johnsons, you get three points. The idea is that your score on this test should roughly represent how social you are. It's a simple way of estimating how many friends and acquaintances you have.

> Algazi, Alvarez, Alpern, Ametrano, Andrews, Aran, Arnstein, Ashford, Bailey, Ballout, Bamberger, Baptista, Barr, Barrows, Baskerville, Bassiri, Bell, Bokgese, Brandao, Bravo, Brooke, Brightman, Billy, Blau, Bohen, Bohn, Borsuk, Brendle, Butler, Calle, Cantwell, Carrell, Chinlund, Cirker, Cohen, Collas, Couch, Callegher, Calcaterra, Cook, Carey, Cassell, Chen, Chung, Clarke, Cohn, Carton, Crowley, Curbelo, Dellamanna, Diaz, Dirar, Duncan, Dagostino, Delakas, Dillon, Donaghey, Daly, Dawson, Edery, Ellis, Elliott, Eastman, Easton, Famous, Fermin, Fialco, Finklestein, Farber, Falkin, Feinman, Friedman, Gardner, Gelpi, Glascock, Grandfield, Greenbaum, Greenwood, Gruber, Garil, Goff, Gladwell, Greenup, Gannon, Ganshaw, Garcia, Gennis, Gerard, Gericke, Gilbert, Glassman, Glazer, Gomendio, Gonzalez, Greenstein, Guglielmo, Gurman, Haberkorn, Hoskins, Hussein, Hamm, Hardwick, Harrell, Hauptman, Hawkins, Henderson, Hayman, Hibara, Hehmann, Herbst, Hedges, Hogan, Hoffman, Horowitz, Hsu, Huber, Ikiz, Jaroschy, Johann, Jacobs, Jara, Johnson, Kassel, Keegan, Kuroda, Kavanau, Keller, Kevill, Kiew, Kimbrough, Kline, Kossoff, Kotzitzky, Kahn, Kiesler, Kosser, Korte, Liebowitz, Lin, Liu, Lowrance, Lundh, Laux, Leifer, Leung, Levine, Leiw, Lockwood, Logrono, Lohnes, Lowet, Laber, Leonardi, Marten, McLean, Michaels, Miranda, Moy, Marin, Muir, Murphy, Marodon, Matos, Mendoza, Muraki, Neck, Needham, Noboa, Null, O'Flynn, O'Neill, Orlowski, Perkins, Pieper, Pierre, Pons, Pruska, Paulino, Popper, Potter, Purpura, Palma, Perez, Portocarrero, Punwasi, Rader, Rankin, Ray, Reyes, Richardson, Ritter, Roos, Rose, Rosenfeld, Roth, Rutherford, Rustin, Ramos, Regan, Reisman, Renkert, Roberts, Rowan, Rene, Rosario, Rothbart, Saperstein, Schoenbrod, Schwed, Sears, Statosky, Sutphen, Sheehy, Silverton, Silverman, Silverstein, Sklar, Slotkin, Speros, Stollman, Sadowski, Schles, Shapiro, Sigdel, Snow, Spencer, Steinkol, Stewart, Stires, Stopnik, Stonehill, Tayss, Tilney, Temple, Torfield, Townsend, Trimpin, Turchin, Villa, Vasillov, Voda, Waring Weber, Weinstein, Wang, Wegimont, Weed, Weishaus.

I have given this test to at least a dozen groups of people. One was a freshman World Civilizations class at City College in Manhattan. The students were all in their late teens or early twenties, many of them recent immigrants to America, and of middle and lower income. The average score in that class was 20.96, meaning that the average person in the class knew 21 people with the same last names as the people on my list. I also gave the test to a group of health educators and academics at a conference in Princeton, New Jersey. This group were mostly in their forties and fifties, largely white, highly educated—many had Ph.D.'s—and wealthy. Their average score was 39. Then I gave the test to a relatively random sample of my friends and acquaintances, mostly journalists and professionals in their late twenties and thirties. The average score was 41. These results shouldn't be all that surprising. College students don't have as wide a circle of acquaintances as people in their forties. It makes sense that between the ages of twenty and forty the number of people you know should roughly double, and that upper-income professionals should know more people than lower-income immigrants. In every group there was also quite a range between the highest and the lowest scorers. That makes sense too, I think. Real estate salesmen know more people than computer hackers. What was surprising, though, was how enormous that range was. In the college class, the low score was 2 and the high score was 95. In my random sample, the low score was 9 and the high score was 118. Even at the conference in Princeton, which was a highly homogenous group of people of similar age, education, and income—who were all, with a few exceptions, in the same profession—the range was enormous. The lowest score was 16. The highest score was 108. All told, I have given the test to about 400 people. Of those, there were two dozen or so scores under 20, eight over 90, and four more over 100. The other surprising thing is that I found high scorers in every social group I looked at. The scores of the students at City College were less, on average, than adult scores. But even in that group there are people whose social circle is four or five times the size of other people's. Sprinkled among every walk of life, in other words, are a handful of people with a truly extraordinary knack of making friends and acquaintances. They are Connectors.

3.

Connectors are important for more than simply the number of people they know. Their importance is also a function of the kinds of people they know. Perhaps the best way to understand this point is through the popular parlor game "Six Degrees of Kevin Bacon." The idea behind the game is to try to link any actor or actress, through the movies they've been in, to the actor Kevin Bacon in less than six steps. So, for example, O.J. Simpson was in *Naked Gun* with Priscilla Presley, who was in *Ford Fairlane* with Gilbert Gottfried, who was in *Beverly Hills Cop II* with Paul Reiser, who was in *Diner* with Kevin Bacon. That's four steps. Mary Pickford was in *Screen Snapshots* with Clark Gable, who was in *Combat America* with Tony Romano, who, thirty-five years later, was in *Starting Over* with Bacon. That's three steps. Recently, a computer scientist at the University of Virginia by the name of Brett Tjaden actually sat down and figured out what the average Bacon number is for the quarter million or so actors and actresses who have played in television films or major motion pictures and came up with 2.8312 steps. Anyone who has ever acted, in other words, can be linked to Bacon in an average of under three steps. That sounds impressive, except that Tjaden then went back and performed an even more heroic calculation, figuring out what the average degree of connectedness was for everyone who had ever acted in Hollywood. For example, how many steps on average does it take to link everyone in Hollywood to Robert DeNiro or Shirley Temple or Adam Sandler? Tjaden found that when he listed all Hollywood actors in order of their "connectedness," Bacon ranked only 669th. Martin Sheen, by contrast, can be connected to every other actor in 2.63681 steps, which puts him almost 650 places higher than Bacon. Elliot Gould can be connected even more quickly, in 2.63601. Among the top fifteen are people like Robert Mitchum and Gene Hackman and Donald Sutherland and Shelley Winters and Burgess Meredith. The best-connected actor of all time? Rod Steiger.

Why is Kevin Bacon so far behind these actors? One big factor is that Bacon is a lot younger than most of them and as a result has made fewer movies. But that explains only some of the difference. There are lots of people, for example, who have made lots of movies and aren't particularly well connected. John Wayne, for example, made an extraordinary 179 movies in his sixty-year career and still ranks only 116th, at 2.7173. The problem is that more than half of John Wayne's movie were Westerns, meaning that he made the same kind of movie with the same kind of actors over and over again.

But take someone like Steiger: he has made a great movies like the Oscar-winning *On the Waterfront* and dreadful movies like *Car Pool*. He won an Oscar for his role in *In the Heat of the Night* and also made "B" movies so bad they went straight to video. He's played Mussolini, Napoléon, Pontius Pilate, and Al Capone. He's been in thirty-eight dramas, twelve crime pictures and comedies, eleven thrillers, eight action films, seven Westerns, six war movies, four documentaries, three horror flicks, two sci-fi films, and a musical, among others. Rod Steiger is the best-connected actor in history because he has managed to move up and down and back and forth among all the different worlds and subcultures and niches and levels that the acting profession has to offer.

This is what Connectors are like. They are the Rod Steigers of everyday life. They are people whom all of us can reach in only a few steps because, for one reason or another, they manage to occupy many different worlds and subcultures and niches. In Steiger's case, of course, his high connectedness is a function of his versatility as an actor and, in all likelihood, some degree of good luck. But in the case of Connectors, their ability to span many different worlds is a function of something intrinsic to their personality, some combination of curiosity, self-confidence, sociability, and energy.

This is in some ways the archetypal Lois Weisberg story. First she reaches out to somebody, to someone outside her world. She was in drama at the time. Arthur Clarke wrote science fiction. Then, equally important, that person responds to her. Lots of us reach out to those different from ourselves, or to those more famous or successful than we are, but that gesture isn't always reciprocated. Then there's the fact that when Arthur Clarke comes to Chicago and wants to be connected, to be linked up with someone else, Weisberg comes up with Isaac Asimov. She says it was a fluke that Asimov was in town. But if it wasn't Asimov, it would have been someone else.

One of the things that people remember about Weisberg's Friday night salons back in the 1950s was that they were always, effortlessly, racially integrated. The point is not that without that salon blacks wouldn't have socialized with whites on the North Side. It was rare back then, but it happened. The point is that when blacks socialized with whites in the 1950s in Chicago, it didn't happen by accident; it happened because a certain kind of person made it happen. That's what Asimov and Clarke meant when they said that Weisberg has this thing—whatever it is—that brings people together.

"She doesn't have any kind of snobbery," says Wendy Willrich, who used to work for Weisberg. "I once went with her on a trip to someone's professional photography studio. People write her letters and she looks at all of her mail, and the guy who owned the studio invited her out and she said yes. He was basically a wedding photographer. She decided to check it out. I was thinking, ohmigod, do we have to hike out forty-five minutes to this studio? It was out by the airport. This is the Commissioner of Cultural Affairs for the City of Chicago we're talking about. But she thought he was incredibly interesting." Was he actually interesting? Who knows? The point is that Lois found him interesting, because, in some way, she finds everyone interesting. Weisberg, one of her friends told me, "always says—'Oh, I've met the most wonderful person. You are going to love her,' and she is as enthused about this person as she was about the first person she has met and you know what, she's usually right." Helen Doria, another of her friends, told me that "Lois sees things in you that you don't even see in yourself," which is another way of saying the same thing, that by some marvelous quirk of nature, Lois and the other people like her have some instinct that helps them relate to the people they meet. When Weisberg looks out at the world or when Roger Horchow sits next to you on an airplane, they don't see the same world that the rest of us see. They see possibility, and while most of us are busily choosing whom we would like to know, and rejecting the people who don't look right or who live out near the airport, or whom we haven't seen in sixty-five years, Lois and Roger like them all.

4.

There is a very good example of the way Connectors function in the work of the sociologist Mark Granovetter. In his classic 1974 study *Getting a Job*, Granovetter looked at several hundred professional and technical workers from the Boston suburb of Newton, interviewing them in some detail on their employment history. He found that 56 percent of those he talked to found their job through a personal connection. Another 18.8 percent used formal means—advertisements, headhunters—and roughly 20 percent applied directly. This much is not surprising; the best way to get in the door is through a personal contact. But, curiously, Granovetter found that of those personal connections, the majority were "weak ties." Of those who used a contact to find a job, only 16.7 percent saw that contact "often"—as they would if the contact were a good friend—and 55.6 percent saw their contact only "occasionally." Twenty-eight percent saw the contact "rarely." People weren't getting their jobs through their friends. They were getting them through their acquaintances.

Why is this? Granovetter argues that it is because when it comes to finding out about new jobs—or, for that matter, new information, or new ideas—"weak ties" are always more important than strong ties. Your friends, after all, occupy the same world that you do. They might work with you, or live near you, and go to the same churches, schools, or parties. How much, then, would they know that you wouldn't know? Your acquaintances, on the other hand, by definition occupy a very different world than you. They are much more likely to know something that you don't. To capture this apparent paradox, Granovetter coined a marvelous phrase: the strength of weak ties. Acquaintances, in short, represent a source of social power, and the more acquaintances you have the more powerful you are. Connectors like Lois Weisberg and Roger Horchow—who are masters of the weak tie—are extraordinarily powerful. We rely on them to give us access to opportunities and worlds to which we don't belong.

This principle holds for more than just jobs, of course. It also holds for restaurants, movies, fashion trends, or anything else that moves by word of mouth. It isn't just the case that the closer someone is to a Connector, the more powerful or the wealthier or the more opportunities he or she gets. It's also the case that the closer an idea or a product comes to a Connector, the more power and opportunity it has as well. Could this be one of the reasons Hush Puppies suddenly became a major fashion trend? Along the way from the East Village to Middle America, a Connector or a series of Connectors must have suddenly become enamored of them, and through their enormous social connections, their long lists of weak ties, their role in multiple worlds and subcultures, they must have been able to take those shoes and send them in a thousand directions at once—to make them really tip. Hush Puppies, in a sense then, got lucky. And perhaps one of the reasons why so many fashion trends don't make it into mainstream America is that simply, by sheerest bad fortune, they never happen to meet the approval of a Connector along the way.

Horchow's daughter, Sally, told me a story of how she once took her father to a new Japanese restaurant where a friend of hers was a chef. Horchow liked the food, and so when he went home he turned on his computer, pulled up the names of acquaintances who lived nearby, and faxed them notes telling them of a wonderful new restaurant he had discovered and that they should try it. This is, in a nutshell, what word of mouth is. It's not me telling you about a new restaurant with great food, and you telling a friend and that friend telling a friend. Word of mouth begins when somewhere along that chain, someone tells a person like Roger Horchow.

9.

The one thing that a Maven is not is a persuader. Alpert's motivation is to educate and to help. He's not the kind of person who wants to twist your arm. As we talked, in fact, there were several key moments when he seemed to probe me for information, to find out what I knew, so he could add it to his own formidable database. To be a Maven is to be a teacher. But it is also, even more emphatically, to be a student. Mavens are really information brokers, sharing and trading what they know. For a social epidemic to start, though, some people are actually going to have to be persuaded to do something. A good number of the young people who bought Hush Puppies, for instance, were people who once upon a time wouldn't have been caught dead in them. Similarly, after Paul Revere had passed on his news, you can imagine that all of the men in the militia movement gathered around and made plans to confront the British the following morning. But it can't have been an automatic process. Some people were probably gung ho. Some may have doubted the wisdom of confronting a trained, professional army with a homegrown militia. Others—who may not have known Revere personally—might have been skeptical about the accuracy of his information. That almost everyone, in the end, fell in line is something that we would normally credit to peer pressure. But peer pressure is not always an automatic or an unconscious process. It means, as often as not, that someone actually went up to one of his peers and pressured him. In a social epidemic, Mavens are data banks. They provide the message. Connectors are social glue: they spread it. But there is also a select group of people—Salesmen—with the skills to persuade us when we are unconvinced of what we are hearing, and they are as critical to the tipping of world-of-mouth epidemics as the other two groups.

12.

In the early hours of April 19, 1775, the men of Lexington, Massachusetts, began to gather on the town common. They ranged in age from sixteen to sixty and were carrying a motley collection of muskets and swords and pistols. As the alarm spread that morning, their numbers were steadily swelled by groups of militia from the surrounding towns. Dedham sent four companies. In Lynn, men left on their own for Lexington. In towns further west that did not get the news until morning, farmers were in such haste to join the battle in Lexington that they literally left their plows in the fields. In many towns, virtually the whole male population was mustered for the fight. The men had no uniforms, so they wore ordinary clothes: coats to ward off the early morning chill and large-brimmed hats.

As the colonists rushed toward Lexington, the British Regulars (as they were known) were marching in formation toward the town as well. By dawn, the advancing soldiers could see figures all around them in the half-light, armed men running through the surrounding fields, outpacing the British in their rush to get to Lexington. As the Regulars neared the town center, they could hear drums beating in the distance. Finally the British came upon Lexington Common and the two sides met face-to-face: several hundred British soldiers confronting less than a hundred militia. In that first exchange, the British got the best of the colonists, gunning down seven militiamen in a brief flurry of gunshots on the common. But that was only the first of what would be several battles that day. When the British moved on to Concord, to systematically search for the cache of guns and ammunition they had been told was stored there, they would clash with the militia again, and this time they would be soundly defeated. This was the beginning of the American Revolution, a war that before it was over would claim many lives and consume the entire American colony. When the American colonists declared independence the following year, it would be hailed as a victory for an entire nation. But that is not the way it began. It began on a cold spring morning, with a word-of-mouth epidemic that spread from a little stable boy to all of New England, relying along the way on a small number of very special people: a few Salesmen and a man with the particular genius of both a Maven and a Connector.

The Saints and the Roughnecks

William J. Chambliss

Eight promising young men—children of good, stable, white upper-middle-class families, active in school affairs, good pre-college students—were some of the most delinquent boys at Hanibal High School. While community residents knew that these boys occasionally sowed a few wild oats, they were totally unaware that sowing wild oats completely occupied the daily routine of these young men. The Saints were constantly occupied with truancy, drinking, wild driving, petty theft, and vandalism. Yet no one was officially arrested for any misdeed during the two years I observed them.

This record was particularly surprising in light of my observations during the same two years of another gang of Hanibal High School students, six lower-class white boys known as the Roughnecks. The Roughnecks were constantly in trouble with police and community even though their rate of delinquency was about equal with that of the Saints. What was the cause of this disparity? the result? The following consideration of the activities, social class, and community perceptions of both gangs may provide some answers.

The Saints from Monday to Friday

The Saints' principal daily concern was with getting out of school as early as possible. The boys managed to get out of school with minimum danger that they would be accused of playing hookey through an elaborate procedure for obtaining "legitimate" release from class. The most common procedure was for one boy to obtain the release of another by fabricating a meeting of some committee, program or recognized club. Charles might raise his hand in his 9:00 chemistry class and ask to be excused—a euphemism for going to the bathroom. Charles would go to Ed's math class and inform the teacher that Ed was needed for a 9:30 rehearsal of the drama club play. The math teacher would recognize Ed and Charles as "good students" involved in numerous school activities and would permit Ed to leave at 9:30. Charles would return to his class, and Ed would go to Tom's English class to obtain his release. Tom would engineer Charles's escape. The strategy would continue until as many of the Saints as possible were freed. After a stealthy trip to the car (which has been parked in a strategic spot), the boys were off for a day of fun.

Over the two years I observed the Saints, this pattern was repeated nearly every day. There were variations on the theme, but in one form or another, the boys used this procedure for getting out of class and then off the school grounds. Rarely did all eight of the Saints manage to leave school at the same time. The average number avoiding school on the days I observed them was five.

Having escaped from the concrete corridors, the boys usually went either to a pool hall on the other (lower-class) side of town or to a cafe in the suburbs. Both places were out of the way of people the boys were likely to know (family or school officials), and both provided a source of entertainment. The pool hall entertainment was the generally rough atmosphere, the occasional hustler, the sometimes drunk proprietor and, of course, the game of pool. The cafe's entertainment was provided by the owner. The boys would "accidentally" knock a glass on the floor or spill cola on the counter—not all the time, but enough to be sporting. They would also bend spoons, put salt in sugar bowls and generally tease whoever was working in the cafe. The owner had opened the cafe recently and was dependent on the boys' business which was, in fact, substantial since between the horsing around and the teasing they bought food and drinks.

The Saints on Weekends

On weekends the automobile was even more critical than during the week, for on weekends the Saints went to Big Town—a large city with a population of over a million 25 miles from Hanibal. Every Friday and Saturday night most of the Saints would meet between 8:00 and 8:30 and would go into Big Town. Big Town activities included drinking heavily in taverns or nightclubs, driving drunkenly through the streets, and committing acts of vandalism and playing pranks.

By midnight on Fridays and Saturdays the Saints were usually thoroughly high, and one or two of them were often so drunk they had to be carried to the cars. Then the boys drove around town, calling obscenities to women and girls; occasionally trying (unsuccessfully so far as I could tell) to pick girls up; and driving recklessly through red lights and at high speeds with their lights out. Occasionally they played "chicken." One boy would climb out the back window of the car and across the roof to the driver's side of the car while the car was moving at high speed (between 40 and 50 miles an hour); then the driver would move over and the boy who had just crawled across the car roof would take the driver's seat.

Searching for "fair game" for a prank was the boys' principal activity after they left the tavern. The boys would drive alongside a foot patrolman and ask directions to some street. If the policeman leaned on the car in the course of answering the question, the driver would speed away, causing him to lose balance. The Saints were careful to play this prank only in an area where they were not going to spend much time and where they could quickly disappear around the corner to avoid having their license plate number taken.

Construction sites and road repair areas were the special province of the Saints' mischief. A soon-to-be-repaired hole in the road inevitably invited the Saints to remove lanterns and wooden barricades and put them in the car, leaving the hole unprotected. The boys would find a safe vantage point and wait for an unsuspecting motorist to drive into the hole. Often, though not always, the boys would go up to the motorist and commiserate with him about the dreadful way the city protected its citizenry.

Leaving the scene of the open hole and the motorist, the boys would then go searching for an appropriate place to erect the stolen barricade. An "appropriate place" was often a spot on a highway near a curve in the road where the barricade would not be seen by an on-coming motorist. The boys would wait to watch an unsuspecting motorist attempt to stop and (usually) crash into the wooden barricade. With saintly bearing the boys might offer help and understanding.

A stolen lantern might well find its way onto the back of a police car or hang from a street lamp. Once a lantern served as a prop for a reenactment of the "midnight ride of Paul Revere" until the "play," which was taking place at 2:00 A.M. in the center of a main street of Big Town, was interrupted by a police car several blocks away. The boys ran, leaving the lanterns on the street, and managed to avoid being apprehended.

Abandoned houses, especially if they were located in out-of-the-way places, were fair game for destruction and spontaneous vandalism. The boys would break windows, remove furniture to the yard and tear it apart, urinate on the walls and scrawl obscenities inside.

Through all the pranks, drinking, and reckless driving the boys managed miraculously to avoid being stopped by police. Only twice in two years was I aware that they had been stopped by a Big City policeman. Once was for speeding (which they did every time they drove whether they were drunk or sober), and the driver managed to convince the policeman that it was simply an error. The second time they were stopped they had just left a nightclub and were walking through an alley. Aaron stopped to urinate and the boys began making obscene remarks. A foot patrolman came into the alley, lectured the boys and sent them home. Before the boys got to the car one began talking in a loud voice again. The policeman, who had followed them down the alley, arrested this boy for disturbing the peace and took him to the police station where the other Saints gathered. After paying a $5 fine, and with the assurance that there would be no permanent record of the arrest, the boy was released.

The boys had a spirit of frivolity and fun about their escapades. They did not view what they were engaged in as "delinquency," though it surely was by any reasonable definition of that word. They simply viewed themselves as having a little fun and who, they would ask, was really hurt by it? The answer had to be no one, although this fact remains one of the most difficult things to explain about the gang's behavior. Unlikely though it seems, in two years of drinking, driving, carousing and vandalism no one was seriously injured as a result of the Saints' activities.

The Saints in School

The Saints were highly successful in school. The average grade for the group was "B" with two of the boys having close to a straight "A" average. Almost all of the boys were popular and many of them held offices in the school. One of the boys was vice president of the student body one year. Six of the boys played on athletic teams.

At the end of their senior year, the student body selected ten seniors for special recognition as the "school wheels"; four of the ten were Saints. Teachers and school officials saw no problem with any of these boys and anticipated that they would all "make something of themselves."

How the boys managed to maintain this impression is surprising in view of their actual behavior while in school. Their technique for covering truancy was so successful that teachers did not even realize that the boys were absent from school much of the time. Occasionally, of course, the system would backfire and then the boy was on his own. A boy who was caught would be most contrite, would plead guilty and ask for mercy. He inevitably got the mercy he sought.

Cheating on examinations was rampant, even to the point of orally communicating answers to exams as well as looking at one another's papers. Since none of the group studied, and since they were primarily dependent on one another for help, it is surprising that grades were so high. Teachers contributed to the deception in their admitted inclination to give these boys (and presumably others like them) the benefit of the doubt. When asked how the boys did in school, and when pressed on specific examinations, teachers might admit that they were disappointed in John's performance, but would quickly add that they "knew that he was capable of doing better," so John was given a higher grade than he had actually earned. How often this happened is impossible to know. During the time that I observed the group, I never saw any of the boys take homework home. Teachers may have been "understanding" very regularly.

One exception to the gang's generally good performance was Jerry, who had a "C" average in his junior year, experienced disaster the next year, and failed to graduate. Jerry had always been a little more nonchalant than the others about the liberties he took in school. Rather than wait for someone to come get him from class, he would offer his own excuse and leave. Although he probably did not miss any more class than most of the others in the group, he did not take the requisite pains to cover his absences. Jerry was the only Saint whom I ever heard talk back to a teacher. Although teachers often called him a "cut up" or a "smart kid," they never referred to him as a troublemaker or as a kid headed for trouble. It seems likely, then, that Jerry's failure his senior year and his mediocre performance his junior year were consequences of his not playing the game the proper way (possibly because he was disturbed by his parents' divorce). His teachers regarded him as "immature" and not quite ready to get out of high school.

The Police and the Saints

The local police saw the Saints as good boys who were among the leaders of the youth in the community. Rarely, the boys might be stopped in town for speeding or for running a stop sign. When this happened the boys were always polite, contrite, and pled for mercy. As in school, they received the mercy they asked for. None ever received a ticket or was taken into the precinct by the local police.

The situation in Big City, where the boys engaged in most of their delinquency, was only slightly different. The police there did not know the boys at all, although occasionally the boys were stopped by a patrolman. Once they were caught taking a lantern from a construction site. Another time they were stopped for running a stop sign, and on several occasions they were stopped for speeding. Their behavior was as before: contrite, polite, and penitent. The urban police, like the local police, accepted their demeanor as sincere. More important, the urban police were convinced that these were good boys just out for a lark.

The Roughnecks

Hanibal townspeople never perceived the Saints' high level of delinquency. The Saints were good boys who just went in for an occasional prank. After all, they were well dressed, well mannered, and had nice cars. The Roughnecks were a different story. Although the two gangs of boys were the same age, and both groups engaged in an equal amount of wild-oat sowing, everyone agreed that the not-so-well-dressed, not-so-well-mannered, not-so-rich boys were heading for trouble. Townspeople would say, "You can see the gang members at the drugstore, night after night, leaning against the storefront (sometimes drunk) or slouching around inside buying Cokes, reading magazines, and probably stealing old Mr. Wall blind. When they are outside and girls walk by, even respectable girls, these boys make suggestive remarks. Sometimes their remarks are downright lewd."

From the community's viewpoint, the real indication that these kids were in trouble was that they were constantly involved with the police. Some of them had been picked up for stealing, mostly small stuff, of course, "but still it's stealing small stuff that leads to big time crimes." "Too bad," people said. "Too bad that these boys couldn't behave like the other kids in town; stay out of trouble, be polite to adults, and look to their future."

The community's impression of the degrees to which this group of six boys (ranging in age from 16 to 19) engaged in delinquency was somewhat distorted. In some ways the gang was more delinquent than the community thought; in other ways they were less.

The fighting activities of the group were fairly readily and accurately perceived by almost everyone. At least once a month, the boys would get into some sort of fight, although most fights were scraps between members of the group or involved only one member of the group and some peripheral hanger-on. Only three times in the period of observation did the group fight together: once against a gang from across town, once against two blacks, and once against a group of boys from another school. For the first two fights the group went out "looking for trouble"—and they found it both times. The third fight followed a football game and began spontaneously with an argument on the football field between one of the Roughnecks and a member of the opposition's football team.

Jack had a particular propensity for fighting and was involved in most of the brawls. He was a prime mover of the escalation of arguments into fights.

More serious than fighting, had the community been aware of it, was theft. Although almost everyone was aware that the boys occasionally stole things, they did not realize the extent of the activity. Petty stealing was a frequent event for the Roughnecks. Sometimes they stole as a group and coordinated their efforts; other times they stole in pairs. Rarely did they steal alone.

The thefts ranged from very small things like paperback books, comics, and ballpoint pens to expensive items like watches. The nature of the thefts varied from time to time. The gang would go through a period of systematically shoplifting items from automobiles or school lockers. Types of thievery varied with the whim of the gang. Some forms of thievery were more profitable than others, but all thefts were for profit, not just thrills.

Roughnecks siphoned gasoline from cars as often as they had access to an automobile, which was not very often. Unlike the Saints, who owned their own cars, the Roughnecks would have to borrow their parents' cars, an event which occurred only eight or nine times a year. The boys claimed to have stolen cars for joy rides from time to time.

Ron committed the most serious of the group's offenses. With an unidentified associate the boy attempted to burglarize a gasoline station. Although this station had been robbed twice previously in the same month, Ron denied any involvement in either of the other thefts. When Ron and his accomplice approached the station, the owner was hiding in the bushes beside the station. He fired both barrels of a double-barreled shotgun at the boys. Ron was severely injured; the other boy ran away and was never caught. Though he remained in critical condition for several months, Ron finally recovered and served six months of the following year in reform school. Upon release from reform school, Ron was put back a grade in school, and began running around with a different gang of boys. The Roughnecks considered the new gang less delinquent than themselves, and during the following year Ron had no more trouble with the police.

The Roughnecks, then, engaged mainly in three types of delinquency: theft, drinking, and fighting. Although community members perceived that this gang of kids was delinquent, they mistakenly believed that their illegal activities were primarily drinking, fighting, and being a nuisance to passersby. Drinking was limited among the gang members, although it did occur, and theft was much more prevalent than anyone realized.

Drinking would doubtless have been more prevalent had the boys had ready access to liquor. Since they rarely had automobiles at their disposal, they could not travel very far, and the bars in town would not serve them. Most of the boys had little money, and this, too, inhibited their purchase of alcohol. Their major source of liquor was a local drunk who would buy them a fifth if they would give him enough to buy himself a pint of whiskey or a bottle of wine.

The community's perception of drinking as prevalent stemmed from the fact that it was the most obvious delinquency the boys engaged in. When one of the boys had been drinking, even a casual observer seeing him on the corner would suspect that he was high.

There was a high level of mutual distrust and dislike between the Roughnecks and the police. The boys felt very strongly that the police were unfair and corrupt. Some evidence existed that the boys were correct in their perception.

The main source of the boys' dislike for the police undoubtedly stemmed from the fact that the police would sporadically harass the group. From the standpoint of the boys, these acts of occasional enforcement of the law were whimsical and uncalled for. It made no sense to them, for example, that the police would come to the corner occasionally and threaten them with arrest for loitering when the night before the boys had been out siphoning gasoline from cars and the police had been nowhere in sight. To the boys, the police were stupid on the one hand, for not being where they should have been and catching the boys in a serious offense, and unfair on the other hand, for trumping up "loitering" charges against them.

From the viewpoint of the police, the situation was quite different. They knew, with all the confidence necessary to be a policeman, that these boys were engaged in criminal activities. They knew this partly from occasionally catching them, mostly from circumstantial evidence ("the boys were around when those tires were slashed"), and partly because the police shared the view of the community in general that this was a bad bunch of boys. The best the police could hope to do was to be sensitive to the fact that these boys were engaged in illegal acts and arrest them whenever there was some evidence that they had been involved. Whether or not the boys had in fact committed a particular act in a particular way was not especially important. The police had a broader view; their job was to stamp out these kids' crimes; the tactics were not as important as the end result.

Over the period that the group was under observation, each member was arrested at least once. Several of the boys were arrested a number of times and spent at least one night in jail. While most were never taken to court, two of the boys were sentenced to six months' incarceration in boys' schools.

The Roughnecks in School

The Roughnecks' behavior in school was not particularly disruptive. During school hours they did not all hang around together, but tended instead to spend most of their time with one or two other members of the gang who were their special buddies. Although every member of the gang attempted to avoid school as much as possible, they were not particularly successful and most of them attended school with surprising regularity. They considered school a burden—something to be gotten through with a minimum of conflict. If they were "bugged" by a particular teacher, it could lead to trouble. One of the boys, Al, once threatened to beat up a teacher and, according to the other boys, the teacher hid under a desk to escape him.

Teachers saw the boys the way the general community did, as heading for trouble, as being uninterested in making something of themselves. Some were also seen as being incapable of meeting the academic standards of the school. Most of the teachers expressed concern for this group of boys and were willing to pass them despite poor performance, in the belief that failing them would only aggravate the problem.

The group of boys had a grade point average just slightly above "C." No one in the group failed either grade, and no one had better than a "C" average. They were very consistent in their perception of the boys' achievement.

Two of the boys were good football players. Herb was acknowledged to be the best player in the school and Jack was almost as good. Both boys were criticized for their failure to abide by training rules, for refusing to come to practice as often as they should, and for not playing their best during practice. What they lacked in sportsmanship they made up for in skill, apparently, and played every game no matter how poorly they had performed in practice or how many practice sessions they had missed.

Two Questions

Why did the community, the school, and police react to the Saints as though they were good, upstanding, nondelinquent youths with bright futures but to the Roughnecks as though they were tough, young criminals who were headed for trouble? Why did the Roughnecks and the Saints in fact have quite different careers after high school—careers which, by and large, lived up to the expectations of the community?

The most obvious explanation for the differences in the community's and law enforcement agencies' reactions to the two gangs is that one group of boys was "more delinquent" than the other. Which group *was* more delinquent? The answer to this question will determine in part how we explain the differential responses to these groups by the members of the community and, particularly, by law enforcement and school officials.

In sheer number of illegal acts, the Saints were the more delinquent. They were truant from school for at least part of the day almost every day of the week. In addition, their drinking and vandalism occurred with surprising regularity. The Roughnecks, in contrast, engaged sporadically in delinquent episodes. While these episodes were frequent, they certainly did not occur on a daily or even a weekly basis.

The difference in frequency of offenses was probably caused by the Roughnecks' inability to obtain liquor and to manipulate legitimate excuses from school. Since the Roughnecks had less money than the Saints, and teachers carefully supervised their school activities, the Roughnecks' hearts may have been as black as the Saints', but their misdeeds were not nearly as frequent.

There are really no clear-cut criteria by which to measure qualitative differences in antisocial behavior. The most important dimension is generally referred to as the "seriousness" of the offenses.

If seriousness encompasses the relative economic cost of delinquent acts, then some assessment can be made. The Roughnecks probably stole an average of about $5 worth of goods a week. Some weeks the figure was considerably higher, but these times must be balanced against long periods when almost nothing was stolen.

The Saints were more continuously engaged in delinquency but their acts were not for the most part costly to property. Only their vandalism and occasional theft of gasoline would so qualify. Perhaps once or twice a month they would siphon a tankful of gas. The other costly items were street signs, construction lanterns and the like. All of these acts combined probably did not quite average $5 a week, partly because much of the stolen equipment was abandoned and presumably could be recovered. The difference in cost of stolen property between the two groups was trivial, but the Roughnecks probably had a slightly more expensive set of activities than did the Saints.

Another meaning of seriousness is the potential threat of physical harm to members of the community and to the boys themselves. The Roughnecks were more prone to physical violence; they not only welcomed an opportunity to fight, they went seeking it. In addition, they fought among themselves frequently. Although the fighting never included deadly weapons, it was still a menace, however minor, to the physical safety of those involved.

The Saints never fought. They avoided physical conflict both inside and outside the group. At the same time, though, the Saints frequently endangered their own and other people's lives. They did so almost every time they drove a car, especially if they had been drinking. Sober, their driving was risky; under the influence of alcohol it was horrendous. In addition, the Saints endangered the lives of others with their pranks. Street excavations left unmarked were a very serious hazard.

Evaluating the relative seriousness of the two gangs' activities is difficult. The community reacted as though the behavior of the Roughnecks was a problem, and they reacted as though the behavior of the Saints was not. But the members of the community were ignorant of the array of delinquent acts that characterized the Saints' behavior. Although concerned citizens were unaware of much of the Roughnecks' behavior as well, they were much better informed about the Roughnecks' involvement in delinquency than they were about the Saints'.

Visibility

Differential treatment of the two gangs resulted in part because one gang was infinitely more visible than the other. This differential visibility was a direct function of the economic standing of the families. The Saints had access to automobiles and were able to remove themselves from the sight of the community. In as routine a decision as to where to go to have a milkshake after school, the Saints stayed away from the mainstream of community life. Lacking transportation, the Roughnecks could not make it to the edge of town. The center of town was the only practical place for them to meet since their homes were scattered throughout the town and any noncentral meeting place put an undue hardship on some members. Through necessity the Roughnecks congregated in a crowded area where everyone in the community passed frequently, including teachers and law enforcement officers. They could easily see the Roughnecks hanging around the drugstore.

The Roughnecks, of course, made themselves even more visible by making remarks to passersby and by occasionally getting into fights on the corner. Meanwhile, just as regularly, the Saints were either at the cafe on one edge of town or in the pool hall at the other edge of town. Without any particular realization that they were making themselves inconspicuous, the Saints were able to hide their time-wasting. Not only were they removed from the mainstream of traffic, but they were almost always inside a building.

On their escapades the Saints were also relatively invisible, since they left Hanibal and traveled to Big City. Here, too, they were mobile, roaming the city, rarely going to the same area twice.

Demeanor

To the notion of visibility must be added the difference in the responses of group members to outside intervention with their activities. If one of the Saints was confronted with an accusing policeman, even if he felt he was truly innocent of a wrongdoing, his demeanor was apologetic and penitent. A Roughnecks' attitude was almost the polar opposite. When confronted with a threatening adult authority, even one who tried to be pleasant, the Roughneck's hostility and disdain were clearly observable. Sometimes he might attempt to put up a veneer of respect, but it was thin and was not accepted as sincere by the authority.

School was no different from the community at large. The Saints could manipulate the system by feigning compliance with the school norms. The availability of cars at school meant that once free from the immediate sight of the teacher, the boys could disappear rapidly. And this escape was well enough planned that no administrator or teacher was nearby when the boys left. A roughneck who wished to escape for a few hours was in a bind. If it were possible to get free from class, downtown was still a mile away, and even if he arrived there, he was still very visible. Truancy for the Roughnecks meant almost certain detection, while the Saints enjoyed almost complete immunity from sanctions.

Bias

Community members were not aware of the transgressions of the Saints. Even if the Saints had been less discreet, their favorite delinquencies would have been perceived as less serious than those of the Roughnecks.

In the eyes of the police and school officials, a boy who drinks in an alley and stands intoxicated on the street corner is committing a more serious offense than is a boy who drinks to inebriation in a nightclub or a tavern and drives around afterwards in a car. Similarly, a boy who steals a wallet from a store will be viewed as having committed a more serious offense than a boy who steals a lantern from a construction site.

Perceptual bias also operates with respect to the demeanor of the boys in the two groups when they are confronted by adults. It is not simply that adults dislike the posture affected by boys of the Roughneck ilk; more important is the conviction that the posture adopted by the Roughnecks is an indication of their devotion and commitment to deviance as a way of life. The posture becomes a cue, just as the type of the offense is a cue, to the degree to which the known transgressions are indicators of the youths' potential for other problems.

Visibility, demeanor, and bias are surface variables which explain the day-to-day operations of the police. Why do these surface variables operate as they do? Why did the police choose to disregard the Saints' delinquencies while breathing down the backs of the Roughnecks?

The answer lies in the class structure of American society and the control of legal institutions by those at the top of the class structure. Obviously, no representative of the upper class drew up the operational chart for the police which led them to look in the ghettos and on street corners—which led them to see the demeanor of lower-class youth as troublesome and that of upper-middle-class youth as tolerable. Rather, the procedures simply developed from experience—experience with irate and influential upper-middle-class parents insisting that their son's vandalism was simply a prank and his drunkenness only a momentary "sowing of wild oats"—experience with cooperative or indifferent, powerless, lower-class parents who acquiesced to the laws' definition of their son's behavior.

Adult Careers of the Saints and the Roughnecks

The community's confidence in the potential of the Saints and the Roughnecks apparently was justified. If anything, the community members underestimated the degree to which these youngsters would turn out "good" or "bad."

Seven of the eight members of the Saints went on to college immediately after high school. Five of the boys graduated from college in four years. The sixth one finished college after two years in the army, and the seventh spent four years in the air force before returning to college and receiving a B.A. degree. Of these seven college graduates, three went on for advanced degrees. One finished law school and is now active in state politics, one finished medical school and is practicing near Hanibal, and one boy is now working for a Ph.D. The other four college graduates entered submanagerial, managerial or executive training positions with large firms.

The only Saint who did not complete college was Jerry. Jerry had failed to graduate from high school with the other Saints. During his second senior year, after the other Saints had gone on to college, Jerry began to hang around with what several teachers described as a "rough crowd"—the gang that was heir apparent to the Roughnecks. At the end of his second senior year, when he did graduate from high school, Jerry took a job as a used-car salesman, got married and quickly had a child. Although he made several abortive attempts to go to college by attending night school, when I last saw him (ten years after high school) Jerry was unemployed and had been living on unemployment for almost a year. His wife worked as a waitress.

Some of the Roughnecks have lived up to community expectations. A number of them were headed for trouble. A few were not.

Jack and Herb were the athletes among the Roughnecks and their athletic prowess paid off handsomely. Both boys received unsolicited athletic scholarships to college. After Herb received his scholarship (near the end of his senior year), he apparently did an about-face. His demeanor became very similar to that of the Saints. Although he remained a member in good standing of the Roughnecks, he stopped participating in most activities and did not hang around on the corner as often.

Jack did not change. If anything, he became more prone to fighting. He even made excuses for accepting the scholarship. He told the other gang members that the school had guaranteed him a "C" average if he would come to play football—an idea that seems far-fetched, even in this day of highly competitive recruiting.

During the summer after graduation from high school, Jack attempted suicide by jumping from a tall building. The jump would certainly have killed most people trying it, but Jack survived. He entered college in the fall and played four years of football. He and Herb graduated in four years, and both are teaching and coaching in high schools. They are married and have stable families. If anything, Jack appears to have a more prestigious position in the community than does Herb, though both are well respected and secure in their positions.

Two of the boys never finished high school. Tommy left at the end of his junior year and went to another state. That summer he was arrested and placed on probation on a manslaughter charge. Three years later he was arrested for murder; he pleaded guilty to second degree murder and is serving a 30-year sentence in the state penitentiary.

Al, the other boy who did not finish high school, also left the state in his senior year. He is serving a life sentence in a state penitentiary for first degree murder.

Wes is a small-time gambler. He finished high school and "bummed around." After several years he made contact with a bookmaker who employed him as a runner. Later he acquired his own area and has been working it ever since. His position among the bookmakers is almost identical to the position he had in the gang; he is always around but no one is really aware of him. He makes no trouble and he does not get into any. Steady, reliable, capable of keeping his mouth closed, he plays the game by the rules, even though the game is an illegal one.

That leaves only Ron. Some of his former friends reported that they had heard he was "driving a trunk up north," but no one could provide any concrete information.

Reinforcement

The community responded to the Roughnecks as boys in trouble, and the boys agreed with that perception. Their pattern of deviancy was reinforced, and breaking away from it became increasingly unlikely. Once the boys acquired an image of themselves as deviants, they selected new friends who affirmed that self-image. As that self-conception became more firmly entrenched, they also became willing to try new and more extreme deviances. With their growing alienation came freer expression of disrespect and hostility for representatives of the legitimate society. This disrespect increased the community's negativism, perpetuating the entire process of commitment to deviance. Lack of a commitment to deviance works the same way. In either case, the process will perpetuate itself unless some event (like a scholarship to college or a sudden failure) external to the established relationship intervenes. For two of the Roughnecks (Herb and Jack), receiving college athletic scholarships created new relations and culminated in a break with the established pattern of deviance. In the case of one of the Saints (Jerry), his parents' divorce and his failing to graduate from high school changed some of his other relations. Being held back in school for a year and losing his place among the Saints had sufficient impact on Jerry to alter his self-image and virtually to assure that he would not go on to college as his peers did. Although the experiments of life can rarely be reversed, it seems likely in view of the behavior of the other boys who did not enjoy this special treatment by the school that Jerry, too, would have "become something" had he graduated as anticipated. For Herb and Jack outside intervention worked to their advantage, for Jerry it was his undoing.

Selective perception and labeling—finding, processing, and punishing some kinds of criminality and not others—means that visible, poor, nonmobile, outspoken, undiplomatic "tough" kids will be noticed, whether their actions are seriously delinquent or not. Other kids, who have established a reputation for being bright (even though under-achieving), disciplined, and involved in respectable activities, who are mobile and monied, will be invisible when they deviate from sanctioned activities. They'll sow their wild oats—perhaps even wider and thicker than their lower-class cohorts—but they won't be noticed. When it's time to leave adolescence most will follow the expected path, settling into the ways of the middle class, remembering fondly the delinquent but unnoticed fling of their youth. The Roughnecks and others like them may turn around, too. It is more likely that their noticeable deviance will have been so reinforced by police and community that their lives will be effectively channeled into careers consistent with their adolescent background.

UNIT THREE

Our daily lives steadily involve the increasing variety of people we live and work with. This social diversity is easily seen. Yet, the process by which we come into increasing contact with others and the social meanings used to differentiate groups are not simple. Such meanings vary from the enrichment of American life with different forms of music, art, food, and cultural ideas, to the stereotypical bigotry so evident in hate crimes. How visible differences such as skin color and sex become the focus of the meanings by which authority and opportunity are structured and by which some people are considered "good" or "bad" or "capable" or "incapable" show the social roots of bigotry and discrimination. As we will show, such invidious and arbitrary distinctions among people underlie the more subtle inequalities that exist in the ways banks provide loans and mortgages; stores and other retail outlets extend credit and many organizations including some police departments operate every day, as shown in the Pincus reading on structural discrimination.

In this unit we also show the social processes that define what is appropriate behavior for each sex. Such processes start very early and persist throughout the adult life course, as is shown in the Gould reading. In this part of our book we also discuss the social complexity to patterns of sexual behavior and relationships. In contrast to the popular image of sex in soap operas, magazines, and other media, human sexuality is much more diverse and complex.

Finally, in this unit we present one of the most enduring and important dimensions of diversity in any society, the various levels of living represented in the social classes that comprise a society's stratification system. All societies have social classes and they all develop social ideologies or widely held beliefs that justify and explain such differences. Often these beliefs concern supposed aspects of character, like hard work and intelligence, that explain levels of living. Sociology will help you see, however, that such stereotypic thinking is no explanation of the vast differences in levels of living. Instead we hope to make you more aware of the social trends and social forces that change the mix of well-paying jobs and lesser paying employment opportunities. Such opportunity (or lack of it) caused by firm relocation, expanding technology, and other social forces is called structural mobility.

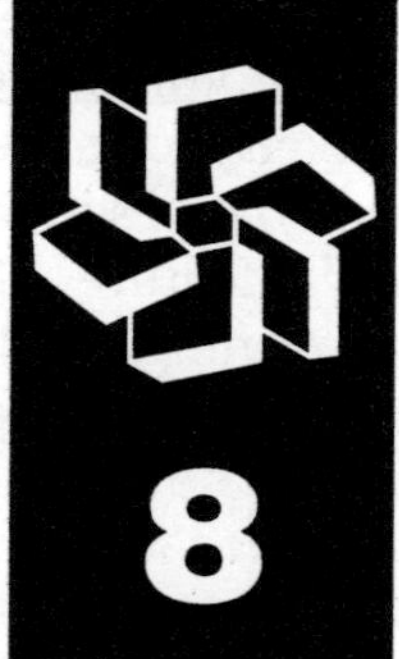

8

Race and Multiculturalism

Sociologists study race by analyzing the social meanings individuals, governments, and societies give to biological heritage. Like death and paying taxes, we can do nothing to change ancestral effects on some of our biological traits. People do not choose their biological ancestors, nor the divergent effects of their ancestry such as skin color, eye fold shape, hair type, and so on. In spite of these biological effects due to ancestry, scientific evidence shows that all human beings share nearly all the same genetic material (DNA). Genetic research has determined that humans now and in the past have had a genetic commonality and all people are of the same biological species.

To sociologists, what is important about ancestry is not the biological variation, but the different social meanings that emerge in social life in relation to ancestral effects, especially those easily observable differences such as skin coloration. Like the "dumb blond" stereotype, observable differences among people, such as facial features or skin coloration, became the basis for developing social meanings for "race" by organizing different social experiences and opportunities based on biological heritage (Loveman 1999). For example, various government policies toward Native Americans have been based upon different definitions of being an "Indian." These definitions have been based upon various so-called "blood quantum rules," based upon attempts to verify through "official" records how many immediate ancestors were "full-blooded." In the later 1800s Native Americans were required to show at least one "full-blooded" parent to gain ownership to federal land. In the 1920s, people with any Native American ancestry at all became "citizens" and subject to individual rather than tribal contract laws regarding land and mineral rights. The first definition made it difficult for Native Americans to claim legitimate ownership of land, and the second definition made it much easier for the government to negotiate mineral rights with individual landowners. In recent years, the "one-fourth" blood quantum or having at least one "full-blooded grandparent," defines the eligibility of Native Americans for various federal services including health care (Jaimes 1992). Throughout all the periods of different usage, many controversies have erupted concerning the "official" records used to establish the blood quantum rules. Similarly, views of Irish and Italian Americans as races were quite common around 1900 (Loveman 1999).

Sociologists also study the way in which social judgments based upon ancestral background are used to categorize people and develop different and unequal opportunities because of such categorizations. In the United States, in contrast to other parts of the world including Latin America, racial categorization has been dichotomized and social experiences have been organized based on being "white" or "nonwhite." The so-called "one-drop role" has meant that people with any nonwhite ancestry were considered "nonwhite." This dichotomization has had important social consequences for all people, but especially for people of mixed race ancestry, who have either had to act as if they were "white" or accept the discriminating experiences in social life accorded all "nonwhites," despite biological heritage, skin tone, or other physical features. The social experiences of these mixed-race people in the U.S. illustrate the restrictive meanings that race has had in America, while in Latin America there have always been many more people of mixed race and the meanings of race have not been dichotomized there (Marger, 1994).

While confusing race and ethnicity is easy, to sociologists the latter term refers to the countries in which people were born, and not necessarily where they grow up or live as adults. In the United States, where immigration laws have allowed the entry and citizenship of many people born in various parts of the world, there are many Americans with quite divergent ethnicity. Today, for example, about 30 million American families include people born outside the U.S. who do not speak English at home. Despite the great diversity of ethnicity among Americans, the social meanings created for ethnicity are similar to the dichotomized meaning of "race." For example, Spanish-speaking Americans are often referred to in social life and in public affairs including government programs as "Hispanics" rather than by their ethnicity as having been born in Cuba, Puerto Rico, or Mexico. Such collective references distort the cultural differences among these groups, which are important to them (Marin and Marin, 1991). Similarly, "Asian Americans" is often used when referring to Americans who themselves or their ancestors were born in the Philippines (Filiponos), South Korea, Taiwan, China, and Japan. When different ethnic groups are treated similarly, despite their different geographical origins and other cultural dissimilarities, sociologists call such a process aggregation. Like the dichotomization of race, aggregation oversimplifies large differences in culture and experience, and also important socioeconomic differences (Trueba, 1999).

Despite a long history of racial dichotomization and ethnic aggregation in the United States, multiculturalism has increased in the United States in recent years. To sociologists multiculturalism involves two ideas that are less contradictory than they seem. First, multiculturalism means an acceptance and an appreciation of social life in the United States of the cultural differences related to people's ancestry and ethnicity. Appreciation of difference in groups' foods, types of entertainment, sports and recreation, and holiday celebrations is part of the increased multiculturalism in the U.S. International days on campuses and in communities recognize such cultural diversity, as does the celebration of Kwanzaa at Christmas time. The freedom to practice various types of religious expression is an important part of the U.S. Constitution and historically has been the foundation of legal support for divergent cultural styles in the U.S. The second idea, also guaranteed through the equal protection clause of the U.S. Constitution and various Equal Rights Amendments, is that differences of ancestry, ethnicity, and gender should not and will not prevent qualified people from getting an equal opportunity to get jobs, enter politics, purchase houses, and so on. Multiculturalism is being reflected in the increasing diversity of American universities, business firms, hospitals, and government agencies.

While multiculturalism in the U.S. is far from becoming as developed as it could be or should be, recent changes in education and business, for example, show a spread of multiculturalism beyond sports and entertainment into sectors such as business that have traditionally employed mostly white men. For example, African-American men and women have recently been appointed to high executive positions in businesses and in government. That such appointments have occurred without fanfare and without consideration of ancestral heritage, but rather based on qualifications and performance hopefully represents the rapid expansion of multiculturalism. These sorts of social processes represent the elimination of previous social meanings of "race" in the U.S. Sociologists call this the "social deconstruction" of "race." As of the 2000 census, people in the U.S. could refer to any number of races in defining their biological heritage. This is further evidence of the social processes that let people define their own ancestral backgrounds for no other purpose than self-identification.

Multiculturalism in the U.S. has been increased by various types of diversity training programs and other programs to increase awareness of multiculturalism. Such programs have been used throughout the 1990s by many businesses and universities. In business, workshops and training sessions on appreciation of diversity have included issues such as gender, race, and age. In universities such programs have included women's studies programs, African-American studies programs, diversity courses in many departments, and diversity workshops. Sociologists have studied the positive effects of diversity appreciation programs in universities (Astin 1993) and in businesses (Taylor, 1995). These evaluation studies have found positive direct and indirect effects. The direct positive effects have been that people who experience more cultural diversity training are more understanding of and respectful toward other groups and have greater interest in improving intergroup relationships (Taylor 1995). The positive indirect effects have been that university learning and employment experience are more satisfying when schools and firms operate without the legacies of racial dichotomization and ethnic aggregation (Astin 1993).

Programs offering sensitivity training with respect to race, gender, sexual orientation and other aspects of diversity are intended to influence people's opinions in more accepting directions. However, like other areas of multilevel sociological research (see Chapter 15 and 16), sociologists also stress the need for reducing institutional discrimination, or the discriminatory ways organizations and agencies continue to operate in everyday life. For example, in spite of increasing incomes among blacks in the U.S., research still shows that home mortgage applicants who are black are rejected more frequently compared with whites, even when controlling for income and quality of the neighborhood (Gotham 1998). Firms may hire minorities, but only in positions where they supervise other minorities or deal with them as clients, with little opportunity to advance to top chief executive positions from such ghettoized departments (Powell 1999). Institutional forms of discrimination also include the unequal treatment of black versus white criminals and the way many schools and agencies accept middle class minorities but are less accepting of or able to help poor minorities. (See Chapters 7, 10, 17 and 18.) Affirmative action, or governmental mandates to change long existent discriminatory patterns in hiring have helped break down sexual and racial barriers in employment (Tomaskovic-Devey 1993). However, affirmative action increasingly has been challenged by courts interested in equal protection under current hiring policies and by less sympathetic views of whites who themselves have more problems in obtaining good jobs (Sears, Sidonious and Bobo 2000). Consequently, affirmative action directed toward compensating for past discrimination has waned and affirmative action to recruit qualified people of all backgrounds has continued actively. Clearly, how to promote fairer hiring policies and patterns will be a major problem in the U.S. as the labor force becomes increasingly diverse. (See Chapters 15, 16, 17 and 18.)

Name: ______________________________

Quiz Questions: Race and Multiculturalism

1. Humans share mostly the same genetic backgrounds. (True or False?)
2. Sociologists are mostly interested in the biological differences created by ancestral effects. (True or False?)
3. Which of the following was used by the Federal Government to define "Indians" in the U.S.?
   a. the self-defined choices in the 2000 census
   b. the one-drop rule
   c. various blood quantum rules
   d. "Indians" have never been defined by the government
4. Ethnicity refers to which of the following?
   a. native language
   b. religious beliefs
   c. country of birth
   d. present citizenship
5. The term "Hispanics" illustrates which of the following?
   a. blood quantum rules
   b. dichotomization
   c. aggregation
   d. multiculturalism
6. Racial dichotomization oversimplifies the biological variation among Americans. (True or False?)
7. In the 2000 Census, people had to choose one of six main groups to define their biological ancestry in answering the "race" question. (True or False?)
8. Sociological studies show the diversity experiences on college campuses help people feel better about other groups but result in graduates being less satisfied with their college experience. (True or False?)
9. Institutional discrimination is a continuing problem in the U.S. (True or False?)
10. Affirmative action in the U.S. now focuses more on changing past patterns of hiring rather than on fair hiring of new employees. (True or False?)

Name: ______________________________

Exercise: Race and Multiculturalism

1. In the space provided, clearly explain a real life example of racial dichotomization or ethnic aggregation you have read about or seen happen.

Name: ___________________________

Exercise: Race and Multiculturalism

2. In the space provided, clearly explain a diversity experience you had as you went through grade school or middle school.

Name: ___________________________

Exercise: Race and Multiculturalism

3. Think back to your experiences in school including those in college. In the space provided, discuss examples of the social deconstruction of race, diversity appreciation programs, and institutional discrimination.

Name: ______________________________

Exercise: Race and Multiculturalism

4. Think back on the experiences you and other students have had in school including college. In the space provided, discuss examples of racial dichotomization, ethnic aggregation, and multiculturalism.

Name: ______________________________

Exercise: Race and Multiculturalism

5. Watch the classic movie *Guess Who's Coming to Dinner*. In the space provided, discuss how the movie illustrated dichotomization of race, the social deconstruction of race, and multiculturalism.

Name: ______________________________

Exercise: Race and Multiculturalism

6. Watch the movie *Save the Last Dance for Me.* In the space provided, discuss how the movie illustrated dichotomization of race, the social deconstruction of race, and multiculturalism.

Name: ______________________________

Exercise: Race and Multiculturalism

7. Go to the campus library or online and select an article from the *Journal of Black Studies*. Select any article, read it, and in the space provided, discuss how the article illustrated the social construction of race, racial dichotomization, and multiculturalism.

Name: ______________________________

Exercise: Race and Multiculturalism

8. Go to the campus library or online and select an article from *Black Scholar*. Select an article, read it, and in the space provided, discuss how the article dealt with social construction of race, multiculturalism, and institutional discrimination.

Name: ______________________________

Exercise: Race and Multiculturalism

9. Go online to the website of any bank or mortgage company. Based upon information on the website, in the space provided, discuss any evidence of multiculturalism, the absence of institutional discrimination, and equal protection under the U.S. Constitution.

Name: ______________________

Exercise: Race and Multiculturalism

10. Go online to the website of any large retail sales firm like Sears or JC Penney's. Based upon information at the website, in the space provided, discuss any evidence of multiculturalism, the absence of institutional discrimination, and equal protection under the U.S. Constitution.

Gender and Sexuality

A common controversy among observers of human behavior is the nature vs. nurture debate (Schaefer 2001). The issue is whether human behavior is largely dictated by nature or biology, or by the environment or our nurturing. Followers of the nature perspective argue that genetics, hormones, instincts or other traits one has at birth dictate human behavior. The other side of the debate is the nurture position. This view contends that human behavior is largely shaped by our environment or socialization. (See Chapter 4.) According to this view, the situations we find ourselves in, the culture within which we are raised and what we are taught, have a larger influence on our behavior. Within this broad controversy, several topics are debated frequently. For example, many people debate whether IQ is inherited, or taught. Others debate the origin of homosexuality. Was one born with a homosexual orientation (nature), or does one become a homosexual through his or her experiences (nurture)? Of course, the cause of gender differences is debated. This debate explores whether the differences between men and women in American society are caused by biology, perhaps hormones or genetic make-up, or whether men and women behave differently because they were taught to do so. Sociologists generally believe that socialization, or nurture, is responsible for most of the behavioral differences between males and females. Sociologists argue that one is born as a particular sex, which refers to one's biological characteristics. Depending upon the sex you are born with, you are taught to express an appropriate gender role, that is the expected attitudes and behaviors a society associates with each sex. A gender role includes the patterns of social positions, activities, and ways of thinking that societies instruct for the appropriate ways to "be male" or "be female." Gender roles, such as certain types of occupations and types of family-related activities including household chores and childcare are traditionally relegated to males or to females. These are called traditional gender roles and reflect a social world divided into areas of "female" activity and areas of "male" involvement. In the labor market this is called a gender-segregated market or the dual labor market (Hodson and Sullivan 2002).

All major social institutions, including the family, education and the media, are involved in gender role socialization or teaching boys and girls the appropriate way to behave for their sex. Gender role socialization begins immediately upon birth. Studies have shown that within 24 hours of birth, parents of boys rate them as stronger and tougher than parents of girls rate their children (Rubin, Provenzano and Luria 1974). Other evidence of early gender socialization by parents has been examined through experiments. One such experiment was conducted where a mother was given a child dressed in either boy clothes or girl clothes. Depending upon how the child was dressed, the mother played with the child differently. The child the mother thought was a girl, was cuddled and cooed to (Will, Self and Datan 1976; Bonner 1984). The child dressed as a boy was bounced around and admired for his strength. Overall, boys are socialized to presume or anticipate mastery, efficacy and instrumental competence. In a sense, boys are given wings. Parents of girls socialize their daughters to maintain proximity. They discourage independent problem solving, restrict exploration and discourage active play. Girls, in a sense, are given roots (Block 1984).

The education system socializes girls and boys differently as well. When children begin school, they form some of their first peer groups. Peers are a very strong socializing agent of children. It is children themselves who enforce strict adherence to gender roles in the primary grades (Lips 1989). Beyond peers, educators themselves reinforce traditional gender roles. Teachers treat girls and boys differently. Teachers respond more to boys who act aggressive and girls who act dependent (Serbin and O'Leary 1975). Boys are given more individual instruction. When girls are noncompliant with teachers, they are evaluated more harshly than boys who are noncompliant with teachers (Gold, Crombie and Noble 1987). Boys are praised for their academic performance, while girls are praised for their appearance (Dweck 1975; Dweck Goetz and Strauss 1980). Books and information in the curriculum also tend to be sexist with prominent roles primarily played by males (Best 1983; Grossman and Grossman 1994; Orenstein 1997).

The media also reinforces typical notions of gender roles. On television, women are more frequently seen involved in household chores, such as cleaning and childcare. Men portray aggressive and authoritarian roles. The media also socializes the two genders into ideal body types, often depicting ideal types that are genetically impossible for most people to attain (Peacock 2000). (See Chapter 4.)

When gender roles become more androgynous, they are not reversed, but the fuller range of human activities and attitudes from males and females are expressed. More androgyny is seen in the recent entry of women into business and professional employment including positions of major executive responsibility in U.S. airlines and entertainment companies. More androgyny is also seen among the millions of young fathers who split shifts of work with their spouses and care for the children while their wives work (Hodson and Sullivan 2002). Nevertheless, the delimiting features of traditional roles endure in the U.S. and elsewhere in the world. For example, the Family Medical Leave Act of 1993 allows workers in the U.S. to take up to twelve weeks of unpaid leave (with full health insurance benefits) to care for family members. Research suggests that many women fear that if they take such leave they will appear less career-committed and be passed over in future promotions (Hochschild 1997). Furthermore, although most women cannot afford to stay home with young children, since two incomes are necessary for household resource needs, most husbands do not share most household chores and child care with their wives (Hochschild and Manchung 1989; Reskin and Padavic 1994). Many older professional women face the dilemma of the biological limits to birthing because they have remained unmarried while pursuing their careers. Finally, evidence suggests that the men and women who break through traditional gender barriers at work are not viewed positively. They are sometimes viewed as deviant and receive stigmatized reactions from fellow workers (Kanter 1977). Consequently, more androgynous roles are slowly emerging in social life, but we still have a long way to go before they become fully androgynous.

Our three main sociological theories address gender. Functionalists focus on how gender differentiation is beneficial for society. Opposite gender roles allow men and women to specialize and become very good at their appropriate tasks. Symbolic interactionist theory argues that people "do" gender. If a man were simply to have a close shave and put on a dress, he would not fool anyone that he was a woman. To "pass" as a woman, that man would have to appear as a woman, but also adopt the mannerisms of a woman. For example, his posture, his gestures, his eye contact, must all be like a woman's before anyone would mistake him for a woman. Conflict theory illustrates how gender differentiation contributes to gender inequality. Conflict theorists assert the United States is organized as a patriarchy, which is a form of social organization in which males dominate females.

Because of this domination, women have suffered inequality. There are a variety of measures of this inequality. One of the clearest is in the workplace. First, the workplace is segregated. Women are extremely over represented in jobs that are similar to their gender role. Half of all women employed outside the home work in "pink collar" positions, such as clerical or service work (Bellas 1993; Kaufman 1995; Thornborrow and Sheldon 1995). When women do break into "male jobs" they tend to choose specialties that are lower in prestige and income. Women also experience a glass ceiling, an invisible barrier that blocks the promotion of a qualified individual. In 1995 a bipartisan congressional commission uncovered a variety of reasons for the existence of the glass ceiling, such as women experiencing a lack of mentoring, having little access to critical development assignments, being subject to different standards of evaluation, and having little access to informal communication networks (Department of Labor 1995). Ultimately inequality in the workplace is measured by the gender wage gap, or the ratio of women's income to men's, which has stayed at a rate of 76 percent for about twenty years (Bureau of Labor Statistics 1999). This disparity in income comes from four main social sources. First, gender discrimination, secondly, women's domestic responsibilities, including time off for pregnancy and childcare, and third, the difference in average job qualifications of women compared to men. Finally, work done by women is valued less in American culture than work done by men and therefore receives a lower salary (Brym and Lie 2003).

Women in the U.S. have been active in changing their position in the social world. The women's movement first began in the mid-1800s with the goal of achieving suffrage (the right to vote) for women. This movement was not successful until 1920. The women's movement continues to fight for equality. (See Chapter 18.) Feminism is the term used to refer to individuals who are advocating for the equal rights of women. Although feminism is expressed in a variety of forms, from very radical demands for equal rights to fairly conservative efforts, most forms of feminism adopt the following principles: the importance of social change, the expansion of human choice, the elimination of gender stratification, the ending of sexual violence and the control of women's sexuality and reproduction (Macionis 2003). (See Chapter 18.)

Gender, sex, sexual orientations, and sexuality must carefully be distinguished. Sex refers to the biological differences between males and females. Physical differences such as men being able to impregnate women and women giving birth to children are called primary sex traits. Physical differences between men and women, such as muscular-skeletal and body hair not related to reproduction, are secondary sex traits. Sexual orientations are the preferences that people have for sharing emotional close relationships including sexual activity with others. Sexuality refers to sexual activity people have with partners and may or may not coincide with sexual preferences, and sexual activity can be influenced by many social factors related to sexual orientations such as the emotional quality of relationships or factors unrelated to sexual orientations such as aging and health. (See Chapters 12, 13 and 14.) Intersexuals are people born with some reproductive organs of both sexes and transsexuals are people who have surgery to alter their primary sex traits. Sexual orientations are much more complex than many people think. Since Kinsey and his colleagues conducted the first scientific study of sexual orientations (Kinsey 1948), several types of orientations are known to exist among Americans. Heterosexuals are people who prefer close and sexually related relationships with people of the opposite sex, while homosexuals have such preferences for same-sex partners. The State of Vermont and various employers in the U.S. have recognized same-sex partners' legal rights for inheritance and health benefits, albeit in legal unions rather than legalized "marriages." Bisexuals are people who desire emotionally close and/or sexual relationships with partners of both sexes. Fuller understanding of sexual orientations and sexuality is necessary to understand the complexity of sexuality, especially in comparison to the typical treatment of it in the media, and to understand health issues better such as safe sex and sexually transmitted diseases (STD's) (Garrett 1994).

Actual scientific research on sexual activity is scarce. Most people see social representations of sexuality in the media such as on soap operas and in movies. The popular press also tends to highlight the unusual or bizarre aspects of sexuality related to crime including serial killings as well as to the instances of promiscuity involving famous personalities including professional athletes.

Kinsey's (1948) early scientific study of sexuality showed the diverse forms it then took in the U.S. and contributed to a more open discussion of sexuality in America (Macionis 2003). While Kinsey's study showed much more premarital sex among men than women, recent research shows that about two thirds of both sexes have had premarital sex by their senior year of high school. Thus, despite concerns about family values and health problems related to unsafe sex, considerable proportions of American youth have premarital sex (Laumann et al. 1994). Such research also shows that sexual activity continues to vary widely among adults in the United States. Best estimates suggest that about one-third of adults report sex with a partner a few times per year or not at all, another third reports such activity once to several times per month and the remaining third reports sex with a partner two or more times per week. Married people have sex with partners most frequently and married people also report the highest levels of satisfaction with their partners (Laumann et al. 1994). Thus, many media images of sexual experiences do not coincide with the overall patterns of sexuality in the United States. For example, scientific research shows that extra marital activity is not as frequent as many people believe, or as frequent as it is portrayed in the media. About 75 percent of men and 90 percent of women remain sexually faithful to their partners throughout their married lives (Laumann et al. 1994; NORC 2001: 1135).

Name: ______________________________

Exercise: Gender and Sexuality

2. In the space provided, describe an instance where you felt inequality due to your gender.

Name: ______________________________

Exercise: Gender and Sexuality

3. Think back on your family experiences when you were growing up. In the space provided, discuss traditional gender roles, gender role socialization, and any evidence of androgyny.

Name: ______________________________

Exercise: Gender and Sexuality

4. Think back on your experiences with people you went to school with growing up. In the space provided, discuss sexual orientations, homosexuality, heterosexuality, and feminism.

Name: ___________________________

Exercise: Gender and Sexuality

5. Watch any of Armistead Maupin's episodes of *Tales of the City*. After watching an episode, in the space provided, discuss <u>sexual orientations</u>, <u>homosexuality</u>, <u>transsexuality</u>, and <u>bisexuality</u>.

Name: ______________________________

Exercise: Gender and Sexuality

6. Watch the film *Mrs. Doubtfire*. After watching the film discuss in the space provided, gender segregated work, gender roles, patriarchy, and androgyny.

Name: ______________________________

Exercise: Gender and Sexuality

7. Go to the campus library or online and select an article from the journal *Gender Roles*. Select any one article, read it, and in the space provided, discuss traditional gender roles, gender role socialization, and androgyny.

Name: ______________________________

Exercise: Gender and Sexuality

8. Go to the campus library or online and select an article from the *Journal of Homosexuality*. Select any one article, read it, and in the space provided, discuss sexual orientations, homosexuality, and bisexuality.

Name: ______________________________

Exercise: Gender and Sexuality

9. Go to the website of any gay rights group. Based upon the information available on the site, in the space provided, discuss same-sex partners' legal rights, sexual orientations, and safe sex.

Name: ______________________________

Exercise: Gender and Sexuality

10. Go to the website of any women's rights group. Based upon the information available on the site, in the space provided, discuss feminism, patriarchy, and androgyny.

Poverty and Stratification

Every society has processes of distributing its work. Work in modern society gets divided out or differentiated into many individual jobs (Rosenfeld 1992). Jobs that require many years of skilled training are often highly valued by society's members. Thus, some jobs come to be more valued than others over time. Highly valued jobs are usually rewarded well in comparison to less valued jobs. Rewards can vary by society, but they can usually be thought of as forms of power, prestige and wealth. The outcome of this distribution of jobs and rewards is a stratification system—a hierarchy of groups and individuals (Kerbo 1991). Every society has some system of stratification. Throughout history different stratification systems including primitive communalism, slavery, feudalism, caste, and class systems have existed in various societies (Wallace and Wallace 1989).

In America, the citizenry is stratified into a hierarchical arrangement of social classes—social categories whose members are believed to have common economic, political or social interests (Wanner 1986). These classes reflect significant inequalities in life-chances, or amounts of social resources like money, homes, health care, dietary habits, recreational activity, and so on. One way of looking at social class is to examine changes in average earned income differences as reflected by the income disparity number (Census 2001). The income disparity number is how many times higher the average income of the top 20 percent of families is compared to the average income of the lowest 20 percent of families. In 1980, the top 20 percent of families made $103,044 on average while the bottom 20 percent averaged $13,414. This means that the upper 20 percent averaged 7.2 times more money than the bottom 20 percent averaged. In 2000, the average income of the top 20 percent of families was $155,527 and the average income of the lowest 20 percent was $14,232, meaning that the income disparity number had increased to almost 11, reflecting the increasing differences in income in the U.S. (Carruthers and Babb 2000).

Another way sociologists differentiate social classes is to use family income ranges and types of employment that have increasing levels of earnings versus occupations with more limited earnings potential. While several class typologies have been developed, a common one follows (Macionis 2002). Upper Class (UC) families are the 5 percent of Americans whose individual earnings exceed $160,000 per year. While many have inherited their earnings, such as the Rockefellers or the Mellons, many like Bill Gates have become very rich in their own lifetimes. The Upper-Middle Class (UMC) includes more than 20 percent of American families who are well educated and have a family member in a profession with an income between $80,000 and $160,000. The Average Middle Class (AMC) includes more than 20 percent of the U.S. population with incomes from $40,000 to $80,000. Many

AMC members are in middle management and sales work or in skilled trades such as plumbers. The Working Class (WC) includes about 30 percent of American families with incomes ranging from $25,000 to $40,000. Many are in lower skilled jobs in manufacturing and services and their incomes have fallen. The remaining American families are in the Lower Class (LC). The proportions of Americans in various social classes fluctuate with the trends in employment in better paying and lesser paying jobs. Sociologists often examine the structural mobility of a society—the ability of individuals to move within and across social classes as job opportunities change.

While all the strata of the American class structure are of interest to sociologists, the lowest class is of particular interest (Wynn 2001). Sociologists have further differentiated three subgroups within the lower class: the near-poor, the poor, and the underclass. Macro-level sociologists are concerned because the size of these groups can serve as an indicator of the health of the society (Best 2001). For example, the Reagan presidency (1980–1988) brought on an immense rise in the number of individuals who could no longer afford housing which clearly demonstrated a societal decline (Appelbaum 1989; Davey 1992; Rubin, Wright and Devine 1992; Young 1988). Micro-level sociologists are also concerned with the lower strata of society because people's position in the social structure affects people's life risks—what risks they will be exposed to over their lifetimes—and their life chances—the trajectory that their lives will follow. For example, sociologists have found that poorer people are exposed to more health risks in their living environments and they have fewer resources with which to maintain health and avoid illness (Cockerham 2001).

One major concern of sociologists is in the definition of what poverty means. Poverty is defined in one of two ways (Blackwood and Lynch 1994). In some societies, poverty is viewed as relative. That is, relative poverty is defined as how much money or resources one has in relation to others. For instance, in Western Europe and Scandinavia, a family is considered poor if their income is less than half the national median income for a family of their size (Rodgers 2000). Absolute poverty, on the other hand, is defined objectively, usually by calculating some minimum amount of resources necessary to live. Of course, the calculation of such a line can vary depending on criteria used. For example, the International Fund for Agriculture Development (IFAD) defines poverty as the condition of being so deprived of resources—food, housing, clothes, and essential health care—that a person's life is endangered (International Fund for Agriculture Development 2001). IFAD's extreme consumption poverty line equates to 1 U.S. dollar a day. According to IFAD (2001), approximately 1.2 billion people around the world consume less than one dollar's worth of resources a day. The United States government also uses an absolute poverty standard (Rodgers 2000). In the U.S. case, the government calculates a dollar figure for a basic diet for different-sized families. These numbers are then multiplied times three to include other necessities like clothing and housing. Families making less than the calculated amount of money for their family size are defined as being poor.

How the poverty line is calculated is, of course, a political issue. Government officials would prefer to identify fewer people in poverty so that societal processes will reflect well upon their administration. Therefore, they would like a very low poverty line. Activists would prefer to identify more individuals in poverty so that poverty becomes a basis for social reform (in America we often rank our political reform issues in terms of how many people they affect). This legitimates activists' recommendations for alleviating poverty. (See the Best reading.) Social scientists who believe that the U.S. government measure is too low often use from 125 percent to 200 percent of the official poverty level to identify people in social distress. These individuals, whose income is just above the poverty level, are called the near poor (Eitzen and Smith 2003, Gorey and Vena 1994). The near poor are seen as earning enough money to meet their basic needs but are still at risk of sliding into poverty if an emergency strikes (Nelson and Smith 1999). Such people are vulnerable to all sorts of economic downturns. (See Chapters 16 and 17.)

Sociologists are often involved in the debates over the definition of poverty because they attempt to calculate better poverty measures. One way sociologists have accomplished this is by calculating a more realistic set of budget criteria. For example, Zimmerman, Kershaw, and Garkovich (2000) calculated a minimum monthly budget for a family of three (an employed mother and two children) to be self-sufficient was $1,685.92 a month. Working full-time this would require a job earning $10.89 an hour. A person working a minimum wage job would actually need to work two such full-time jobs to meet this monthly budgetary goal.

Another way that sociologists are involved with poverty research is in identifying relationships between poverty and other social characteristics. Demographers, sociologists who specialize in the study of the size, composition, and distribution of society, have shown that every person in society does not have the same chance of being poor. For example, when asked to describe the poor, most Americans would probably describe poverty as an urban black phenomenon. It is interesting that in America while the number of metropolitan people in poverty is larger than the number of nonmetropolitan people in poverty, sociologists have found that the chance of a metropolitan person being in poverty is lower than the chance of a nonmetropolitan person (Rural Sociological Society 1993). Moreover, more whites are poor than blacks; however, the chance that a randomly selected African-American is poor is much higher than the chance that a randomly selected white is poor. Furthermore, sociologists note that findings like these do not discuss how far below the poverty line people are. William Julius Wilson (1987, 1996) points out that many poor urban blacks are members of the underclass, the poor who are chronically unemployed or who can only find minimum wage work, if any.

Sociologists are also active in determining the reasons why poverty exists. This is important because identifying causes is the first step toward the solution of limited opportunity. Causes of poverty can usually be divided into reasons that focus on either the individual or the place (Fitchen 1981, 1991; Jargowsky 1997). Person poverty emphasizes individual choices to commit or not commit to schooling, training or work (Rural Sociological Society 1993). From a person poverty perspective, if a place has a high poverty rate it is because the local labor force is less productive. The workers lack traits that lead to more lucrative employment and therefore result in a higher likelihood of being poor. At the other extreme, place poverty emphasizes the number of high-quality, available jobs in a place as a determining factor of poverty. If there are no good jobs in a place, there is no reason to be educated (unless one is planning on moving) (Falk and Lyson 1988). If a place has good jobs and they are in high demand, then individuals will have more motivation to credential themselves with a degree or certificate. Thus, from a place poverty standpoint, community and economic development are extremely important processes. (See Chapters 7, 16, 17 and 19.)

Lastly, sociologists are involved in current government efforts to move the poor off welfare and make them more self-sufficient. Efforts to reform the U.S. welfare system have been underway since the 1960s. Sociologists have been involved in implementing and evaluating test projects such as the Negative Income Tax Experiments (Nathan 1988, Rossi and Lyall 1976) and the Housing Allowance Experiments (Friedman 1985, Hamilton 1979). More recently sociologists have also been involved in assessing the outcomes of changes caused by the most recent welfare reform legislation (Dyk and Zimmerman 2000; Edin, Harris, Sandefur 1998). Among the positive aspects of such reforms is that more former welfare recipients are employed and contributing to the total output of the economy or Gross Domestic Product (GDP). Among the negative aspects of such reforms is that many of these new employees are in low-wage jobs and are among the near-poor.

Name: ______________________

Quiz Questions: Poverty and Stratification

1. Work in modern society gets:
   a. bid out into many jobs
   b. differentiated into many individual jobs
   c. divided into a few, large categories
   d. all of the above
2. A hierarchy of groups and individuals divided by jobs is known as:
   a. a class system
   b. a feudal system
   c. a stratification system
   d. a typology system
3. What percent of families currently comprise the Upper Middle Class in the United States?
   a. 15 percent
   b. 5 percent
   c. 20 percent
   d. 10 percent
4. The actual proportions of U.S. citizens in social classes varies due to:
   a. trends in the stock market
   b. trends in better paying and lesser paying jobs
   c. population
   d. none of the above
5. The United States defines poverty as consuming less than a dollar's worth of resources a day. (True or False?)
6. Demographers are sociologists who study the size, composition and distribution of society. (True or False?)
7. Relative poverty is defined as being so deprived of resources that a person's life is endangered. (True or False?)
8. Government officials, social scientists, and activists often disagree over how poverty should be calculated. (True or False?)
9. Place poverty stresses how committed people act toward work. (True or False?)
10. The income disparity number in the U.S. is increasing. (True or False?)

Name: ______________________________

Exercise: Poverty and Stratification

1. Think back on the hometown or area of a city that you grew up in. In the space provided, discuss how where you grew up illustrated <u>near poor</u>, <u>person poverty</u> and <u>place poverty</u>.

Name: ______________________________

Exercise: Poverty and Stratification

2. Using your campus town, in the space provided, illustrate absolute poverty, relative poverty and the near poor.

Name: ______________________________

Exercise: Poverty and Stratification

3. Consider members of your family including aunts, uncles, and cousins. In the space provided, discuss the social class of the wealthiest part of your family is in and compare it to the poorest part of your family. Discuss how structured mobility is related to social class difference in your family.

Name: ______________________

Exercise: Poverty and Stratification

4. In the space provided, discuss the social class level you hope to attain. Discuss how you hope to achieve and maintain this social class level. Discuss how you would avoid the sources of person poverty and place poverty.

Name: ______________________________

Exercise: Poverty and Stratification

5. Watch the classic movie *The Grapes of Wrath*. In the space provided, discuss how the movie illustrates absolute poverty, person poverty, place poverty, and the underclass.

Name: ______________________

Exercise: Poverty and Stratification

6. Watch the movie *The Breakfast of Champions*. In the space provided, discuss how the movie illustrates income disparity, social class, absolute poverty, and person poverty.

Name: ________________________________

Exercise: Poverty and Stratification

7. Go to the campus library or online to select an article from the sociological journal *Work and Occupations*. Select any one article and in the space provided, discuss how the article illustrates income disparity, person poverty, relative poverty, and the near poor.

Name: ______________________________

Exercise: Poverty and Stratification

8. Go to the campus library or online to select an article from the journal *The Monthly Labor Review*. Select any one article and discuss in the space provided, how the article illustrates the near poor, person poverty, place poverty, and recent welfare reform legislation.

Name: ______________________________

Exercise: Poverty and Stratification

9. Go online to a website that deals with the homeless and homelessness. Use information on the website to discuss in the space provided, the underclass, absolute poverty, person poverty, and programs for the homeless.

Name: ______________________________

Exercise: Poverty and Stratification

10. Go to the website of any organization that exists to help poor people, such as Habitat for Humanity or Feed the Children. Using information on the website, discuss, in the space provided, person poverty, the underclass, absolute poverty, and the life risks of the poor.

From Individual to Structural Discrimination

Fred L. Pincus

People often think of racial discrimination in terms of the actions of individual prejudiced white people against individual people of color. However, . . . prejudice (an attitude) does not necessarily lead to discrimination (an overt behavior), and discrimination is not always caused by prejudice.

Group discrimination can exist at many different levels. An individual teacher who mistreats a Hispanic student is different from a school system that refuses to admit Hispanics. An individual personnel officer who decides not to hire a qualified black applicant is different from an entire state police department that refuses to hire black officers.

In their influential book *Black Power*, which was published more than a quarter of a century ago, Stokely Carmichael and Charles Hamilton differentiated "individual racism" from "institutional racism." The former involved the behavior of white individuals toward blacks and other minorities, and the latter involved the behavior of the entire white society and its institutions toward people of color.

Since *racism* is a pejorative word often used imprecisely, I shall modify the Carmichael/Hamilton typology and apply it to the concept of discrimination. My discussion here deals with three different types of race/ethnic discrimination: individual, institutional, and structural.

1. *Individual discrimination* refers to the behavior of individual members of one race/ethnic group that is intended to have a differential and/or harmful effect on the members of another race/ethnic group. This category includes a wide range of behavior by majority-group individuals or small groups—from anti-Asian graffiti and name calling, to an employer's refusal to hire blacks or a landlord's refusal to rent to Hispanics, to physical attacks against Native Americans.

According to this definition, actions by individual minority-group members against the majority group can also be characterized as "individual discrimination." Examples might include antiwhite graffiti by blacks, physical attacks against whites by Hispanics, or employment discrimination by Asians against whites. Each of these actions entails intentional antiwhite treatment that has a differential and/or harmful impact.

2. *Institutional discrimination* is quite different in that it refers to the policies of majority institutions, and the behavior of individuals who implement these policies and control these institutions, that are intended to have a differential and/or harmful effect on minority groups. A major goal of institutional discrimination is to keep minority groups in a subordinate position within society. Hence this concept is much broader than that of individual discrimination.

Sometimes, institutional discrimination is embodied in laws and government policy. From the 1890s until the 1950s, for example, most southern states had laws that *legally* discriminated between blacks and whites in all areas of life—from voting, education, and employment to religion, public accommodations, and restaurants. These laws had broad support among the white population and were even given the stamp of approval by the U.S. Supreme Court in 1896.[1] Legal segregation, which has been referred to as the "Jim Crow System," is a clear example of institutional discrimination, and it goes far beyond the level of individual actions.

Blacks are not the only victims of institutional discrimination in the United States. Whites seized the land of Native Americans by brutally defeating them on the battlefield and then confining them to reservations. Treaties with Indian Nations were routinely broken by the government, and entire tribes were forcibly moved from one reservation to another, often with fatal results.

Asians have also been victims. After Japan attacked Pearl Harbor in 1941, all Japanese people on the West Coast were taken from their homes and placed in internment camps for the duration of the war. Both citizens and noncitizens were forced to sell their property at a great loss.

Although most discrimination by federal, state, and local governments is now illegal, examples of institutional discrimination can still be found. One such example is "gerrymandering," the illegal drawing of electoral districts in such a way as to intentionally minimize the electoral power of minority groups. Police and fire departments in many cities across the country have illegally refused to hire and promote *qualified* blacks and Hispanics at the same rate as comparably qualified whites. (This practice has resulted in a series of lawsuits and controversial affirmative action programs. . . .) And even the prestigious Federal Bureau of Investigation illegally discriminated against black and Hispanic agents until 1992, when the FBI entered into a consent decree to end a lawsuit by black agents.

Institutional discrimination can be detected in the private sector as well. Real estate associations often "steer" blacks away from white neighborhoods and show them houses and apartments in predominantly minority neighborhoods. Banks in various cities have "redlined" certain minority areas (that is, they have refused to grant mortgages to people who live in these areas regardless of whether they meet the financial qualifications specified), and they have granted smaller mortgages at higher interest rates. Moreover, large corporations have been convicted of racial discrimination in hiring and promotion, and private social clubs often refuse to admit minority members.

Since the majority group generally controls the major institutions, institutional discrimination is almost always carried out by the majority group against the minority group—not the other way around. For the most part, minority groups lack the power with which to practice institutional discrimination. Nevertheless, the refusal by a black-controlled city government to hire whites would be an example of institutional discrimination.

3. Finally, there is a third type of discrimination that some would say is not really discrimination at all. *Structural discrimination* refers to the policies of majority institutions, and the behavior of the individuals who implement these policies and control these institutions, that are race-neutral in intent but have a differential and/or harmful effect on minority groups. The key element in structural discrimination is not the intent but the effect of keeping minority groups in a subordinate position.

Although it is sometimes difficult to determine whether a particular phenomenon is an example of institutional or structural discrimination, the differences between the two are important both conceptually and in terms of social policy. Both types have the *effect* of keeping minority groups subordinate, but only institutional discrimination is *intended* to keep minority groups subordinate. Some examples of structural discrimination follow.

It is well known that blacks and Hispanics are underrepresented on the nation's college campuses. Most colleges, however, have what appear to be race-neutral meritocratic entrance requirements: Anyone who meets the requirements will be admitted regardless of race, ethnicity, gender, and so on. Requirements usually include high school grades, scores on SAT or ACT tests, teacher recommendations, and the like. And most educators sincerely believe that schools with the most rigorous entrance requirements offer the highest-quality educations.

It is also well known that, for a variety of reasons, blacks and Hispanics on the average tend to get lower high school grades and to score lower on the SAT then do whites. Accordingly, a smaller proportion of blacks and Hispanics than whites are admitted to college, especially to the more prestigious schools. In this case, we can say that college entrance requirements constitute an example of structural discrimination because they have a negative effect on blacks and Hispanics.

The criteria that educators believe to be important are less accessible to black and Hispanic students than to whites. As a rule, college managers and faculty members do not intend to be racially discriminatory, and many even feel quite badly about the harm done to black and Hispanic students as a result of these requirements. However, most also do not want to change the requirements.

It is possible, of course, that the under-representation of blacks and Hispanics on college campuses is being caused by institutional discrimination. A few colleges may still refuse to admit any black students. Others may purposely inflate entrance requirements as a way of screening out most minority students. Individual discrimination may also be taking place, as when a recruiting officer chooses to avoid black high schools when looking for potential students.

Another example of structural discrimination can be found in the context of job qualifications. Many employers require new employees to have earned a bachelor's degree even though there may be no direct connection between a college education and the skills required for the job in question. The employer, of course, may *believe* that college-educated people will be better workers. Since a smaller percentage of blacks and Hispanics get bachelor's degrees than do whites, blacks will be underrepresented among those who qualify for the job. This is a case of structural discrimination because blacks and Hispanics are negatively affected by the educational requirement for the job, even though there may be no intent to subordinate them.

On the other hand, an employer who used the bachelor's degree requirement intentionally to screen out blacks and Hispanics would be committing a form of institutional discrimination. And an individual personnel manager who refused to hire a qualified black applicant would be guilty of individual discrimination.

Consider yet another example: Insurance rates for homes, businesses, and cars are generally higher in black communities than in white communities, in part because of the higher rates of street crime in lower-income black communities. Insurance companies argue that it is good business to charge higher rates in areas where they will have to pay out more in claims, and they insist that they charge high rates in high-crime white areas as well. Yet in spite of the apparently race-neutral determination of insurance rates, the average black ends up paying more than the average white. So this, too, is an example of structural discrimination.

The "good business" argument can also be seen in the banking practice of granting loans and mortgages. The lower an individual's income, the less likely that individual is to be able to pay back the loan. Banks, therefore, are reluctant to give loans to lower-income people; and if they grant any at all, the loans are likely to be small. Since blacks tend to earn lower incomes than whites, they find it more difficult to get loans. Consequently, they have a harder time buying homes and starting businesses. Accordingly, the lending practices of banks are examples of structural discrimination, even though the banks themselves may be following standard business procedures.

Although banks and insurance companies routinely use the "good business" argument to justify structural discrimination, they sometimes practice institutional discrimination as well. Banks often "redline" black communities, and insurance companies have been known to charge higher rates in black communities than in white ones, even after controlling for crime rates.

Many social scientists and much of the general public would be reluctant to apply the term *structural discrimination* to the examples listed here, given the absence in these examples of any intent to harm minority groups or keep them subordinate. I assert, however, that the negative *effects* constitute discrimination. Thus even policies that are intended to be race-neutral and are carried out by well-intentioned people can perpetuate racial inequality.

Like institutional discrimination, structural discrimination is almost always a matter of majority group against minority group, not the other way around. Again, since most social institutions work to the advantage of the majority group, few if any institutional policies favor the minority group. Groups with little power are generally unable to implement policies that are structurally discriminatory.

Although it is sometimes difficult to know whether a given policy that negatively affects minority-group members is a case of individual, institutional, or structural discrimination, an understanding of the conceptual differences among these three categories is important. Since the different types of discrimination have different origins, different policies are required for their elimination. In trying to eliminate individual and institutional discrimination, for example, activists can appeal to the moral and legal principles of equal opportunity and racial fairness. In particular, they might argue that race-neutral meritocratic policies that promote equal opportunity should be the rule in education, employment, housing, and so on.

Where structural discrimination is concerned, however, policies that are race-neutral in intent are not race-neutral in effect. Since policymakers involved with structural discrimination have not tried to harm or subordinate minorities, it makes no sense for activists to appeal to their sense of racial fairness. The policymakers already believe that they are being racially fair. Instead, activists must convince these policymakers to reevaluate some of the fundamental policies upon which their institutions are based.

If banks are practicing institutional discrimination by "redlining" minority areas, for example, activists can demand that the banks treat each person in that area as a distinct individual. All individuals, inside or outside the redlined area, who meet the banks' universal credit requirements should receive a mortgage. Race or neighborhood should not be a factor.

Confronting the profit-oriented business practices of banks, which I have included in the category of structural discrimination, is more problematic. Even without redlining, banks grant fewer mortgages to blacks than to whites because of racial differences in income and wealth. Bankers can argue that they are simply being good race-neutral capitalists and may even express sincere regret that more blacks do not qualify for loans and mortgages. To deal with this problem, activists must confront the profit-oriented business practices themselves, not the racial views of the bank officials. Perhaps banks have to forgo some of their profits in order to help poor black communities. Perhaps the federal government must subsidize more loans to low-income blacks and create not-for-profit banks in low-income areas.

Alternative arguments are also needed to confront racial inequality in higher education. Colleges that refuse to admit Hispanics who meet their admissions standards are practicing institutional discrimination. If activists can successfully show that qualified Hispanics are not being admitted, they can try to bring public pressure on the colleges to get them to stop discriminating. If this effort failed, the activists could probably sue the colleges in a court of law.

Combating structurally discriminatory admissions standards in higher education requires a different approach. Educators can justify admissions standards by saying that certain grade-point averages and SAT scores are essential to the mission of academic excellence in their institutions, even though a relatively small percentage of Hispanics are able to qualify.

Activists must call on educators to modify their standards, not their racial views. (Certainly Hispanics do not benefit from the standards currently in place.) Indeed, colleges should devote more resources to remedial and support programs for Hispanics who do not meet the entrance requirements. Also needed are new pedagogical techniques, including a more multicultural curriculum, that would be more suited to Hispanic students. And perhaps colleges could shoulder some of the responsibility for improving the quality of high schools attended by Hispanic students.

All three types of discrimination coexist as major problems in American society. And all three must be confronted if racial equality is to be achieved. Individual and institutional discrimination are the most visible. Yet even if they were completely eliminated, the prospect of racial equality would be jeopardized by continuing structural discrimination.

Note

1. . . . *1896*: In the landmark case, Plessy v. Ferguson, the Supreme Court upheld southern segregation laws.

X: A Fabulous Child's Story

Lois Gould

Once upon a time, a baby named X was born. This baby was named X so that nobody could tell whether it was a boy or a girl. Its parents could tell, of course, but they couldn't tell anybody else. They couldn't even tell Baby X, at first.

You see, it was all part of a very important Secret Scientific Xperiment, known officially as Project Baby X. The smartest scientists had set up this Xperiment at a cost of Xactly 23 billion dollars and 72 cents, which might seem like a lot for just one baby, even a very important Xperimental baby. But when you remember the prices of things like strained carrots and stuffed bunnies, and popcorn for the movies and booster shots for camp, let alone 28 shiny quarters from the tooth fairy, you begin to see how it adds up.

Also, long before Baby X was born, all those scientists had to be paid to work out the details of the Xperiment, and to write the *Official Instruction Manual* for Baby X's parents and, most important of all, to find the right set of parents to bring up Baby X. These parents had to be selected very carefully. Thousands of volunteers had to take thousands of tests and answer thousands of tricky questions. Almost everybody failed because, it turned out, almost everybody really wanted either a baby boy or a baby girl, and not Baby X at all. Also, almost everybody was afraid that a Baby X would be a lot more trouble than a boy or a girl. (They were probably right, the scientists admitted, but Baby X needed parents who wouldn't *mind* the Xtra trouble.)

There were families with grandparents named Milton and Agatha, who didn't see why the baby couldn't be named Milton or Agatha instead of X, even if it *was* an X. There were families with aunts who insisted on knitting tiny dresses and uncles who insisted on sending tiny baseball mitts. Worst of all, there were families that already had other children who couldn't be trusted to keep the secret. Certainly not if they knew the secret was worth 23 billion dollars and 72 cents—and all you had to do was take one little peek at Baby X in the bathtub to know if it was a boy or a girl.

But, finally, the scientists found the Joneses, who really wanted to raise an X more than any other kind of baby—no matter how much trouble it would be. Ms. and Mr. Jones had to promise they would take equal turns caring for X, and feeding it, and singing it lullabies. And they had to promise never to hire any baby-sitters. The government scientists knew perfectly well that a baby-sitter would probably peek at X in the bathtub, too.

The day the Joneses brought their baby home, lots of friends and relatives came over to see it. None of them knew about the secret Xperiment, though. So the first thing they asked was what kind of a baby X was. When the Joneses smiled and said, "It's an X!" nobody knew what to say. They couldn't say, "Look at her cute little dimples!" And they couldn't say, "Look at his husky little biceps!" And they couldn't even say just plain "kitchy-coo." In fact, they all thought the Joneses were playing some kind of rude joke.

But, of course, the Joneses were not joking. "It's an X" was absolutely all they would say. And that made the friends and relatives very angry. The relatives all felt embarrassed about having an X in the family. "People will think there's something wrong with it!" some of them whispered. "There *is* something wrong with it!" others whispered back.

"Nonsense!" the Joneses told them all cheerfully. "What could possibly be wrong with this perfectly adorable X?"

Nobody could answer that, except Baby X, who had just finished its bottle. Baby X's answer was a loud, satisfied burp.

Clearly, nothing at all was wrong. Nevertheless, none of the relatives felt comfortable about buying a present for a Baby X. The cousins who sent the baby a tiny football helmet would not come and visit any more. And the neighbors who sent a pink-flowered romper suit pulled their shades down when the Joneses passed their house.

The *Official Instruction Manual* had warned the new parents that this would happen, so they didn't fret about it. Besides, they were too busy with Baby X and the hundreds of different Xercises for treating it properly.

Ms. and Mr. Jones had to be Xtra careful about how they played with little X. They knew that if they kept bouncing it up in the air and saying how *strong* and *active* it was, they'd be treating it more like a boy than an X. But if all they did was cuddle it and kiss it and tell it how *sweet* and *dainty* it was, they'd be treating it more like a girl than an X.

On page 1,654 of the *Official Instruction Manual*, the scientists prescribed: "plenty of bouncing and plenty of cuddling, *both*. X ought to be strong and sweet and active. Forget about *dainty* altogether."

Meanwhile, the Joneses were worrying about other problems. Toys, for instance. And clothes. On his first shopping trip, Mr. Jones told the store clerk, "I need some clothes and toys for my new baby." The clerk smiled and said, "Well, now, is it a boy or a girl?" "It's an X," Mr. Jones said, smiling back. But the clerk got all red in the face and said huffily, "In *that* case, I'm afraid I can't help you, sir." So Mr. Jones wandered helplessly up and down the aisles trying to find what X needed. But everything in the store was piled up in sections marked "Boys" or "Girls." There were "Boys' Pajamas" and "Girls' Underwear" and "Boys' Fire Engines" and "Girls' Housekeeping Sets." Mr. Jones went home without buying anything for X. That night he and Ms. Jones consulted page 2,326 of the *Official Instruction Manual*. "Buy plenty of everything!" it said firmly.

So they bought plenty of sturdy blue pajamas in the Boys' Department and cheerful flowered underwear in the Girls' Department. And they bought all kinds of toys. A boy doll that made pee-pee and cried, "Pa-pa" And a girl doll that talked in three languages and said, "I am the Pres-i-dent of Gen-er-al Mo-tors." They also bought a storybook about a brave princess who rescued a handsome prince from his ivory tower, and another one about a sister and brother who grew up to be a baseball star and a ballet star, and you had to guess which was which.

The head scientists of Project Baby X checked all their purchases and told them to keep up the good work. They also reminded the Joneses to see page 4,629 of the *Manual*, where it said, "Never make Baby X feel *embarrassed* or *ashamed* about what it wants to play with. And if X gets dirty climbing rocks, never say "Nice little Xes don't get dirty climbing rocks.'"

Likewise, it said, "If X falls down and cries, never say 'Brave little Xes don't cry.' Because, of course, nice little Xes *do* get dirty, and brave little Xes *do* cry. No matter how dirty X gets, or how hard it cries, don't worry. It's all part of the Xperiment."

Whenever the Joneses pushed Baby X's stroller in the park, smiling strangers would come over and coo: "Is that a boy or a girl?" The Joneses would smile back and say, "It's an X." The strangers would stop smiling then, and often snarl something nasty—as if the Joneses had snarled at *them*.

By the time X grew big enough to play with other children, the Joneses' troubles had grown bigger, too. Once a little girl grabbed X's shovel in the sandbox, and zonked X on the head with it. "Now, now, Tracy," the little girl's mother began to scold, "little girls mustn't hit little—"

and she turned to ask X, "Are you a little boy or a little girl, dear?"

Mr. Jones, who was sitting near the sandbox, held his breath and crossed his fingers.

X smiled politely at the lady, even though X's head had never been zonked so hard in its life. "I'm a little X," X replied.

"You're a *what*?" the lady exclaimed angrily. "You're a little b-r-a-t, you mean!"

"But little girls mustn't hit little Xes, either!" said X, retrieving the shovel with another polite smile. "What good does hitting do, anyway?"

X's father, who was still holding his breath, finally let it out, uncrossed his fingers, and grinned back at X.

And at their next secret Project Baby X meeting, the scientists grinned, too. Baby X was doing fine.

But then it was time for X to start school. The Joneses were really worried about this, because school was even more full of rules for boys and girls, and there were no rules for Xes. The teacher would tell boys to form one line, and girls to form another line. There would be boys' games and girls' games, and boys' secrets and girls' secrets. The school library would have a list of recommended books for girls, and a different list of recommended books for boys. There would even be a bathroom marked BOYS and another one marked GIRLS. Pretty soon boys and girls would hardly talk to each other. What would happen to poor little X?

The Joneses spent weeks consulting their *Instruction Manual* (there were 249½ pages of advice under "First Day of School"), and attending urgent special conferences with the smart scientists of Project Baby X.

The scientists had to make sure that X's mother had taught X how to throw and catch a ball properly, and that X's father had been sure to teach X what to serve at a doll's tea party. X had to know how to shoot marbles and how to jump rope and, most of all, what to say when the Other Children asked whether X was a Boy or a Girl.

Finally, X was ready. The Joneses helped X button on a nice new pair of red-and-white checked overalls, and sharpened six pencils for X's nice new pencilbox, and marked X's name clearly on all the books in its nice new bookbag. X brushed its teeth and combed its hair, which just about covered its ears, and remembered to put a napkin in its lunchbox.

The Joneses had asked X's teacher if the class could line up alphabetically, instead of forming separate lines for boys and girls. And they had asked if X could use the principal's bathroom, because it wasn't marked anything except BATHROOM. X's teacher promised to take care of all those problems. But nobody could help X with the biggest problem of all—Other Children.

Nobody in X's class had ever known an X before. What would they think? How would X make friends?

You couldn't tell what X was by studying its clothes—overalls don't even button right-to-left, like girls' clothes, or left-to-right, like boys' clothes. And you couldn't guess whether X had a girl's short haircut or a boy's long haircut. And it was very hard to tell by the games X liked to play. Either X played ball very well for a girl, or else X played house very well for a boy.

Some of the children tried to find out by asking X tricky questions, like "Who's your favorite sports star?" That was easy. X had two favorite sports stars: a girl jockey named Robyn Smith and a boy archery champion named Robin Hood. Then they asked, "What's your favorite TV program?" And that was even easier. X's favorite TV program was "Lassie," which stars a girl dog played by a boy dog.

When X said that its favorite toy was a doll, everyone decided that X must be a girl. But then X said that the doll was really a robot, and that X had computerized it, and that it was programmed to bake fudge brownies and then clean up the kitchen. After X told them that, the other children gave up guessing what X was. All they knew was they'd sure like to see X's doll.

After school, X wanted to play with the other children. "How about shooting some baskets in the gym?" X asked the girls. But all they did was make faces and giggle behind X's back.

"How about weaving some baskets in the arts and crafts room?" X asked the boys. But they all made faces and giggled behind X's back, too.

That night, Ms. and Mr. Jones asked X how things had gone at school. X told them sadly that the lessons were okay, but otherwise school was a terrible place for an X. It seemed as if Other Children would never want an X for a friend.

Once more, the Joneses reached for their *Instruction Manual*. Under "Other Children," they found the following message: "What did you Xpect? *Other Children* have to obey all the silly boy-girl rules, because their parents taught them to. Lucky X—you don't have to stick to the rules at all! All you have to do is be yourself. P.S. We're not saying it'll be easy."

X liked being itself. But X cried a lot that night, partly because it felt afraid. So X's father held X tight, and cuddled it, and couldn't help crying a little, too. And X's mother cheered them both up by reading an Xciting story about an enchanted prince called Sleeping Handsome, who woke up when Princess Charming kissed him.

The next morning, they all felt much better, and little X went back to school with a brave smile and a clean pair of red-and-white checked overalls.

There was a seven-letter-word spelling bee in class that day. And a seven-lap boys' relay race in the gym. And a seven-layer-cake baking contest in the girls' kitchen corner. X won the spelling bee. X also won the relay race. And X almost won the baking contest, except it forgot to light the oven. Which only proves that nobody's perfect.

One of the Other children noticed something else, too. He said: "Winning or losing doesn't seem to count to X. X seems to have fun being good at boys' skills *and* girls' skills."

"Come to think of it," said another one of the Other Children, "maybe X is having twice as much fun as we are!"

So after school that day, the girl who beat X at the baking contest gave X a big slice of her prizewinning cake. And the boy X beat in the relay race asked X to race him home.

From then on, some really funny things began to happen. Susie, who sat next to X in class, suddenly refused to wear pink dresses to school any more. She insisted on wearing red-and-white checked overalls—just like X's. Overalls, she told her parents, were much better for climbing monkey bars.

Then Jim, the class football nut, started wheeling his little sister's doll carriage around the football field. He'd put on his entire football uniform, except for the helmet. The he'd put the helmet *in* the carriage, lovingly tucked under an old set of shoulder pads. Then he'd start jogging around the field, pushing the carriage and singing "Rock-abye Baby" to his football helmet. He told his family that X did the same thing, so it must be okay. After all, X was now the team's star quarterback.

Susie's parents were horrified by her behavior, and Jim's parents were worried sick about his. But the worst came when the twins, Joe and Peggy, decided to share everything with each other. Peggy used Joe's hockey skates, and his microscope, and took half his newspaper route. Joe used Peggy's needlepoint kit, and her cookbooks, and took two of her three baby-sitting jobs. Peggy started running the lawn mower, and Joe started running the vacuum cleaner.

Their parents weren't one bit pleased with Peggy's wonderful biology experiments, or with Joe's terrific needlepoint pillows. They didn't care that Peggy mowed the lawn better, and that Joe vacuumed the carpet better. In fact, they were furious. It's all that little X's fault, they agreed. Just because X doesn't know what it is, or what it's supposed to be, it wants to get everybody *else* mixed up, too!

Peggy and Joe were forbidden to play with X any more. So was Susie, and then Jim, and then *all* the Other Children. But it was too late; the Other Children stayed mixed up and happy and free, and refused to go back to the way they'd been before X.

Finally, Joe and Peggy's parents decided to call an emergency meeting of the school's Parents' Association, to discuss "The X Problem." They sent a report to the principal stating that X was a "disruptive influence." They demanded immediate action. The Joneses, they said, should be *forced* to tell whether X was a boy or a girl. And then X should be *forced* to behave like whichever it was. If the Joneses refused to tell, the Parents' Association said, then X must take an Xamination. The school psychiatrist must Xamine it physically and mentally, and issue a full report. If X's test showed it was a boy, it would have to obey all the boys' rules. If it proved to be a girl, X would have to obey all the girls' rules.

And if X turned out to be some kind of mixed-up misfit, then X should be Xpelled from the school. Immediately!

The principal was very upset. Disruptive influence? Mixed-up misfit? But X was an Xcellent student. All the teachers said it was a delight to have X in their classes. X was president of the student council. X had won first prize in the talent show, and second prize in the art show, and honorable mention in the science fair, and six athletic events on field day, including the potato race.

Nevertheless, insisted the Parents' Association, X is a Problem Child. X is the Biggest Problem Child we have ever seen!

So the principal reluctantly notified X's parents that numerous complaints about X's behavior had come to the school's attention. And that after the psychiatrist's Xamination, the school would decide what to do about X.

The Joneses reported this at once to the scientists, who referred them to page 85,759 of the *Instruction Manual*. "Sooner or later," it said, "X will have to be Xamined by a psychiatrist. This may be the only way any of us will know for sure whether X is mixed up—or whether everyone else is."

The night before X was to be Xamined, the Joneses tried not to let X see how worried they were. "What if—?" Mr. Jones would say. And Ms. Jones would reply, "No use worrying." Then a few minutes later, Ms. Jones would say, "What if—?" and Mr. Jones would reply, "No use worrying."

X just smiled at them both, and hugged them hard and didn't say much of anything. X was thinking, What if—? And then X thought: No use worrying.

At Xactly 9 o'clock the next day, X reported to the school psychiatrist's office. The principal, along with a committee from the Parents' Association, X's teacher, X's classmates, and Ms. and Mr. Jones, waited in the hall outside. Nobody knew the details of the tests X was to be given, but everybody knew they'd be *very* hard, and that they'd reveal Xactly what everyone wanted to know about X, but were afraid to ask.

It was terribly quiet in the hall. Almost spooky. Once in a while, they would hear a strange noise inside the room. There were buzzes. And a beep or two. And several bells. An occasional light would flash under the door. The Joneses thought it was a white light, but the principal thought it was blue. Two or three children swore it was either yellow or green. And the Parents' Committee missed it completely.

Through it all, you could hear the psychiatrist's low voice, asking hundreds of questions, and X's higher voice, answering hundreds of answers.

The whole thing took so long that everyone knew it must be the most complete Xamination anyone had ever had to take. Poor X, the Joneses thought. Serves X right, the Parents' Committee thought. I wouldn't like to be in X's overalls right now, the children thought.

At last, the door opened. Everyone crowded around to hear the results. X didn't look any different; in fact, X was smiling. But the psychiatrist looked terrible. He looked as if he was crying! "What happened?" everyone began shouting. Had X done something disgraceful? "I wouldn't be a bit surprised!" muttered Peggy and Joe's parents. "Did X flunk the *whole* test?" cried Susie's parents. "Or just the most important part?" yelled Jim's parents.

"Oh, dear," sighed Mr. Jones.

"Oh dear," sighed Ms. Jones.

"*Sssh*," ssshed the principal. "The psychiatrist is trying to speak."

Wiping his eyes and clearing his throat, the psychiatrist began, in a hoarse whisper. "In my opinion," he whispered—you could tell he must be very upset—"in my opinion, young X here—"

"Yes? Yes?" shouted a parent impatiently.

"*Sssh*!" ssshed the principal.

"Young *Sssh* here, I mean young X," said the doctor, frowning, "is just about—"

"Just about *what*? Let's have it!" shouted another parent.

". . . just about the *least* mixed-up child I've ever Xamined!" said the psychiatrist.

"Yay for X!" yelled one of the children. And then the others began yelling, too. Clapping and cheering and jumping up and down.

"*SSSH!*" SSShed the principal, but nobody did.

The Parents' Committee was angry and bewildered. How *could* X have passed the whole Xamination? Didn't X have an *identity* problem? Wasn't X mixed up at *all*? Wasn't X *any* kind of a misfit? How could it *not* be, when it didn't even *know* what it was? And why was the psychiatrist crying?

Actually, he had stopped crying and was smiling politely through his tears. "Don't you see?" he said. "I'm crying because it's wonderful!

X has absolutely no identity problem! X isn't one bit mixed up! As for being a misfit—ridiculous! X knows perfectly well what it is! Don't you, X?" The doctor winked, X winked back.

"But what *is* X?" shrieked Peggy and Joe's parents. "*We* still want to know what it is!"

"Ah, yes," said the doctor, winking again. "Well, don't worry. You'll all know one of these days. And you won't need me to tell you."

"What? What does he mean?" some of the parents grumbled suspiciously.

Susie and Peggy and Joe all answered at once. "He means that by the time X's sex matters, it won't be a secret any more!"

With that, the doctor began to push through the crowd toward X's parents. "How do you do," he said, somewhat stiffly. And then he reached out to hug them both. "If I ever have an X of my own," he whispered, "I sure hope you'll lend me your instruction manual."

Needless to say, the Joneses were very happy. The Project Baby X scientists were rather pleased, too. So were Susie, Jim, Peggy, Joe, and all the Other Children. The Parents' Association wasn't, but they had promised to accept the psychiatrist's report, and not make any more trouble. They even invited Ms. and Mr. Jones to become honorary members, which they did.

Later that day, all X's friends put on their red-and-white checked overalls and went over to see X. They found X in the back yard, playing with a very tiny baby that none of them had ever seen before. The baby was wearing very tiny red-and-white checked overalls.

"How do you like our new baby?" X asked the Other Children proudly.

"It's got cute dimples," said Jim.

"It's got husky biceps, too," said Susie.

"What kind of baby is it?" asked Joe and Peggy.

X frowned at them. "Can't you tell?" Then X broke into a big, mischievous grin. *"It's a Y!"*

Poverty, Place, and Community

Frank D. Beck

In August of 2000 I drove from my hometown of Bloomington, Illinois to the annual conference of the Rural Sociological Society in Washington, DC. Because I wanted some time off the beaten path, I chose to travel on two-digit state routes or smaller country roads as much as possible. Though I am a community sociologist, I did not choose this path in order to see small town America; however, that is the America that I traveled. For the most part the trip across the mid-west was cathartic, a chance to step outside my normal life and its cares; however, it was the rural communities in West Virginia that shocked and jarred my sociological imagination.

As I crossed from Belpre, Ohio, to Parkersburg, West Virginia, the difference between life on one side of the river and the other was palpable. The disparity in economic resources between the two states is readily apparent. Parkersburg itself looked older than most other comparable cities in the year 2000. It reminded me of an old mining and industrial town with a run-down look indicating a place left behind. On the outskirts of Parkersburg were some nicer homes, residences of white collar or well-paid blue-collar workers who commuted to the city. Farther out of town, Route 47 started to wind through the hills.

Soon the houses grew smaller and more unkempt and I began to see mobile homes interspersed among the small houses. I am intimately familiar with mobile home life. My family and I spent several years living in a trailer park while I finished graduate school. But these mobile homes were not like the one in which we had lived. Several of the mobile homes I passed were 30 to 40 years old and were still being used as permanent residences; however, there was a sense of transience about them. These trailers had no skirting covering the wheels, there was no lawn art present, and the hitches still poked out from under the dwellings. At least three times, 1960s era house trailers—the kind originally built for family camping trips—were on blocks with weathered porches attached. Sometimes children were visible around the homes I passed. They did not seem to know their circumstances were closer to those of third world children than to the kids growing up in affluent American suburbs.

Not since family vacations and school "mission" trips as an adolescent had I seen poverty like this. I remember my father once warning me about the condition of some homes we were going to pass as we traveled south out of my childhood Ohio home. I should have called him for a reminder before embarking on this journey. Yes, occasionally, there were the well-kept, larger homes of wealthier people tucked between two decidedly different structures. These were rare, however, relative to the number of people I saw living on the fringes of the new American economy. The standard of living enjoyed by many in my hometown seemed well beyond the residents of these places.

West Virginia is not alone in this circumstance; I am told the Mississippi Delta is similar. On another trip (driving through Leesburg, IL) I saw poor families living near each other in similar trailers, cut-off from needed services and opportunity. But those were small pockets of poverty, up to five trailers at most. What I saw in West Virginia was thousands of families, tens of thousands of souls. And this was only on the state route; there were numerous roads up into the hollows and other dirt driveways, where the mailbox was the only visible sign of life. What was life like off Route 47? Was it more of the same, or worse?

I also wondered whether these people were poor at all. Did they see themselves as poor? I am not sure. At one point, I saw two teenagers walking bare foot on Route 47. It appeared as though they did not have a care in the world even though their clothes were absent of a designer label but, clearly, hand-me-downs or thrift shop purchases. Occasionally around dusk, I would catch up to a pickup truck driving slowly down the switchbacks. The driver would shine a light into the trees, while another man in back held a gun, hoping for some fresh deer meat. They were alive, probably near their kin and connected to what they might care most about—the woods and a way of life. Moreover, I was happy to spend my money at a Marathon station with an old-fashioned general store and gas pumps like ones I remember from childhood. I even had the pleasure of passing a church social. Cars (and trucks) lined the road and a large white festival tent and stage served as the focus of attention that Saturday. Who am I to judge their life?

As a sociologist, however, I am concerned about life chances. The quality of education, health care, and strength of a local economy are not random. They are social creations. Circumstances exist as they do because of the interpretations people generate and use as they interact with others and their environment. We create and perpetuate this world. We created the communities that line West Virginia Route 47, we continue to allow their existence, and we know they affect the resident's life chances. This is what disturbed me most.

When I finally arrived in Washington, DC, I was surrounded by marble stairs, brass railings, and cherry walls. The differences between West Viriginia Route 47 and Connecticut Avenue were stunning. At the sociology conference we spoke to each other about poverty, about economic stagnation, and about rural policy. I know that the people surrounding me at the meeting cared about rural people and rural communities, and many of them have cared about rural communities for years. But somehow the ivory tower and those West Virginia valleys occupied different dimensions of reality. The academic work of a discipline was not working, at least not for the people I had so recently passed, on that road, in West Virginia. Once I got past my dismay and depression over washing my face in a sink of marble and drinking a five dollar beer, I began to wonder why our work has not worked.

The poverty in the places I passed through has been there for decades. As shown in Table 1, the poverty rates for most of the counties I traveled through have changed little from 1970 to 1990.[1] Six of the ten counties I traveled through had poverty rates higher than the state average over three decennial censuses (Bureau of the Census, 1970, 1980 and 1990). In sociology we refer to this as persistent poverty (Duncan and Coles, 2000). Three other counties had rates above the state average in two of those censuses. All ten were above the state average at least once.

Included in Table 1 are the poverty rates for four of the places I traveled through. In almost every case, the poverty rate for the county is higher than that of the urban area. It is clear that poverty was higher in the more remote places like Lorenz and Ellamore in Upshur County and Womelsdorf, Norton, Bowden, and Wymer in Randolph County. Poverty in Parkersburg never exceeded the state average and poverty in Elkins and Bunkhannon exceeded it only once. By and large, it is the larger places that offered a stronger economy. The rural areas, those places with less than 2,500 people were more isolated and removed from economic opportunity.

The poorest counties (see Table 1 and Figure 1)—those with the highest rates and most persistent poverty—are in the center of the state. Areas just south of these are included in a federal Enterprise Community—a program aimed at increasing economic opportunity and the

Table 1. Percent of Persons in Poverty for Counties and Places Containing West Virginia Route 47, US Route 33 and West Virginia Route 55 (1970–1990).[1]

Counties (Places)	1970	1980	1990	Number of Times Rate Exceeds State Average
Gilmer	42.6	32.0	33.5	3
Grant	32.8	29.9	15.5	2
Hardy	32.1	26.9	14.6	2
Lewis	28.8	25.5	23.7	3
(Weston)	22.6	18.1	26.3	3
Pendleton	33.1	30.3	17.0	2
Randolph	28.6	24.2	21.9	3
(Elkins)	19.5	15.0	21.0	1
Ritchie	29.2	25.2	26.0	3
Upshur	29.4	23.6	21.2	3
(Bunkhannon)	21.0	17.1	19.1	1
Wirt	33.4	30.0	22.0	3
Wood	12.1	15.7	14.1	1
(Parkersburg)	13.4	14.1	19.0	0

[1]Data come from the US Census 1970,1980, and 1990.

possibilities of sustainable development in persistently poor areas. Wood County (with poverty rates consistently less than 16 percent) borders Ohio. Hardy and Pendleton counties border Virginia; Grant borders Maryland. The difference in the communities I saw as I approached the Virginia state line is confirmed by the data. The Spruce Knob-Seneca Rocks National Recreation Area and numerous ski resorts are found there. The economies of Hardy, Pendleton, and Grant are tied to tourism. It was in these areas that I saw signs for bed and breakfasts, lodges, and cabins for weekend getaways. It is clear the rise of a personal service economy has benefited some places in the state and not others. There is something about the geographic isolation of central West Virginia that appears to be associated with higher and more persistent poverty.

It should be noted that this discovery is not new. Eleanor Roosevelt saw disturbing signs of stifling poverty in this state during the depression and even successfully lobbied for the movement and rebuilding of an entire town—Scot's Run. John Kennedy saw the poverty of West Virginia first hand when he was campaigning in the 1960 Democratic primary. The Kennedy Task Force recommended only one planning commission by name—it was for the depressed areas of the Appalachians (Harrington, 1962). In the groundbreaking work, *The Other America*, Harrington (1962) spent considerable effort describing the poverty of West Virginia communities. The issues facing these people and their places are not new.

The Community Connection

Poverty is related to life's chances, and poverty is not the same in every place. We know that poverty can be quite persistent (Duncan and Coles, 2000; Fitchen, 1981 and 1991; Wilson, 1987 and 1996). And we know how poverty is related to health, child education, and overall well-being. These facts make it clear that place matters. Further, because poverty varies by place, it is a community problem. The social environment adversely affects people in certain places. Yet, these days social scientists are placing increased emphasis on personal communities (Wellman and Wortley, 1990) or communities of identity.

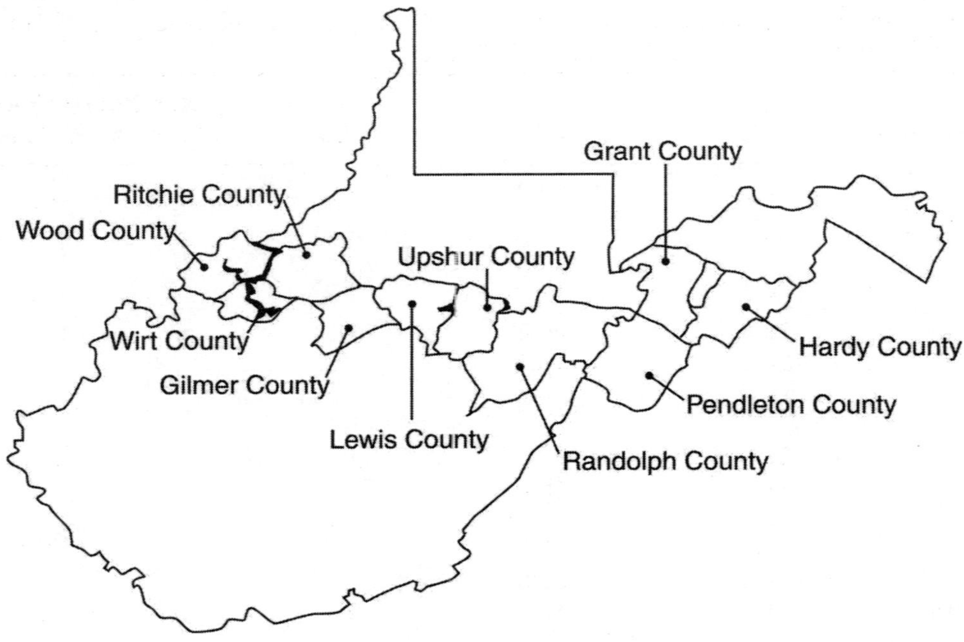

Figure 1. West Virginia Counties Containing Portions of State Route 47, U.S. 33, and State Route 55.

Both of these types of association exist and I do not intend to exclusively hold the word community for my own devices; however, there is something terribly wrong in what I see as an overemphasis on these other two forms of community at the expense of communities of place. It is true that an individual's well-being is most proximately affected by those closest to them—their family, friends, and neighbors. However, the characteristics of the local space that someone inhabits matter just as much. The quality of health care and education available to children, diversity and strength of an economy, safety, and pollution are, by some mechanism, locally created with local consequences. Even identity and global processes are interpreted and acted upon locally (Robertson, 1995). To those who say that chat rooms are community, I say fine; but when you log-off the Internet, you are still affected by local crime and poverty rates and whether or not racial prejudice hangs in the air around you.

Another very important reason for why communities of place still matter flows from the work of Kenneth P. Wilkinson (1991). To Wilkinson and his mentor Harold Kaufman, community is a field of interaction—the web of connections we live within. In fact it is the most generalizable field of interaction that has the most bearing on our day-to-day quality of life. For it is within places that people experience their society. The mesh of social relations in a place create its culture, institutions, and the generalized other that each of us relies upon in judging our behavior. Children know the world first through the significant others immediately around them, but as they grow older, it is friends, friends of parents, teachers, and others they learn from as they interpret their world. The children growing up in rural West Virginia communities and other persistently poor places experience a different society than children in wealthy suburbs and gated neighborhoods. Place matters.

Something else I realized on my trip was that interstate highways deafen community differences. We now pass by exits with names of places we only know from the map. If we choose an exit, we are often faced with fast food and hotel choices similar to those of the last exit or the night before. Interstate travel numbs us to local architecture, economic circumstances, and cultural expressions. Just as interstates raise the valleys and lower the mountains, they also level socioeconomic differences by allowing us to rush past them. It would not surprise me if the move away from talking about communities of place is linked to the lack of difference we experience during our travels. The people residing along West

Virginia's Route 47 demand that we still talk about communities of place. The poverty seen there still demands that something be said.

Communities of place have become less important to sociology over time. All one has to do is examine the table of contents for some recently released Introduction to Sociology texts to see this. Community, if at all present, is tucked within the urbanization and population chapters (for examples, see Andersen and Taylor, 2002 and Macionis, 1997). Nowhere in these texts will you see community treated as a special form of group. Community is also not presented (as I once learned) as the lowest social institution consisting of all other institutions needed for meeting daily needs and improving well-being. It is also obvious that sociologists have much work to do. The work of community scholars has not changed the reality of Route 47.

I do not pretend to have the answers. Much has already been written about what communities do and do not need. My belief is that local responses are the best-suited means of dealing with local issues. People in places know what those places need. Some may be thinking this is an argument for the devolution of decision-making and resources to the smallest unit possible, a trend recently promulgated by numerous federal administrations. According to Wilkinson (1991), local decision-making needs to be helped with extra-local resources. Social capital offers little help here. The people living along Route 47 may have social capital; yet, it is unlikely that they could afford medical or dental care for their children. My guess is that these people live according to certain norms of reciprocity and that they do trust one another (two key components to social capital), but what the people of rural West Virginia communities need most are jobs. That will require efforts aimed at more even and progressive economic development. In response to some recent trends in sociology, let me add that attention to personal communities and communities of identity will not help with these issues either. Communities of place still exist and still matter.

References

Andersen, M. L. and H. F. Taylor. 2002. *Sociology: Understanding a Diverse Society*. Belmont, CA: Wadsworth.

Bureau of the Census. 1970, 1980, and 1990. *Census of Population: Social and Economic Characteristics*. Washington: U.S. Department of Commerce.

Duncan, C. M. and Coles, R. 2000. *Worlds Apart: Why Poverty Persists in Rural America*. New Haven: Yale University Press.

Fitchen, J. M. 1981. *Poverty in Rural America: A Case Study*. Boulder, CO: Westview.

Fitchen, J. M. 1991. *Endangered Spaces, Enduring Places: Change, Identity, and Survival in Rural America*. Boulder, CO: Westview.

Harrington, M. 1962. *The Other America: Poverty in the United States*. New York: Macmillan.

Macionis, J. J. 1997. *Sociology*. 6th edition. Upper Saddle River, NJ: Prentice Hall.

Robertson, R. 1995. "Glocalization: Time-space and homogeneity-heterogeneity." In *Global Modernities*. ed. M. Featherstone. London: Sage.

Wellman, B. and S. Wortley. 1990. "Different strokes from different folks: community ties and social support (second East York study). *American Journal of Sociology*. 96: 558–88.

Wilkinson, K. P. 1991. *The Community in Rural America*. New York: Greenwood Press.

Wilson, W. J. 1987. *The Truly Disadvantaged*. University of Chicago Press.

Wilson, W. J. 1996. *When Work Disappears: The World of the New Urban Poor*. New York: Alfred A. Knopf.

Any society, including our own, is sustained and shaped by societal institutions, those nationwide patterns of activity that address major aspects of collective survival. Any society needs an economy to produce and distribute goods and services, and a political order to regulate social life and organize defense. Societies also need the family as the societal institution that recruits and socializes new societal members through birth or marriage and is the primary unit of economic organization.

In this unit we will deal with how evolving and adapting family structures are attempting to deal with the increasingly complex demands of family, parenthood, and employment outside the home, as in the reading from Hochschild's *The Second Shift*. Better understanding how family life and marriage succeed or fail will hopefully help you make good choices in your own relationships.

In this unit we also include treatment of aging and health, two other fundamental aspects of evaluating the nature and quality of life in a society. While all people age, some societies, such as ours, experience "aging" as larger and larger percentages of the population are made up of people more than 65 years of age. The rapid increase in such groups is resulting in new social meanings for "being old" and greater diversity among older groups. The social meanings of being elderly are a key concern of social gerontologists. In this part of our book we also show how sociology will help you better understand illness and premature death. While sickness and dying have biological reasons, the social factors behind contracting illnesses and dying in an accident are a key concern of medical sociology. Another important thing you will learn in this unit is that many ideas about health, disability, and older people are myths that help justify indifference to or unfair treatment of elderly and disabled people.

We will be showing that better social programs to deal with health, illness, and disability will be needed, since the American workforce, like the U.S. population as a whole, is aging (see reading). Disabled Americans are perhaps the largest minority group in the U.S., a group denied full access to social opportunity and usually treated as profoundly different. We hope to show that disabled people are much more capable than most social environments allow them to be. Even when elderly Americans become unable to care for themselves on a daily basis, most are cared for by family members and not in institutions like nursing homes. (See reading.)

Family

The family is the major social institution, meaning it is a very important way of organizing social activity to meet societal needs. (See Chapters 16, 17 and 18.) The family is also a cultural universal, which means all cultures have some form of a kinship network. The culture within which family life occurs determines what form the family will take and the norms and values surrounding the family. Some cultures have encouraged large families with many children and several generations living together to operate family businesses and farms. Other cultures have encouraged small, mobile families with fewer children and with smaller kinship networks to move in search of food or in tending animals. Whether several generations of the groom's or the bride's family live together, depends upon the nature of economic needs and warfare needs, such as keeping sons close for defense (Ember and Ember 1991).

In the United States, the primary family form is the nuclear family. The nuclear family is one in which parents and children live together in one household. Although never the dominant family form, occasionally in the United States there exist extended family households. This is when parents, children and other relatives, such as grandparents or aunts and uncles reside in the same household. Marital relationships in the United States are monogamous. An individual can only be married to one person at a time. Other cultures allow polygamy, or one person may have more than one spouse. There are also guidelines within a culture regarding mate selection, or who a person is allowed to marry. Marriages in the United States are primarily endogamous, since we tend to choose a mate that has the same race, class, and religion as us. However, other cultures demand that individuals marry outside particular local groups, or form exogamous relationships. Finally, within a culture there are norms of where a newly married couple should set up their household. In the United States, it is a neolocal pattern. Couples set up their own household away from their families of origin. Other cultures are matrilocal, the couple resides with the bride's family, or patrilocal, the couple resides with the groom's family (Ember and Ember 1991).

The American family of the 21st century is best understood within its historical context. According to Cherlin (1996), the family in colonial times, before 1776, was a public family. The family performed many public services, such as hospitals, orphanages and poorhouses (Demos 1970). All members of the family were expected to contribute to the family as an economic unit, including wives and children. Between 1776 and 1900, our current family form began to emerge with the beginning of capitalism. Capitalism moved work away from the home, which then also resulted in separate social domains for men and women. Men's domain was working outside the home, while women remained in the home, becoming responsible for care of the home and children. However, women still contributed economically to the family by doing piecework, laundry or taking in boarders (Degler 1980). Individualism emerged, resulting in more freedom to choose spouses, along with the idea that marriage should be based upon love. Since 1900 the importance of these values has continued to rise. Families throughout the 20th century have focused on emotional satisfaction as criteria for a good marriage (Cherlin 1996). Also significant during this century have been the numbers of women who have begun to work outside the home. This has added needed family income but has complicated the traditional separation of male employment vs. female home management. One source of marital dissatisfaction and frustration is the complex demands of working outside the home and raising children. The division of labor still leaves women doing more than men, but there has also been a decline in the hours available for housework (Bianchi et al. 2000). Women's work outside the home is also related to couples having fewer children and an increasing proportion of childless couples in the U.S.

In the United States, many of today's marriages are still based upon romantic love. Despite images of cupid randomly shooting his arrow, however, romantic love is no random event. The person one chooses as a mate is shaped by many social influences. For example, the resources that one brings to the marriage market affect who is going to be a likely mate, such as one's education, physical attractiveness or socioeconomic status. The groups that one belongs to are also likely to shape interaction patterns that affect mate selection. Religious groups and school groups are likely to influence a mate selection from within that group, as a part of the socialization process. (See Chapter 5.) Demographic and population compositional factors also influence mate selection, since relative sizes of marriageable populations influence who and when people marry (Brym and Lie 2003). Marriages in the U.S. increasingly consist of spouses with similar levels of education and interests (homogamy), and the number of marriages with mixed race or mixed religious couples is also increasing (heterogamy).

Despite our culture's emphasis on romantic love, and the popularity of marriage, marriages in the United States frequently end in divorce, but probably not as frequently as the media leads us to believe. Typically a divorce rate of 50 percent is quoted throughout popular media (Henslin 2002). This statistic is calculated by dividing all the marriages occurring in one year by all the divorces granted in one year. This is misleading, as these are not the same people who are getting divorced as who were married. Perhaps one could use the number of divorces granted in one year divided by the number of all the married couples that exist in one year, but that is a difficult figure to determine accurately. A final way to conceptualize the pervasiveness of divorce is to ask of all married people, what percent have been divorced at some point in their life? (Henslin 2002). Whichever way the divorce rate is calculated, the United States has the highest divorce rate of all the industrialized nations (Statistical Abstract 1998; Table 1346). Interestingly, however, the rate of divorce has declined somewhat per 1000 people since the early 1980s. Possible reasons include people waiting longer to first marry—around 27 years for men and 25 years for women—and the increased resources of dual earner couples (Shepard 2002).

Sociologists look to cultural factors existing in the United States to explain the relative high rate of divorce in the U.S. For example, marriages in the United States are based upon romantic love, which can fade. Individualism is on the rise and women are less dependent upon men. When one's personal happiness is a priority there is little incentive to stay in an unhappy marriage. As women have gained independence, they have other options to support themselves than through marriage. Divorce in the United States is socially acceptable and easier to get legally. Despite the relatively high U.S. divorce rate and cultural conditions that lead Americans to be prone to divorce, not all American marriages are equally likely to end in divorce. Those who marry young, or experience an unexpected pregnancy before marriage, are more likely to divorce (Macionis 2002). When both partners have successful careers, each person has the option of living independently and are more likely to divorce.

Due to the stress of blended families, those who have divorced before are also at higher risk for divorcing a second time (Shepard 2002).

In the past 40 years, other notable changes in the family have taken place. Men and women have both delayed marriage and parenthood to 100 year highs. Cohabitation and remaining single have replaced the trend of early marriage during the post WWII era (Henslin 2002). The delay in marriage is largely due to changes in the economy and women working. Both men and women have had to delay marriage to gain financial stability, usually by achieving a higher education (see Koontz's article in this reader). There has also been an increase in single parenthood, primarily due to divorce, but also by unmarried persons. Also an increasing proportion of marriages in the U.S., now nearly half, are made up of at least one previously married partner. These marriage patterns are rapidly increasing the percentage of blended families and children living in them (Shepard 2002). In such a dynamic situation it probably is too early to characterize the enduring nature of blended families definitively. For better or worse, such families increasingly will make up an important form of family in the U.S. and are helping socialize many children.

The family is one of the most violent social institutions (Strauss 1980). Specific conditions are found in families that make them susceptible to violence (Strauss and Gelles 1979). We have the right to influence our family members and a cultural norm exists that says outsiders should not intrude on family life. We also spend more time with our families than we do with our peers or colleagues. There is an intensity of involvement with families not present in other social situations, so actions and decisions within the family affect all family members. In this intensified interactional environment, the effect of employment problems, job losses and inability to secure stable employment may compound stress and increase the likelihood of violence. All states have enacted marital rape laws and many communities across the United States have established safe haven shelters where family members who have suffered violence can go for aid. Ironically violent family members are most likely to be people who themselves experienced violence in their families (Blankenborn 1995). This can lead to high levels of stress within families.

Despite the continuing complexity and problems with which American families have to deal, there are encouraging signs that the various forms of family life in the United States are adapting to the current needs of parents and children. Many grandparents are either caring for young children or continue raising them. The number of cohabitors and same-sex partners raising children has increased. The increasing variety of conditions under which children are being cared for and socialized may help explain the decline in the infant mortality rate in the U.S., now lower than ever before. With most divorced people remarrying, the numbers of children being raised in part by stepparents will also increase. Thus, family life in the U.S. involves an increased variety of socializers of preschool children (Shepard 2002).

Name: ______________________________

Quiz Questions: Family

1. A household in which parents, children and an aunt are all living, is considered by sociologists to be:

   a. a nuclear family
   b. a polygamous family
   c. an extended family
   d. an exogamous family

2. If a person of the Jewish faith were to marry a person of the Catholic faith, the marriage would be:

   a. endogamous
   b. exogamous
   c. extended
   d. neo-local

3. During what period of time did separate spheres for men and women first emerge?

   a. prior to 1776
   b. between 1776 and 1900
   c. since 1900
   d. no separate spheres emerged

4. Modern-day marriages are based on romantic love. (True or False?)

5. Which of the following is an explanation for the relatively high rates of divorce in the United States?

   a. individualism
   b. women's increasing independence
   c. divorce is more socially acceptable.
   d. all of the above

6. Who is at higher risk for divorce?

   a. partners who both have successful careers
   b. those who marry young
   c. those who have divorced previously
   d. all of the above

7. One reason families experience violence is because of the intensity of involvement in family relationships. (True or False?)

8. If a newly married couple move in with the groom's parents, they are part of a patrilocal culture. (True or False?)

9. The widely quoted divorce rate of 50 percent is calculated in which of the following ways?

   a. as a ratio of the number of divorces per 1000 people in a society
   b. by determining what percent of individuals have ever been divorced
   c. by dividing all the marriages in one year, by all the divorces in that same year
   d. by dividing all the divorces that happen in a year by all the married people in that year

10. Currently, the divorce rate in the United States is still increasing. (True or False?)

Name: ______________________

Exercise: Family

1. Using the words underlined in paragraph two of this chapter, describe, in the space provided, your mate and current family or your future mate and family. For example, what endogamous characteristics do you share? Will you live as a nuclear or extended family?

Name: ______________________________

Exercise: Family

2. In the space provided, describe how our culture constructs romantic love. How do people feel and how do they behave when they are "in love"? Talk to a person from a culture different than your own. How does he or she describe romantic love?

Name: ______________________________

Exercise: Family

3. Consider your family, including grandparents, uncles, aunts, and cousins. In the space provided, use your family to discuss endogamous relationships, homogamy, and blended families.

Name: ________________________________

Exercise: Family

4. Consider the family you would like to have or now have through your marriage and/or parenthood. Use your own immediate family or the one you would like to have eventually to discuss in the space provided, homogamy, individualism, and neolocalism.

Name: ______________________________

Exercise: Family

5. Watch the classic movie *The Philadelphia Story*. Use the content of the movie to discuss, in the space provided, homogamy, individualism, extended family households, and kinship ties.

Name: ______________________________

Exercise: Family

6. Watch the movie *Frequency*. Use the content of the movie to discuss, in the space provided, endogamy, homogamy, extended family ties, and family violence.

Name: ______________________________

Exercise: Family

7. Go to the campus library or online and select an article from the sociological journal, *Marriage and Family*. Select any one article and use the article content to discuss, in the space provided, neolocalism, homogamy, divorce, and remarriage.

Name: ______________________________

Exercise: Family

8. Go to the campus library or online and select an article from the *Journal of Divorce and Remarriage*. Select any one article and use the contents of the article to discuss, in the space provided, divorce, individualism, remarriage, and blended families.

Name: ______________________________

Exercise: Family

9. Consider the recent Internet correspondence you have had with members of your family. Use the contents of the communication to discuss, in the space provided, kinship networks, blended family and divorce, and childcare.

Name: ______________________________

Exercise: Family

10. Go to the website of a family services agency in your hometown or university town. Use the information at the website to discuss, in the space provided, marital dissatisfaction, family violence, and safe haven shelters.

12

Aging

Social gerontology is the study of the social aspects of aging. Most commonly, gerontologists focus on aging as it applies to periods later in the life course, especially old age. Yet what is old age? How is it that we decide that someone counts as "old"? Old age is a social construction, meaning a culture determines what old age is for that culture. For example, one hundred years ago, a person who reached age 50 would have been considered an old person, while today, our culture views that person as middle aged. Since there is no set time when old age begins, gerontologists define someone as old by using three social criteria: chronological age, social roles, and functional age (Quadagno 1999). Chronological age defines someone as old simply by how many years he or she has been alive, such as reaching age 65 or age 80. Social roles define a person as older because that individual fulfills roles that are typically occupied by people who are older, such as retiree, or grandmother. Functional age is a little less specific than the previous constructions, and measures age by how well a person is functioning. For example, is a person active and full of vitality or has he or she slowed, or is he or she suffering from a chronic illness such as arthritis or diabetes. Using any one of these social constructions to define a person as old has drawbacks. Furthermore, a person may or may not seem old depending upon the construction used, such as a person who may be "old" because he or she is aged 70, but his or her functional age may be more like a 40-year-old. For its simplicity, gerontologists most commonly use chronological age when studying aging. Chronological old age is then divided into three categories: the young old are 65–74, the middle old are age 75–84 and the oldest old are over age 85 (Quadagno 1999).

Sociology began its formal exploration of aging during the 1960s when the first formal theory of aging was developed. It was a functional theory of aging, which suggested that as a process of aging, older people and society mutually disengage from one another. Thus, the theory was coined disengagement theory (Cumming and Henry 1961). This disengagement was said to be mutual, normal, universal and inevitable. It was considered functional for society for older individuals to step out of the way of younger people so that death and impairments would not be disruptive to the functioning of society. At earlier stages of disengagement people who approach the age of 65 are encouraged to retire. The retirement of elderly workers creates replacement positions for younger workers. This allows for a smooth replacement process when retirement occurs. Therefore, older people should naturally want to retire, to give up community involvement and to lessen their social ties. This theory was tested and it was found that older people who were disengaged from society were the least happy, therefore, contradicting the theory at least as to its being acceptable for elderly people (Maddox 1965).

Following disengagement theory, activity theory, a symbolic interactionist theory, has been used to describe aging in America (Havighurst 1968). This theory argues that as we age, we have the same social and psychological needs as we did when we were younger. Therefore, the most well adjusted aging individuals will be those who continue to lead active and involved lives. (See Chapter 4 and 5.) Activity theory argues that this does not necessarily mean that older individuals will always want or be able to participate in the same activities as when they were younger, but a person will find appropriate substitute activities for those in which he or she no longer participates. While activity theorists acknowledge that some older Americans do disengage from social roles, they explore the question of why some older Americans are more likely to disengage than others (Quadagno 1999). For example, becoming a widow, being poor, or having poor health all contribute to disengagement (Maddox 1964; Hochshild 1975; Ball and Whittington 1995). Other factors may include whether or not family members stay close enough to remain in daily contact, or at least celebrate birthdays and other family events.

The last theory that is frequently used to address issues of aging in America is a conflict perspective. This perspective examines the inequality of older Americans in a variety of social contexts, including social policy. Medicare is a national health insurance program for individuals over the age of 65. It is heavily critiqued for its lack of prescription drug coverage and coverage of long term care expenses (Quadagno 1999). It is very important to remember that Medicare involves considerable out-of-pocket expenses and that elderly people are most likely to need multiple medications in treatments for multiple chronic conditions. Consequently, the failure of Medicare to maintain adequate health care coverage for the health needs of the elderly is seen as an exploitive device to ration health care. Such a strategy is a good indication of the minority status of older Americans, especially those in relatively poorer health.

Many consider older Americans to be a minority group. One reason for this is that older Americans experience ageism. Ageism is the systematic stereotyping of and discrimination against people just because they are old. Ageism, like other forms of prejudice and discrimination, finds its roots in stereotypes. These stereotypes can be either positive or negative images. For example, Hummert et al (1994) determined through surveys three "positive" stereotypes exist in American culture: the "golden ager," the perfect grandparent, and the John Wayne conservative. Similarly, she developed three categories of negative stereotypes: older people as a shrew, a recluse or an elitist. These stereotypes are important to uncover as they lead individuals who hold them to deny the individuality of older Americans. Just as with younger Americans, older Americans represent a diverse range of personalities, ethnicities and social statuses. Stereotypes that demean and degrade the elderly serve as the basis for their exclusion and denial of their participation in social life. It makes much more sense to enhance their roles in many productive ways such as part-time workers, mentors and caregivers to preschool children. Clearly, despite stereotypes, many older Americans are living active lives and are contributing in important ways to younger Americans. Older Americans actively volunteer with community organizations and a great many U.S. grandparents are raising preschool children as the children's primary caregivers (Crispell 1993).

Perhaps attitudes toward and discrimination against older Americans will change in the very near future due to the dramatic changes that are occurring in the age distribution of the United States. The United States population is aging. This means the median age of the United States population is increasing. This "population aging" is due to three things. First, birthrates have declined; second, people are living longer; and third, we have a large cohort, a group of people born during the same time period, now entering old age, the baby boomers, who were born between 1946 and 1964. The percent of people more than 65 years of age in 1900 was just 4 percent; in the 1990s this percentage had grown to 13 percent; and by the year 2023, the proportion of those more than 65 is expected to be 20 percent (U.S. Bureau of the Census 1993). This aging will cause dramatic changes in American society. It will affect Americans of all ages, and those who are part of the baby boom will be redefining what old age is all about. No career will remain unaffected by this change in the age structure. The United States has no historical precedence to address the needs of a population that has so many elderly. On the contrary, the United States has been a young population.

The United States will be facing many challenges with this dramatic change in the age distribution of the population. One major public policy question is the increasing fund requirements to serve the needs of the elder and youth. While some may think that the elderly are not as important or as in need of programs to help them, this argument will be difficult to sustain given the large number of elderly who, though not dependent, will have disabilities that require changes in how transportation, commerce and entertainment operate. (See Chapter 14.) Another challenge will be to try to match up the many retirees and other elders who can give to communities, families and organizations in communities that need such help. Volunteer and elder hostel programs will be very important ways to coordinate the needs of younger people with the capabilities of those who are older. Social Security currently has more money being paid into it than money going out to beneficiaries. As the boomers age, Social Security will face a crisis. There will not be enough money coming in to pay the level of benefits promised to the beneficiaries. Consequently, other means of generating money for employment benefits must be developed, or revenues will be taken from other programs.

While the change in the age structure will be dramatic and have dramatic consequences, there is good news. While we are living longer, we are also living healthier (Manton, Corder and Stallard 1997). Although the United States still has very high rates of cardiovascular disease, these rates have been going down. However, there are still some older Americans—particularly among the fastest growing age segment, the oldest old—who need assistance in their activities of daily living. Although the preferred living arrangement of adult children and their parents is to maintain their own separate households, adult children have not abandoned their parents in their old age (U.S. Congressional Budget Office 1988). Rather the opposite is true. The frontline of assistance to older Americans comes through family members, especially wives, as they live longer than their husbands, and adult daughters and daughters in law (Stone, Cafferata, and Sange 1987). Only about 5 percent of the elderly are in nursing homes, and this rate is expected to remain stable into the future. However, due to the aging of society, there will be more people in nursing homes in actual numbers (Cowart and Quadagno 1995). It is very important, therefore, to remember that healthy elderly people may have physical ailments and disabilities but are hardly dependent. (See Chapter 14.)

Name: ______________________________

Quiz Questions: Aging

1. Octogenarians (people in their 80s) who have no major disabilities and are active in family and community life are "old" in terms of which of these social constructions?

   a. functional age
   b. social roles
   c. chronological age
   d. census definition

2. Most older Americans over the age of 65 have disengaged from all aspect of social life including employment. (True or False?)

3. Providing more social activity for the elderly would probably contribute to their feeling healthier and living longer. Which of these theories do these postulates reflect?

   a. disengagement theory
   b. conflict theory
   c. activity theory
   d. ageism

4. The median age of the U.S. population is going down. (True or False?)

5. Most negative stereotypes of the elderly are true. (True or False?)

6. In general older Americans are healthier then ever before. (True or False?)

7. Most dependent elderly in the U.S. are in nursing homes. (True or False?)

8. Communities could increase the use of elderly to help run many community agencies. (True or False?)

9. Medicare covers most health needs of the elderly. (True or False?)

10. By the year 2023 the percent of the U.S. population over the age of 65 is expected to be:

    a. 10
    b. 20
    c. 30
    d. 40

Name: ________________________________

Exercise: Aging

1. In the space provided, describe some examples of stereotypical behaviors toward elderly people you have witnessed.

Name: ______________________________

Exercise: Aging

2. In the space provided, describe how you and your present or future spouse should prepare for your post-retirement years.

Name: ______________________________

Exercise: Aging

3. Think about elderly people in your own family and or friends' families. In the space provided, discuss ageism, functional age, disengagement theory and activity theory.

Name: ______________________________

Exercise: Aging

4. Think about elderly people in your hometown. In the space provided, discuss community programs in relation to activity theory, functional age, ageism, and using elders to help meet communities' needs.

Name: ______________________________

Exercise: Aging

5. Watch the classic movie *Sunset Boulevard*. In the space provided, discuss how the movie illustrated functional age, disengagement theory, ageism, and activity theory.

Name: ______________________________

Exercise: Aging

6. Watch the movie *Driving Miss Daisy*. In the space provided, discuss disengagement theory, chronological old age, conflict perspective and ageism.

Name: ______________________________

Exercise: Aging

7. Go to the campus library or online and select an article from the journal *Aging and Society*. Select any one article and in the space provided, how the article illustrated functional age, activity theory, ageism, and disengagement theory.

Name: ___________________________

Exercise: Aging

8. Go to campus or library or on line and select an article from the journal, *Research on Aging*. Select any one article and in the space provided, discuss how the article illustrates ageism, disengagement theory, activity theory, and functional age.

Name: ______________________________

Exercise: Aging

9. Think of the elderly people you see at malls and other public places. In the space provided, discuss how the elderly in public places illustrate functional age, disengagement theory, ageism, and activity theory.

Name: ___________________________

Exercise: Aging

10. Think of the last family event or reunion you went to. Based on how elderly people were treated at the event, in the space provided, discuss disengagement theory, conflict theory, ageism, and the elderly living independently.

Health and Health Care

Medical sociologists study the social patterns to diseases, the causes of death among different groups, and the ways people maintain wellness and/or are treated for illness. All diseases and deaths have biological features, from the decay and infections that cause tooth aches to the complex biochemical processes that cause cancer tumors to grow, to the slowed reflexes of drunken drivers that result in accidental deaths. However, important social factors are involved in people's becoming ill or being injured in accidents. Whether people drive while intoxicated, and whether they work in dangerous occupations such as commercial fishing or meat cutting, are primary explanations of why people get injured (brain injuries among drunk drivers and loss of fingers among meat cutters). People's beliefs about the importance of staying healthy and people having the economic resources to obtain all the health care that they need are also very important social factors in explaining why modern life has not brought the disappearance of disabling diseases and premature deaths. Tobacco usage, poor diets, and excessive alcohol consumption are among the major causes of people dying prematurely, and such behaviors not only endanger those engaged in them but also others who come into contact with the risk takers. People who inhale passive smoke are sicker than people who do not live with smokers, and drunk drivers kill thousands of Americans yearly. Nevertheless, while risk behaviors are important reasons for illness, injury and death in contemporary society, the economic resources necessary for living healthfully and preventing illness including living in a wealthier community are just as important (Robert 1988).

In 1900, the three leading causes of death in the United States—influenza (the flu), pneumonia, and tuberculosis—were infectious diseases spread from person to person. Symptoms like fever and coughing developed before these diseases became well advanced. In contrast, the top three killers in the U.S. now are very different: heart disease, cancer, and cerebrovascular (brain blood-vessel-related) diseases (especially strokes) (Cockerham 2001). Contemporary diseases take much longer to show their symptoms (have longer latency periods). So, the only way for people to know they have such diseases before symptoms are noticed is to use early detection procedures like blood tests, ultra sound or other internal imaging procedures including X-rays, urine tests, and so on. These detection methods are called health screens. These sorts of tests can be very expensive and with their busy schedules many people wait until they feel quite ill before they check for any illness. In addition, complexities of contemporary managed health insurance make it difficult for many people to get screens and other health services that they need (Kronenfeld 2001). There also is evidence that some people deny symptoms of illness that they clearly feel (such as pains in their left arms), believing that it is merely indigestion. This tendency to avoid screens and to ignore symptoms of serious illness is often related to the assumption that doctors and other caregivers can fix anything that may be wrong. This overreliance on the powers of medicine is one negative consequence of the contemporary reliance upon caregivers called medicalization (Cockerham 2001).

How to get people more aware of and concerned about illness before their symptoms become noticeable is a worldwide problem. The problem is compounded by the fact that awareness may be irrelevant if people do not have the economic resources or other means for living healthfully, eating properly, and living in pollution-free environments. (See Chapters 7, 10 and 20.) Moreover, recently sociologists have found increasing ways in which good health care that potentially may be available gets disrupted or degraded. The latter process has occurred recently in the former Russian Federation, in the political and economic disarray following the collapse of communism (Cockerham 1999). The former is illustrated even in countries such as England with government-provided universal (or single payer) health insurance and health care, where large differences in disease and death rate exist between highly paid workers and poorly paid employees (Marmot 1996). The multipayer system in the U.S. means that workers are insured by a variety of health benefit programs offered by the various employers who offer such benefits. When offered to workers, such plans usually require subscribers to pay monthly premiums and deductibles and other non-covered expenses just like other forms of insurance including coverage for homes and automobiles. Thus, being employed does not necessarily mean having employer-provided insurance or health insurance adequate for a households' needs (Smith, Grimm and Brewster 2002).

Health insurance in the U.S. increasingly depends upon workers having longer-term employment with firms that offer health insurance benefits. Job loss, downsizing, and relocating plants overseas not only take jobs away from American workers but such events prevent them and their families from having health insurance (Seccombe and Amey 1995). While Federal laws now allow workers who lose their jobs to continue paying monthly health insurance premiums at their former (lower) group rates, workers must still pay such increased expenses themselves. The U.S. probably will never have a single-payer health care system, but the government does run two public health insurance programs: Medicaid for families with incomes below the official poverty line and Medicare for people 65 years or older (Skocpal 1995). Remembering that these public programs pay only a fraction of health care costs of their members and their families is important. Many vitally necessary components of care such as prescribed medications, extensive follow up procedures with specialists, and others are not well covered. Nearly 40 million people in the U.S. have no health insurance at all. The major reasons for this are that their employers do not provide health insurance benefits and their family incomes are above the official poverty line. Thus, programs encouraging people to leave public assistance and become employed have made it difficult for the working poor to obtain any kind of health insurance. Many states in the U.S. are developing state and local programs to offer low costs or free care to the families of the working poor. Even so, many low and even moderate income households cannot afford to pay for all their health needs (Smith, Grimm and Brewster 2002).

During the last twenty years health care in the U.S. has changed from being administered by the so-called fee for service system in which patients paid doctors and other providers of their choice, to a managed care system (Kronenfeld 2001). Overall, most workers in the U.S. who have private health insurance now are participants (or subscribers) in some form of managed health care. Their care is organized and yearly contracted arrangements between employers and insurance companies or other so-called "third parties" who manage health care by linking their subscribers with providers (e.g., physicians, nonphysician clinicians such as optometrists, and pharmacists) and determine its costs. One major form of these contracted relationships occurs in Health Maintenance Organizations (HMOs) where third parties encourage subscribers to use health screens and live healthfully and limit the payments to providers in ways that discourage unnecessary procedures. Another form occurs in the Preferred Provider Organizations (PPOs) in which contracting agents charge subscribers predetermined premiums and other so-called out-of-pocket expenses like deductibles and contract limited and discounted prices for service with specific providers and pharmacies. The PPO contract links providers and patients in a network, where prices are much cheaper than if patients get services outside the network.

Sociologists are finding that managed care involves a new and increasingly complex set of problems in and barriers to obtaining appropriate health care (Kronenfeld 2001). While managed care has reduced the yearly amount of increases to health care costs, it has involved disruptions in family physicians, denials of necessary care especially for women, and more problems in maintaining adequate care for chronic illness (Furlong and Wilken 2001). Disruptions of treatment and other administrative problems in obtaining necessary care have resulted in many states of the U.S. passing laws guaranteeing patients their right to choose their family physician and setting up state offices that can be contacted by patients and subscribers who wish to complain about their managed health care (Kronenfeld 2001). Future health care reforms in the U.S., therefore, must be directed to improving public health insurance programs, improving managed health care for employees who have such options, and determining how to provide health care to the increasing member of Americans who cannot afford to buy health insurance and are not eligible for public health insurance due to their income (Marshall 2001). With the importance of health care for all American families and with the great variety of options in the U.S. for providing necessary health care, a better distribution of comprehensive health care hopefully will be coming soon. (See Chapters 10, 13, 15, 17 and 18.)

Name: ______________________________

Quiz Questions: Health and Health Care

1. Medical Sociologists focus on which of the following in explaining patterns to diseases and deaths?

   a. economic resources
   b. beliefs about healthfulness
   c. risk behaviors like smoking
   d. all of the above

2. The major causes of premature deaths in the U.S. are infectious diseases. (True or False?)

3. Modern diseases like cancer have shorter latency periods than diseases like the flu that caused more deaths in the U.S. around 1900. (True or False?)

4. Medicalization is usually associated with people getting all the health screens that they should get. (True or False?)

5. Which of the following is <u>false</u> in describing the U.S. system of health care?

   a. is a multipayer system
   b. has some public health insurance programs
   c. is a single-payer system
   d. has some employers who don't provide health insurance

6. Most people in the U.S. now have fee-for-service health care. (True or False?)

7. A network is the main component of which of these health care programs?

   a. fee-for-service
   b. HMOs
   c. PPOs
   d. single-payer system

8. Sociologists have found that managed care has less disrupted services, especially for women, than fee-for-service health care. (True or False?)

9. The working poor in the U.S. are generally eligible for Medicaid. (True or False?)

10. Increasing the health insurance benefits for the working poor is an important way to improve health care in the U.S. (True or False?)

Name: ______________________________

Exercise: Health and Health Care

1. In the space provided, discuss health issues, including health screens that should be important to college students.

Name: ______________________________

Exercise: Health and Health Care

2. In the space provided, explain any recent problems that you or the members of your family have had in obtaining managed health care.

Name: ______________________

Exercise: Health and Health Care

3. Think of adults in your family who have had health problems. In the space provided, discuss how the health experiences of these family members illustrate risk behaviors, latency, medicalization, and managed care.

Name: ______________________________

Exercise: Health and Health Care

4. Think of illness you yourself have had. In the space provided, discuss how your illness experience, illustrate health screens, latency, medicalization, and provider networks.

Name: ______________________________

Exercise: Health and Health Care

5. Watch the classic dark comedy movie *The Hospital*. Use the content of the movie to discuss in the space provided, health screens, medicalization, health insurance, and administrative problems in obtaining care.

Name: ______________________

Exercise: Health and Health Care

6. Watch the movie *Philadelphia*. Use the content of the movie to discuss, in the space provided, medicalization, latency, infectious disease, and problems in maintaining care for chronic illness.

Name: ______________________________

Exercise: Health and Health Care

7. Go to the campus library or online and select an article from the sociological journal, *Health and Social Behavior*. Select any one article, read it, and use the content to discuss, in the space provided, latency, health screens, medicalization, and managed care.

Name: ______________________________

Exercise: Health and Health Care

8. Go to the campus library or online and select an article from the journal *Family and Community Health*. Select any one article, read it, and use the contents to illustrate, in the space provided, medicalization, health screens, health insurance, and managed care.

Name: ____________________

Exercise: Health and Health Care

9. Go to the website of a hospital or clinic in town. Use the information on the website to discuss, in the space provided, managed care, networks of providers, health screens, and medicalization.

Name: ______________________________

Exercise: Health and Health Care

10. Go to the website of the public health clinic in your county or city. From information on the website discuss, in the space provided, health screens, medicalization, care for people without health insurance and either Medicare or Medicaid.

14

Disabilities

Disabilities commonly are viewed through the types of impairments, such as blindness or deafness, or the parts of the body disabled, such as paraplegia when there is paralysis of the lower half of the body including both legs. Disabled people are often viewed as profoundly different, and they are usually considered the mostly helpless victims of their physical or mental problems. Consequently, most people with disabilities are viewed as unable to participate in social life without assistance (Brown 2000). In contrast, sociologists who study disabilities focus upon the social activities and social environments that can lead to people having impairments, such as the birth defects caused by pregnant women using drugs and drinking alcoholic beverages. Showing how unsafe workplaces, dangerous recreational behavior like driving high-speed boats while drunk, and how drug usage including smoking result in disabilities illustrates how sociologists focus upon the social etiology of disabilities (their social causes) (Ross and Wu 1995). Another sociological focus is upon the natural progression of impairments such as those related to arthritis that accompany normal aging (Cockerham 1997).

Sociologists also stress the idea that definitions of disabilities and policy decisions based upon such definitions vary among different social contexts. For example, disabilities among youth are usually defined concerning school-related activities, while among elderly people disabilities are more related to problems with daily activities such as personal hygiene. Among working-age adults, disabilities mean people having problems doing or being unable to do various types of daily activities that non-disabled people take for granted and can do quite easily (Bury 2000). The U.S. government defines adult disabilities as either moderate or severe, by using daily personal tasks like bathing and dressing called Activities of Daily Living (ADLs) or non-personal daily activities like using the telephone, shopping, and handling money, called Instrumental Activities in Daily Living (IADLs). People with moderate disabilities have trouble doing ADLs and/or IADLs, and people who are unable to complete them are considered to have severe disabilities. A similar distinction is used among adults with respect to functional activities like lifting ten pounds, reading a newspaper, climbing stairs, and speaking understandably. At least thirty million adults in the U.S. have some type of disability (National Center for Health Statistics 1998).

Sociologists also study and try to improve social environments like schools and universities, theaters and sports arenas, and cars and other motor vehicles so that disabled people can become more active and independent in social activities other people take for granted. Social environments constructed or arranged in ways that exclude the disabled are called disabling social environments (Higgins 1992). While most people would not willingly prevent a disabled person from coming to a public event, this is exactly what disabling social environments do. For example, at a public event like a political speech or a commencement, most deaf people not sitting close enough to the speaker to lip read are unable to understand anything said. Stores often provide motorized carts for disabled shoppers, but most of the shelving is too high for those seated in the carts to reach. Schools may or may not provide school transportation for disabled students. Even when such transportation is available it may not suit the needs of all types of disabled students, and school facilities may not enable disabled students to change clothing for a play or performance, get around in the hallways and classroom aisles, or get to the blackboard to write out the answer to a math problem. How better to design and to renovate environments and equipment for disabled people will be extremely important goals for the future, especially for new social movements striving for equal rights for all citizens (Gostin, Fieldblum, and Webber 1999). (See Chapter 18.)

Sociologists stress the difference between the stereotypes and misperceptions many people use in relating to disabled people with the actual capabilities of people with disabilities. Many people see disabled people such as the blind as generally helpless in all areas of activity, or as dependent. However, among people with visual impairments, and all other forms of disability, there are various forms and degrees of disability. Some people have trouble seeing to the side, others with focusing on close objects, and still others see shapes and colors while some can see nothing. Thus, some visually impaired people can walk outside without the need of assistance but are unable to read a newspaper or the printing on a label. Treating an impaired shopper as completely dependent may therefore not only be incorrect but it may also be demeaning. Moreover, contrary to the idea that disabled people see themselves as pitiable and abnormal, most people with disabilities do not define themselves primarily through what they are unable to do, provided their environments have been made less disabling. Wheelchair moms, for example, do just fine once their homes have been adapted so that appliances, bathroom fixtures, cabinets, and so on can be reached from their chairs. Disabled workers make good employees once they are in workplaces and in jobs that are not disabling (Higgins 1992).

Sociologists also study the various groups and reform organizations that have been and continue to be a part of the Disability Rights Movement. Among the disabled themselves the Independent Living Movement that emerged in the 1970s continues to have the goal of providing community service to disabled people so they will not be confined in institutions or their own homes. Increasingly, American households are providing family care-giving to disabled family members rather than placing them in institutions including nursing homes. There is increasing evidence that retirees including very elderly people are not only living healthier lives in the community but they are more actively participating in community organizations and in the life of their family including providing considerable care for their grandchildren (Rowe and Kahn 1998). (See Chapter 12.) Another group, Disability Rights Advocates (DRA), is a nonprofit legal organization that started in California and during the 1990s spread nationwide, bringing various legal services to the disabled including lawsuits for their rights (Weitz 2001, p. 156). (See Chapters 16, 17 and 18.) Sociologists pay particular attention to the continuous legal and social processes in interpreting and implementing the Americans with Disabilities Act (ADA), which was passed by the U.S. Congress in 1990 and put into effect in 1992. This law prohibits discrimination against all disabled people including those with mental impairments and with AIDS in all private and public enterprises. The law also mandates that public transportation and buildings be accessible to the disabled. It also requires employers to make reasonable accommodations in assigning work to qualified disabled people, so the work environment and job activities are non-disabling. Making workplaces and job activities less disabling has not been easy. Improving the rights of the disabled in workplaces primarily depends on challenges of job assignments from the disabled themselves or through lawsuits related to complaints brought before the Equal Employment Opportunity Commission (EEOC), the government regulatory agency that interprets workplace grievances before legal action begins. Most of the ADA-related complaints before the EEOC since 1992 have not been resolved in favor of the disabled. Primarily this is because the courts have redefined most work-related disabilities as medical conditions treatable through either medication or mechanical aids like special eyeglasses. These more medicalized definitions allow employers much greater latitude in hiring and firing disabled people (Gostin et al. 1999). (See Chapter 12, 13, and 16.)

Many social factors are a part of the etiology behind the increasing number of disabled people in modern society. Accidents and work-related injuries disable many people. Accidents and injuries from recreational activity impair many others. Advances in medicine increasingly allow many impaired infants to live who in the past would not have survived. Risk behaviors and especially drug usage and cigarette smoking continue to lead to impairments and to premature deaths. Illnesses like arthritis and ailments like hearing loss are a normal part of the aging process and increasing numbers of the elderly live with such disabling conditions. In the future, therefore, continuing efforts will be necessary so that the disabled may as actively and completely as they can participate in aspects of social life that the rest of us, thankfully, do not have problems with (Shapiro 1993).

Name: ____________________

Quiz Questions: Disabilities

1. Sociologists agree with the common viewpoint that disabilities are primarily understandable through what part of the body is useless. (True or False?)
2. Among which of these groups are ADLs and/or IADLs the primary basis for defining disabilities?
   a. youth
   b. the elderly
   c. working-age adults
   d. infants
3. Which of the following activities is a functional activities disability?
   a. bathing
   b. dressing
   c. using the telephone
   d. climbing stairs
4. Lack of public bus transportation for wheelchair users creates a disabling social environment. (True or False?)
5. Most disabled people see themselves as being dependent. (True or False?)
6. The Independent Living Movement was started by whom?
   a. government agencies
   b. the disabled themselves
   c. lawyers representing the disabled
   d. the EEOC
7. The primary piece of federal law that is used to decide legal issues with respect to the disabled is which of the following?
   a. ADA
   b. ADLs
   c. IADLs
   d. EEOC
8. Most complaints related to disability that have come before the EEOC since 1992 have been resolved in favor of the disabled. (True or False?)
9. Various social factors such as accidents and injuries as well as impairments among the elderly are increasing the number of disabled people in modern society. (True or False?)
10. Acceptance of disabled people in most social settings is now pretty much accomplished. (True or False?)

Name: ________________________________

Exercise: Disabilities

1. In the space provided, discuss in a couple of sentences each, five ways that your college campus could be made less disabling for disabled students.

Name: ______________________________

Exercise: Disabilities

2. Go to a large discount store and observe five major ways that the store disables people. Clearly list and explain in a sentence or so each of the five ways, in the space provided.

Name: ______________________________

Exercise: Disabilities

3. Think about the disabled students that you went to school with or that you are going to college with now. In the space provided, discuss disabling social environments, degrees of disability, and the rights of the disabled.

Name: ______________________________

Exercise: Disabilities

4. Think about the places of public entertainment and dining in your town. In the space provided, discuss how they could be made less disabling and how disabled people could participate in them without being dependent.

Name: ______________________________

Exercise: Disabilities

5. Watch the classic movie, *The Best Years of Our Lives*. Based upon the movie's content, in the space provided, discuss disability, disabling social environments, being dependent, and the rights of the disabled.

Name: ______________________________

Exercise: Disabilities

6. Watch the movie, *My Left Foot*. Based upon the movie's content, in the space provided, discuss the capabilities of disabled people, disabling social environments, dependency, and the rights of the disabled.

Name: ________________________________

Exercise: Disabilities

7. Go to the campus library or online, and select an article related to disabilities from the journal *Family and Community Health*. Use the content of the article to discuss, in the space provided, disabling social environments, rights of the disabled, and the ADA.

Name: ______________________________

Exercise: Disabilities

8. Go to the campus library or online, and select an article from the journal *AIDS and Public Policy*. Use the article's content to discuss, in the space provided, disabling social environments, the rights of the disabled, and ADA.

Name: ______________________________

Exercise: Disabilities

9. Go online to the website devoted to disability rights. Use the content of the site to discuss, in the space provided, the independent living movement, rights of the disabled, and use of the ADA to increase employment opportunity for the disabled.

Name: ______________________________

Exercise: Disabilities

10. Go online to the website of Disability Rights Education and Defense Fund, www.dredf.org, and use the content to discuss, in the space provided, disability rights advocates, the disability rights movement, and increasing the employment opportunity for the disabled.

The Second Shift, Part One
When Working Wives Get Home

Arlie Russell Hochschild with Anne Machung

Introduction

She is not the same woman in each magazine advertisement, but she is the same idea. She has that working-mother look as she strides forward, briefcase in one hand, smiling child in the other. Literally and figuratively, she is moving ahead. Her hair, if long, tosses behind her; if it is short, it sweeps back at the sides, suggesting mobility and progress. There is nothing shy or passive about her. She is confident, active, "liberated." She wears a dark tailored suit, but with a silk bow or colorful frill that says, "I'm really feminine underneath." She has made it in a man's world without sacrificing her femininity. And she has done this on her own. By some personal miracle, this image suggests, she has managed to combine what 150 years of industrialization have split wide apart—child and job, frill and suit, female culture and male.

When I showed a photograph of a supermom like this to the working mothers I talked to in the course of [my] research, many responded with an outright laugh. One daycare worker and mother of two, ages three and five, threw back her head: "Ha! They've got to be *kidding* about her. Look at me, hair a mess, nails jagged, twenty pounds overweight. Mornings, I'm getting my kids dressed, the dog fed, the lunches made, the shopping list done. That lady's got a maid." Even working mothers who did have maids couldn't imagine combining work and family in such a carefree way. "Do you know what a baby *does* to your life, the two o'clock feedings, the four o'clock feedings?" Another mother of two said: "They don't show it, but she's whistling"—she imitated a whistling woman, eyes to the sky—"so she can't hear the din." They envied the apparent ease of the woman with the flying hair, but she didn't remind them of anyone they knew.

The women I interviewed—lawyers, corporate executives, word processors, garment pattern cutters, daycare workers—and most of their husbands, too—felt differently about some issues: how right it is for a mother of young children to work a full-time job, or how much a husband should be responsible for the home. But they all agreed that it was hard to work two full-time jobs and raise young children.

How well do couples do it? The more women work outside the home, the more central this question. The number of women in paid work has risen steadily since before the turn of the century, but since 1950 the rise has been staggering. In 1950, 30 percent of American women were in the labor force; in 1986, it was 55 percent. In 1950, 28 percent of married women with children between six and seventeen worked outside the home; in 1986, it had risen to 68 percent. In 1950, 23 percent of married women with children under six worked. By 1986, it had grown to 54 percent. We don't know how many women with children under the age of one worked outside the home in 1950; it was so rare that the Bureau of Labor kept no statistics on it. Today half of such women do. Two-thirds of all mothers are now in the labor force; in fact, more mothers have paid jobs (or are actively looking for one) than nonmothers. Because of this change in women, two-job families now make up 58 percent of all married couples with children.

Since an increasing number of working women have small children, we might expect an increase in part-time work. But actually, 67 percent of the mothers who work have full-time jobs—that is, thirty-five hours or more weekly. That proportion is what it was in 1959.

If more mothers of young children are stepping into full-time jobs outside the home, and if most couples can't afford household help, how much more are fathers doing at home? As I began exploring this question I found many studies on the hours working men and women devote to housework and childcare. One national random sample of 1,243 working parents in forty-four American cities, conducted in 1965–66 by Alexander Szalai and his coworkers, for example, found that working women averaged three hours a day on housework while men averaged seventeen minutes; women spent fifty minutes a day of time exclusively with their children; men spent twelve minutes. On the other side of the coin, working fathers watched television an hour longer than their working wives, and slept a half hour longer each night. A comparison of this American sample with eleven other industrial countries in Eastern and Western Europe revealed the same difference between working women and working men in those countries as well. In a 1983 study of white middle-class families in greater Boston, Grace Baruch and R. C. Barnett found that working men married to working women spent only three-quarters of an hour longer each week with their kindergarten-aged children than did men married to housewives.

Szalai's landmark study documented the now familiar but still alarming story of the working woman's "double day," but it left me wondering how men and women actually felt about all this. He and his coworkers studied how people used time, but not, say, how a father felt about his twelve minutes with his child, or how his wife felt about it. Szalai's study revealed the visible surface of what I discovered to be a set of deeply emotional issues: What should a man and woman contribute to the family? How appreciated does each feel? How does each respond to subtle changes in the balance of marital power? How does each develop an unconscious "gender strategy" for coping with the work at home, with marriage, and, indeed, with life itself? These were the underlying issues.

But I began with the measurable issue of time. Adding together the time it takes to do a paid job and to do housework and childcare, I averaged estimates from the major studies on time use done in the 1960s and 1970s, and discovered that women worked roughly fifteen hours longer each week than men. Over a year, they worked an *extra month of twenty-four-hour days a year*. Over a dozen years, it was an extra year of twenty-four-hour days. Most women without children spend much more time than men on housework; with children, they devote more time to both housework and childcare. Just as there is a wage gap between men and women in the workplace, there is a "leisure gap" between them at home. Most women work one shift at the office or factory and a "second shift" at home.

Studies show that working mothers have higher self-esteem and get less depressed than housewives, but compared to their husbands, they're more tired and get sick more often. In Peggy Thoits's 1985 analysis of two large-scale surveys, each of about a thousand men and women, people were asked how often in the preceding week they'd experienced each of twenty-three symptoms of anxiety (such as dizziness or hallucinations). According to the researchers' criteria, working mothers were more likely than any other group to be "anxious."

In light of these studies, the image of the woman with the flying hair seems like an upbeat "cover" for a grim reality, like those pictures of Soviet tractor drivers smiling radiantly into the distance as they think about the ten-year plan. The Szalai study was conducted in 1965–66. I wanted to know whether the leisure gap he found in 1965 persists, or whether it has disappeared. Since most married couples work two jobs, since more will in the future, since most wives in these couples work the extra month a year, I wanted to understand what the wife's extra month a year meant for each person, and what it does for love and marriage in an age of high divorce.

With my research associates Anne Machung and Elaine Kaplan, I interviewed fifty couples very intensively, and I observed in a dozen homes. We first began interviewing artisans, students, and professionals in Berkeley, California, in the late 1970s. This was at the height of the women's movement, and many of these couples were earnestly and self-consciously struggling to modernize the ground rules of their marriages. Enjoying flexible job schedules and intense cultural support to do so, many succeeded. Since their circumstances were unusual they became our "comparison group" as we sought other couples more typical of mainstream America. In 1980 we located more typical couples by sending a questionnaire on work and family life to every thirteenth name—from top to bottom—of the personnel roster of a large, urban manufacturing company. At the end of the questionnaire, we asked members of working couples raising children under six and working full time jobs if they would be willing to talk to us in greater depth. Interviewed from 1980 through 1988, these couples, their neighbors and friends, their children's teachers, daycare workers and baby-sitters, form the heart of this [research].

When we called them, a number of baby-sitters replied as one woman did, "You're interviewing us? Good. We're human too." Or another, "I'm glad you consider what we do work. A lot of people don't." As it turned out, many daycare workers were themselves juggling two jobs and small children, and so we talked to them about that, too.

We also talked with other men and women who were not part of two-job couples; divorced parents who were war-weary veterans of two-job marriages, and traditional couples, to see how much of the strain we were seeing was unique to two-job couples.

I also watched daily life in a dozen homes during a weekday evening, during the week-end, and during the months that followed, when I was invited on outings, to dinner, or just to talk. I found myself waiting on the front doorstep as weary parents and hungry children tumbled out of the family car. I shopped with them, visited friends, watched television, ate with them, walked through parks, and came along when they dropped their children at daycare, often staying on at the baby-sitter's house after parents waved good-bye. In their homes, I sat on the living-room floor and drew pictures and played house with the children. I watched as parents gave them baths, read bedtime stories, and said good night. Most couples tried to bring me into the family scene, inviting me to eat with them and talk. I responded if they spoke to me, from time to time asked questions, but I rarely initiated conversations. I tried to become as unobtrusive as a family dog. Often I would base myself in the living room, quietly taking notes. Sometimes I would follow a wife upstairs or down, accompany a child on her way out to "help Dad" fix the car, or watch television with the other watchers. Sometimes I would break out of my peculiar role to join in the jokes they often made about acting like the "model" two-job couple. Or perhaps the joking was a subtle part of my role, to put them at ease so they could act more naturally. For a period of two to five years, I phoned or visited these couples to keep in touch even as I moved on to study the daily lives of other working couples—black, Chicano, white, from every social class and walk of life.

I asked who did how much of a wide variety of household tasks. I asked who cooks? Vacuums? Makes the beds? Sews? Cares for plants? Sends Christmas or Hanukkah cards? I also asked: Who washes the car? Repairs household appliances? Does the taxes? Tends the yard? I asked who did most household planning, who noticed such things as when a child's fingernails need clipping, cared more how the house looked or about the change in a child's mood.

Inside the Extra Month a Year

The women I interviewed seemed to be far more deeply torn between the demands of work and family than were their husbands. They talked with more animation and at greater length than their husbands about the abiding conflict between them. Busy as they were, women more often brightened at the idea of yet another interviewing session. They felt the second shift was *their* issue and most of their husbands agreed. When I telephoned one husband to arrange an interview with him, explaining that I wanted to ask him about how he managed work and family life, he replied genially, "Oh, this will *really* interest my *wife*."

It was a woman who first proposed to me the metaphor, borrowed from industrial life, of the "second shift." She strongly resisted the *idea* that homemaking was a "shift." Her family was her life and she didn't want it reduced to a job. But as she put it, "You're on duty at work. You come home, and you're on duty. Then you go back to work and you're on duty." After eight hours of adjusting insurance claims, she came home to put on the rice for dinner, care for her children, and wash laundry. Despite herself her home life *felt* like a second shift. That was the real story and that was the real problem.

Men who shared the load at home seemed just as pressed for time as their wives, and as torn between the demands of career and small children. . . . But the majority of men did not share the load at home. Some refused outright. Others refused more passively, often offering a loving shoulder to lean on, an understanding ear as their working wife faced the conflict they both saw as hers. At first it seemed to me that the problem of the second shift was hers. But I came to realize that those husbands who helped very little at home were often indirectly just as deeply affected as their wives by the need to do that work, through the resentment their wives feel toward them, and through their need to steel themselves against the resentment. Evan Holt, a warehouse furniture salesman, did very little housework and played with his four-year-old son, Joey, at his convenience. Juggling the demands of work with family at first seemed a problem for his wife. But Evan himself suffered enormously from the side effects of "her" problem. His wife did the second shift, but she resented it keenly, and half-consciously expressed her frustration and rage by losing interest in sex and becoming overly absorbed with Joey. One way or another, most men I talked with do suffer the severe repercussions of what I think is a transitional phase in American family life.

One reason women take a deeper interest than men in the problems of juggling work with family life is that even when husbands happily shared the hours of work, their wives felt more *responsible* for home and children. More women kept track of doctors' appointments and arranged for playmates to come over. More mothers than fathers worried about the tail on a child's Halloween costume or a birthday present for a school friend. They were more likely to think about their children while at work and to check in by phone with the baby-sitter.

Partly because of this, more women felt torn between one sense of urgency and another, between the need to soothe a child's fear of being left at daycare, and the need to show the boss she's "serious" at work. More women than men questioned how good they were as parents, or if they did not, they questioned why they weren't questioning it. More often than men, women alternated between living in their ambition and standing apart from it.

As masses of women have moved into the economy, families have been hit by a "speed-up" in work and family life. There is no more time in the day than there was when wives stayed home, but there is twice as much to get done. It is mainly women who absorb this "speed-up." Twenty percent of the men in my study shared housework equally. Seventy percent of men did a substantial amount (less than half but more than a third), and 10 percent did less than a third. Even when couples share more equitably in the work at home, women do two-thirds of the *daily* jobs at home, like cooking and cleaning up—jobs that fix them into a rigid routine. Most women cook dinner and most men change the oil in the family car. But, as one mother pointed out, dinner needs to be prepared every evening around six o'clock, whereas the car oil needs to be changed every six months, any day around that time, any time that day. Women do more childcare than men, and men repair more household appliances. A child needs to be tended daily while the repair of household appliances can often wait "until I have time." Men thus have more control over *when* they make their contributions than women do. They may be very busy with family chores but, like the executive who tells his secretary to "hold my calls," the man has more control over his time. The job of the working mother, like that of the secretary, is usually to "take the calls."

Another reason women may feel more strained than men is that women more often do two things at once—for example, write checks and return phone calls, vacuum and keep an eye on a three-year-old, fold laundry and think out the shopping list. Men more often cook dinner *or* take a child to the park. Indeed, women more often juggle three spheres—job, children, and housework—while most men juggle two—job and children. For women, two activities compete with their time with children, not just one.

Beyond doing more at home, women also devote *proportionately more* of their time at home to housework and proportionately less of it to childcare. Of all the time men spend working at home, more of it goes to childcare. . . . Since most parents prefer to tend to their children than clean house, men do more of what they'd rather do. More men than women take their children on "fun" outings to the park, the zoo, the movies. Women spend more time on maintenance, feeding and bathing children, enjoyable activities to be sure, but often less leisurely or "special" than going to the zoo. Men also do fewer of the "undesirable" household chores: fewer men than women wash toilets and scrub the bathroom.

As a result, women tend to talk more intently about being overtired, sick, and "emotionally drained." Many women I could not tear away from the topic of sleep. They talked about how much they could "get by on" . . . six and half, seven, seven and a half, less, more. They talked about who they knew who needed more or less. Some apologized for how much sleep they needed—"I'm afraid I need eight hours of sleep"—as if eight were "too much." They talked about the effect of a change in baby-sitter, the birth of a second child, or a business trip on their child's pattern of sleep. They talked about how to avoid fully waking up when a child called them at night, and how to get back to sleep. These women talked about sleep the way a hungry person talks about food.

All in all, if in this period of American history, the two-job family is suffering from a speed up of work and family life, working mothers are its primary victims. It is ironic, then, that often it falls to women to be the "time and motion expert" of family life. Watching inside homes, I noticed it was often the mother who rushed children, saying, "Hurry up! It's time to go," "Finish your cereal now," "You can do that later," "Let's go!" When a bath is crammed into a slot between 7:45 and 8:00 it was often the mother who called out, "Let's see who can take their bath the quickest!" Often a younger child will rush out, scurrying to be first in bed, while the older and wiser one stalls, resistant, sometimes resentful: "Mother is always rushing us." Sadly enough, women are more often the lightning rods for family aggressions aroused by the speed-up of work and family life. They are the "villains" in a process of which they are also the primary victims. More than the longer hours, the sleeplessness, and feeling torn, this is the saddest cost to women of the extra month a year.

Marriage in the Stalled Revolution

Each marriage bears the footprints of economic and cultural trends which originate far outside marriage. A rise in inflation which erodes the earning power of the male wage, an expanding service sector which opens up jobs for women, new cultural images—like the woman with the flying hair—that make the working mother seem exciting, all these changes do not simply go on *around* marriage. They occur *within* marriage, and transform it. Problems between husbands and wives, problems which seem "individual" and "marital," are often individual experiences of powerful economic and cultural shock waves that are not caused by one person or two. Quarrels that erupt . . . result mainly from a friction between faster-changing women and slower-changing men, rates of change which themselves result from the different rates at which the industrial economy had drawn men and women into itself.

There is a "his" and "hers" to the economic development of the United States. In the latter part of the nineteenth century, it was mainly men who were drawn off the farm into paid, industrial work and who changed their way of life and their identity. At that point in history, men became more different from their fathers than women became from their mothers. Today the economic arrow points at women; it is women who are being drawn into wage work, and women who are undergoing changes in their way of life and identity. Women are departing more from their mothers' and grandmothers' way of life, men are doing so less.[1]

Both the earlier entrance of men into the industrial economy and the later entrance of women have influenced the relations *between* men and women, especially their relations within marriage. The former increase in the number of men in industrial work tended to increase the power of men, and the present growth in the number of women in such work has somewhat increased the power of women. On the whole, the entrance of men into industrial work did not destabilize the family whereas *in the absence of other changes*, the rise in female employment has gone with the rise in divorce. . . . Beneath the image of the woman with the flying hair, there has been a real change in women without much change in anything else.

The exodus of women into the economy has not been accompanied by a cultural understanding of marriage and work that would make this transition smooth. The workforce has changed. Women have changed. But most workplaces have remained inflexible in the face of the family demands of their workers, and at home, most men have yet to really adapt to the changes in women. This strain between the change in women and the absence of change in much else leads me to speak of a "stalled revolution."

A society which did not suffer from this stall would be a society *humanely* adapted to the fact that most women work outside the home. The workplace would allow parents to work part time, to share jobs, to work flexible hours, to take parental leaves to give birth, tend a sick child, or care for a well one. As Delores Hayden has envisioned in *Redesigning the American Dream*, it would include affordable housing closer to places of work, and perhaps community-based meal and laundry services. It would include men whose notion of manhood encouraged them to be active parents and share at home. In contrast, a stalled revolution lacks social arrangements that ease life for working parents, and lacks men who share the second shift.

If women begin to do less at home because they have less time, if men do little more, if the work of raising children and tending a home requires roughly the same effort, then the questions of who does what at home and of what "needs doing" become key. Indeed they may become a source of deep tension in the marriage, tensions I explore here one by one.

My first question about who does what gave way to a series of deeper questions: What leads some working mothers to do all the work at home themselves—to pursue what I call a supermom strategy—and what leads others to press their husbands to share the responsibility and work of the home? Why do some men genuinely want to share housework and childcare, others fatalistically acquiesce, and still others actively resist?

How does each husband's ideas about manhood lead him to think he "should feel" about what he's doing at home and at work? What does he really feel? Do his real feelings conflict with what he thinks he should feel? How does he resolve the conflict? The same questions apply to wives. What influence does each person's consequent "strategy" for handling his or her feelings and actions with regard to the second shift affect his or her children, job, and marriage? Through this line of questioning, I was led to the complex web of ties between a family's needs, the sometime quest for equality, and happiness in modern marriage. . . .

We can describe a couple as rich or poor and that will tell us a great deal about their two-job marriage. We can describe them as Catholic, Protestant, Jewish, black, Chicano, Asian, or white and that will tell us something more. We can describe their marriage as a combination of two personalities, one "obsessive compulsive," say, and the other "narcissistic," and again that will tell us something. But knowledge about social class, ethnicity, and personality takes us only so far in understanding who does and doesn't share the second shift, and whether or not sharing the work at home makes marriages happier.

When I sat down to compare one couple that shared the second shift with another three that didn't, many of the answers that would seem obvious—a man's greater income, his longer hours of work, the fact that his mother was a housewife or his father did little at home, his ideas about men and women—all these factors didn't really explain why some women work the extra month a year and others don't. They didn't explain why some women seemed content to work the extra month, while others were deeply unhappy about it. When I compared a couple who was sharing and happy with another couple who was sharing but miserable, it was clear that purely economic or psychological answers were not enough. Gradually, I felt the need to explore how *deep* within each man and woman gender ideology goes. I felt the need to understand the ways in which some men and women seemed to be egalitarian "on top" but traditional "underneath," or the other way around. I tried to sensitize myself to the difference between shallow ideologies (ideologies which were contradicted by deeper feelings) and deep ideologies (which were reinforced by such feelings). I explored how each person reconciled ideology with his or her own behavior, that of a partner, and with the other realities of life. I felt the need to explore what I call loosely "gender strategies."

The Top and Bottom of Gender Ideology

A gender strategy is a plan of action through which a person tries to solve problems at hand, given the cultural notions of gender at play. To pursue a gender strategy, a man draws on beliefs about manhood and womanhood, beliefs that are forged in early childhood and thus anchored to deep emotions. He makes a connection between how he thinks about his manhood, what he feels about it, and what he does. It works in the same way for a woman.

A woman's gender ideology determines what sphere she *wants* to identify with (home or work) and how much power in the marriage she wants to have (less, more, or the same amount). I found three types of ideology of marital roles: —traditional, transitional, and egalitarian. Even though she works, the "pure" traditional wants to identify with her activities at home (as a wife, a mother, a neighborhood mom), wants her husband to base his at work and wants less power than he. The traditional man wants the same. The "pure" egalitarian, as the type emerges here, wants to identify with the same spheres her husband does, and to have an equal amount of power in the marriage. Some want the couple to be jointly oriented to the home, others to their careers, or both of them to jointly hold some balance between the two. Between the traditional and the egalitarian is the transitional, any one of a variety of types of blending of the two. But, in contrast to the traditional, a transitional woman wants to identify with her role at work as well as at home. Unlike the egalitarian, she believes her husband should base his identity more on work than she does. A typical transitional wants to identify *both* with the caring for the home, and with helping her husband earn money, but wants her husband to focus on earning a living. A typical transitional man is all for his wife working, but expects her to take the main responsibility at home too. Most men and women I talked with were "transitional." At least, transitional ideas came out when I asked people directly what they believed.

In actuality, I found there were contradictions between what people said they believed about their marital roles and how they seemed to *feel* about those roles. Some men seemed to me egalitarian "on top" but traditional "underneath." Others seemed traditional on top and egalitarian underneath.[2] Often a person attached deep feelings to his or her gender ideology in response to what I call early "cautionary tales" from childhood, as well as in response to his or her present situation. Sometimes these feelings *reinforced* the surface of a person's gender ideology. For example, the fear Nancy Holt was to feel of becoming a submissive mother, a "doormat," as she felt her mother had been, infused emotional steam into her belief that her husband Evan should do half the second shift.

On the other hand, the dissociation Ann Myerson was to feel from her successful career undermined her ostensible commitment both to that career and to sharing the second shift. Ann Myerson's surface ideology was egalitarian; she *wanted* to feel as engaged with her career as her husband was with his. This was her view of the "proper experience" of her career. She thought she *should* love her work. She *should* think it mattered. In fact, as she confessed in a troubled tone, she didn't love her work and didn't think it mattered. She felt a conflict between what she thought she ought to feel (according to her surface ideology)—emotionally involved in her career—and what she did feel—uninvolved with it. Among other things, her gender strategy was a way of trying to resolve that conflict.

The men and women I [interviewed], seem to have developed their gender ideology by unconsciously synthesizing certain cultural ideas with feelings about their past. But they also developed their ideology by taking opportunity into account. Sometime in adolescence they matched their personal assets against the opportunities available to men or women of their type; they saw which gender ideology best fit their circumstances, and—often regardless of their upbringing—they identified with a certain version of manhood or womanhood. It "made sense" to them. It felt like "who they were." For example, a woman sizes up her education, intelligence, age, charm, sexual attractiveness, her dependency needs, her aspirations, and she matches these against her perception of how women like her are doing in the job market and the "marriage market." What jobs could she get? What men? What are her chances for an equal marriage, a traditional marriage, a happy marriage, any marriage? Half-consciously, she assesses her chances—chances of an interesting, well-paid job are poor? her courtship pool has very traditional men? She takes these into account. *Then* a certain gender ideology, let's say a traditional one, will "make sense" to her. She will embrace the ideology that suits her perception of her chances. She holds to a certain version of womanhood (the "wilting violet," say). She identifies with its customs (men opening doors), and symbols (lacy dress, long hair, soft handshakes, and lowered eyes). She tries to develop its "ideal personality" (deferential, dependent), not because this is what her parents taught her, not because this corresponds to how she naturally "is," but because these particular customs now *make sense* of her resources and of her overall situation in a stalled revolution. The same principle applies to men. However wholehearted or ambivalent, a person's gender ideology tends to fit their situation.

Gender Strategies

When a man tries to apply his gender ideology to the situations that face him in real life, unconsciously or not he pursues a gender strategy.[3] He outlines a course of action. He might become a "superdad"—working long hours and keeping his child up late at night to spend time with him or her. Or he might cut back his hours at work. Or he might scale back housework and spend less time with his children. Or he might actively try to share the second shift.

The term "strategy" refers both to his plan of action and to his emotional preparations for pursuing it. For example, he may require himself to suppress his career ambitions to devote himself more to his children, or suppress his responsiveness to his children's appeals in the course of steeling himself for the struggle at work. He might harden himself to his wife's appeals, or he might be the one in the family who "lets" himself see when a child is calling out for help.

In the families I [interviewed], then, I have tried to be sensitive to the fractures in gender ideology, the conflicts between what a person thinks he or she ought to feel and what he or she does feel, and to the emotional work it takes to fit a gender ideal when inner needs or outer conditions make it hard.

As this social revolution proceeds, the problems of the two-job family will not diminish. If anything, as more couples work two jobs these problems will increase. If we can't return to traditional marriage, and if we are not to despair of marriage altogether, it becomes vitally important to understand marriage as a magnet for the strains of the stalled revolution, and to understand gender strategies as the basic dynamic of marriage.

The Economy of Gratitude

The interplay between a man's gender ideology and a woman's implies a deeper interplay between his gratitude toward her, and hers toward him. For how a person wants to identify himself or herself influences what, in the back and forth of a marriage, will seem like a gift and what will not. If a man doesn't think it fits the kind of "man" he wants to be to have his wife earn more than he, it may become his "gift" to her to "bear it" anyway. But a man may also feel like the husband I interviewed, who said, "When my wife began earning more than me I thought I'd struck gold!" In this case his wife's salary is the gift, not his capacity to accept it "anyway." When couples struggle, it is seldom simply over who does what. Far more often, it is over the giving and receiving of gratitude.

Family Myths

As I watched couples in their own homes, I began to realize that couples sometimes develop "family myths"—versions of reality that obscure a core truth in order to manage a family tension.[4] Evan and Nancy Holt managed an irresolvable conflict over the distribution of work at home through the myth that they now "shared it equally." Another couple unable to admit to the conflict came to believe "we aren't competing over who will take responsibility at home; we're just dreadfully busy with our careers." Yet another couple jointly believed that the husband was bound hand and foot to his career "because his work demanded it," while in fact his careerism covered the fact that they were avoiding each other. Not all couples need or have family myths. But when they do arise, I believe they often manage key tensions which are linked, by degrees, to the long hand of the stalled revolution.

[Toward the end of my twelve years of interviewing, I found that] more couples *wanted* to share and imagined that they did. Dorothy Sims, a personnel director, summed up this new blend of idea and reality. She eagerly explained to me that she and her husband Dan "shared all the housework," and that they were "equally involved in raising their nine-month-old son Timothy." Her husband, a refrigerator salesman, applauded her career and "was more pleased than threatened by her high salary"; he urged her to develop such competencies as reading ocean maps, and calculating interest rates (which she'd so far "resisted learning") because these days "a woman should." But one evening at dinner, a telling episode occurred. Dorothy had handed Timothy to her husband while she served us a chicken dinner. Gradually, the baby began to doze on his father's lap. "When do you want me to put Timmy to bed?" Dan asked. A long silence followed during which it occurred to Dorothy—then, I think, to her husband—that this seemingly insignificant question hinted to me that it was *she*, not he, or "they," who usually decided such matters. Dorothy slipped me a glance, put her elbows on the table, and said to her husband in a slow, deliberate voice, "So, what do *we* think?"

When Dorothy and Dan described their "typical days," their picture of sharing grew even less convincing. Dorothy worked the same nine-hour day at the office as her husband. But she came home to fix dinner and tend Timmy while Dan fit in a squash game three nights a week from six to seven (a good time for his squash partner). Dan read the newspaper more often and slept longer.

Compared to the early interviews, women in the later interviews seemed to speak more often in passing of relationships or marriages that had ended for some other reason but of which it "was also true" that he "didn't lift a finger at home." Or the extra month alone did it. . . . But women like Dorothy Sims, who simply add to their extra month a year a new illusion that they aren't doing it, represent a sad alternative to the woman with the flying hair—the woman who doesn't think that's who she is.

Notes

1. This is more true of white and middle-class women than it is of black or poor women, whose mothers often worked outside the home. But the trend I am talking about—an increase from 20 percent of women in paid jobs in 1900 to 55 percent in 1986—has affected a large number of women.
2. In a 1978 national survey, Joan Huber and Glenna Spitze found that 78 percent of husbands think that if husband and wife both work full time, they should share housework equally (*Sex Stratification: Children, Housework and Jobs*. New York: Academic Press, 1983). In fact, the husbands of working wives at most average a third of the work at home.
3. The concept of "gender strategy" is an adaptation of Ann Swidler's notion of "strategies of action." In "Culture in Action—Symbols and Strategies," *American Sociological Review* 51 (1986): 273–86, Swidler focuses on how the individual uses aspects of culture (symbols, rituals, stories) as "tools" for constructing a line of action. Here, I focus on aspects of culture that bear on our ideas of manhood and womanhood, and I focus on our emotional preparation for and the emotional consequences of our strategies.
4. For the term *family myth* I am indebted to Antonio J. Ferreira, "Psychosis and Family Myth," *American Journal of Psychotherapy* 21 (1967): 186–225.

References

Baruch, Grace K., and Rosalind Barnett

1983 "Correlates of Fathers' Participation in Family Work: A Technical Report." Working paper no. 106. Wellesley College, Center for Research on Women, Wellesley, Mass.

Szalai, Alexander (ed.).

1972 *The Use of Time: Daily Activities of Urban and Suburban Populations in Twelve Countries*. The Hague: Mouton.

Thoits, Peggy.

1986 "Multiple Identities: Examining Gender and Marital Status Differences in Distress." *American Sociological Review* 51: 259–72.

Health and Illness Issues Facing an Aging Workforce in the New Millennium

Nancy L. Marshall
Center for Research on Women, Wellesley College, Wellesley, Massachusetts, USA

This article raises key social issues facing an aging workforce, including the increasing levels of employment after retirement, the concentration of older workers in the service industries and in part-time work, and the impact of technological innovation on older workers. The article examines the experiences of older workers in the context of the other major social roles occupied by women and men aged 55 and older. This review provides medical sociologists several suggestions for new or continued areas for research as we move into the new millennium on health and illness issues relevant to older workers in the United States.

There are over 14 million older workers[1] in the United States (Commonwealth Fund 1993). The National Occupational Research Agenda has estimated that the "number of workers aged 55 and older is expected to grow twice as fast as the total workforce for the next several years as the 'baby boomer' population matures and life expectancy increases" (National Institute for Occupational Safety and Health [NIOSH] 1996). In 1990, 65% of men aged 55–64 and 14% of men aged 65 or older were in the labor force. For women, 42% of women aged 55–64 and 7% of women aged 65 or older were in the labor force (Sterns 1995). Increasingly greater proportions of women are employed in their later years, as the cumulative impact of younger women's rising employment carries over into older ages. As a result of this and other factors, the older worker labor force is increasingly female (Kinsella and Gist 1995).

The average age of retirement in the United States has been declining from the average age of 65 in the mid-1960s. At the same time, the variability in the age of retirement is actually increasing, reflecting the fact that some categories of workers are retiring at earlier and earlier ages, and others continue employment long beyond the "normative" age of retirement (Han and Moen 1998). The declining average age of retirement is more evident among men. Women's average age of retirement has actually shown less decline than men's average age, reflecting women's different career patterns.[2] And retirement does not always signal the end of employment: Various studies have suggested that approximately one third of older workers become reemployed postretirement—especially likely among workers with a college degree and among women who have been intermittently employed before "retirement" (Han and Moen 1998).

This rise in older workers coincides with the shift in the United States from a manufacturing economy to a service economy. The number of jobs in the service industries is rising faster than in any other area of the economy. In 1970, 26% of civilian jobs were in manufacturing, and 26% were in the service industries. By 1990, only 18% of civilian jobs were in manufacturing, and 33% were in the service industries. This shift to a service economy is of particular relevance to older workers, as older workers are over-represented in many of the service industries and in part-time work (which is itself more common in service industries; see Blau, Oser, and Stephens 1983).

These factors combine to create a pressing need for a better understanding of older workers and the nature and magnitude of the health risks they face. As the National Occupational Research Agenda (NIOSH 1996:1) noted,

> Information and service industries are replacing manufacturing jobs. The workforce is aging rapidly and becoming increasingly diverse. Re-engineering and downsizing continue unabated, and temporary and part-time jobs are increasingly common. These trends may adversely affect work organization, and may result, for example, in increased workload demands, longer and more varied work shifts, and job insecurity. However, the actual effects of these trends on the conditions of work and the well-being of workers have received little study.

Medical sociologists should heed this call for further study. Medical sociology can make important contributions to the understanding of health and illness issues for older workers in the new millennium.

Work Conditions

Although various studies have shown that employment, per se, is positively associated with health among older workers (see Ross and Mirowsky 1995), a central question remains largely unanswered: To what extent do the *characteristics* of older workers' jobs constitute health risk factors? Understanding the links between work conditions, full-time or part-time employment, technological innovation, and older workers' psychological and physical health may help to reduce both health costs and loss of productivity.

Although there has been a rise in occupational health studies over the past two decades, there have been only a few studies that have specifically examined the role of work conditions *in older workers'* health. Hayward et al. (1989) found that older adults with jobs that were substantively complex were less likely to leave the workforce because of disability. Staats et al. (1994) found that work stressors were correlated with a less hopeful outlook and poorer quality of life in a sample of 217 workers over 50 years of age. In a 1995 survey of 2,592 respondents aged 18–95, Ross and Van Willigen (1997) found that individuals with challenging, nonalienated work reported less emotional distress and less physical distress.

One of the leading theoretical models in the field of occupational health is the demand-control model, developed by Karasek and Theorell (1990). The demand-control model posits that the *combination* of heavy demands and limited control or decision latitude to moderate those demands results in job strain, and job strain, in turn, leads to negative health consequences. Earlier studies have supported this model; for example, in a study of random national samples of male workers in the United States and Sweden, Karasek (1979) found that high demands combined with low decision latitude were associated with greater depression. The demand-control model has also been confirmed in studies of specific occupations, including clerical workers in the finance industry, employees in manufacturing, and German metal workers (Karasek and Theorell 1990; Dwyer and Ganster 1991). In addition, Karasek's job characteristics scales seem to be limited to domains more characteristic of traditional industrial jobs (Muntaner, Eaton, and Garrison 1993). Thus, the majority of studies that have confirmed the demand-control model were conducted on data collected from samples drawn from the manufacturing industry, before the recent rise in the service industries. Because they were conducted with traditionally aged workforce samples, there is a need to explore the associations between job characteristics and health outcomes for older workers further.

Existing research on the occupational health of younger workers has identified the importance of social support, particularly work-related social support. Studies of work conditions and work-related social support among men have found that work-related support buffers the impact of work conditions on people's health. For example, LaRocco, House, and French (1980) found that coworker and supervisor support buffered the impact of work conditions on men's levels of psychological strain. Marshall and Barnett (1992) found that work-related social support from the supervisor was important to women's physical health and support from the spouse was important to their emotional well-being. Given the salience of social support factors for the physical and mental well-being of workers in general, these types of studies need to be replicated with populations of older workers.

Technological Innovation

The introduction of new technologies is changing the workplace. The high-tech industry's share of the Gross Domestic Product has grown from 5.5% in 1990 to 6.2% in 1996 (Atkinson and Court 1998). Although this change is significant, the rise in the use of computers and other advanced technology in virtually all sectors of the economy has had, potentially, the biggest impact on workers. Many of the new jobs in goods production and distribution are office jobs, where the most commonly used tools are computers, fax machines, and copiers. Almost half (46%) of all workers used a computer at work in 1993 (U.S. Bureau of the Census 1993). Computers are more likely to be used by workers with at least some college education, managers, and professionals. Older workers, however, are less likely to use computers, with only 37% of older workers using computers at work. In addition, only 20% of older workers have computers in their homes, and only 56% of those with computers at home actually use them, compared with 34% of workers aged 35–44 years with computers in the home, of whom 68% actually use them (U.S. Bureau of the Census 1993).

Various arguments have been advanced about the impact of technological development on individual workers. The data have suggested that the organizational structures of computerized workplaces are different from those of non-computerized workplaces (fewer hierarchical levels, less formal, with a bifurcated workforce) and vary in worker control and autonomy as a function of the specific organizational context. In addition, jobs at the top (managers and professionals) tend to be "upskilled," whereas jobs at the bottom of the ladder may experience some de-skilling (Burris 1998). Given the existing research on worker control and on skill discretion, these aspects of technological innovation could have an impact on worker health. Potential decreases in work capacity among some older workers and the reality of limited exposure to computer technology among many older workers combine to raise concerns about the ability of older workers to quickly adapt to technological changes. However, empirical study may provide evidence to the contrary.

Part-Time Employment

Older workers are more likely to work part time or reduced hours compared with younger workers. Although most (90 percent) part-time workers are not contingent workers (temporary, time limited), they share some of the same work conditions as contingent workers, including lower wages and fewer benefits than their "permanent" counterparts receive (U.S. General Accounting Office 1991).

There are several studies of the relationship of part-time work to health. Ross and Mirowsky (1995) examined the reciprocal effects of employment on health and health on employment in a longitudinal study of workers aged 20–64. They found that although full-time employment predicted a slower decline in health over time, part-time employment was unrelated to health. On the other hand, in a study of 2,672 workers in Texas who were aged 55 or older, Blau et al. (1983) found that part-time workers—both male and female—reported more physical health problems, and higher depression scores, than full-time workers, although the gap narrowed at older ages. This study, however, used cross-sectional data, and the change with age may reflect the reciprocal effects of health on employment status and work schedule, with less healthy workers leaving the labor force or reducing their hours. The relationship between part-time employment and older workers' health status needs further exploration.

Concurrent Social Roles

Employment cannot be understood in isolation; individual workers are also involved in other social roles that have consequences for their health and well-being. Research in the life course tradition has identified a range of social roles occupied by older adults, including paid employment, but also including significant investments of time in caregiving and volunteer work (Moen 1996). These social roles are key components of older Americans' productivity, particularly women (Herzog and Morgan 1992). They are also potential sources of both stressors and resources that may be associated with older workers' health. For example, Moen, Robison, and Dempster-McClain (1995) found that women in their 50s and 60s who were currently caregiving reported a higher sense of mastery than their counterparts who were not currently caregivers.

In a similar vein, the research on multiple roles has generally found that men and women with more roles tend to be in better health. Further, the health of individuals who are employed but do not occupy another major social role is more strongly affected by work conditions (see Barnett et al. 1995).[3] Thus, medical sociologists need to know more about the varied roles taken by older workers and the association of other major roles with health and illness outcomes.

Emerging Health and Illness Issues and Research Questions

As we enter the 21st century, we face a society unlike any we have seen before, with a significant proportion of the U.S. population over the age of 55 and an increasing proportion of the older population actively engaged in paid employment. As sociologists, we are provided a pressing opportunity to further explore emerging health and illness issues for an aging workforce. Does employment help to keep people healthy, or do health limitations keep certain older Americans out of the labor force? What are the consequences of the service economy for older workers? Is a job in the service sector a good fit for postretirement employment, or does it contribute to lower well-being? Is the rise in part-time employment among older workers driven by the changing economy, or by the needs and wishes of individuals seeking only a limited engagement with the workplace? How does the workplace respond to older workers? How does employment fit with the other social roles traditionally occupied by older Americans—caregivers for kin and others, volunteers, grandparents? Do the changing work experiences of older Americans contribute to happier, healthier, and more productive older years or to poorer functioning and poorer health? Medical sociology can help provide the answers to these questions related to working in the new millennium.

Notes

[1] "older workers" includes all workers age 55 and older

[2] Calculated from Table No. 682 from U.S. Bureau of the Census (1985) and Table 1, United States, from U.S. Bureau of the Census (1990).

[3] The one exception to this is parenting young children, suggesting that the stresses associated with parenting young children may outweigh the benefits associated with multiple roles.

References

Atkinson, Robert D. and Randolph D. Court. 1998. *The New Economy Index: Understanding America's Economic Transformation.* Washington, DC: The Progressive Policy Institute Technology, Innovation and the New Economy Project. Retrieved 27 December 2000, from the World Wide Web: www.neweconomyindex.org/

Barnett, R. C., S. W. Raudenbush, T. T. Brennan, J. H. Pleck, and N. L. Marshall. 1995. "Change in Job and Marital Experiences and Change in Psychological Distress: A Longitudinal Study of Dual-Earner Couples." *Journal of Personality and Social Psychology* 69:839–50.

Blau, Z. S., G. T. Oser, and R. C. Stephens. 1983. "Older Workers: Current Status and Future Prospects." *Research in Sociology of Work: Peripheral Workers* 2:101–124.

Burris, B. H. 1998. "Computerization of the Workplace." *Annual Review of Sociology* 24:141–57.

Commonwealth Fund. 1993. *The Untapped Resource: The Final Report of the Americans over 55 at Work Program*. New York: The Fund.

Dwyer, C. J., and D. C. Ganster. 1991. "The effect of Job Demands and Control on Employee Attendance and Satisfaction." *Journal of Organizational Behavior* 12:595–608.

Han, S. and P. Moen. 1998. "Clocking Out: Multiplex time in Retirement." *Cornell Employment and Family Careers Institute*. BLCC Working Paper #98-03. Ithaca, NY: Cornell University.

Hayward, M. D., W. R. Grady, M. A. Hardy, and D. Sommers. 1989. "Occupational Influences on Retirement, Disability, and Death." *Demography* 26(3):393–409.

Herzog, A. R., and J. N. Morgan. 1992. "Age and Gender Differences in the Value of Productive Activities: Four Different Approaches." *Research on Aging* 14(2): 169–98.

Karasek, R. A. 1979. "Job Demands, Job Decision Latitude, and Mental Strain: Implications for Job Redesign." *Administrative Science Quarterly* 24:285–307.

Karasek, R. and T. Theorell. 1990. *Healthy Work*. New York: Basic Books.

Kinsella, K. and Y. J. Gist. 1995. *IPC/95-2 Older Workers, Retirement, and Pensions: A Comparative International Chartbook*. Washington, DC: U.S. Department of Commerce, Bureau of the Census.

LaRocco, J. M., J. S. House, and J. R. P. French, Jr. 1980. "Social Support, Occupational Stress, and Health." *Journal of Health and Social Behavior* 21:202–18.

Marshall, N. L. and R. C. Barnett. 1992. "Work-Related Support among Women in Caregiving Occupations." *Journal of Community Psychology* 20:36–42.

Marshall, N. L., A. Sayer, and R. C. Barnett. 1997. "The Changing Workforce, Job Stress and Psychological Distress." *Journal of Occupational Health Psychology* 2:99–107.

Moen, P. 1996. "A Life Course Perspective on Retirement, Gender, and Well-Being." *Journal of Occupational Health Psychology* 1:131–44.

Moen, P., J. Robison, and D. Dempster-McClain. 1995. "Caregiving and Women's Well-Being: A Life Course Approach." *Journal of Health and Social Behavior* 36:259–73.

Muntaner, C., W. M. Eaton, and R. Garrison. 1993. "Dimensions of the Psychosocial Work Environment in a Sample of the US Metropolitan Population." *Work and Stress* 7(4):351–63.

National Institute for Occupational Safety and Health. 1996. *National Occupational Research Agenda*. Washington, DC: U.S. Government Printing Office.

Ross, E. E. and J. Mirowsky. 1995. "Does Employment Affect Health?" *Journal of Health and Social Behavior* 36(3):230–43.

Ross, C. E. and M. Van Willigen. 1997. "Education and the Quality of Life." *Journal of Health and Social Behavior* 38(3):275–97.

Staats, S., C. Partlo, M. Armstrong-Stassen, and L. Plimpton. 1994. "Older Working Widows: Present and Expected Experiences of Stress and Quality of Life in Comparison to Married Workers." Pp. 181–195 in *Job Stress in a Changing Workforce: Investigating Gender, Diversity and Family Issues*, edited by G. P. Keita and J. J. Hurrell, Jr. Washington, DC: American Psychological Association.

Sterns, H. L. 1995. "The Aging Worker in a Changing Environment: Organizational and Individual Issues." *Journal of Vocational Behavior* 47:248–68.

U.S. Bureau of the Census. 1985. *Statistical Abstract of the United States*: 1986.

U.S. Bureau of Census, 1990. *1970 Census Data*. Retrieved 27 December 2000, from Database C90STF3C1, Summary Level: Nation, on the World Wide Web: http://www.census.gov/cdrom/lookup.

U.S. Bureau of the Census. 1993. *Table B. Use of Computers at Home, School, and Work by Persons 18 years and Older*: October 1993. Retrieved 27 December 2000, from the World Wide Web: http://www.census.gov/popu-.gov/population/socdemo/computer/compuseb.txt

U.S. General Accounting Office. 1991. *Workers at Risk: Increased Numbers in Contingent Employment Lack Insurance, Other Benefits*. Report to the Chairman, Subcommittee on Employment and Housing: Committee on Government operations, House of Representatives, Washington, DC: U.S. General Accounting Office.

The Caregivers' Perspective

Emily K. Abel

Much of the literature on aging emphasizes the strains of caring for an elder. We have a hierarchy of care in the United States—care for a long-term spouse is obligatory, care for a demented parent admirable, care for a developmentally disabled adult child, necessary. But care for an aged aunt or a neighbor is either saintly or suspect. The long, thin hierarchy of care goes straight down the generations. The extent of responsibility women now take for elders with frail health is relatively new historically—people died more quickly much younger in the early part of this century. As the women in Emily Abel's research show, a sense of responsibility for the health and safety of elders easily conflicts with concern for their autonomy and quality of life.

Abel provides an important corrective to the concept of "caregiver burden" embraced by gerontologists. Like some earlier works, Abel finds that a strong bond overrides the burden, love outweighs the loss. For these caregivers, protecting dignity meant maintaining pretense. Otherwise failing memory, loss of function, and dependence might become visible and mortifying. Caregivers learn new ways to cope with emotions, though not without difficulty and often without professional validation. Look carefully at these caregivers' statements and think how you might assess the strains and rewards of caregiving.

When we hear women talk about the experience of caring for elderly parents, it is clear that caregiving does not conform to the classic distinction between instrumental tasks and affective relations. Caregivers try to provide love as well as labor, "caring about" while "caring for" (Graham 1983; Ungerson 1983). . . . Researchers frequently define caregivers in terms of the tasks they fulfill because tasks are the feature of caregiving that can be quantified most easily. This chapter will explore the various ways caregivers themselves understand their endeavors.

Not surprisingly, the importance that women in this study accorded to chores depended partly on the amount they performed. Women whose parents required few services or who had delegated the most difficult chores to paid helpers tended to speak dismissively of the tasks involved in care. The following are two representative comments by women who had hired aides to help tend their mothers with Alzheimer's disease:

> The direct care isn't really anything. Anyone can dress, give medication. What is the big deal? That is physical. The hardest thing is talking to someone who no longer can respond, where there is no reaching with one another.

From "The Caregivers' Perspective," as it appears in *Who Cares for the Elderly: Public Policy and the Experiences of Adult Daughters* by Emily K. Abel. Reprinted by permission of Temple University Press.

> That's the part that really hurts. The instrumental kinds of things—finding places and buying her things—that's not what I find so difficult about caring for her. What I find the difficult part is coming to terms with the course of a human being's life at this point.

Women without onerous practical responsibilities occasionally saw helping with household tasks as a way to escape what they considered the more emotionally demanding aspects of care. One woman described visits to her mother's home: "I start cleaning her house the minute I go there, making food, cooking things in her refrigerator, making the food that's rotting away. I'm not my best self. I find that I do things rather than talk to her." Women who cared for seriously impaired parents with little outside assistance were far more likely to focus on concrete tasks. One of the five women living alone with parents reported, "My day is filled up with little chores—non stop, no break until the night, when I fall asleep in front of the television." A second woman, interviewed a few weeks after the death of her father, described the daily grind in a similar way: " A typical day was complete drudgery, from the time I got up in the morning until I went to bed."

Nevertheless, even women whose days were consumed by a range of chores stressed other aspects of the caregiving experience. When asked to estimate the number of hours they devoted to caregiving tasks, most women responded that it would be impossible to make such a calculation, explaining that they remained preoccupied with their parents' well-being even when not actually rendering instrumental assistance. In their eyes, caregiving was a boundless, all-encompassing activity, rather than a clearly demarcated set of discrete tasks. The dominant element in caregiving was their overall sense of responsibility for their parents' lives, not particular chores.

Responsibility

Because the phrase "filial responsibility" appears frequently in the writings of policy analysts, it is important to understand how caregivers themselves defined this term. When some women said that they felt responsible for their parents, they meant that they had taken charge of decisions affecting their parents' lives. Some still were pondering decisions they had made months and occasionally years before, and they used the interviews as opportunities to reassess their choices.

But the meaning of responsibility typically extended much farther. Once women had begun to make decisions on their parents' behalf, they felt accountable not just for the consequences of these decisions but for virtually every aspect of their parents' lives. Several believed that they should be able to protect their parents from all physical harm. Two, for example, viewed themselves as culpable when their parents hurt themselves in falls, although they acknowledged that they could not possibly have prevented such mishaps. One woman, interviewed a few months after she and her husband had moved into her mother's house, remarked: "I felt really bad one day. I came home from work, and she'd gone in her bedroom, and I heard her fall down. It was such a shock because I thought, if I'm living here, I can protect her from this. It was so shocking to just hear her fall, and I was 20 feet away, just in the next room and not be able to do anything." Three others faulted themselves for not having been able to halt or at least slow the progress of their parents' disease. A woman whose mother suffered from episodes of depression stated:

> When she goes to the hospital, I seem to think there should have been something I could have done to stop that from happening—that I should have better control of the situation; I should have called the doctor sooner; I should have gotten her more medicine; I should have told the other doctors to stay out of things; I should have been able to help her more, somehow.

. . . Several women considered themselves answerable for any deficiencies in medical or social service programs they arranged. And in some cases the daughters' sense of responsibility encompassed their parents' emotional as well as physical well-being. Although their parents suffered from intractable physical or mental health problems and had experienced losses that could not be repaired, the daughters believed that they should be able to make their parents happy.

How can we account for the overwhelming sense of responsibility these women felt? Nancy Chodorow argues that because women in this society fail to differentiate themselves from others, they often assume responsibility even for events they could not possibly control (Chodorow 1974). According to Elaine M. Brody (1985), women caring for aging parents measure themselves against the all-embracing care they received as children. Hilary Graham (1985:35) offers a very different explanation. Women consider themselves responsible for anything that befalls the recipients of their care because caregiving is defined as a private endeavor. In the absence of governmental responsibility for care of dependents, "experiences become personalized with problems seen as self-inflicted and failures seen as a cause for self-recrimination and blame."

The chasm between women's overriding sense of responsibility and their ultimate powerlessness is one of the major difficulties caregivers experienced. One woman recalled: "In the beginning, I cried every night. Because you feel so powerless to do anything. And I think that's the worst thing, to see a person who's been very active, very personable, and all of a sudden, right in front of your eyes, they're just totally deteriorating." Policymakers frequently exhort adult children to display greater responsibility toward their aging parents. We will see, however, that the women in this study frequently expressed a desire to do just the opposite—to reduce their sense of involvement in their parents' lives and lower their expectations of what they could accomplish.

Dignity

Daughters also refused to define caregiving as a series of concrete chores because their primary objective was to preserve their parents' dignity. In a study of daughters caring for aging parents, Barbara Bowers (1990:279) concluded that women "conceptualized their caregiving work in terms of purpose, rather than tasks. The adult daughters . . . placed a priority on protective care (protecting or preserving the parent's sense of self and the parent-child relationship). This was especially true when their parents had either a mild or moderate form of dementia." This analysis illuminates the experiences of the women I interviewed. . . . Many women had their own reasons for seeking to protect their parents' individuality and self image. Some also invoked the authority of experts to support their definitions of good care. Books and lectures counseled them to preserve their parents' sense of competence and uniqueness and not compel them to confront their disabilities. The women interpreted this injunction in various ways.

When parents suffered little or no mental impairment, daughters defined their goal as respecting their parents' autonomy and encouraging them to remain in control of their lives. Thus, although some caregivers tried to protect their parents from all hazards, others deferred to their parents' judgment and refrained from intervening, even when the parents placed themselves in dangerous situations.

When dementia progressed, women found it more difficult to view their parents as self-governing and to leave major decisions in their hands. The daughters thus increasingly viewed their mission as pretending that nothing had changed. One woman who spoke emphatically about the need to respect her mother's dignity explained that this meant preventing her mother from realizing that she had lost control over decisions affecting her life: "I let her think she had made the decision, or that she was taking care of herself. I don't ever let her feel that she couldn't survive if she wasn't here with me. To some people, that would be a comfort, but not to someone like my mother. If she could really come back and look and see, it would be the worst thing in the world." The daughters tried to conceal other changes in their parents' status. Women whose parents had been professionals sought to create the illusion that the parents continued to command the respect they previously had enjoyed. One woman was pleased when an aide was willing to cater to her father's professional pride, despite his severely impaired mental capacities: "This man makes an effort to be sensitive, and he is very willing to say, 'Yes, sir;' and 'Doctor this' and 'doctor that,' kind of play to my father's authoritarianism." Another woman asserted: "My mother had been on the faculty at the university. I didn't want her ever to know that she is losing her memory, which she is; that she is losing her hearing, which she is; because her conception of herself is someone still on the faculty. I won't allow her to see that anything is wrong."

Women caring for mothers who had been housewives encouraged their mothers to believe that they still could make valuable contributions to household services. One woman discussed her mother's visits to her house:

> Part of what I try and do when she's here is make sure that I have accumulated things she can do so she feels useful. For example, I may just leave a pile of laundry totally unfolded, because that's something she can do and do easily. Last time she came, I was trying to iron, and she insisted she wanted to iron, so I let her; and she ironed. I will let her do whatever I feel she can do. Sometimes it interferes because it's not exactly what I had planned to do that day, but that's the way it is.

When this woman returned from the hospital after a serious illness, she worked to foster the pretence that her mother could care for her in meaningful ways:

> By the time I came home, I could cope with her trying to take care of me. She could bring me a cup of coffee and she could bring me some food, because I made sure everything was prepared. She had the feeling she was helping because I set it up, knowing what she could do, and I think that helped her. I could just as well have gotten up and gotten a drink as have her bring me a drink, but she felt better because she was bringing me the drinks.

But women not only tried to prevent their parents from acknowledging their disabilities. Those who believed that the disease had ravaged their parents' sense of personhood viewed themselves as guardians of the people they remembered. One woman recalled a ritual she conducted during the two years she tended her mother, who suffered from Alzheimer's disease: "I kissed her goodnight every night, but it was never returned. I always felt like I'm just doing it because when she was herself, she liked that."

. . . Two women asserted that caregiving was a means of expressing loyalty to the mothers they had known. Said one:

> I loved my mother a lot when I was growing up. . . . When her memory went so poor, I realized that I really loved the lady she was. This is a different lady. This is not the mother that was, this is someone else. I can't really say that I love this person that is now, but what I do love is the memory of the person that was before, and because of that love, I have a tremendous sense of obligation to her, and I'll take care of her till the day she dies. Sometimes there's guilt involved because I don't love her in the way that I did. And sometimes I'm sad about it because I really remember the way that she was, and that's a curse and a blessing, at the same time.

The other commented: "I try to validate some of the things she tried to raise, ideals in me, things that she tried to teach us as we were growing up, that it was important to care about other people." By acting in accordance with the ideals her mother had sought to instill in her, this woman reaffirmed her bond with a mother she feared she had lost.

Finally, daughters viewed themselves as promoting their parents' self-respect when they helped their parents conceal evidence of physical frailty. . . . A key reason some women hired aides was that they did not want their parents to be compelled to reveal the extent of their physical impairments to their daughters. In addition, many daughters did not insist that their parents use walkers or wheelchairs, even when their parents had serious problems with ambulation. In a society that places a high value on independence, weakness of any kind is considered shameful; caregivers promote the dignity of recipients by hiding all signs of dependence.

Medical Diagnosis

In trying to foster their parents' dignity, the daughters in this study were following one line of advice frequently offered to caregivers. But daughters of parents with dementia also received a contradictory message—to define their relatives in terms of their diseases. Such popular advice books as *The 36-Hour Day* (Mace and Rabins 1981) stress the importance of viewing the behavior of demented adults as symptoms of disease rather than as deliberate acts. Women whose parents suffered from some form of dementia thus faced a problem that has been common since the rise of scientific medicine at the end of the nineteenth century and the new understanding of disease specificity. To what extent should patients be viewed as a configuration of symptoms and to what extent as whole and unique individuals? Because a diagnosis of dementia can call into question an individual's sense of self, this issue emerges in particularly urgent form for their caregivers. This section thus will focus on women caring for parents with dementia.

Diagnosis typically follows an evaluation by a physician. In most cases, family members initiate the process of obtaining an evaluation. One daughter in this study, however, had not even considered the possibility of dementia until she saw her mother's insurance form and learned that her mother had sought a consultation for memory loss.

Obtaining the diagnosis marked a turning point for many women. Three who had hoped that their parents had problems that could be treated (such as depression or alcohol or drug-induced dementia) were shocked to learn that their parents were suffering from an irreversible form of dementia. The reactions of two others revealed the stigma attached to Alzheimer's disease; they stated that they were relieved to learn that their parents had other types of dementia, although there still was no possibility of a cure.

But the precise designation was less important than learning that something was the matter. Although the diagnosis often confirmed daughters' worst fears, it also could be a source of reassurance. One woman explained why she and her siblings had insisted that their mother receive an evaluation:

> We suspected, and we didn't think we had a right to suspect without a professional opinion. . . . We used to swap stories of "guess what mother did now?" and it wasn't cruel. [The diagnosis] reconfirms that it's not you, because sometimes when you're in with someone who's not dealing with things properly, you begin to feel: "Was it me? Did I hear that? I don't believe she said that."

A second woman also initially had considered it improper to question her mother's mental capacities: "We just didn't know what was going on. She would say things that were strange, and I thought, 'My mama has really been very bright and now. . . .' I didn't say the word stupid, but you get the idea. I really thought that was not the respectable thing to say because it was my mother." Once their parents were labeled sick, women could trust their own instincts, make sense of their parents' behavior, and consider the best way to provide care.

After receiving a diagnosis, most women tried to learn more about the nature of their parents' impairments, seeking information from books, friends, support groups, and professionals. As their knowledge grew, many increasingly interpreted behavior in light of the disease. Some began to associate their parents with other victims of dementia. In answer to questions about their own parents, they discussed adults with dementia in general, occasionally referring to "them" or "these people." One woman lamented her inability to spend more time talking with her mother "because this is what an Alzheimer's disease patient needs." Another woman explained why she had found the right aide for her father: "She is aware of how to take care of Alzheimer's people. It would be a real problem for some if they didn't understand Alzheimer's disease and the nature of it and how people are when they have that disease. She knows never to confront my dad head on, that there are other ways of getting him to do what you want." The women also used their new understanding to develop techniques for dealing with their parents themselves. One woman explained how she coped with her father's repetitive questions:

> His memory is so poor that he'll ask me the same questions over again, like, "What are you doing in your life now?" and "Do you have a job?" So I have to answer him a lot. And one thing I feel proud of myself is that, because I understand his situation, I don't put a lot of energy into answering the questions, I mean I just say the same thing over and over again. . . . I don't expect him to understand. I just answer it so he'll get the answer at that moment, but I don't expect him to remember five minutes later, and I expect it to come up again and again and again.

Another woman realized that, because her mother had the same disease as members of a day care center she observed, the daughter could learn techniques from the center staff:

> I learned so much about what must be the fright or the fear that the old people feel, the threat at the loss, even if they don't know what they're losing or what they lost. There's something that's so interesting that happens. If there's stress in the room, they pick it up like children. And what I saw at the day care center were the workers always touching the people. They give them a hug, or a pat, or hold their hand, or a kiss. Lovely, lovely. And I've learned to do that with my mother. When she's real agitated or upset, if I just sit down and put my arm around her, she calms right down.

Several women also claimed that information about the genesis of behaviors helped them to gain greater control over their own emotions. Thus one woman reported:

> We always viewed my mother as somewhat crazy and tried to get her to see a psychiatrist, but to have it be a clear dementia in some ways makes it easier to relate to her. Even though some of the things she does it's hard not to take personally, it's clearly not personal and doesn't have anything to do with who I am. . . . My coping mechanism had always been to distance myself, but there was always some doubt that maybe that was invalid, it always got to me eventually. This way, it's objective, so there is no way it could get to me.

When caregivers learned that their parents' actions were unintentional, some of their anger faded. One woman recalled:

> I took [my mother] to the doctor and he's the one that told me about the book, *The 36-Hour Day*. I went and got that book, I read it from cover to cover. And after I read that book, I started to understand some of the things that were happening to me. I started to understand why it is when she calls me and I would have her come here that she would want to go home again. It was because she felt totally uncomfortable, she wasn't in surroundings that she's used to, she would forget where rooms were. Just all these things started to come together, and I started to understand. . . .

Not all women found it . . . easy to translate information about dementia into appropriate emotional responses. Arlie Russell Hochschild (1975:289) has coined the phrase "feeling rules" to describe rules that "define what we should feel in various circumstances." An understanding of the relationship between parental behavior and disease processes convinced women that they should not be angry; but many acknowledged the difficulty of conforming their feelings to the knowledge they had gained. Looking back on the two years she spent caring for her mother, one woman stated: "I wish it hadn't upset me. I wish that I could have coped with it. I wish I could have just said, 'She can't help it,' and that was that, but I couldn't. I couldn't do it." Another woman noted that it was "hard to put insights into practice." Nevertheless, a medical label did help women gain at least some of the emotional distance they considered critical.

Caregivers also noted the importance of learning what to expect. A diagnosis of dementia leaves many questions unanswered: How rapidly will the disease progress? What symptoms will emerge? To what extent will the individual's disease follow the widely recognized stages? Nevertheless, most women believed that the diagnosis dispelled some of the uncertainty surrounding their parents' care and enabled them to make preparations for the future. One woman remarked: "At the hospital, there was a wonderful doctor, and he said: 'Watch for these signs. When you come to pick her up and she has to brush her hair or brush her teeth, she's beginning to deteriorate. And then watch for her doing this and wandering off and not being able to get home.' So we watched for all the signs to come." Because many women insisted that their parents' illness had caught them by surprise, their ability to make plans gave them a sense of greater control over their lives.

Finally, women who attached a medical label to their parents found it easier to consult physicians about a broad range of issues. Aside from prescribing medications to control agitation, there was little that medical science could do in most cases. Physicians could neither cure the disease nor slow its progress. As one woman said, "You can't put the mind back." Nevertheless, many women sought guidance from physicians for problems that required human, not technical solutions. Women invoked physician recommendations to explain such varied steps as consulting a psychiatrist, joining a support group, enrolling their parents in day care centers, bringing their parents to live in the same city as themselves, and hiring aides and attendants.

But it is important to note that the comments of several women revealed that women were motivated less by trust in professional judgment than by their desire to use physicians to bolster their own authority. They sought professional advice in order to justify actions they already had decided were correct. Asked whether she had considered placing her father in a nursing home, one woman responded:

> I don't think he's quite ready yet, and I don't want to move him until he really is, because I think once the move is made, that will be it, that will be where he'll remain. And I just feel that right now, it's just much more pleasant for him to be where he is. This is why I think I've been so insistent on finding one of these geriatric assessment services and doing the tests again, to try to get someone else to say to me, "He's not ready to go yet. He's not ready to move yet." I just wanted to put that burden, that responsibility on someone else. I'm halfway through one of these assessments, and they agree that he should stay where he is for now. And I'm relieved to hear them say that. I would like to keep him where he is as long as I can.

. . . Several other women relied on doctors in order to avoid conflicts with their parents. . . . Caregivers often must assert authority over parents and prevent them from engaging in certain activities traditionally considered basic to adulthood in our society. When physicians recommended that parents stop driving or managing their own money, the daughters were relieved of responsibility for the decision. And one woman used a consultation with a physician to puncture her brother's denial about their father's condition:

> My brother kept insisting that my father's just having anxiety attacks. So I made my brother go to the doctor with my father. And he sat and watched how his father could not remember to do three things that the doctor had told him to do and how he couldn't do things properly. And he watched the whole process, and then he was willing to accept the fact that he was really sick, that there was something wrong with him. Then my brother was willing to set up a conservatorship.

In short, a diagnostic label served women in various ways—enabling them to muster resources for dealing with their parents' problems, helping them develop techniques for coping with bizarre or troublesome behavior; permitting them to gain critical emotional distance from their parents, and enabling them to rely on the authority of physicians. Nevertheless, the women in this study resisted reducing their parents to a set of symptoms. If they "watched for all the signs to come," they also continued to respond to their parents as individuals. One woman commented:

> I've just realized that there are things [my mother] can't grasp. My dad set up a trust in his will when he was ill, and I explained it to her so many times over so many months, and she still doesn't understand it. My husband finally just said, "Listen, let's just tell her it's just complicated legal stuff and you're never going to understand it, and just don't worry about it. Your husband took good care of you, and you don't need to worry about any of it." But my first impulse is always to treat her the way I've always treated her. I still try and get her preferences for things. She can't try on anything in stores anymore, it's just too hard, so I just charge everything and take it home so she can try it on. I kind of say, "Well, which one do you think looks better on you, and which colors do you like best?" I'd also like to ask her advice. I think in matters of the heart she probably could still advise me. She just can't balance her checkbook very well.

As this woman struggled to accept the fact that her mother's mental capacities had diminished, she remained attentive to her mother's wishes and sought to convince herself that her mother still possessed wisdom. Another woman described her determination not to treat her mother like every other victim of Alzheimer's disease, even as the progression of the disease threatened to destroy her mother's uniqueness:

> What I find difficult is trying to figure out what's best for her, which is what a parent does for a small child, but there are many more clear directives for a parent than there are in this situation. And it's hard to separate what I would want for me in that situation [from how she might] choose for herself in a former time or now. We are dealing with a person that is different from the person that I know how to make choices for. I can't easily say that my mother would like this, this, and this, based on what she appears to want, because she can't communicate. . . . I was clear that I wanted her to have as much of her own furniture in her place around her as possible, because furniture was a big part of her life, and she loved antiques, and she got her self worth from her surroundings. There was a three-week delay in getting her furniture to where she was staying, and she'd forgotten it all. . . .

Jaber F. Gubrium and Robert L. Lynott (1987:271) argue that medical assessments of demented adults serve to construct as well as detect disease. Once evaluations have been conducted, caregivers tend to "see impairment everywhere." But a study by Betty Risteen Hasselkus (1988) suggests that family members are less easily swayed by medical labels. The caregivers she interviewed occasionally used their special knowledge of elderly relatives to cast doubt on their diagnoses. A few women I spoke to pointed to faculties their parents retained in order to question a medical diagnosis. One expressed doubts about whether her mother actually had Alzheimer's disease because she still could play the violin so well. Some who accepted the diagnosis nevertheless argued that certain behaviors experts attributed to disease actually were exaggerations of lifelong personality traits. The comments of one woman illustrate the difficulty of determining which behaviors should be attributed to a disease and which to a parent's distinctive personality:

> When my mother's brother was visiting, my father had no idea who this man was, but he was quite indignant that this strange man had come to visit. My mother left the car lights on in the car; and my uncle said, "Give me the keys and I will go and turn them off," but my father said no. He told my mother that she had to go out, that she was the one who left them on, and she was going to have to turn

> them off. This kind of behavior was a side of him always, but it was not always so naked in front of my uncle. He would not have been totally unconscious about it. He would have veiled it in the past. But he never was a good person to get along with. It's hard to tell now when his personality is deteriorating. It is very difficult to tell whether or not it is the crankiness they talk about or the nastiness related to Alzheimer's disease or if it is just him.

A second woman noted that as long as she could remember, her mother had had angry outbursts, although they now seemed to take an exaggerated form. A third was uncertain that even more aberrant behavior could be classified as a disease symptom:

> The first hint that she was sick was an incident that clearly had a paranoid element because she imagined helicopters landing in her yard. But the distinction was very difficult, because she always had crazy-making behavior: For example, she changed her will and gave all her money to Harvard. It always was hard to know how much was her craziness, which always was there, and how much was a definable diagnosis. . . . She does very inappropriate things. For example, she'll say in a loud voice: "There's Helen. Don't talk to Helen; she has nothing going on upstairs." It's embarrassing. What's so funny is she might have said the same thing toned down six levels when she was more coherent. She used to say obviously embarrassing things in the middle of large groups. So in that sense it is just an exaggeration of how she is or was.

Many women also asserted that their parents' personalities transcended the disease. One woman explained why she enjoyed the time she spent with her father: "He's real sweet, he's not like sometimes Alzheimer's people get, kind of angry. He was a real sweet person to begin with, and he's still really nice. I mean, to me, he's fun, and even with his Alzheimer's, he'll say really funny things." Finally, rather than assuming that the disease had transformed their parents' personalities, three women reassessed their prior view of their parents in light of the changes that had occurred. "It's as if I've been fooled all these years," one said.

Women who emphasized their parents' uniqueness tended to be less impressed by advice books than others. One, for example, had little praise for *The 36-Hour Day*:

> There's nothing human about it. The discussions about how you pick a place are all very instrumental, and none of it deals with the concerns about how you know what's good for a person. Nobody has described to me what would be the impact on me of walking for the very first time into a nursing home, the impact of seeing these very old women who were sitting and kind of nodding. I would see *my* mother in every single one of the women, and it's very hard.

Some women considered other types of professional expertise equally irrelevant. One mentioned that her husband had suggested that she consult a geriatric specialist to give her guidance about the way to care for her father. She explained why she had demurred: "We're dealing with a uniquely strong personality." Women also gained the confidence to override physicians' advice by relying on their own intimate knowledge of their parents. Some argued that physicians, acting on the basis of universalistic knowledge, missed unique aspects of their parents' experiences. Thus one woman scoffed at a physician who recommended that she give her mother a sense of security by imposing routines on her mother's life, "My mother never has lived by routines." The recommendation most commonly rejected was that parents be placed in nursing homes. Virtually all women in the study were staunchly opposed to institutionalization. One woman who did accept a physician's counsel to put her mother in a home told an unusually harrowing story:

> My husband started getting terrible pains, just unbearable pains, and we went for months to doctors. They all said, "Your husband has terrible headaches because your mama is living with you." Finally, we went to a neurologist for my mother, and he examined her and took a CAT scan and he gave us the verdict that she had Alzheimer's. He said, "Let me tell you what that means." I will never forget those words. He said to me: "You have to put your mama in a nursing home because if you don't your marriage is at risk. Your husband is suffering very much. It's going to destroy your marriage. . . ." We ended up putting my mom in a nursing home about ten minutes away. I went to see her every day, and I couldn't bear seeing my mama in the situation they had her in. . . . I'll never forgive myself for letting her go there, but I was so desperate and my husband was getting worse. A few months later he collapsed, and then he found out that it was a brain tumor, and he had twelve and one-half hour surgery and we almost lost him. . . . The worst thing I ever did was to put her in a nursing home and not let her stay with me anymore. I was given advice by professional people that I respected. . . .

During a period of enormous stress, she had allowed the judgment of physicians and other professionals to prevail, disregarding her own knowledge about both her husband and her mother. She bitterly regretted acquiescing in professional expertise and remained convinced of the importance of personalized, as opposed to scientific, knowledge.

Role Reversal

If caregivers of persons with dementia viewed their parents simultaneously as disease victims and unique individuals, they also referred to their parents as both adults and children. A cardinal principle of gerontology is that the elderly should not be considered children; despite any disabilities they may experience, they should be accorded all the rights and privileges of other adults in our society. But Karen Lyman (1988) found that at least some staff in adult day care centers for dementia patients violate this principle; believing that demented adults degenerate by regressing to the level of young children, the staff members she observed routinely infantilized their patients. From a study of 15 women caring for frail elderly parents, Lucy Rose Fischer (1986:165) reported: "All but one of the daughters declared specifically that they had experienced a role reversal."

In this study as well, women labeled their relationships as "role reversal," said "I'm the parent now," and described the "childlike" qualities of their parents. Women used such phrases to signify that their parents depended on them for care. One commented: "The day that he couldn't find his way to my house in his car was when I felt like I had really lost my father. It was almost like a dying of my father. And it was sort of like all of a sudden, I'm the big one now, and he's the little one, and I've got to take care of him. Women who were mothers themselves reported that certain caregiving activities—tucking their parents in at night, bathing them, and hiring sitters—were reminiscent of their experiences as mothers of small children: "A couple of years ago, my mother was in the hospital, and she kept climbing out of the bed and would fall. It was very difficult. I had to tell them it was O.K. to tie her down. That was so hard for me. I remembered having to make similar decisions when my child was young. Something just has to be done. I immediately went into that mode." Women without children were convinced that they would be better equipped to give directions and make decisions if they had raised children. One said:

> My sister told me that when she was visiting here that she just went back to her days of having a toddler and treated Mom very much in the same way. She'd say, "Well, it's time for your bath now," and "Dinner's ready." Because she's raised a child, that's a posture she's more familiar with. For me, this has been a little harder because I haven't had any kids. I wonder if you find that women who

> have had children, if it's easier for them somehow.

Defining parents with dementia as children also may have enabled the women to deny some of the emotions the experience of care provoked. One woman stated: "The problems may just be me and my reactions to things. If I can try and keep the attitude that she's really just a little girl who needs to be treated gently and lovingly, then I kind of have fun with it. But if I expect her to be an adult and fend for herself, then it's much harder."

Nevertheless, all the women I interviewed emphasized the vast differences between caring for children and aging parents. Instead of fostering growth and development, they witnessed deterioration:

> When my mother first came to live with me, I thought: "Oh, this isn't going to be difficult. I can manage this, I've raised six kids." I kept seeing the relationship in terms of that, she acted very much like a 3- or 4-year-old. And, goodness, I had six children, ten grandchildren, and so I could handle this. And it wasn't the same, because with children you know they're going to grow, and you know there's a future, and with this you know it's the opposite.

Caring for the elderly also lacks familiar milestones; thus, although caregivers typically have an enormous investment in providing good care, they have few ways of evaluating their work:

> You expect small children to show progress. If small children don't show progress, then you really have to take steps to see what's wrong with them. The difference is that here there is no progress, there's only a slow deterioration, almost an invisible deterioration, but I know it's there. It's very different from taking care of kids. If you're doing a good job with kids, they move along, they progress, their world expands. My mother's world is contracting.

Women also pointed out that, although parents seek to produce socially acceptable children (see Ruddick 1982), they were not trying to mold their aging parents.

But the major reason women did not confuse parent care with child care is that . . . caregiving often revived powerful elements of the original parent-child relationship; several women reported that the emotional relationship with their parents remained unchanged. The term "role reversal" thus can be considered more an indication of women's discomfort at the inversion of responsibilities than an expression of their belief that they actually had traded places with their parents (see Brody 1985).

Reciprocity

It often is assumed that care for elderly parents is rooted in reciprocity—children repay parents for the care they received when young (see Bulmer 1987; Qureshi and Walker 1989; Ungerson 1987). The notion of reciprocity meshes with social exchange theory (Blau 1964). As Tamara Hareven (1987:73) writes, "The classic exchange along the life course is that between parents and children, based on parents' expectation of old age support in return for their investment in childbearing."

Six women in this study explained their motivation in terms of filial gratitude. Said one, "She was there for me, I'll be there for her." Another woman felt an obligation to repay her mother for services the daughter received when she already was an adult:

> She made me go back to college after I had graduated to become a teacher because I didn't take my education courses, and she came an hour and a half train ride to take care of my kids in the morning so I could go to school. It was three different trains for her. In snow and sleet, she carried food, and she cleaned my house and my windows and everything while I was in school, so I really owe her. I wanted to pay her back.

But, just as adult children do not simply reverse roles when caring for parents, so most women I interviewed did not perceive themselves as giving payment for services rendered. As noted, all discussed the enormous differences between parent care and care for children. Moreover, eight stated that they were rendering care in spite of rather than because of their treatment as children. They claimed that their parents either had given them insufficient love or had entrusted their care to outsiders, such as nannies or governesses. One woman mused, "My brother says to me, 'She was so awful to you, why are you so interested in taking such good care of her now?' and I can't really answer that."

Most women also did not believe that their parents had a special right to care because of the services they had rendered their own parents. The great majority asserted that they were the first in their families to care for elderly parents. And, just as some women said that they cared for their parents despite the poor care they had received as children, so some women claimed that their parents' treatment of their own parents constituted a negative, rather than a positive, model. One woman explained why she brought her mother with her when she moved across the country:

> We were originally from southern Germany, and my mother cared for her mother. By the time we emigrated from Germany, which was in the spring of [19]38, very late, my grandma had had a stroke, and my mother left her behind, and she ended up in a concentration camp, and she was killed, as far as we know. It was something my mother never talked about. But I certainly don't want to treat my mother the way she treated her mother.

Nor did women believe that they could expect payment in the form of services from their own children when they themselves grew old. Although two women asserted that they were setting an example for their children, most were fare less sanguine about their future. All the childless women expressed fears that they would have no one to care for them in old age. Most mothers shared these fears, either because they had sons rather than daughters or because they were convinced that all young people had rejected an ethic of care. "We're the last generation to provide this care," one woman asserted.

By emphasizing the reciprocal nature of caregiving, we miss its essential meaning. The notion of reciprocity rests on the assumption that individuals view each other as instrumental resources for discrete tasks, coming together primarily to exchange specific goods and services (see Glenn 1987; see Hartsock 1983). By contrast, writers such as Nancy Chodorow (1974) and Carol Gilligan (1982) argue that women experience themselves as embedded in social relationships and derive their sense of identity from such relationships. According to most women I spoke with, caregiving flowed from a sense of connection to their parents, not from a desire to repay services previously rendered or to make an investment in their own futures.

Appreciation

Partly because these women did not view themselves as either returning services or accumulating credit for their own old age, they believed that their care deserved appreciation. One women who recently had moved with her husband into her mother's house was dismayed to discover how desperately she sought thanks:

> I think people have told her that it's good for the kids, that we won't have to pay rent, that we'll be able to save money. So I think in some ways she didn't see that it was a sacrifice for us. . . . One day she could tell I was just upset, I was kind of banging dishes around when I was cleaning up, and it's terrible, she was saying, "Well, if you don't want to be here, you don't have to be." It was strange for me, because I realized I wanted her to be grateful, I wanted her to appreciate the sacrifice I was making. It sounds terrible. She just kind of said, "If you don't want to live here, you can leave." She's never brought it up again, but it's like she was doing us a favor. I don't like that in myself, that I want her to be grateful. I feel like a real jerk to want her to be grateful, to just kind of

> acknowledge that this isn't all fun and games and that I was happy with the life I had before, that I liked my privacy and my freedom, and it's a sacrifice.

A woman caring for a father also revealed an intense desire for appreciation:

> Once he said to me, after we had a very good day together, he said, "Thank you for everything." I cried all the way home. It touched me, because he doesn't say thank you and sometimes I don't believe that he's aware of what's happening. Just having him say that meant that he was aware, that he appreciated it. It was such a nice thing that it moved me to tears, it doesn't happen often. In fact I even had talked to a close friend of mine, "If once he'd say thank you, if he'd say thank you just once, I would feel somewhat that he was cognizant of what was going on." And it was several days after that, that he said that. So it was very poignant. It was striking at the time he said that, although he has no idea that he has turned my life absolutely upside down, that he's caused such an upheaval and disturbance to my life.

These women were not alone in receiving less gratitude than they wanted. The great majority of women in the study complained of inadequate appreciation. Some explained that, because their parents suffered from dementia, they had little conception of what was being done for them. As we have seen, some women also took pains to conceal their contributions in order to foster their parents' self-image. In addition, women noted that their parents resented their dependency and resisted all offers of help; they could not show gratitude for services that were being rendered over their objections. Finally, some women believed that their parents simply took their daughters' efforts for granted. One woman commented:

> I keep expecting her to see that it's too much for me, that's what I'd like. My aunt and uncle do that. They fuss and fume and take care of me and say, "This is just too much for you." But the more I do for mother, the more she seems to expect. I'd like even a little concern that I'm doing too much. One day I was lugging all these groceries up the stairs, and she looked at me and said, "Smile when I smile at you." Every time you look at her she smiles, and she wants a smile back. And I didn't smile. I said, "I'm tired" and her response was, "Well, sit down." She thinks it's that easy, you just sit down. But it's not that easy.

A second woman voiced a similar complaint: "From time to time she expresses her appreciation, but on the whole I think she expects it. She expects me to be there for her. I think she does appreciate what my husband does, and she says thank you to him. I think she thinks I'm her daughter, and I should just be there for her. Women like these tended to interpret their parents' failure to appreciate their efforts as evidence of their own worthlessness in their parents' eyes.

Responses to Care

When women assessed their responses to caregiving, they agreed that stress was a major component. I have noted that stress consumes much of the attention of students of informal caregiving. Comments about stress also were constant refrains in the interviews I conducted with caregivers. As Allan Young (1980:133) writes: "'Stress' and ancillary concepts such as 'coping' have permeated everyday discourse. . . . Information on stress is now widely available to lay audiences . . . through frequent articles in mass circulation magazines, self-help books, television programs, lectures, and pharmaceutical advertising for vitamins and sleep preparations." Although the women were not asked directly about the stresses of caregiving, nine volunteered that they had consulted therapists to help cope with the problems of caregiving, and another commented that she was considering doing so. Twenty-four women also were members of support groups, where they discussed the strains involved in rendering care. Several women attributed physical problems to stress. Three stated that the stress of caregiving created fatigue, and three others claimed that it contributed to eating problems. Four women believed that stress had precipitated even more serious health problems, including chronic back pain and cancer. Two additional women wondered if stress had exacerbated their difficulties with infertility. Women who lived apart from their parents described physical symptoms that occurred either while visiting their parents or after returning home. One woman, for example, remarked:

> I had a bad experience a couple of months ago. Boy, it taught me a lesson. I thought my mother would enjoy going to the arboretum. They had a special spring show of flowers, and I wanted to see them myself. The only problem is that it was 50 minutes in the car. I didn't realize that I couldn't sit in the car with her for 50 minutes. She talked on and on, and she says the same things over and over and over again. What happens to me when I am stressed out or anxious is I get very sleepy. I almost couldn't make it home. There were times on the freeway coming back where I thought, "If I don't pull over and take a nap, I'm going to fall asleep." If she drove, I would have said, "Please drive." I really almost couldn't make it. I'd never gotten that bad before. I got her home and I sat in the car and took a little nap before I came back home, which was only another ten minutes. I realized I can't do that anymore.

Another woman noted: "I find the day is better if I visit mother in the morning and then go about my business, and then I come home refreshed. But the majority of days I go toward the end of the day, and then I come home beaten because it takes a lot out of me. I normally am very organized, but I am not then. I drive very carefully because I'm just not all there." A woman interviewed a few days after institutionalizing a mother with whom she had lived for two years reported:

> When I woke up, I thought, oh, another day, and when I went to bed it was the same thing. All day I could keep busy, coping, but at night it was terrible. It got to the point where I was not myself anymore. One of my daughters said, "You were just driving a car with empty," and that's the way I felt. Any little thing that happened was a major catastrophe to me, and I'm not that way. I'm an easy-going person. Usually I'm not a worrier, but I couldn't relax. I was becoming uptight, neurotic. I felt someone else was coming inside and controlling me.

But, if stress was a key concern of women in this study, most insisted that it did not define their experience of caregiving. When asked how life would be different without the responsibility of care, one woman caring for her mother responded:

> I think I could plan more trips. I like to travel. I could think about moving away, which I would never do now, moving to a quieter, simpler community. I guess I'd eventually feel less burdened. But I also think that I'd miss her very much, and her presence and all the cherished moments that you have. All the family occasions and the times you want to share with a parent, that you want them to be there to see and be a part of.

Another commented: "I'd have a lot more free time and a lot more freedom of movement. I think I'd feel a lot more carefree. But, you know, it's like this is thinking back to the past, because in the future, if I'm not caring for her it means that she's not well enough for me to care for her anymore, and so I'm sure there's going to be a lot more sadness mixed in with it." And a third remarked: "It would be one less responsibility but also one less joy. I am just lucky to have her." To women such as these, a one-sided focus on the problems of caregiving denied the value of their parents' lives. They viewed caregiving as the inevitable consequence of having elderly parents and an expression of their attachment to their parents. As a result, it was a privilege as well as a burden.

When asked if caregiving offered satisfactions, a few women laughed dismissively. One angrily retorted, "You don't expect rewards for caring for your mother." Nevertheless, most women identified at least some gratifications from caregiving. Although many women said that they felt uncertain about how best to proceed when they first assumed caregiving responsibilities, four said that caregiving eventually provided them with an opportunity to display competence. Several women also took pride in making an important difference in their parents' lives. A woman who was interviewed shortly after she placed her mother in a nursing home assessed her contribution this way:

> I think I helped her just to retain her dignity a little longer, just to hang onto it a little bit. She was always a very dignified lady. It's sort of like seeing your mother stripped naked when they don't care for themselves. Their clothes are dirty; they have this look on their face of total rejection. It's like seeing them standing there naked. So I was able to, in a way, clothe her for two years.

If some women had grandiose expectations about what they could accomplish, this woman believed that she had fulfilled her desire to foster her mother's self-respect. In addition, caregiving enabled women to reaffirm their sense of themselves as good people. For example: "I don't know if I would be doing all this if I didn't get some sense that I'm helping and that I'm worthwhile for doing it, that I'm a good person, that I'm someone that can be relied on." Some women asserted that caregiving was a humanizing experience. Said one, "You gain a lot of wisdom and insight and compassion for other people's suffering and problems." Another commented: "I've always been very religious all my life, but I've always had a very wonderful life. I haven't had any massive burdens or catastrophes, just your normal things that happen in life. But because of this problem with my mother, I've had to search and realize what my faith means to me. I look at it like this was mother's final gift to me."

Conclusion

This chapter suggests that many of the concepts commonly used to describe caregiving fail to capture the experience of women engaged in this activity. Rather than perceiving caregiving as a series of chores, the women I interviewed emphasized their overall responsibility for their parents' lives and their determination to foster their parents' self-respect. Although several spoke in terms of role reversal and reciprocity, these terms did not adequately describe the way most daughters defined their endeavor. And, despite their emphasis on the strains that caregiving generated, the majority of women resisted viewing caregiving solely in terms of stress and burdens. This chapter also demonstrates the complexities of women's relationship to professional expertise. Although some daughters whose parents suffered from dementia believed that the jurisdiction of physicians extended very broadly, most did not simply relinquish authority. Instead, they used professional opinion to enhance their own authority over their parents. Because they viewed their parents as unique individuals rather than simply victims of disease, they retained faith in their own ability to determine how care should be rendered.

References

Blau, P. 1964. *Exchange in Social Life*. New York: John Wiley.

Bowers, B. 1990. "Family Perceptions of Care in a Nursing Home." In *Circles of Care: Work and Identity in Women's Lives*, ed. E.K. Abel and M.K. Nelson, pp. 278–89. Albany: State University of New York Press.

Brody, E.M. 1985. "Parent Care as a Normative Family Stress." *The Gerontologist* 25(1):19–28.

Bulmer, M. 1987. *The Social Basis of Community Care*, London: Allen & Unwin.

Chodorow, N. 1974. "Family Structures and Feminine Personality." In *Woman, Culture and Society*, ed. M.Z. Rosaldo and L. Lamphere, pp. 43–66. Stanford: Stanford University Press.

Fischer, L. R. 1986. *Linked Lives: Adult Daughters and Their Mothers*. New York: Harper & Row.

Gilligan, C. 1982. *In a Different Voice: Psychological Theory and Women's Development*. Cambridge: Harvard University Press.

Glenn, E.N. 1987. "Gender and the Family." In *Analyzing Gender: A Handbook of Social Science Research*, ed. B.B. Hess and M.M. Ferree, pp. 348–80. Newbury Park, CA: Sage.

Graham, H. 1983. "Caring: A Labour of Love." In *A Labour of Love: Women, Work and Caring*, eds. J. Finch and D. Groves, pp. 13–30. London: Routledge and Kegan Paul.

———. 1985. "Providers, Negotiators, and Mediators: Womena as the Hidden Carers." In *Women, Health and Healing: Toward a New Perspective*, ed. E. Lewin and V. Olesen, pp. 25–52. New York: Tavistock.

Gubrium, J.F., and R.J. Lynott. 1987. "Measurement and Interpretation of Burden in the Alzheimer's Disease Experience." *Journal of Aging Studies* 1(3):265–85.

Hareven, T.K. 1987. "The Dynamics of Kin in an Industrial Community." In *Families and Work*, ed. N. Gerstel and H.E. Gross, pp. 55–83. Philadelphia: Temple University Press.

Hartsock, N.C.M. 1983. *Money, Sex and Power: Toward a Feminist Historical Materialism*. Boston: Northeastern University Press.

Hasselkus, B.R. 1988. "Meaning in Family Caregiving: Perspectives on Caregiver/Professional Relationships." *The Gerontologist* 28(5):686–91.

Hochschild, A.R. 1975. "The Sociology of Feeling and Emotion: Selected Possibilities." In *Another Voice: Feminist Perspectives on Social Life and Social Science*, ed. M. Millman and R.M. Kanter, pp. 280–307. Garden City, NY: Anchor Press/Doubleday.

Lyman, K.A. 1988. "Infantilization of Elders: Day Care for Alzheimer's Disease Victims." *Research in the Sociology of Health Care* 7:71–103.

Mace, N.L., and P.V. Rabins. 1981. *The 36-Hour Day: A Family Guide to Caring for Persons with Alzheimer's Disease, Related Dementing Illnesses, and Memory Loss in Later Life*. Baltimore: Johns Hopkins University Press.

Qureshi, H., and A. Walker: 1989. *The Caring Relationship: Elderly People and Their Families*. Philadelphia: Temple University Press.

Ruddick, S. 1982. "Maternal Thinking." In *Rethinking the Family: Some Feminist Questions*, ed. B. Thorne, pp. 76–94. New York: Longman.

Ungerson, C. 1983. "Women and Caring: Skills, Tasks and Taboos." In *The Public and the Private*, ed. E. Gamarnikow et al., pp. 62–77. London: Heinemann.

———. 1987. *Policy Is Personal: Sex, Gender, and Informal Care*. London: Tavistock.

Young, A. 1980. "The Discourse on Stress and the Reproduction of Conventional Knowledge." *Social Science and Medicine*, 14B:133–46.

Any society also is dependent upon societal institutions like religion, for moral order, and education, for organizing necessary learning. These institutions and the interrelationships between the economy and the political order, or the political economy, are dealt with in this unit, along with the causes and types of societal change.

Increasingly, sociologists study how societal institutions interrelate and change together. How governmental regulations and economic activity interrelate to preserve a proper balance between commercial gains and public interest is a good example of that research. Sociologists also are developing multilevel theories that show how institutional processes and the experiences of people are interrelated. In this unit we develop multilevel treatments of religion and education. We hope to show how and why public issues and personal experiences (and personal problems) are interrelated as C. Wright Mills argued in *The Sociological Imagination*.

Social life does not stand still any more than our daily lives stay the same. Studying the key ingredients in societal change has been a long-standing focus of sociology, from the times of the sociological founders like Auguste Comte, Karl Marx, Emile Durkheim, and others. In this unit we will deal with major sociological theories of societal change. We will also be showing that worldwide social changes allowing an integrated and equitable world will be an important social goal for the future.

Religion and Education

Sociologists apply C. Wright Mills' (1959) sociological imagination (see Chapter 1) in theoretical explanations that involve interrelated processes at the interpersonal (micro) and societal (macro) levels of analysis. (See Chapter 1, 5, 15, 16, and 17.) As conceptualized by Mills, the sociological imagination involved analytical links between people's personal experiences (or their personal problems) and societal trends and problems (or public issues). Contemporary sociologist George Ritzer has expanded the use of Mills' approach to help develop his multilevel approach to sociological theory (Ritzer 2000). Ritzer (1995) has analyzed how people's overextended credit card debt contributes to the proliferation of credit card companies extending pre-approved (easily obtainable) credit and the widespread use of bankruptcy rather than fiscal management to deal with debt. In turn, the widespread offering of pre-approved credit and widespread use of bankruptcy prompt ever more people and companies to consider undergoing bankruptcy (Ritzer 1995). In developing his multilevel theory Ritzer (2000) has pointed out that personal troubles can become public issues if they occur frequently enough, and a public issue such as a major disruption of societal or community economic order (employers leaving a community) can greatly increase personal troubles.

The multilevel approach to sociological explanation is the use of interrelated ideas to explain how people's experiences (which are subjective) reflexively are related to societal processes (which are objective) (Ritzer 2000). Such an explanatory approach avoids giving causal priority to either component (avoiding whether it was the chicken or the egg that came first). The whole point of the multilevel approach is that personal problems and public issues, to use Mills' terms, are inherently related to each other. While there can be a dialectical relationship between levels, as in the overextended consumer credit example, the interconnections between micro and macro levels may also be positive, as when families' experiences with particular community health care services configure the community health programs they support with volunteer activity and financial support (Grimm and Brewster 2002; Wellman and Frank 2001). Thus, multilevel explanations can accommodate the integrative focus of functionalism in sociology or the inherent problems of inequality and power of the conflict perspective (Ritzer 2000).

While multilevel theorists agree with Durkheim (1895) that social reality exists in its own realm, the nature of that reality is shaped by and does also shape people's experiences. This complex idea is important for beginning students to understand, to avoid false and unneeded arguments over whether micro or macro issues are more important. If they are inherently related, then both are of equal and continuing importance. A successful football team, for example, is not just the added skills of all the members. Teams win not because of the skills and accomplishments (records) of individuals, though such statistics are kept. Football teams (or workplaces, or hospitals) accomplish more when collective strategies are used in game plans, strength and conditioning, and in games (when even the best players need occasional rest). On the other hand, the individuals' levels of skill, especially offensive and defensive linemen, though seldom noticeable to fans and media, are crucial for team success. These interlocking explanations between individual experiences and collective processes and vice versa are an important trend in American sociology (Ritzer 2000).

Multilevel explanation in sociology can be illustrated with the importance of religion as a social institution for society and religiosity for people. As a social institution (see Chapters 15, 16 and 17) religion refers to the ways in which religious organizations and belief systems spread through societies and shape general moral order. At the individual level, religiosity is the various ways that religion is important in people's lives (Macionis 2002). While religion is generally important in all societies (civil religion is the general symbolization of religiousness in any society, like "In God We Trust" on U.S. coins), societies vary as to their being politically structured by a particular religion. So-called state churches mean that a particular religion such as Islam in Morocco or Judaism in Israel is the major basis of government, of political order, and moral order. Religious pluralism refers to societies like the United States where a diverse number of religions and religious organizations contribute not only to collective moral order (even if based upon different faiths and practices) but to the evolving diversity of American society. (See Chapters 5, 8, 16, 17, and 18.) As immigrant groups enter and remain in the U.S., they bring traditional religious ideas expressed in new ways as they settle in the United States. The increased diversity of the U.S. society is reflected in this so-called religious innovation. Likewise, the growth of the less traditional and more demonstrative religion activity in sects in the U.S. reflects the desire among many Americans for intense religious experiences (Iannaccone 1994). Sociologists use the term denominations to refer to the well-established religious groups like Catholics and Methodists, while sects are the less established more informal groups with more personally expressive forms of religious rituals. Cults are the least well-established religious groups, often based on the personal attraction people that feel toward a particular individual (Macionis 2002).

At the interpersonal or micro-level, religiosity is very important in shaping people's ideas and the ways they act in everyday life. Many people in the U.S. believe in God and in life after death (NORC 2001). How many Americans regularly attend church is difficult to determine, since some people do not attend every Sunday, some attend services outside their neighborhood and residential communities, others attend when visiting relatives, and many watch services on TV who cannot or do not attend in person. However, sociologists agree that many Americans belong to churches and attend services rather regularly (Hout and Greeley 1998). These affiliations and activities in turn support and enable Americans to give donations and other aid to the needy, to visit people in hospitals, and provide meals on wheels and other activities in volunteer programs. Consequently, in the U.S. churches are a major link between people's personal experiences and how communities deal with public issues such as poverty, home visitation needs, and homelessness. Churches also link people's beliefs and their participation in protest movements that have the goals of extending due process and equality of opportunity and reducing institutionalized forms of discrimination (Jasper 1998). (See Chapters 12, 17, and 18.)

Education is both a social institution and a guiding force in people's lives. The educational institution is made up of societal processes including schooling with formal instruction and trained teachers that impart knowledge, skills, information, and appropriate ways of behaving. All states in the United States have mandatory education laws that require young people to attend school until the age of sixteen or the completion of the eighth grade (Macionis 2002). Youth receive more than information and skills training in schooling since they also experience the hidden curriculum, or activities that impart proper forms of behavior such as politeness, timeliness, orderly discussion, and leadership. Education, despite the problems schools have had and continue to have, is very much related to economic development, and the continued linkage between qualified workers and increasingly technical jobs in modern economies (Nolan and Lenski 1999). (See Chapters 5, 7, 10, and 16.) Likewise, and despite the need for better access to equal resources for schools, education is still a major factor in increasing lifetime incomes and more stable employment experiences (Shepard 2002). Reflecting the increasingly diverse forms of education in the U.S. is home schooling for children of parents who would rather teach their own children, programs designed to provide incentives for youth to stay in school and remain drug free, and the variety of training programs and funding for degrees provided by employees in the U.S. (Shepard 2002). In addition, learning at all levels is increasingly influenced by Internet access and the ways in which access to learning has become available to many more people (Ritzer 1998). All these forms of educational experiences make American society increasingly dependent upon but also increasingly able to provide educational experiences that help avoid social problems such as dropping out of school, functional illiteracy, and mismatches between employment requirements and people's skills.

People's educational experiences shape much more than their skills and employment opportunities. Children's participation in the locally administered but federally funded Head Start programs for underprivileged children improve their readiness to learn and interest in learning and influence what they subsequently do learn and the types of improved job experiences they have as well (Mills 1998). Education is still the major reason that some Americans earn more and have less long-term deprivation than others do. However, what is more important, well-educated people have the knowledge and the motivation to live more healthfully. While the effects of economic advantage for health cannot be discounted, sociologists have found that better educated people often limit their risk by not smoking and are more likely to live healthfully as to their choices such as diet (Ross and Wu 1995). (See Chapter 13.) The more willing and more able people are to get educated or to be retrained, the better the fit between employment needs and the availability of workers will be. Sociologists stress that a major cause of unemployment is the technological changes and other social changes that create mismatches between job skills and workers' skills, or structural unemployment. (See Chapters 7, 10, 16, 19, and 20). It makes a great deal of sense for employers to retain some employees and retrain them, rather than relying on new workers or hiring temporary workers (Snizek and Kostel 1999). Consequently, educational programs designed to better train and retrain Americans of all ages will do much to help the American economy avoid stagnation. It will also enhance the commitment of more workers to their employers.

Name: ______________________________

Quiz Questions: Religion and Education

1. Multilevel explanations usually involve focusing on either the micro or macro level only. (True or False?)
2. The macro level is what sociologists call personal troubles or personal experiences. (True or False?)
3. Which of these terms is related to religion as a social institution?
   a. religiosity
   b. churchgoing
   c. state churches
   d. beliefs in God and Heaven
4. The U.S. illustrates which of the following?
   a. state churches
   b. the disappearance of religion
   c. religious innovation
   d. none of the above
5. Most Americans do not ever attend religious services. (True or False?)
6. The most well-established religious organization in the U.S. is which of the following?
   a. sect
   b. cult
   c. church
   d. none of the above
7. Churches are important links between religiosity and public issues like poverty and visiting elderly people who can't leave their homes. (True or False?)
8. The more education people have the more money they earn, but, in general, the more education people have the less healthy they are especially from stress. (True or False?)
9. Which of these would be the hidden curriculum?
   a. reading skills
   b. proper discussion rules
   c. arithmetic
   d. writing skills
10. It makes sense for employers to get rid of or downsize all older workers and hire new ones that can be better trained. (True or False?)

Name: ______________________________

Exercise: Religion and Education

1. Discuss, in the space provided, how campus organizations might better address public issues.

Name: ____________________

Exercise: Religion and Education

2. Explain, in the space provided, the aspects of campus life that involve the hidden curriculum.

Name: ______________________________

Exercise: Religion and Education

3. Think about the religious activity of members of your family. In the space provided, discuss how religion in your family illustrates denomination, church attendance patterns, and how church activities relate to community issues.

Name: ____________________

Exercise: Religion and Education

4. Think about your educational experiences before coming to college. Use your experiences to discuss, in the space provided, schooling, hidden curriculum, preparation for employment, and technological training.

Name: ______________________________

Exercise: Religion and Education

5. Watch the movie *Elmer Gantry*. Use the contents of the movie to discuss, in the space provided, religiosity, sects, and religious activity.

Name: ________________________________

Exercise: Religion and Education

6. Watch the movie *Stand and Deliver*. Use the contents of the movie to discuss, in the space provided, schooling, hidden curriculum, staying in school, and technical skills.

Name: ______________________________

Exercise: Religion and Education

7. Go to the campus library or online and select an article from the *Journal for the Scientific Study and Religion*. Select any article, read it and use the contents to discuss, in the space provided, religiosity, denominations, and church attendance.

Name: ______________________________

Exercise: Religion and Education

8. Go to the campus library or online and select an article from the *Journal of Educational Research*. Select any one article, read it, and use the contents to discuss in the space provided, staying in school, hidden curriculum, and education increasing employability and income.

Name: ______________________________

Exercise: Religion and Education

9. Go to the web site of a church in your community. Use information on the web site to discuss, in the space provided, religiosity, denominations, church attendance, and church involvement in community problems.

Name: ______________________________

Exercise: Religion and Education

10. Go to the web site of a high school in your community. Use information on the web site to discuss, in the space provided, schooling, staying in schools, and the payoffs of education.

Political Economy

The events of 9/11 and their aftermath are clear reminders that Americans do not take the tenets of their society for granted. Renewed patriotism in the U.S., symbolized in renewed flag flying and sayings such as "United We Stand," reflects the importance to Americans of their social institutions. Social institutions are the societal arrangements for dealing with necessary aspects of societal continuance (Thompson and Hickey 2002). An ongoing society must have a religious institution to coordinate moral order and a family institution (see Chapter 11) to organize and sustain family life and child raising. These necessary societal configurations are called requisite institutions, while others that characterize the fundamental character of society but are not necessary for societal existence are emerging institutions. Televised sports and entertainment are an emergent institution in the U.S.

The economy, the institution that organizes the production of goods and services and the political order, the institution that coordinates legal authority and defense, have very interrelated importance in societies. The interrelated dynamics of these two requisite social institutions is called the political economy. How culture and social values as well as characteristics of markets shape political economies are major areas of sociological research. (See Chapters 1 and 2.) There are no purely capitalistic or socialist political economies, although in the U.S. most laws reflect a capitalistic economy in that they support free enterprise, market competition, and so-called employment-at-will under which either workers or employers may end work relations anytime. In a socialistic economy like China most forms of commerce are controlled and operated by agencies of government, and while some profit-taking is allowed, most economic gain is distributed by the government in ways that enable economic development and benefits like education, housing, and health care for all citizens (Macionis 2002). While some political economies are more capitalistic and others are more socialistic, sociologists who study political economics have often found a great variety of combinations of both elements, especially among developing nations and newly emergent transnational networks of trading partners (Carruthers and Babb 2000).

The political economy of the United States continues to display many fundamental principles of individual entrepreneurship dating back to the days of the traveling peddlers (Biggart 1989). While legal regulations allow secret ballot elections among workers to decide if a union will represent their interests to management, laws prevent union membership from being a precondition of employment, laws disallow sympathy strikes among workers other than those at a particular work-site, and allow the President of the U.S. to order striking workers back to work in the national interest (Hodson and

Sullivan 2002). Nevertheless, especially in the public sector employment of teachers, postal workers, and firefighters, strikes are prohibited but collective bargaining with binding arbitration is required. Essentially, regulations require employee and employer representatives to present their views on employment contracts before a judge or other third party whose decisions about the final agreement must be accepted by both sides. These regulations have allowed a steady dynamic to employment relationships without disruptive strikes, making public sector employment in the U.S. one of the most progressive and stable (Hodson and Sullivan 2002).

In the political economy of the United States, government regulations influence commerce, work conditions, environmental impact, and other aspects of economic activity. Regulation refers to legal restrictions that require compliance with public interest laws that deal with workplace safety, illegal pricing and fraud, product safety, and so on. At local levels, public interest regulations have involved restrictions on the public concessions such as free electricity and tax exemptions that corporations want before they decide to locate in a community (Adler 2000). The Equal Employment Opportunity Commission (EEOC) continues to extend due process to the workplace by encouraging laws that forbid unnecessary criteria for employment such as weight or English speaking when they are not required for the work (Edelman 1990). Deregulation refers to easing the restrictions on commerce such as removing geographical limits on commerce. Nationwide branch banking, for example, has brought many types of alternative and competitive banking services to regions of the country previously denied them. Reregulation is possible when commerce threatens competition and employee benefits, such as when huge corporations in related business merge to control an industry and the workers in it (Tilly and Tilly 1998). Recent financial scandals involving major corporate executives and accounting firms have increased the likelihood of regulation of business reporting. Unregulated work is work in the U.S. done by so-called day laborers and others who are often paid in cash and employers do not report employees' income and avoid payroll taxes. That such work is unregulated makes it a source of employment for illegal immigrants and other undocumented workers who want to avoid taxes (Hodson and Sullivan 2002).

Sociological studies of political economies in socialist states have found them to be complex and diverse, containing various combinations of capitalist and socialist features (Hamilton and Biggart 1988). Moreover, some like China have expanding productivity and increasingly healthy populations, while others like some Eastern European countries in the former Soviet Union have stagnating productivity and declining health (Cockerham 1999). China's political economy involves marketized productivity. The expanding production and distribution of goods and services in China is controlled and coordinated by local government agencies. These agencies operate like capitalist firms in that they respond to localized needs and demands. Managers and workers retain some residual profit, but much economic gain throughout China is given to the central government for investment in development and provision of free social services like health care (Walder 1995). The efficiency of the marketized productivity in China is because traditional local networks based upon kinship and cultural tradition are still used (Boisot and Child 1996). For sociologists, China exemplifies how traditional culture, socialized social services, and marketized production have combined to sustain remarkable economic development and improved health (Carruthers and Babb 2000).

Sociological studies of the so-called Asian Tigers—Hong Kong, South Korea, Taiwan, and Singapore—have found diversity in the way these socialist states have successfully managed rapid economic development (Hamilton and Biggart 1998). The diversity, like in China, is explained by the difference in cultural traditions of doing business and governing. The strong centralized government in South Korea has encouraged and aided the emergence of very large domestic firms like Hyundai in automobile manufacturing. These large firms became exporters as South Korea opened its market, thus allowing rapid economic growth. The model of the centralized Confucian state in South Korea contrasts with the traditional control of wealth by families and family networks in Taiwanese culture. Government help has therefore characterized development in Taiwan for family firms that split and diversify as they grow (Hamilton and Biggart 1988). The development among the Asian Tigers has been characterized by the combination of modernized production and finance with traditional cultural traditions. (See Chapters 13, 17, 19 and 20.)

Transnational political economies are the newly formed groups of trading partners that have emerged with globalization. So far, these alliances have involved countries in the same geographical area, such as the European Economic Community (EEC) and Mexico, Canada, and the United States linked by the North American Fair Trade Act (NAFTA). Sociological studies have shown diversity in the way these transnational political economies have emerged and developed. Despite cultural differences, the economic similarities among countries like Germany, France, and Portugal allowed them to agree regarding their collective commerce. A common currency, the Eurodollar, was agreed upon, as were regulatory standards for working conditions and environmental protection (Metcalf 2000). In contrast, NAFTA involved many more agreed-upon reductions in trade barriers, and fewer agreements concerning working conditions, the environment, or strategies to equalize standards of living (Dreiling 2000). Consequently, while trade among the NAFTA partners has increased, wage disparities between Mexico and the other partners as well as other differences in regulatory standards remain. Labor groups like the World Confederation of Labor (WCL) with large memberships in Canada and Latin America, like other new social movements, actively have sought to reform NAFTA with international labor standards and environmental protection agreements (Hodson and Sullivan 2002). (See Chapters 17, 19 and 20.)

Globalized manufacturing involves producing parts of finished products in various countries and assembling them in countries where they are not sold, to save labor costs. It also involves huge flows of money and other forms of capital such as loans and new technology among producers in various countries. This, in turn, has led to an integration of the capital holdings and managerial staffs of transnational corporations (TNCs) that operate simultaneously in many nations. Through interlocking directorates, or the same set of managers and executives, such giant corporations amass great power and massive wealth. For example, in car manufacturing General Motors owns Opel in Germany, Ford owns Jaguar in England, Saab in Sweden is closely linked with General Motors, and so is Isuzu in Japan. Many of those companies have more wealth than many countries of the world. Yet to evolve are the regulatory standards that control the TNCs in the ways transnational trading agreements have. Until such regulations emerge, TNCs can and do operate without uniform labor standards or environmental protection guidelines. Some of them, in fact, produce and assemble goods in less developed countries under very poor working conditions. Again, labor organizations such as the WCL are actively seeking world labor standards, especially regarding the exploitation of children. (See Chapter 20.)

New Social Movements actively seeking worldwide labor standards and agreements regarding environmental protection (see Chapter 18) will be very important. Such efforts will be needed to offset the political influence of the TNCs and business interests generally on political leaders throughout the world. In the United States business interests are very disproportionately represented in the money collected and distributed by Political Action Committees (PACs). These organizations raise and spend huge sums to elect particular candidates to offices in all levels of government in the U.S. The vast sum of money to run political campaigns in the United States makes the influence of contributors extremely important for successful candidates at all levels of government. The political counterpart to the influence of business interests in the U.S. elections will continue to be various new social movements (Jenkins and Wallace 1996). Two impediments in amassing political support among voters in the U.S. are their apathy especially younger well-educated citizens and voter registration laws that require being registered well before Election Day (Brians and Grofman 2001). (See Chapter 18.)

Name: ______________________________

Quiz Questions: Political Economy

1. Televised sports and entertainment in the U.S. is a requisite institution. (True or False?)
2. Binding arbitration in collective bargaining applies mostly to unionized workers in skilled positions in manufacturing. (True or False?)
3. Day laborers and workers paid in cash like maids and gardeners illustrate which of these forms of work in the U.S.?

   a. regulated work
   b. deregulated work
   c. reregualted work
   d. unregulated work
4. Marketized production operated by local agencies of government characterize which of these countries?

   a. Taiwan
   b. South Korea
   c. China
   d. Japan
5. Small to medium size family business characterize the political economy of which of these countries?

   a. Taiwan
   b. South Korea
   c. China
   d. Japan
6. The EEC has fewer regulations on work standards than NAFTA does. (True or False?)
7. TNCs are better regulated than the EEC is. (True or False?)
8. Traditional culture plays a very minor role in the ways that Asian Tigers have developed. (True or False?)
9. New social movements in the U.S. are primarily the opposing force to which of the following?

   a. Republicans
   b. Democrats
   c. PACs
   d. transactional political economies
10. Sociological studies show that political economies are pretty much the same throughout the world. (True or False?)

Name: ______________________________

Exercise: Political Economy

1. Based upon experiences in your family or among people you know, in the space provided, describe the benefits they have lost because of employment problems.

Name: ______________________________

Exercise: Political Economy

2. In the space provided, briefly describe how students on your campus could participate more in the political economy of the U.S.

Name: ______________________________

Exercise: Political Economy

3. Think about the jobs the adults in your family have had. In the space provided, describe how family members' employment illustrated the capitalistic economy, regulation, and unregulated work.

Name: ______________________________

Exercise: Political Economy

4. Think about your community and the jobs available in it. In the space provided, discuss any evidence of manufacturing, transitional corporations, and regulations.

Name: ______________________________

Exercise: Political Economy

5. Watch the movie *All the King's Men*. Using material in the film, in the space provided, discuss how the movie illustrated regulation, political corruption, and capitalistic economy.

Name: ______________________________

Exercise: Political Economy

6. Watch the movie *Erin Brockovich*. In the space provided, discuss regulation, unregulated work, and environmental protection laws.

Name: ______________________

Exercise: Political Economy

7. Go to the campus library or online to select an article from the journal *Administrative Science Quarterly*. Select any one article, read it, and use the contents to discuss, in the space provided, regulation, capitalistic economy, and interlocking directorates.

Name: ______________________________

Exercise: Political Economy

8. Go to the campus library or online to select an article from the journal *Economy and Society*. Select any one article, read it, and use the contents to discuss, in the space provided, regulation, unregulated work, and TNCs.

Name: ____________________

Exercise: Political Economy

9. Go to the web site of a TNC like Ford Motor Company, General Motors, or General Electric. Use information on the web site to illustrate, in the space provided, globalized manufacturing, TNCs, and political power.

Name: ______________________________

Exercise: Political Economy

10. Go to the campus library or online to the web site of any environmental protection group such as the Sierra Club or Green Peace. Using information on the web site, discuss, in the space provided, TNCs, political power of the TNCs, and new social movements that are concerned with all citizens' rights.

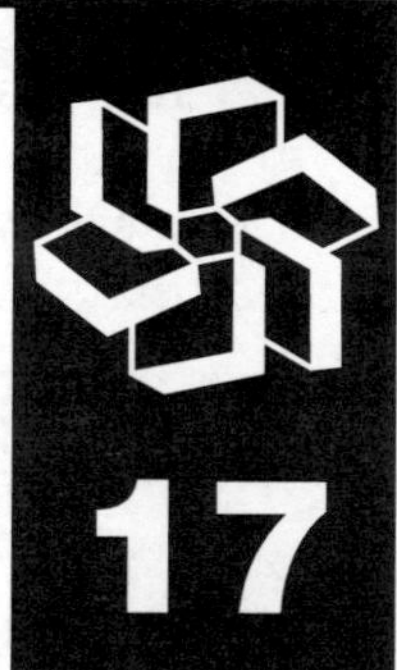

Social Change

Everyday social life involves many changes including the seasonal changes in clothes and sports, such as football in the fall and baseball in the spring and summer. Many people adopt changes in clothing styles that are new and hairstyles, body piercing, and tattooing also represent the changes apparent in fads, fashions, and styles of body adornment like types of jewelry. While social life can and does involve such changes, sociologists consider social change to be the more pervasive and permanent types of changes not only in what people do and think, but also in society itself. Social change can begin with a new invention or technology like the computer and microprocessor. Through a process called diffusion the new devices spread throughout a society in ways that basically restructure the way people live and the way society is organized. These longer-term effects of social change usually extend throughout most basic aspects of society influencing changes in education, family life, laws and government, work and travel, and leisure and recreation. The invention and mass production of affordable cars (the Ford Model T in the early 1900s) fundamentally altered the way Americans worked, lived, traveled, and communicated.

Sociologists have developed several important theoretical explanations of various types of social change. Technological change like that illustrated by the early mass production of affordable cars is explained by sociologists in terms of how rapid and completely new devices are adopted in a so-called diffusion curve. In addition, sociologists analyze and map the enduring ways the new devices change basic aspects of social life including housing, transportation, family activities, manufacturing, and alterations in the social class structure. In the Middle Ages, for example, the invention and diffusion of the stirrup allowed knights on horseback to hold lances during combat rather than merely to throw them. As much more effective combatants, knights became a powerful elite and in the service of landowners and other rich people they restructured social relationships among various social classes in medieval society (White 1972). Similarly, the successful mass production and diffusion of Ford cars influenced the spread of assembly line production throughout the economy, changed the basic nature of work and family life, and helped the emergence of a large working and middle class in the United States. It also helped contribute significantly to the domination of smaller firms by bigger ones, which is still a basic characteristic of economies throughout the world (Averitt 1968).

Sociologists who focus upon the ways in which technological and economic forms of social change contribute to continuing and increased social inequality and other consequences for society have developed the social class conflict theory. Karl Marx (1867) focused upon the early emergence of mass production in large firms as creating vast differences in wealth and influence between owners and workers. This increased economic inequality was accompanied by the great influence of rich capitalists in developing the major ideas and laws that Marx called cultural hegemony. He and other sociologists also have analyzed the degree to which the perspectives of the rich toward social life are usually widely accepted by the non-rich, in a process called false consciousness (Giddens 1997). Such perspectives in the United States as the ideas that the rich are more intelligent and hardworking and that poorer people are less hardworking (if not lazy and morally corrupt) illustrate the ways in which stereotypic viewpoints of rich and influential people diffuse throughout society and sustain cultural hegemony.

Many sociologists accept the importance of both technological and economic social change, but agree with Weber that new ideas are as important in social change as are technology and amassing wealth. Weber's classic work *The Protestant Ethic and the Spirit of Capitalism* (1958, original 1904–1905) and his other massive historical analyses of world religions, demonstrated how Calvinist beliefs in worldly success as evidence of predestined salvation fueled the emergence of capitalism. Weber also stressed the role that charismatic leaders of social movements have played in social changes in the laws and authority of societies throughout history (Weber 1978, original 1921). (See Chapters 15 and 18.) Another comprehensive explanation of the role of ideas in social change throughout history is the theory of cyclical change of Pitirim Sorokin (1937–1941). His "principle of limit" refers to his conclusion based upon historical trends he found in art, music, sculpture, books, and other aspects of culture that societies can become too immersed in certain ideas and this overemphasis prompts change. Ideational societies that emphasized philosophical and religious concerns remain stable as long as they also deal with practical matters. If not, social change ensues and societies move in the direction of sensate societies concerned primarily with practical matters. Yet these societies, too, can become too hedonistic, which triggers a swing back in the direction of ideational change.

Still, other sociologists, demographers and economists use the demographic transition theory in focusing their explanation of social change. This perspective stresses the changes in population size and composition that accompany and contribute toward economic development and technological change (Macionis 2002). As mass production and new knowledge and devices, especially things like the ways to cure and prevent diseases, develop and spread, population size increases. The increase is due in part to the facts that more people avoid early deaths and people on average live longer. The increase also comes from the fact that families may continue to have larger numbers of children like they did when many children were needed to help run farms and small businesses. Nevertheless, as societies continue to experience the effects of modern economic and technological change including effective means of birth control, population growth slows, allowing continued advances to avoid the hindrance of many more people. Currently, some sociologists have defined the second demographic transition to be the decline of population in some well-developed countries of Europe (Shepard 2002).

Many sociologists focus their explanation of social change especially upon the processes by which economic development and technological change and its attendant changes in social life and have occurred and continue to occur among the less developed countries (LDCs). Theories of development or modernization focus upon how LDCs such as countries in Africa and Asia including China are developing economies, transportation, health care, education systems, and other societal features more like more developed countries (MDCs). Modernization refers to explanations of the most significant and successful components in LDCs development especially those that make the LDCs less dependent upon the MDCs such as the United States, Canada, Europe, and Japan (Fukuyama 1999). (See Chapters 18, 19 and 20.) Of particular interest to these theorists is the remarkable progress among the so-called Asian Tigers including Hong Kong, South Korea, Taiwan, and Singapore. One important feature of their development is the variety of exports and increasing types of domestic goods they have produced for their own people. They have not become too dependent upon loans from the MDCs or upon imports. On the contrary, the Asian Tigers have continued and multifaceted trade relationships with the MDCs (Carruthers and Babb 2000). (See Chapter 16.)

Besides modernization, sociologists and others study the interrelated changes in relationships between the LDCs, the developing nations such as the Asian Tigers including China, and the MDCs. Globalization refers to the increasing interconnectedness among and interrelationships between various countries of the world (Giddens 1990). (See Chapter 20.) Such connections take many forms but an important one involves transnational corporations (TNCs) that produce and assemble the components of products in various nations and market them in ways that extend across national boundaries. In fact, the structure and operation of TNCs by definition means that the capital they own and manage and the goods that they make and distribute flow increasingly freely across national boundaries (Carruthers and Babb 2000). In addition, other aspects of culture such as sports, entertainment, fast food services, clothing styles, and tourism increasingly link all countries of the world (Andrews et al 1996). The increasing number of relationships between universities in the U.S. and those throughout the world including those in China illustrates the globalization of higher education in the U.S. (Brody 1997). (See Chapters 16, 19, and 20.)

Distinguishing globalization from the presumption of cultural universalism that would occur if the LDCs became mere carbon copies of the MDCs is important. While some convergence among all nations occurs as certain consumer products and aspects of society like health care spread, such spread does not occur in identical ways. Thus, most sociologists stress that the diffusion of technology, goods, and services throughout LDCs fosters divergence as well as similarity. The increasingly free flow of capital and goods, and capitalism as a whole, throughout the world creates increasing ways for traditional cultural differences to assert themselves (Carruthers and Babb 2000). Variations in capitalism and niches of trade among subsets of nations that reflect traditional cultural values add an increasingly diverse number and form of enterprises throughout the world. (See Chapters 16, 17, 19 and 20.) A good example of this diversity is the way that McDonald's fast food has become popular in China as snack food rather than as complete meals (Yan 1997). (See Chapter 20.)

Name: ______________________

Quiz Questions: Social Change

1. The number of marriages, divorces, and job losses in a year represent good examples of social change. (True of False?)
2. Pitirim Sorokin's theory of social change focused on which of these?
   a. technology
   b. social class conflict
   c. ideas
   d. economic production
3. Cultural hegemony is a concept in which of these sociologist's theory of social change?
   a. Max Weber
   b. Pitirim Sorokin
   c. Karl Marx
   d. Henry Ford
4. Population changes in relation to economic development is the focus of demographic transition theory. (True or False?)
5. The second demographic transition refers to the economic development occurring among the Asian Tigers. (True or False?)
6. Modernization usually destroys most aspects of traditional culture in the LDCs. (True or False?)
7. Globalization is resulting in most of the countries of the world having the same basic aspects of culture. (True of False?)
8. The Asian Tigers have developed largely by means of loans from the MDCs. (True or False?)
9. Globalization involves worldwide relationships among universities and locations for entertainment and entertainers as well as relationships based upon TNCs. (True or False?)
10. The effect of an important source of social change in terms of its spread is indicated by which of these concepts?
    a. class conflict
    b. cultural hegemony
    c. diffusion curve
    d. false consciousness

Name: ______________________________

Exercise: Social Change

1. In the space provided, identify and briefly discuss the three most important ways that your social life differs from the social life when elderly members of your family were your age.

Name: ______________________________

Exercise: Social Change

2. In the space provided, identify and briefly discuss three aspects of globalization that you have encountered on campus.

Name: ______________________________

Exercise: Social Change

3. Think about the town or part of a city or other metropolitan area you grew up in. In the space provided, discuss social change in your town or urban area in terms of technological change, new ideas, and population changes.

Name: ______________________________

Exercise: Social Change

4. Think about the international students you go to college with now. Discuss, in the space provided, how their native countries illustrate modernization, population changes, and globalization.

Name: ______________________________

Exercise: Social Change

5. Watch the classic movie *Wild River*. Based upon the contents of the movie, in the space provided, discuss how the movie illustrated technological change, diffusion curves, new ideas, and modernization.

Name: ______________________________

Exercise: Social Change

6. Watch the movie *The Air Up There*. Based upon the contents discuss, in the space provided, how the movie illustrated technological diffusion, new ideas, modernization, and globalization.

Name: ____________________

Exercise: Social Change

7. Go to the campus library or online, and select an article from the journal *Economic Development and Cultural Change*. Select any one article, read it, and discuss, in the space provided, how it illustrates population change, modernization, and globalization.

Name: ______________________________

Exercise: Social Change

8. Go to the campus library or online, and select an article from the journal *Technology and Culture*. Select any one article, read it, and discuss, in the space provided, how it illustrates technological change, diffusion curves, and modernization.

Name: ______________________________

Exercise: Social Change

9. Go online to the web site of any developing nation. Using information from the web site, in the space provided, discuss technological change, population changes, and modernization.

Name: ______________________

Exercise: Social Change

10. Go online to the web site of any rural or small town area, such as a county, near you. Based upon information from the web site, discuss, in the space provided, how information illustrates social change, technological change, and population changes.

What We Really Miss about the 1950s

Stephanie Coontz

Popular myth has it that the 1950s were the ideal decade for the American family. In this example of academic writing at its best, Stephanie Coontz provides a clear, well-documented, and insightful analysis of what was really going on and suggests that our nostalgia for the 1950s could mislead us today. Stephanie Coontz teaches history and family studies at The Evergreen State College in Olympia, Washington. An award-winning writer and nationally recognized expert on the family, she has published her work in numerous popular magazines and academic journals, testified before a House Select Committee on families, and appeared in several television documentaries. This selection is from her latest book, *The Way We Really Are: Coming to Terms with America's Changing Families* (1997).

In a 1996 poll by the Knight-Ridder news agency, more Americans chose the 1950s than any other single decade as the best time for children to grow up.[1] And despite the research I've done on the underside of 1950s families, I don't think it's crazy for people to feel nostalgic about the period. For one thing, it's easy to see why people might look back fondly to a decade when real wages grew more in any single year than in the entire ten years of the 1980s combined, a time when the average 30-year-old man could buy a median-priced home on only 15–18 percent of his salary.[2]

But it's more than just a financial issue. When I talk with modern parents, even ones who grew up in unhappy families, they associate the 1950s with a yearning they feel for a time when there were fewer complicated choices for kids or parents to grapple with, when there was more predictability in how people formed and maintained families, and when there was a coherent "moral order" in their community to serve as a reference point for family norms. Even people who found that moral order grossly unfair or repressive often say that its presence provided them with something concrete to push against.

I can sympathize entirely. One of my most empowering moments occurred the summer I turned 12, when my mother marched down to the library with me to confront a librarian who'd curtly refused to let me check out a book that was "not appropriate" for my age. "Don't you *ever* tell my daughter what she can and can't read," fumed my mom. "She's a mature young lady and she can make her own choices." In recent years I've often thought back to the gratitude I felt toward my mother for that act of trust in me. I wish I had some way of earning similar points from my own son. But much as I've always respected his values, I certainly wouldn't have walked into my local video store when he was 12 and demanded that he be allowed to check out absolutely anything he wanted!

Still, I have no illusions that I'd actually like to go back to the 1950s, and neither do most people who express such occasional nostalgia. For example, although the 1950s got more votes than any other decade in the Knight-Ridder poll, it did not win an outright majority: 38 percent of respondents picked the 1950s; 27 percent picked the 1960s or the 1970s. Voters between the ages of 50 and 64 were most likely to choose the 1950s, the decade in which they themselves came of age, as the best time for kids; voters under 30 were more likely to choose the 1970s. African Americans differed over whether the 1960s, 1970s, or 1980s were best, but all age groups of blacks agreed that later decades were definitely preferable to the 1950s.

Nostalgia for the 1950s is real and deserves to be taken seriously, but it usually shouldn't be taken literally. Even people who *do* pick the 1950s as the best decade generally end up saying, once they start discussing their feelings in depth, that it's not the family arrangements in and of themselves that they want to revive. They don't miss the way women used to be treated, they sure wouldn't want to live with most of the fathers they knew in their neighborhoods, and "come to think of it"—I don't know how many times I've recorded these exact words—"I communicate with my kids *much* better than my parents or grandparents did." When Judith Wallerstein recently interviewed 100 spouses in "happy" marriages, she found that only five "wanted a marriage like their parents'." The husbands "consciously rejected the role models provided by their fathers. The women said they could never be happy living as their mothers did."[3]

People today understandably feel that their lives are out of balance, but they yearn for something totally *new*—a more equal distribution of work, family, and community time for both men and women, children and adults. If the 1990s are lopsided in one direction, the 1950s were equally lopsided in the opposite direction.

What most people really feel nostalgic about has little to do with the internal structure of 1950s families. It is the belief that the 1950s provided a more family-friendly economic and social environment, an easier climate in which to keep kids on the straight and narrow, and above all, a greater feeling of hope for a family's long-term future, especially for its young. The contrast between the perceived hopefulness of the fifties and our own misgivings about the future is key to contemporary nostalgia for the period. Greater optimism *did* exist then, even among many individuals and groups who were in terrible circumstances. But if we are to take people's sense of loss seriously, rather than merely to capitalize on it for a hidden political agenda, we need to develop a historical perspective on where that hope came from.

Part of it came from families comparing their prospects in the 1950s to their unstable, often grindingly uncomfortable pasts, especially the two horrible decades just before. In the 1920s, after two centuries of child labor and income insecurity, and for the first time in American history, a bare majority of children had come to live in a family with a male breadwinner, a female homemaker, and a chance at a high school education. Yet no sooner did the ideals associated with such a family begin to blossom than they were buried by the stock market crash of 1929 and the Great Depression of the 1930s. During the 1930s domestic violence soared; divorce rates fell, but informal separations jumped; fertility plummeted. Murder rates were higher in 1933 than they were in the 1980s. Families were uprooted or torn apart. Thousands of young people left home to seek work, often riding the rails across the country.[4]

World War II brought the beginning of economic recovery, and people's renewed interest in forming families resulted in a marriage and childbearing boom, but stability was still beyond most people's grasp. Postwar communities were rocked by racial tensions, labor strife, and a right-wing backlash against the radical union movement of the 1930s. Many women resented being fired from wartime jobs they had grown to enjoy. Veterans often came home to find that they had to elbow their way back into their families, with wives and children resisting their attempts to reassert domestic authority. In one recent study of fathers who returned from the war, four times as many reported painful, even traumatic, reunions as remembered happy ones.[5]

By 1946 one in every three marriages was ending in divorce. Even couples who stayed together went through rough times, as an acute housing shortage forced families to double up with relatives or friends. Tempers frayed and generational relations grew strained. "No home is big enough to house two families, particularly two of different generations, with opposite theories on child training," warned a 1948 film on the problems of modern marriage.[6]

So after the widespread domestic strife, family disruptions, and violence of the 1930s and the instability of the World War II period, people were ready to try something new. The postwar economic boom gave them the chance. The 1950s was the first time that a majority of Americans could even *dream* of creating a secure oasis in their immediate nuclear families. There they could focus their emotional and financial investments, reduce obligations to others that might keep them from seizing their own chance at a new start, and escape the interference of an older generation of neighbors or relatives who tried to tell them how to run their lives and raise their kids. Oral histories of the postwar period resound with the theme of escaping from in-laws, maiden aunts, older parents, even needy siblings.

The private family also provided a refuge from the anxieties of the new nuclear age and the cold war, as well as a place to get away from the political witch-hunts led by Senator Joe McCarthy and his allies. When having the wrong friends at the wrong time or belonging to any "suspicious" organization could ruin your career and reputation, it was safer to pull out of groups you might have joined earlier and to focus on your family. On a more positive note, the nuclear family was where people could try to satisfy their long-pent-up desires for a more stable marriage, a decent home, and the chance to really enjoy their children.

The 1950s Family Experiment

The key to understanding the successes, failures, and comparatively short life of 1950s family forms and values is to understand the period as one of *experimentation* with the possibilities of a new kind of family, not as the expression of some longstanding tradition. At the end of the 1940s, the divorce rate, which had been rising steadily since the 1890s, dropped sharply; the age of marriage fell to a 100-year low; and the birth rate soared. Women who had worked during the Depression or World War II quit their jobs as soon as they became pregnant, which meant quite a few women were specializing in child raising; fewer women remained childless during the 1950s than in any decade since the late nineteenth century. The timing and spacing of childbearing became far more compressed, so that young mothers were likely to have two or more children in diapers at once, with no older sibling to help in their care. At the same time, again for the first time in 100 years, the educational gap between young middle-class women and men increased, while job segregation for working men and women seems to have peaked. These demographic changes increased the dependence of women on marriage, in contrast to gradual trends in the opposite direction since the early twentieth century.[7]

The result was that family life and gender roles became much more predictable, orderly, and settled in the 1950s than they were either twenty years earlier or would be twenty years later. Only slightly more than one in four marriages ended in divorce during the 1950s. Very few young people spent any extended period of time in a nonfamily setting: They moved from their parents' family into their own family, after just a brief experience with independent living, and they started having children soon after marriage. Whereas two-thirds of women aged 20 to 24 were not yet married in 1990, only 28 percent of women this age were still single in 1960.[8]

Ninety percent of all the households in the country were families in the 1950s, in comparison with only 71 percent by 1990. Eighty-six percent of all children lived in two-parent homes in 1950, as opposed to just 72 percent in 1990. And the percentage living with both biological parents—rather than, say, a parent and stepparent—was dramatically higher than it had been at the turn of the century or is today: seventy percent in 1950, compared with only 50 percent in 1990. Nearly 60 percent of kids—an all-time high—were born into male breadwinner-female homemaker families; only a minority of the rest had mothers who worked in the paid labor force.[9]

If the organization and uniformity of family life in the 1950s were new, so were the values, especially the emphasis on putting all one's emotional and financial eggs in the small basket of the immediate nuclear family. Right up through the 1940s, ties of work, friendship, neighborhood, ethnicity, extended kin, and voluntary organizations were as important a source of identity for most Americans, and sometimes a *more* important source of obligation, than marriage and the nuclear family. All this changed in the postwar era. The spread of suburbs and automobiles, combined with the destruction of older ethnic neighborhoods in many cities, led to the decline of the neighborhood social club. Young couples moved away from parents and kin, cutting ties with traditional extrafamilial networks that might compete for their attention. A critical factor in this trend was the emergence of a group of family sociologists and marriage counselors who followed Talcott Parsons in claiming that the nuclear family, built on a sharp division of labor between husband and wife, was the cornerstone of modern society.

The new family experts tended to advocate views such as those first raised in a 1946 book, *Their Mothers' Sons*, by psychiatrist Edward Strecker. Strecker and his followers argued that American boys were infantilized and emasculated by women who were old-fashioned "moms" instead of modern "mothers." One sign that you might be that dreaded "mom," Strecker warned women, was if you felt you should take your aging parents into your own home, rather than putting them in "a good institution . . . where they will receive adequate care and comfort." Modern "mothers" placed their parents in nursing homes and poured all their energies into their nuclear family. They were discouraged from diluting their wifely and maternal commitments by maintaining "competing" interest in friends, jobs, or extended family networks, yet they were also supposed to cheerfully grant early independence to their (male) children—an emotional double bind that may explain why so many women who took this advice to heart ended up abusing alcohol or tranquilizers over the course of the decade.[10]

The call for young couples to break from their parents and youthful friends was a consistent theme in 1950s popular culture. In *Marty*, one of the most highly praised TV plays and movies of the 1950s, the hero almost loses his chance at love by listening to the carping of his mother and aunt and letting himself be influenced by old friends who resent the time he spends with his new girlfriend. In the end, he turns his back on mother, aunt, and friends to get his new marriage and a little business of his own off to a good start. Other movies, novels, and popular psychology tracts portrayed the dreadful things that happened when women became more interested in careers than marriage or men resisted domestic conformity.

Yet many people felt guilty about moving away from older parents and relatives; "modern mothers" worried that fostering independence in their kids could lead to defiance or even juvenile delinquency (the recurring nightmare of the age); there was considerable confusion about how men and women could maintain clear breadwinner-homemaker distinctions in a period of expanding education, job openings, and consumer aspirations. People clamored for advice. They got it from the new family education specialists and marriage counselors, from columns in women's magazines, from government pamphlets, and above all from television. While 1950s TV melodramas warned against letting anything dilute the commitment to getting married and having kids, the new family sitcoms gave people nightly lessons on how to make their marriage or rapidly expanding family work—or, in the case of *I Love Lucy*, probably the most popular show of the era, how *not* to make their marriage and family work. Lucy and Ricky gave weekly comic reminders of how much trouble a woman could get into by wanting a career or hatching some hare-brained scheme behind her husband's back.

At the time, everyone knew that shows such as *Donna Reed*, *Ozzie and Harriet*, *Leave It to Beaver*, and *Father Knows Best* were not the way families really were. People didn't watch those shows to see their own lives reflected back at them. They watched them to see how families were *supposed* to live—and also to get a little reassurance that they were headed in the right direction. The sitcoms were simultaneously advertisements, etiquette manuals, and how-to lessons for a new way of organizing marriage and child raising. I have studied the scripts of these shows for years, since I often use them in my classes on family history, but it wasn't until I became a parent that I felt their extraordinary pull. The secret of their appeal, I suddenly realized, was that they offered 1950s viewers, wracked with the same feelings of parental inadequacy as was I, the promise that there were easy answers and surefire techniques for raising kids.

Ever since, I have found it useful to think of the sitcoms as the 1950s equivalent of today's beer ads. As most people know, beer ads are consciously aimed at men who *aren't* as strong and sexy as the models in the commercials, guys who are uneasily aware of the gap between the ideal masculine pursuits and their own achievements. The promise is that if the viewers on the couch will just drink brand X, they too will be able to run 10 miles without gasping for breath. Their bodies will firm up, their complexions will clear up, and maybe the Swedish bikini team will come over and hang out at their place.

Similarly, the 1950s sitcoms were aimed at young couples who had married in haste, women who had tasted new freedoms during World War II and given up their jobs with regret, veterans whose children resented their attempts to reassert paternal authority, and individuals disturbed by the changing racial and ethnic mix of postwar America. The message was clear: Buy these ranch houses, Hotpoint appliances, and child-raising ideals; relate to your spouse like this; get a new car to wash with your kids on Sunday afternoons; organize your dinners like that—and you too can escape from the conflicts of race, class, and political witch-hunts into harmonious families where father knows best, mothers are never bored or irritated, and teenagers rush to the dinner table each night, eager to get their latest dose of parental wisdom.

Many families found it possible to put together a good imitation of this way of living during the 1950s and 1960s. Couples were often able to construct marriages that were much more harmonious than those in which they had grown up, and to devote far more time to their children. Even when marriages were deeply unhappy, as many were, the new stability, economic security, and educational advantages parents were able to offer their kids counted for a lot in people's assessment of their life satisfaction. And in some matters, ignorance could be bliss: The lack of media coverage of problems such as abuse or incest was terribly hard on the casualties, but it protected more fortunate families from knowledge and fear of many social ills.[11]

There was tremendous hostility to people who could be defined as "others": Jews, African Americans, Puerto Ricans, the poor, gays or lesbians, and "the red menace." Yet on a day-to-day basis, the civility that prevailed in homogeneous neighborhoods allowed people to ignore larger patterns of racial and political repression. Racial clashes were ever-present in the 1950s, sometimes escalating into full-scale antiblack riots, but individual homicide rates fell to almost half the levels of the 1930s. As nuclear families moved into the suburbs, they retreated from social activism but entered voluntary relationships with people who had children the same age; they became involved in PTAs together, joined bridge clubs, went bowling. There does seem to have been a stronger sense of neighborly commonalities than many of us feel today. Even though this local community was often the product of exclusion or repression, it sometimes looks attractive to modern Americans whose commutes are getting longer and whose family or work patterns give them little in common with their neighbors.[12]

The optimism that allowed many families to rise above their internal difficulties and to put limits on their individualistic values during the 1950s came from the sense that America was on a dramatically different trajectory that it had been in the past, an upward and expansionary path that had already taken people to better places than they had even seen before and would certainly take their children even further. This confidence that almost everyone could look forward to a better future stands in sharp contrast to how most contemporary Americans feel, and it explains why a period in which many people were much worse off than today sometimes still looks like a better period for families than our own.

Throughout the 1950s, poverty was higher than it is today, but it was less concentrated in pockets of blight existing side-by-side with extremes of wealth, and, unlike today, it was falling rather than rising. At the end of the 1930s, almost two-thirds of the population had incomes below the poverty standards of the day, while only one in eight had a middle-class income (defined as two to five times the poverty line). By 1960, a majority of the population had climbed into the middle-income range.[13]

Unmarried people were hardly sexually abstinent in the 1950s, but the age of first intercourse was somewhat higher than it is now, and despite a tripling of nonmarital birth rates between 1940 and 1958, more than 70 percent of nonmarital pregnancies led to weddings before the child was born. Teenage birth rates were almost twice as high in 1957 as in the 1990s, but most teen births were to married couples, and the effect of teen pregnancy in reducing further schooling for young people did not hurt their life prospects the way it does today. High school graduation rates were lower in the 1950s than they are today, and minority students had far worse test scores, but there were jobs for people who dropped out of high school or graduated without good reading skills—jobs that actually had a future. People entering the job market in the 1950s had no way of knowing that they would be the last generation to have a good shot at reaching middle-class status without the benefit of postsecondary schooling.

Millions of men from impoverished, rural, unemployed, or poorly educated family backgrounds found steady jobs in the steel, auto, appliance, construction, and shipping industries. Lower middle-class men went further on in college during the 1950s than they would have been able to expect in earlier decades, enabling them to make the transition to secure white-collar work. The experience of shared sacrifices in the Depression and war, reinforced by a New Deal-inspired belief in the ability of government to make life better, gave people a sense of hope for the future. Confidence in government, business, education, and other institutions was on the rise. This general optimism affected people's experience and assessment of family life. It is no wonder modern Americans yearn for a similar sense of hope.

But before we sign on to any attempts to turn the family clock back to the 1950s we should note that the family successes and community solidarities of the 1950s rested on a totally different set of political and economic conditions than we have today. Contrary to widespread belief, the 1950s was not an age of laissez-faire government and free market competition. A major cause of the social mobility of young families in the 1950s was that federal assistance programs were much more generous and widespread than they are today.

In the most ambitious and successful affirmative action program ever adopted in America, 40 percent of young men were eligible for veterans' benefits, and these benefits were far more extensive than those available to Vietnam-era vets. Financed in part by a federal income tax on the rich that went up to 87 percent and a corporate tax rate of 52 percent, such benefits provided quite a jump start for a generation of young families. The GI bill paid most tuition costs for vets who attended college, doubling the percentage of college students from prewar levels. At the other end of the life span, Social Security began to build up a significant safety net for the elderly, formerly the poorest segment of the population. Starting in 1950, the federal government regularly mandated raises in the minimum wage to keep pace with inflation. The minimum wage may have been only $1.40 as late as 1968, but a person who worked for that amount full-time, year-round, earned 118 percent of the poverty figure for a family of three. By 1995, a full-time minimum-wage worker could earn only 72 percent of the poverty level.[14]

An important source of the economic expansion of the 1950s was that public works spending at all levels of government comprised nearly 20 percent of total expenditures in 1950, as compared to less than 7 percent in 1984. Between 1950 and 1960, nonmilitary, nonresidential public construction rose by 58 percent. Construction expenditures for new schools (in dollar amounts adjusted for inflation) rose by 72 percent; funding on sewers and waterworks rose by 46 percent. Government paid 90 percent of the costs of building the new Interstate Highway System. These programs opened up suburbia to growing numbers of middle-class Americans and created secure, well-paying jobs for blue-collar workers.[15]

Government also reorganized home financing, underwriting low down payments and long-term mortgages that had been rejected as bad business by private industry. To do this, government put public assets behind housing lending programs, created two new national financial institutions to facilitate home loans, allowed veterans to put down payments as low as a dollar on a house, and offered tax breaks to people who bought homes. The National Education Defense Act funded the socioeconomic mobility of thousands of young men who trained themselves for well-paying jobs in such fields as engineering.[16]

Unlike contemporary welfare programs, government investment in 1950s families was not just for immediate subsistence but encouraged long-term asset development, rewarding people for increasing their investment in homes and education. Thus it was far less likely that such families or individuals would ever fall back to where they started, even after a string of bad luck. Subsidies for higher education were greater the longer people stayed in school and the more expensive the school they selected. Mortgage deductions got bigger as people traded up to better houses.[17]

These social and political support systems magnified the impact of the postwar economic boon. "In the years between 1947 and 1973," reports economist Robert Kuttner, "the median paycheck more than doubled, and the bottom 20 percent enjoyed the greatest gains." High rates of unionization meant that blue-collar workers were making much more financial progress than most of their counterparts today. In 1952, when eager home buyers flocked to the opening of Levittown, Pennsylvania, the largest planned community yet constructed, "it took a factory worker one day to earn enough money to pay the closing costs on a new Levittown house, then selling for $10,000." By 1991, such a home was selling for $100,000 or more, and it took a factory worker eighteen weeks to earn enough money for just the closing costs.[18]

The legacy of the union struggle of the 1930s and 1940s, combined with government support for raising people's living standards, set limits on corporations that have disappeared in recent decades. Corporations paid 23 percent of federal income taxes in the 1950s, as compared to just 9.2 percent in 1991. Big companies earned higher profit margins than smaller firms, partly due to their dominance of the market, partly to America's post-war economic advantage. They chose (or were forced) to share these extra earnings, which economists call "rents," with employees. Economists at the Brookings Institution and Harvard University estimate that 70 percent of such corporate rents were passed on to workers at all levels of the firm, benefiting secretaries and janitors as well as CEOs. Corporations routinely retained workers even in slack periods, as a way of ensuring workplace stability. Although they often received more generous tax breaks from communities than they gave back in investment, at least they kept their plants and employment offices in the same place. AT&T, for example, received much of the technology it used to finance its postwar expansion from publicly funded communications research conducted as part of the war effort, and, as current AT&T Chairman Robert Allen puts it, there "used to be a life-long commitment on the employee's part and on our part." Today, however, he admits, "the contract doesn't exist anymore."[19]

Television trivia experts still argue over exactly what the fathers in many 1950s sitcoms did for a living. Whatever it was, though, they obviously didn't have to worry about downsizing. If most married people stayed in long-term relationships during the 1950s, so did most corporations, sticking with the communities they grew up in and the employees they originally hired. Corporations were not constantly relocating in search of cheap labor during the 1950s; unlike today, increases in worker productivity usually led to increases in wages. The number of workers covered by corporate pension plans and health benefits increased steadily. So did limits on the work week. There is good reason that people look back to the 1950s as a less hurried age: The average American was working a shorter workday in the 1950s than his or her counterpart today, when a quarter of the workforce puts in 49 or more hours a week.[20]

So politicians are practicing quite a double standard when they tell us to return to the family forms of the 1950s while they do nothing to restore the job programs and family subsidies of that era, the limits on corporate relocation and financial wheeling-dealing, the much higher share of taxes paid by corporations then, the availability of union jobs for noncollege youth, and the subsidies for higher education such as the National Defense Education Act loans. Furthermore, they're not telling the whole story when they claim that the 1950s was the most prosperous time for families and the most secure decade for children. Instead, playing to our understandable nostalgia for a time when things seemed to be getting better, not worse, they engage in a tricky chronological shell game with their figures, diverting our attention from two important points. First, many individuals, families, and groups were excluded from the economic prosperity, family optimism, and social civility of the 1950s. Second, the all-time high point of child well-being and family economic security came not during the 1950s but *at the end of the 1960s*.

We now know that 1950s family culture was not only nontraditional; it was also not idyllic. In important ways, the stability of family and community life during the 1950s rested on pervasive discrimination against women, gays, political dissidents, non-Christians, and racial or ethnic minorities, as well as on a systematic cover-up of the underside of many families. Families that were harmonious and fair of their own free will may have been able to function more easily in the fifties, but few alternatives existed for members of discordant or oppressive families. Victims of child abuse, incest, alcoholism, spousal rape, and wife battering had no recourse, no place to go, until well into the 1960s.[21]

At the end of the 1950s, despite ten years of economic growth, 27.3 percent of the nation's children were poor, including those in white "underclass" communities such as Appalachia. Almost 50 percent of married-couple African-American families were impoverished—a figure far higher than today. It's no wonder African Americans are not likely to pick the 1950s as a golden age, even in comparison with the setbacks they experienced in the 1980s. When blacks moved north to find jobs in the postwar urban manufacturing boom they met vicious harassment and violence, first to prevent them from moving out of the central cities, then to exclude them from public space such as parks or beaches.

In Philadelphia, for example, the City of Brotherly Love, there were more than 200 racial incidents over housing in the first six months of 1955 alone. The Federal Housing Authority, such a boon to white working-class families, refused to insure homes in all-black or in racially mixed neighborhoods. Two-thirds of the city dwellers evicted by the urban renewal projects of the decade were African Americans and Latinos; government did almost nothing to help such displaced families find substitute housing.[22]

Women were unable to take out loans or even credit cards in their own names. They were excluded from juries in many states. A lack of options outside marriage led some women to remain in desperately unhappy unions that were often not in the best interests of their children or themselves. Even women in happy marriages often felt humiliated by the constant messages they received that their whole lives had to revolve around a man. "You are not ready when he calls—miss one turn," was a rule in the Barbie game marketed to 1950s girls; "he criticizes your hairdo—go to the beauty shop." Episodes of *Father Knows Best* advised young women: "The worst thing you can do is to try to beat a man at his own game. You just beat the women at theirs." One character on the show told women to always ask themselves, "Are you after a job or a man? You can't have both."[23]

The Fifties Experiment Comes to an End

The social stability of the 1950s, then, was a response to the stick of racism, sexism, and repression as well as to the carrot of economic opportunity and government aid. Because social protest mounted in the 1960s and unsettling challenges were posed to the gender roles and sexual mores of the previous decade, many people forget that families continued to make gains throughout the 1960s and into the first few years of the 1970s. By 1969, child poverty was down to 14 percent, its lowest level ever; it hovered just above that marker until 1975, when it began its steady climb up to contemporary figures (22 percent in 1993; 21.2 percent in 1994). The high point of health and nutrition for poor children was reached in the early 1970s.[24]

So commentators are being misleading when they claim that the 1950s was the golden age of American families. They are disregarding the number of people who were excluded during that decade and ignoring the socioeconomic gains that continued to be made through the 1960s. But they are quite right to note that the improvements of the 1950s and 1960s came to an end at some point in the 1970s (through not for the elderly, who continued to make progress).

Ironically, it was the children of those stable, enduring, supposedly idyllic 1950s families, the recipients of so much maternal time and attention, that pioneered the sharp break with their parents' family forms and gender roles in the 1970s. This was not because they were led astray by some youthful Murphy Brown in her student rebel days or inadvertently spoiled by parents who read too many of Dr. Spock's child-raising manuals.

Partly, the departure from 1950s family arrangements was a logical extension of trends and beliefs pioneered in the 1950s, or of inherent contradictions in those patterns. For example, early and close-spaced childbearing freed more wives up to join the labor force, and married women began to flock to work. By 1960, more than 40 percent of women over the age of 16 held a job, and working mothers were the fastest growing component of the labor force. The educational aspirations and opportunities that opened up for kids of the baby boom could not be confined to males, and many tight-knit, male-breadwinner, nuclear families in the 1950s instilled in their daughters the ambition to be something other than a homemaker.[25]

Another part of the transformation was a shift in values. Most people would probably agree that some changes in values were urgently needed: the extension of civil rights to racial minorities and to women; a rejection of property rights in children by parents and in women by husbands; a reaction against the political intolerance and the wasteful materialism of 1950s culture. Other changes in values remain more controversial: opposition to American intervention abroad; repudiation of the traditional sexual double standard; rebellion against what many young people saw as the hypocrisy of parents who preached sexual morality but ignored social immorality such as racism and militarism.

Still other developments, such as the growth of me-first individualism, are widely regarded as problematic by people on all points along the political spectrum. It's worth noting, though, that the origins of antisocial individualism and self-indulgent consumerism lay at least as much in the family values of the 1950s as in the youth rebellion of the 1960s. The marketing experts who never allowed the kids in *Ozzie and Harriet* sitcoms to be shown drinking milk, for fear of offending soft-drink companies that might sponsor the show in syndication, were ultimately the same people who slightly later invested billions of dollars to channel sexual rebelliousness and a depoliticized individualism into mainstream culture.

There were big cultural changes brewing by the beginning of the 1970s, and tremendous upheavals in social, sexual, and family values. And yes, there were sometimes reckless or simply laughable excesses in some of the early experiments with new gender roles, family forms, and personal expression. But the excesses of 1950s gender roles and family forms were every bit as repellent and stupid as the excesses of the sixties: Just watch a dating etiquette film of the time period, or recall that therapists of the day often told victims of incest that they were merely having unconscious oedipal fantasies.

Ultimately, though, changes in values were not what brought the 1950s family experiment to an end. The postwar family compacts between husbands and wives, parents and children, young and old, were based on the postwar social compact between government, corporations, and workers. While there was some discontent with those family bargains among women and youth, the old relations did not really start to unravel until people began to face the erosion of the corporate wage bargain and government broke its tacit societal bargain that it would continue to invest in jobs and education for the younger generation.

In the 1970s, new economic trends began to clash with all the social expectations that 1950s families had instilled in their children. That clash, not the willful abandonment of responsibility and commitment, has been the primary cause of both family rearrangements and the growing social problems that are usually attributed to such family changes, but in fact have *separate* origins.

Notes

1 Steven Thomma, "Nostalgia for '50s Surfaces," *Philadelphia Inquirer*, Feb. 4, 1996 [All notes are the author's.]

2 Frank Levy, *Dollars and Dreams: The Changing American Income Distribution* (New York: Russell Sage, 1987), p. 6; Frank Levy, "Incomes and Income Inequality," in Reynolds Farley, ed., *State of the Union: America in the 1990s*, vol. 1 (New York: Russell Sage, 1995), pp. 1–57; Richard May and Kathryn Porter, "Poverty and Income Trends, 1994," Washington, D.C.: Center on Budget and Policy Priorities, March 1996; Rob Nelson and Jon

Cowan, "Buster Power," *USA Weekend*, October 14–16, 1994, p. 10.

[3] Judith Wallerstein and Sandra Blakeslee, *The Good Marriage: How and Why Love Lasts* (Boston: Houghton Mifflin, 1995), p. 15.

[4] Donald Hernandez, *America's Children: Resources from Family, Government and the Economy* (New York: Russell Sage, 1993), pp. 99, 102; James Morone, "The Corrosive Politics of Virtue," *American Prospect* 26 (May–June 1996), p. 37; "Study Finds U.S. No. 1 in Violence," *Olympian*, November 13, 1992. See also Stephen Mintz and Susan Kellogg, *Domestic Revolutions: A Social History of American Family Life* (New York: The Free Press, 1988).

[5] William Tuttle, Jr., *"Daddy's Gone to War": The Second World War in the Lives of America's Children* (New York: Oxford University Press, 1993).

[6] "Marriage and Divorce," *March of Time*, film series 14 (1948).

[7] Arlene Skolnick and Stacey Rosencrantz, "The New Crusade for the Old Family," *American Prospect*, Summer 1994, p. 65; Hernandez, *America's Children*, pp. 128–32; Andrew Cherlin, "Changing Family and Household: Contemporary Lessons from Historical Research," *Annual Review of Sociology* 9 (1983), pp. 54–58; Sam Roberts, *Who We are: A Portrait of America Based on the Latest Census* (New York: Times Books, 1995), p. 45.

[8] Levy, "Incomes and Income Inequality," p. 20; Arthur Norton and Louisa Miller, *Marriage, Divorce, and Remarriage in the 1990s*, Current Population Reports Series P23–180 (Washington, D.C.: Bureau of the Census, October 1992); Roberts, *Who We Are* (1995 ed.), pp. 50–53.

[9] Dennis Hogan and Daniel Lichter, "Children and Youth: Living Arrangements and Welfare," in Farley, ed., *State of the Union*, vol. 2, p. 99; Richard Gelles, *Contemporary Families: A Sociological View* (Thousand Oaks, Calif.: Sage, 1995), p. 115; Hernandez, *America's Children*, p. 102. The fact that only a small percentage of children had mothers in the paid labor force, though a full 40 percent did not live in male breadwinner-female homemaker families, was because some children had mothers who worked, unpaid, in farms or family businesses, or fathers who were unemployed, or the children were not living with both parents.

[10] Edward Strecker, *Their Mothers' Sons: The Psychiatrist Examines an American Problem* (Philadelphia: J. B. Lippincott. 1946), p. 209.

[11] For discussion of the discontents, and often searing misery, that were considered normal in a "good-enough" marriage in the 1940s and 1960s, see Lillian Rubin, *Worlds of Pain: Life in the Working-Class Family* (New York: Basic Books, 1976); Mirra Komarovsky, *Blue Collar Marriage* (New Haven, Conn.: Vintage, 1962); Elaine Tyler May, *Homeward Bound: American Families in the Cold War Era* (New York: Basic books, 1988).

[12] See Robert Putnam, "The Strange Disappearance of Civic America," *American Prospect*, Winter 1996. For a glowing if somewhat lopsided picture of 1950s community solidarities, see Alan Ehrenhalt, *The Lost City: Discovering the Forgotten Virtues of Community in the Chicago of the 1950s* (New York: Basic Books, 1995). For a chilling account of communities uniting against perceived outsiders, in the same city, see Arnold Hirsch, *Making the Second Ghetto: Race and Housing in Chicago, 1940–1960* (Cambridge, Mass.: Harvard University Press, 1983). On homicide rates, see "Study Finds United States No. 1 in Violence," *Olympian*, November 13, 1992; *New York Times*, November 13, 1992, p. A9; and Douglas Lee Eckberg, "Estimates of Early Twentieth-Century U.S. Homicide Rates: A Econometric Forecasting Approach," *Demography* 32 (1995), p. 14. On lengthening commutes, see "It's Taking Longer to Get to Work," *Olympian*, December 6, 1995.

[13] The figures in this and the following paragraph come from Levy, "Incomes and Income Inequality," pp. 1-57; May and Porter, "Poverty and Income Trends, 1994"; Reynolds Farley, *The New American Reality: Who We Are, How We Got Here, Where We Are Going* (New York: Russell Sage, 1996), pp. 83–85; Gelles, *Contemporary Families*, p. 115; David Grissmer, Sheila Nataraj Kirby, Mark Bender, and Stephanie Williamson, *Student Achievement and the Changing American Family*, Ran Institute on Education and Training (Santa Monica, Calif: Rand, 1994), p. 106.

[14] William Chafe, *The Unfinished Journey: America Since World War II* (New York: Oxford University Press, 1986), pp. 113, 143; Marc Linder, "Eisenhower-Era Marxist-Confiscatory Taxation: Requiem for the Rhetoric of Rate Reduction for the Rich," *Tulane Law Review* 70 (1996), p. 917; Barry Bluestone and Teresa Ghilarducci, "Rewarding Work: Feasible Antipoverty Policy," *American Prospect* 28 (1996), p. 42; Theda Skocpol, "Delivering for Young Families," *American Prospect* 28 (1996), p. 67.

[15] Joel Tarr, "The Evolution of the Urban Infrastructure in the Nineteenth and Twentieth Centuries," ed. Royce Hanson, ed., *Perspectives on Urban*

Infrastructure (Washington, D.C.: National Academy Press, 1984); Mark Aldrich, *A History of Public Works Investment in the United States*, report prepared by the CPNSAD Research Corporation for the U.S. Department of Commerce, April 1980.

[16] For more information on this government financing, see Kenneth Jackson, *Crabgrass Frontier: The Suburbanization of the United States* (New York: Oxford University Press, 1985); and *The Way We Never Were*, chapter 4.

[17] John cook and Laura Sherman, "Economic Security Among America's Poor: The Impact of State Welfare Waivers on Asset Accumulation," Center on Hunger, Poverty, and Nutrition Policy, Tufts University, May 1996.

[18] Robert Kuttner, "The Incredible Shrinking American Paycheck," *Washington Post National Weekly Edition*, November 6–12, 1995, p. 23; Donald Bartlett and James Steele, *America: What Went Wrong?* (Kansas City: Andrews McMeel, 1992), p. 20.

[19] Richard Barnet, "Lords of the Global Economy," *Nation*, December 19, 1994, p. 756; Clay Chandler, "U.S. Corporations: Good Citizens or Bad?" *Washington Post National Weekly Edition*, May 20–26, 1996, p. 16; Steven Pearlstein, " No More Mr. Nice Guy: Corporate America Has Done an About-Face in How It Pays and Treats Employees," *Washington Post National Weekly Edition*, December 18–24, 1995, p. 10; Robert Kuttner, "Ducking Class Warfare," *Washington Post National Weekly Edition*, March 11–17, 1996, p. 5; Henry Allen, "Ha! So Much for Loyalty," *Washington Post National Weekly Edition*, March 4–10, 1996, p. 11.

[20] Ehrenhalt, *The Lost City*, pp. 11–12; Jeremy Rifken, *The End of Work: The Decline of the Global Labor Force and the Dawn of the Post-Market Era* (New York: G. P. Putnam's Sons, 1995), pp. 169, 170, 231; Juliet Schorr, *The Overworked American: The Unexpected Decline of Leisure* (New York: Basic Books, 1991).

[21] For documentation that these problems existed, see chapter 2 of *The Way We Never Were*.

[22] The poverty figures come from census data collected in *The State of America's Children Yearbook, 1996* (Washington, D.C.: Children's Defense Fund, 1996), p. 77. See also Hirsch, *Making the Second Ghetto*; Raymond Mohl, "Making the Second Ghetto in Metropolitan Miami, 1940–1960," *Journal of Urban History* 25 (1995), p. 396; Micaela di Leonardo, "Boys on the Hood," *Nation*, August 17–24, 1992, p. 180; Jackson, *Crabgrass Frontier*, pp. 226–227.

[23] Susan Douglas. *Where the Girls Are: Growing Up Female with the Mass Media* (New York: Times Books, 1994), pp. 25, 37.

[24] *The State of America's Children Yearbook, 1966*, p. 77; May and Porter, "Poverty and Income Trends: 1994," p. 23; Sara McLanahan et al., *Losing Ground: A Critique*, University of Wisconsin Institute for Research on Poverty, Special Report No. 38, 1985.

[25] For studies of how both middle-class and working-class women in the 1950s quickly departed from, or never quite accepted, the predominant image of women, see Joanne Meyerowitz, ed., *Not June Cleaver: Women and Gender in Postwar America, 1945–1960* (Philadelphia: Temple University Press, 1994).

UNIT SIX

Modern social life presents all of us with constant media messages about world problems like political upheavals, warfare, rioting, and so on. In this unit we will deal with sociological issues in their global context. We will show how modern social movements increasingly address world issues, how environmental problems really are global in nature, and how globalization involves the social change in economics, government, and culture that increasingly link all nations.

In this part of our book we include crowds and social movements as examples of the types of social actions and social movement organizations (SMOs) that increasingly reflect worldwide disparities in opportunity and resources. Sociology will help you understand that violence, while not condoned, often stems from unfair and intolerable social conditions, including the failure to address sources of people's grievances. Sociology will also help you understand some causes of violent crowd behavior that have many parallels in understanding other forms of violence such as terrorism.

As we ponder our individual futures, we should also ponder the future of the world that we all share. Sociological perspectives on the environment and globalization help to maintain both personal concerns with the quality of our own lives and that of all people of the world. We purposely included these two important issues as the last two chapters in the book to show the ultimate contexts in which multilevel sociological theories and the sociological imagination apply. Whether sociologists or not, all of us must become more aware of and knowledgeable about the sociology of the world.

18

Crowds and Social Movements

Collective behavior refers to less established and less enduring patterns of social activity including rumors and gossip, fashion and fads, crazes and mass hysteria, public opinion, crowd behavior and social movements (Macionis 2002). Sociologists have studied crowd behavior and social movements the most. A crowd is an aggregation of people temporarily gathered at a particular location or event, whose behaviors can change and spread rapidly under certain conditions. Usually the people in crowds act orderly and in consideration of others, such as people waiting in long lines to enter a concert, or people waiting to catch a train. These are examples of conventional crowds. In expressive crowds people's behavior is often loud and emotional yet patterned. For example, organized cheering and singing at soccer matches or the laughter and applause at appropriate times during a play are both emotional and patterned. A key concern of sociologists has been to explain how and why some expressive and conventional crowds become acting crowds in which people act violently as in riots or have violent confrontations with police or panic as when crowds stampede toward exits injuring and killing people.

Several social factors have been found to explain the violent and self-destructive behavior of acting crowds. Cultural circumstances including longstanding tensions and animosities between groups, especially in those countries lacking social reforms to ensure more equal treatment, are related to crowd violence. Many large and very violent race riots in the United States, for example, have occurred during times of war, at home or abroad, and other rapid social changes. These periods include the Civil War (1860–1865), World War One (1914–1918), and World War Two (1940–1945). Another frequent type of crowd violence in the U.S. is represented by the 5,000 lynchings of mostly black men in the post Civil War South from 1880 through 1930. This era was characterized by institutionalized discrimination against blacks in the form of so-called Jim Crow laws that mandated blacks use separate dining and travel facilities and denied many blacks opportunities to vote. The catalysts for lynchings were often alleged instances of blacks committing criminal acts or instances in which blacks deviated from expected behavior. The commonness and cruelty of lynchings, where corpses were often mutilated and left as public displays, were expressed in the poignancy of the title and lyrics of the song Strange Fruit, often sung by the jazz singer Billie Holiday. Lynch mobs were often made up of less educated, poor, white men. This period also saw such people commit acts of violence throughout the South and Midwest as members of the Ku Klux Klan.

Most race riots in the U.S. before the 1960s were riots that involved mobs of whites attacking blacks and often killing them and destroying their homes and neighborhoods. In the years during and after World War One, many blacks migrated northward to states like Indiana and Illinois. Sometimes these newcomers entered jobs traditionally held by whites, and in East St. Louis, Illinois during World War One blacks were employed to replace striking whites. These changes increased tensions between blacks and whites. On July 2, 1919, an incident in which several police officers allegedly were killed by blacks, touched off the very violent East St. Louis riot. About fifty people, mostly blacks, were killed and much property was destroyed. Local newspapers did little to quell the possibilities of violence and instead inflamed it by reporting such falsehoods as stating that armies of blacks were coming from other cities (Rudwick 1966). Riots in the U.S. during and after the 1960s involved black crowds damaging and looting property, often white owned, and engaging in acts of destruction expressing dissatisfaction with urban social conditions, especially with the actions of police in arresting blacks (Jasper 1998). The destruction in these so-called property riots led to attempts at reformi alation of violent behavior. Turner and Killian's (1993) emergent norm theory stresses the emergent nature of violence as suggested by leaders and accepted by members of crowds. This theory has been used successfully to explain various types of crowd violence, especially prison riots led by a core of leaders that occur more often when prison overcrowding makes crowd control more difficult. Preventing overcrowding in theaters and restaurants and at athletic events is a key strategy in avoiding panic among expressive crowds or among conventional crowds during emergencies. Studies of soccer match riots throughout the world show that violence is more likely when many "standing room only" tickets are sold, alcoholic beverages are readily available, and when there are insufficient barriers between spectators and the playing field.

People in crowds do not usually either riot or panic. Nevertheless, the expressiveness of people's behaviors in crowds differs considerably from their everyday public actions. In expressive crowds at athletic events and at rock concerts, for example, fans and spectators yell, scream, curse, make lewd gestures, and so on. Furthermore, the reactions of expressive crowds are often spontaneous and spread very quickly through scores of thousands of people. The standing wave of fans and other collective expressions of crowd support show how rapid and spontaneous expressive crowd behavior can be. Few sociologists today support the early French sociologist Gustave LeBon's (1960) ideas of a "crowd mind" activated by an innate suggestibility like the rapid spread of panic among stampeding cattle. Nevertheless, most sociologists believe that rapid and unified emotional expressions are an important expected part of participation in expressive crowds (Jasper 1998). The anonymity of being among strangers and the belief that authorities will be unable to stop or to find people who escalate expressive actions of violence in destructive directions increases the chances of destructive fan behavior (Tarrow 1994).

Social movements are organized and collective efforts of people who make up social movement organizations (SMOs) to change social life (or resist changing it). More organized and enduring than crowd behaviors, social movements are similar to crowds in the sense that they do not endure beyond the existence of their focal concerns. Progressive movements such as the Gay Rights Movement in the U. S. advocate change, while reactionary movements like the Traditional Values Coalition oppose change. Depending on the scope of the people who would be affected, several important types of SMOs may be distinguished. Alternative social movements want a specific change in a limited sector of society. Promise Keepers in the U.S. desires to increase husbands' and fathers' involvement in family life. Reform social movements advocate delimited change for everyone. The Temperance Movement in the U.S. succeeded in a ban on the legal production and distribution of alcoholic beverages during the Prohibition era in the U.S. from 1920 through 1933 (Gusfield 1963). Revolutionary social movements want broad changes that apply to all. The Russian Revolution of 1918 is an example.

How and why social movements emerge and whether or not they obtain their objectives have been studied extensively by sociologists. Social movements emerge among people with common, frustrating experiences and grievances or who have similar beliefs, such as among people in the U.S. who either favor abortion on demand or feel that all abortion is wrong. The people who join an SMO are the movement's social base. Frustrations and grievances are likely to start SMOs, especially when people perceive that their situations are becoming worse or when they perceive that others' lives are getting better while their own are not. Robert Merton (1968) called such common predispositions relative deprivation. Neil Smelser's (1962) structural strain theory adds other important explanatory factors including the existence of relative disadvantage for long periods, the role of articulate leaders, and the importance of precipitating events such as violence used by police in arresting a suspect like Rodney King. In 1992, the acquittal of Los Angeles police officers who beat Rodney King during his arrest touched off the bloodiest riots in twenty-five years.

Recently, sociologists have focused upon the crucial processes by which SMOs mobilize human and economic resources and how they gain favorable publicity for their causes. Resource mobilization theory has been used successfully in explanations of why in the past some movements have been more successful than others and in explaining how many current movements mobilize and use resources and publicity (McAdam, McCarthy and Zald 1996). The importance of relative deprivation, a social base, an articulate leader but insufficient and unsuccessful management of resources explains the course of the Marcus Garvey Movement in the U.S. during the early 1920s. Garvey was a very charismatic figure and a dynamic speaker who could articulate the grievances of many poorer blacks. He was also able to collect millions of small donations to support his Universal Negro Improvement Association. However, sufficient investment was not forthcoming for his goal of establishing an international steamship line, his Black Star Line Corporation. His efforts to mobilize resources ended in financial turmoil and failure.

In contrast, sociologists expect that the so-called New Social Movements will be both more numerous and more successful in the future in the sense of marshalling and using resources and gaining widespread cultural support (McAdam, McCarthy, and Zald 1996). Several contemporary aspects of social life make it much easier for SMOs to gain resources including economic and legal aid and favorable publicity. For example, legal aid to many SMOs including those in the Gay Rights Movement has been readily provided by The American Civil Liberties Union (ACLU) and the Equal Employment Opportunity Commission (EEOC), the investigative agency that recommends legal action regarding employment grievances to the Justice Department. (See Chapter 16.) The widespread publicity given to trials involving employment grievances and civil challenges of marriage laws have helped extend homosexual rights in workplaces and in civil unions. In fact, such publicity has led many employers in the U.S. to provide employment benefits to the same-sex partners of employees before being legally challenged to do so.

Contemporary SMOs also are unique in the sense that their memberships and social bases are worldwide and include well-educated, economically prosperous, and very well known spokespersons (Pakulski 1993). Bono, the lead singer of the rock group U2, is a good illustration of the role celebrities now play in mobilizing support for SMOs. Widely used modern forms of communication such as cell phones and video recorders also play an important role in publicizing the unpleasant events and circumstance that many SMOs address. The widespread publicity given to workers' demonstrations at the 1999 meeting of the World Trade Organization (WTO) in Seattle is a good example of how the grievances workers have with multinational corporate power have become publicly visible and well known. Surely no event in human history has received more instantaneous, worldwide attention than the tragedy of 9/11. In fact, cell phones played an active role in passengers overcoming the terrorists on the hijacked plane that crashed in the Pennsylvanian countryside. The rapidity with which countries of the world learned about and began dealing with terrorism in relation to 9/11 illustrates how telecommunication networks now simplify the mobilization of worldwide SMO resources (see Chapters 16, 19, and 20).

Name: ______________________________

Quiz Questions: Crowds and Social Movements

1. Crowds in a shopping mall illustrate which of these types of crowds?
   a. expressive crowd
   b. acting crowd
   c. conventional crowd
   d. none of the above
2. Wartime periods have been periods during which riots in the U.S. have been more likely to occur. (True or False?)
3. During and after the 1960s most riots in the U.S. have been mobs of whites attacking blacks. (True or False?)
4. <u>Strange Fruit</u> was a song about riots. (True or False?)
5. Crowd leaders who suggest violence are an important element in emergent norm theory. (True or False?)
6. Overcrowding usually has little effect upon the likelihood that expressive crowds will become violent. (True or False?)
7. Mothers Against Drunk Drivers (MADD) has succeeded in many states passing legislation mandating harsher penalties for drunk driving, especially when drunk drivers kill people. This movement is which of the following types of movements?
   a. an alternative movement
   b. a reform movement
   c. a revolutionary movement
   d. a reactionary movement
8. Which of the following refers to people's perspectives that they are not doing as well as others?
   a. structural strain
   b. a social base
   c. resource mobilization
   d. relative deprivation
9. Current social movements are more able to develop resources than was the case in the Marcus Garvey movement. (True or False?)
10. Current social movements are less likely to become international in scope than was the Marcus Garvey movement. (True or False?)

Name: ______________________________

Exercise: Crowds and Social Movements

1. Observe the behavior of a conventional crowd on your campus, such as students in line waiting to enter an event, or the audience at a campus theater. In the space provided, describe the patterns of behavior that indicated it was a conventional rather than another type of crowd.

Name: ______________________________

Exercise: Crowds and Social Movements

2. Discuss a brief example of behavior on your campus that was similar to SMO activity, such as election campaigns of students running for office, clubs or organizations collecting money for a cause, and so on. In the space provided, discuss patterns of actions that resemble an SMO.

Name: ______________________________

Exercise: Crowds and Social Movements

3. Think about a public event that you have attended and the crowd or audience that you were a part of. In the space provided, use the crowd/audience behavior to discuss expressive activity, conventional behavior, and crowd control measures.

Name: ______________________________

Exercise: Crowds and Social Movements

4. Think about social groups you or members of your family or the family of friends have joined or contributed to. Select one of the groups that resembles a social movement organization (SMO). Based on your knowledge of involvement you or acquaintances had with the group, discuss, in the space provided, the <u>type of movement</u> it seems to have been, the <u>goals it had</u>, and information about <u>resource mobilization</u>.

Name: ______________________________

Exercise: Crowds and Social Movements

5. Watch the movie *Getting Straight*. Using the movie content, in the space provided, discuss the type of SMO the movie dealt with, the goals it had, and resource mobilization strategies.

Name: ______________________________

Exercise: Crowds and Social Movements

6. Watch the movie *Ghosts of Mississippi*. Using movie content, discuss, in the space provided, violent crowd behavior, the social base of the civil rights movement, and resource mobilization.

Name: ______________________________

Exercise: Crowds and Social Movements

7. Go to the campus library or online, and select an article from the journal *International Social Movement Research.* Select any one article, read it, and use the contents to illustrate, in the space provided, resource mobilization, New Social Movements, and spokespersons.

Name: ______________________

Exercise: Crowds and Social Movements

8. Go to the campus library or online, and select an article from the journal *Research in Social Movements, Conflicts and Change*. Select any one article, read it, and use the contents to illustrate, in the space provided, resource mobilization, New Social Movements, and gaining widespread cultural support.

Name: ______________________________

Exercise: Crowds and Social Movements

9. Go to the web site of an SMO, like Amnesty International or Greenpeace. Using information available on the web site, discuss, in the space provided, resource mobilization, worldwide publicity, and New Social Movements.

Name: ______________________________

Exercise: Crowds and Social Movements

10. Go to the web site of a government agency that deals with legal challenges of workplace discrimination, like the web site of the Equal Employment Opportunity Commission or the Justice Department. Use information from the web site to discuss, in the space provided, legal action to extend rights, resource mobilization for legal action, and publicity of case law.

19

Environmental and Natural Resources Sociology

Environmental sociologists study how groups support or oppose each other in gathering resources, developing communities, and dumping their waste products (Dunlap and Catton 2002). We commonly think about our own environment as our supply depot for resources, our waste depository, and/or our home. Environmental sociologists are interested in the conflict and negotiation among two or more of these views. In these ways, sociologists focus upon the ways environmental resources and social life interrelate.

Early European sociologists like Durkheim and Weber, who studied the world at the turn of the last century, looked back on history and saw that their world was moving away from a society where most people made their living through farming, fishing, mining, and forestry to an industrial society, where the economy was based on large-scale manufacturing. The move to manufacturing transformed our society, making it more efficient but also less personal, more bureaucratized, and more reliant on science. (See Chapters 7, 15, 16, and 17.) Increases in the quality of medicine as well as the quantity and quality of food and manufactured goods led many to believe that an industrially based society allowed humans to escape the limits to growth that govern the natural world. Sociologists have come to call this belief exemptionalism and since society was advancing beyond physical limits that governed the natural world, early sociologists believed that social facts or laws could explain human behavior and natural laws could not (Catton and Dunlap 1980).

Early American sociologists preferred to study the ways people lived in the built environment in emerging large cities rather than how people related to the natural environment. These sociologists drew parallels between processes of city growth and the processes found by animal and plant ecologists (Park and Burgess 1925). Such views, which came to be known as human ecology, emphasized the human interaction structured by the interplay of a population, its technological culture, its customs and beliefs, and the natural resources which keep the population biologically and socially healthy (Maines 2001: 78–86).

Rural sociologists distinguished themselves from other early sociologists as an applied branch of sociology that focused on improving the lives of individuals and groups living in rural areas such as farmers, fishers, miners and loggers (Field and Burch 1988). One focus of rural sociological interest was on the extraction of natural resources—particular physical and biological objects that members of a society have defined as useful—from their environment. Thus, rural sociologists studied relationships among the natural resources in a particular place, the technology used to harvest the natural resources, and the ways the resources and the technology affected community relationships and their growth (Field and Burch 1988).

Early natural resource sociologists recognized that natural resources (agricultural plants and animals, forests, rivers, mineral deposits) had an effect on how and where human communities developed (Field, Luloff, and Krannich 2002). They also realized that the technological changes coming from the new mechanized economy changed how natural resources were gathered and used. These changes, in turn, had additional effects on community organization and well-being. One classic study demonstrating these relationships was Walter Goldschmidt's analysis of farm communities (Goldschmidt 1946, 1978). Goldschmidt analyzed communities with different farming orientations. Some communities had primarily small family farms; others had large corporate or commercial farms in the Central Valley of California. In small farm communities, people viewed each other as more equal. In large farm communities, there was a class structure of owners and workers. Thus, the structure of farming affected the class structure in a community and the class structure affected the way community members interacted (Goldschmidt 1978). By the sixties, natural resource sociologists were working both in the U.S. and other countries in efforts designed to develop rural lands and people, while avoiding the creation of further environmental and social problems. Many natural resources sociologists continue to find employment in the government (with the Department of Agriculture, the Forest Service, the Bureau of the Interior and the U.S. Fish and Wildlife), within county extension services, and within international development organizations.

Except for rural sociologists, most American sociologists abandoned or dismissed the environment and its potential effects upon human society until the 1960s, when environmental social movements influenced sociologists to reexamine society's relationship to both the built and the natural environment. Sociologists began rethinking the ways in which societies and their environments were related and began drawing on work from human ecology, geography, and economics as well as urban sociology and natural resources sociology (Humphrey, Lewis and Buttel 2001). Much of the work done by environmental sociologists has been theoretical, trying to mesh the scientific knowledge of the physical sciences with sociological knowledge of society. To some environmental sociologists, this has meant going back to the classical sociological theorists and rereading their works to see how, if at all, the authors had thought about the environment. Others have examined the relationship between environment and society using the most recent theories available (Dunlap, Buttel, Dickens, Gijwijt 2002). Still other sociologists have looked for social scientists previously ignored by sociology who had recognized that human societies were not exempt from natural laws. The work of the Reverend Thomas Malthus (1798) is a good example. Malthus had argued that unless society changed its ways, the human population would grow faster than its food supply. When this happened several negative consequences (disease, war, famine) would be incurred until human populations fell back within the limits of their food. This was one of the earliest studies of human population dynamics as well as political economy. (See Chapter 16 and 17.)

Following the lead of Malthus, most environmental sociology studies examine issues of environmental quality, environmental degradation and sustainability. They deal with real or imagined changes in the environment that affect the beauty, the healthfulness, and/or the ability of individuals to make a living (Hays 1987). Often environmental quality and degradation studies deal with conflict between efforts to preserve the existing environment as is versus efforts to conserve some environmental quality while still engaging in controlled use by humans. This conflict is known as the preservation/conservation debate. Another aspect of environmental quality and degradation studies involves the idea of risk and risk assessment (Clarke and Short 1993, Krimsky and Plough 1988, Perrow 1984). It is argued by some sociologists that the less known or understood about the possible consequences of environmental degradation, the more likely it is that the degradation can lead not only to physical sickness but also to a sense of dread and social breakdown among community members (Erikson 1995). (See Chapter 7.)

Other studies by environmental sociologists emphasize environmental justice. Environmental justice studies examine the power processes surrounding who gets the beneficial goods and who has to deal with the potentially harmful wastes. Many disputes over the siting of new, potentially hazardous land uses focus not only on potential environmental degradation, but also on who will bear the costs and who will be exposed to hazards (Bullard 1994, Crawford 1996).

At the international level environmental justice issues revolve around the north-south debate. The United States and other developed countries in the northern hemisphere import most of their raw materials from less-developed, southern hemisphere countries. The northern hemisphere has begun exporting some of its waste to the southern hemisphere (Frey 2001). When products like pesticides have been banned in the northern hemisphere, they are still sold to southern hemisphere countries (Frey 1995). Southern farmers use the products and sell their produce to the North. Thus, dangerous pesticides that were banned still continue to enter the food stream. Countries of the northern hemisphere are now also asking southern hemisphere nations not to develop their resources for their own citizenry, but to continue exporting them northward. Southern hemisphere countries see this as an environmental justice issue since it was the development of the northern hemisphere nations that have depleted their resources and polluted the environment, yet these same countries do not appear interested in or committed to solving these problems.

Conflicts continue to grow, both nationally and globally, over environmental resources. Achieving sustainable development, which allows for economic growth while protecting the environment, is a difficult task. Environmental sociologists must continue to examine the issues of environmental quality, environmental degradation, and environmental justice to find workable solutions to these conflicts.

Name: ______________________

Quiz Questions: Environmental and Natural Resources Sociology

1. Environmental Sociologists focus on:
   a. how industrialization affects people
   b. the conflict between opposing environmental groups
   c. the conflict between those who support gathering resources and those who oppose development
   d. none of the above.
2. Early European sociologist studied how industrialization affected society. (True or False?)
3. Dangerous products are currently regulated much the same way throughout the world. (True or False?)
4. Rev. Thomas Malthus argued that which problems would occur if population outgrows the food supply?
   a. cities will become overcrowded as people relocate for food
   b. disease, war, and famine will occur
   c. no problems will occur because science will find solutions
   d. all of the above
5. An example of an environmental justice issue would be:
   a. whether or not to allow a farmer to change crops
   b. whether or not to allow a new mall to be built
   c. whether or not to allow a new trash incinerator to be built
   d. all of the above
6. Studies that focus on declines in environmental beauty, health, and livability *and* its costs deals with which of the following?
   a. environmental conservation
   b. environmental degradation
   c. environmental justice
   d. environmental usage
7. Southern hemisphere countries are better developed than are Northern hemisphere countries. (True or False?)
8. Environmental degradation can lead to social breakdown of communities. (True or False?)
9. Early American sociologists studied:
   a. the ways people lived in the built environment in emerging large cities
   b. the ways people relate to the natural environment
   c. the ways communities relate to each other
   d. the way rural societies lived
10. Human societies are exempt from natural laws. (True or False?)

Name: ______________________________

Exercise: Environmental and Natural Resources Sociology

1. In the space provided, discuss environmental degradation in your hometown.

Name: ______________________

Exercise: Environmental and Natural Resources Sociology

2. In the space provided, discuss how worldwide environmental justice could be improved.

Name: ______________________

Exercise: Environmental and Natural Resources Sociology

3. Think about the community, city, or county in a rural area where you grew up. Discuss, in the space provided, how your area of origin illustrates exemptionism, natural resources, and environmental justice.

Name: ______________________

Exercise: Environmental and Natural Resources Sociology

4. Think about the campus community environment, and, in the space provided, discuss environmental quality, the preservation/conservation debate, and environmental resources.

Name: ______________________________

Exercise: Environmental and Natural Resources Sociology

5. Watch the movie *Silkwood*. Based upon the contents of the movie, discuss, in the space provided, exemptionism, environmental degradation, and the preservation/conservation debate.

Name: ______________________________

Exercise: Environmental and Natural Resources Sociology

6. Watch the movie *A Civil Action*. Based upon the contents of the movie, discuss, in the space provided, environmental degradation, environmental justice, and who bears the costs of and hazards of degradation.

Name: ______________________________

Exercise: Environmental and Natural Resources Sociology

7. Go to the campus library or online, and select an article from the journal *Environmental Ethics*. Select any one article, read it, and discuss, in the space provided, how the article illustrated sustainability, the preservation/conservation debate, and environmental justice.

Name: ______________________________

Exercise: Environmental and Natural Resources Sociology

8. Go to the campus library or online, and select an article related to environmental issues from the journal *Social Justice*. Select any one article on the environment, and, in the space provided, discuss how it illustrated sustainability, environmental degradation, and environmental justice.

Name: ______________________________

Exercise: Environmental and Natural Resources Sociology

9. Go to the web site of a town or city near your hometown or the campus. Use information from the web site to illustrate, in the space provided, environmental quality, the preservation/conservation debate, and environmental justice.

Name: ______________________________

Exercise: Environmental and Natural Resources Sociology

10. Go to the web site of a recycling company in your hometown or the campus community area. Using information on the web site, discuss, in the space provided, environmental quality, recycling and sustainability, and environmental justice.

20

Globalization

Over the past 30 years, sociological interest in processes of globalization has increased significantly (Guillen 2001). Globalization refers to the increased number of social relationships occurring across national borders involving more extensive economy, cultural, and political ties (Giddens 1990; Waters 1995). While a worldwide economic system has existed in most of the world for more than 500 years, instantaneous worldwide communication over the Internet and satellite television networks has recently increased people's subjective awareness of and concern about global interconnectedness, especially as this interconnectedness affects their local economy, culture, and environment (Chirot 1977, Robertson 1992, Wallerstein 1974). Sociologists study both the objective and subjective features of globalization and how these cross-society links influence social change. (See Chapter 18.)

Many sociologists focus upon the ways economic globalization has the potential to change social structures. Herbert Blumer (1990) noted that industrialization, whether global or local, can move jobs and people, change group relationships, and foster the development of new groups with new interests. Evaluation of globalization's influences on developed and developing countries is of major interest to sociologists. Some sociologists see globalization processes as affecting relations between individuals and societies (Guillen 2001). For example, at the end of his analysis of global industrialization, Blumer (1990) argues that the processes of globalization are essentially neutral; however, individuals and group actors can use those processes to their own ends.

Other sociologists argue that the effects of globalization are, on the whole, negative. Increasingly, investment capital and the opportunity for investors in one country to invest in the securities of other nations directly characterize the way business is done. Information about worldwide business opportunities is so readily available that the unrestricted flow of capital and goods across national borders occurs in ways that make it difficult for national governments to figure out ownership or productivity. Moreover, while domestic investments are guaranteed through deposit insurance and other governmental safeguards within developed countries, emerging international investment networks that include developing countries do not have as much built-in security or control (Krugman and Obstfeld 1991). In these cases U.S.-based transnational corporations (TNCs) and international investors have relied on the U.S. government to protect their assets either through support of repressive political regimes or through direct or covert military action by the United States (Chirot 1977, Wallerstein 1977).

Transnational corporations have developed close ties through cross investment and other strategies including syndicated investing and interlocking directories (Kuno et al 1998). Governments, on the other hand, cannot regulate globalized production and sales networks, since the political institutions necessary to regulate global commerce have not yet evolved (Western 1997). Many countries have entered the World Trade Organization (WTO) and many regional trade agreements promote freer trade among regional partners such as the North American Free Trade Agreement (NAFTA) between the U.S. and Mexico and the European Union (EU). While such strategies ease trade for disparate economies such as between Mexico and the U.S., there have not been enough attendant agreements on labor standards or investment in the development of Mexico to allow industrialization to develop fully (Dreiling 2000).

To sociologists market forces alone will clearly not enable globalized commerce to foster the common cultural and political ties necessary for better worldwide labor standards, environmental protection agreements, and so on. Without regulatory mechanisms that are a part of domestic political economies (see Chapter 16), TNCs will continue to manufacture and assemble goods in the cheapest labor markets and sell finished products where richer consumers are most plentiful. This process results in poor societies becoming increasingly dependent upon rich nations, a major factor in the worldwide labor protest for more equitable labor regulation (Wallerstein 1979; 1984; Walton and Ragin 1990). Merely to criticize the TNCs for their investment decisions and their other unregulated behavior misses the point that international labor standards and environmental control measures will <u>not</u> emerge until governments agree to adopt and to implement them (Carruthers and Babb 2000). Thus, while globalized production has the potential for increasing worldwide wages and workplace standards (Schwartzman 1998), without regulation as a worldwide political economy, there is no inherent reason for it having any positive effects (Western 1997).

Sociologists also have studied instances of globalized commerce that have operated quite positively. For example, research in China and the East Asian Tigers—Hong Kong, Taiwan, Singapore, and South Korea—has shown how governmental coordination at both state and local levels and also traditional cultural norms for commerce successfully have combined with privatization and globalized commerce to represent many forms of capitalism (Gereffi 1994). Governmental coordination has efficiently fostered and sometimes protected domestic companies as they developed into producers and exporters as well as assemblers and importers. Localized governmental agencies in China have been very effective in the privatization of commerce, dispelling the myth of government as incapable or too bureaucratic (Walters 1995). Use of traditional and often localized networks of commerce also has allowed the ties and trust necessary to establish credible and ongoing commercial networks with the West, especially the United States (Portes 1998). Conversely, American firms have used these same traditional and often localized networks to micro-market their products (Roach 1997). Rather than impeding capitalism in the developing nations, these studies show how government and traditional cultures are vital for diverse political economies to develop. (See Chapter 15.)

Other sociologists have focused upon change evident in global cultural ties as well as political interconnectedness (Waters 1995). Globalization of Western culture will also evolve with the diversity already apparent in globalized capitalism. The media and globalized commerce increasingly make awareness of and access to aspects of America throughout the world. Cultural icons such as famous American athletes and entertainers often endorse U.S. food products and fashion styles leading to their widespread adoption and diffusion. It is very important to remember, however, that use of these products and the meanings of the adopted elements of Western culture may be quite different in other areas of the world. Thus, while McDonald's food products have spread widely throughout the world, cultural diversity in their use and meaning is quite clear. While widely accepted in China, for example, McDonald's fast food outlets are considered places for getting snack foods rather than full meals (Yan 1997). In Japan, such food also is considered snack food lacking rice as the defining culinary characteristic of a meal (Obnuki-Tierney 1997). Moreover, since forms of capitalistic enterprise are developing by means of traditional cultural norms, it is quite unlikely that globalized commerce will homogenize culture; to the contrary, it probably will make such diversity increasingly apparent

(Hamilton and Biggert 1998). During globalized commerce elements of other cultures will probably enter the way business is done in the U.S., as Japan's "just-in-time" production system has been adopted by some American companies (Carruthers and Babb 2000).

In many ways the most problematic features of globalization are the capacity of the environment to sustain development and the growing population of the developing nations (see Chapter 19). The resource-dependent nations of the Northern Hemisphere and the less developed countries of the Southern Hemisphere must adapt better relationships and more sensible ways of resource management. New Social Movements pressing for human rights, international wage standards, and environmental protection agreements will increasingly accompany worldwide commerce (Mielants 2002, Schwartzman 1998). (See Chapter 18.) While world population growth is slowing, the population momentum that exists in the populations of developing nations is a very serious problem. China, Singapore and other nations have employed harsh disincentives like higher taxes to encourage couples to have no more than two children (Weeks 1999). These measures have brought fertility rates down quickly. Furthermore, development itself results in a continuance of a decline in both deaths and number of children born (Weeks 1999). Yet, developing nations have a much larger proportion of youth in their populations, and their populations will grow because of this disproportionate population distribution rather than excessive fertility (Shepard 2002). Consequently, the two biggest challenges of world development will be a better distribution and use of resources and bringing the growth of the world population closer to Zero Population Growth as fast as possible.

It remains to be seen, therefore, whether or not the potential benefits of globalization will be widely realized. Without active concerns between governments and much better agreements among nations concerning resource use and development, it seems likely that there will be fewer rather than more globalization benefits. More appreciation among the developed nations of the needs and concerns of the developing nations also will help maximize the positive aspects of globalization. Collective pursuit of worldwide standards for employment, production, and environmental protection are also essential. Without these attendant features of globalization, the future of the world may involve more inequality among nations than exists now (Schwitzer 2000).

Name: ______________________________

Quiz Questions: Globalization

1. Globalization refers to:

   a. increased number of people moving around
   b. increased number of people migrating to cities
   c. increased number of social relationships occurring across national borders
   d. all of the above

2. Blumer analyzed global industrialization and argues that the process of globalization:

   a. are essentially neutral
   b. are essentially negative
   c. are essentially positive
   d. none of the above

3. National governments have complete control over the flow of capital and goods across national borders. (True or False?)

4. TNCs stands for:

   a. transnational countries
   b. transnational corporations
   c. three nations councils
   d. transinternational councils

5. The North American Free Trade Agreement is an example of a regional trade agreement. (True or False?)

6. One of the most problematic features of globalization is:

   a. the capacity of TNCs to produce goods
   b. the capacity of the environment to sustain development
   c. the capacity of WTOs to create employment
   d. none of the above

7. In Japan, McDonald's meals are considered snacks because they lack soy. (True or False?)

8. Free trade has been more a part of NAFTA than have agreements about wage levels and labor standards. (True or False?)

9. Which of these population issues is very important to the amount of development that can take place in countries like China?

   a. too few store outlets
   b. too much governmental interference
   c. too little education
   d. too much population momentum

10. The two biggest challenges of world development will be better distribution and use of resources and control of WTOs. (True or False?)

Name: ______________________________

Exercise: Globalization

1. Think of news events you have seen recently. In the space provided, discuss how news events increased your awareness of global inter-connectedness.

Name: ______________________________

Exercise: Globalization

2. Discuss, in the space provided, how TNCs can be better regulated.

Name: ______________________________

Exercise: Globalization

3. Think of the product labels on your clothes and on the appliances and devices in your campus dorm room or apartment. Based upon where the items were made, discuss, in the space provided, globalized manufacturing, economic ties among nations, and inequalities among societies.

Name: ______________________________

Exercise: Globalization

4. Think of recent television advertising you have seen while watching sports events or news programs. Use information on the companies that you have seen advertised to discuss, in the space provided, <u>globalized manufacturing</u>, <u>transnational corporations (TNCs)</u>, and <u>world development</u>.

Name: ______________________________

Exercise: Globalization

5. Watch the movie *Local Hero*. Based upon the contents of the movie, discuss, in the space provided, globalized economic ties, developing countries, and cultural ties in globalization.

Name: ______________________________

Exercise: Globalization

6. Watch the movie *Roger and Me*. Based upon the content of the movie, discuss, in the space provided, globalized production, TNCs, and environmental and social justice in globalization.

Name: ______________________________

Exercise: Globalization

7. Go to the campus library or online to select an article from the journal *Global Risk Assessments: Issues, Concepts, and Applications*. Select any one article, read it, and, in the space provided, discuss globalized commerce, regulation of labor standards, and the increased economic ties with globalization.

Name: ______________________________

Exercise: Globalization

8. Go to the campus library or online to select an article from the journal *Economic Development and Cultural Change*. Select any one article, read it, and, in the space provided, discuss how it illustrated diversity in globalized commerce, regulation of TNCs, and environmental justice world-wide.

Name: ______________________________

Exercise: Globalization

9. Go to the web site of any one of the Asian Tigers. Based upon information from the web site, discuss, in the space provided, development of global commerce, efforts to regulate growth, and progress in development.

Name: ______________________

Exercise: Globalization

10. Go to the web site of any less developed country of the world, and, from information available on the web site, discuss, in the space provided, development, globalized commerce, and governmental involvement in development.

The Effects of Free Trade on Development, Democracy, and Environmental Protection

Perry Grossman

Much literature in the social sciences addresses the relationship between economic development and democracy. Many large-scale surveys have found a strong relationship between economic development and democracy, while others indicate a more complex dynamic involving education and inequality. Comparative studies of fewer cases indicate ambiguous results but suggest the importance of historical contingencies, class conflict, unionization, and opposition parties. Free trade advocates argue that trade leads to economic development, which leads to increased demands for and gains in environmental protection. I argue, however, that the relationship needs to be understood in a more complex and dynamic way that takes into account a variety of political, cultural, and economic developments resulting from freer trade. Accordingly, I raise several reasons to be skeptical about claims linking free trade, development, democracy, and environmental protection. I further argue that free trade acts as a cultural constraint upon democratic and environmental protection initiatives.

Introduction

Free trade advocates argue that increased trade results in greater prosperity, which fortifies democracy and helps to provide both the material means and cultural values conducive for such social concerns as environmental protection. Carlos Salinas, former President of Mexico, has stated:

> I believe that on the environment, Mexico and the United States are finally on the same track. And NAFTA will also help in this regard. A country that is stricken by poverty will automatically destroy the environment. A country that can lift itself out of poverty at least has a choice. Mexico is channeling more money toward the environment, more money toward infrastructure, and more funds to improve the quality of life in Mexico. (Salinas 1994, p. 32)

By contrast, critics insist that free trade weakens democracy and environmental protection. As Martin Khor argues:

> The Multilateral Trade Organization (MTO)[1] would erode national sovereignty (national control over domestic policies) as member governments have to alter a wide range of laws and policies to conform to the agreements overseen by the MTO. Particularly affected are policies

From *Sociological Inquiry*, Vol. 72, No. 1, Winter 2002 by Perry Grossman.

> relating to external trade, domestic self-sufficiency (for example, in food or basic manufactured products), foreign investment, intellectual property, technology. But there will be ramifications also for health, safety, environmental, labour and cultural policies. Weak nations (the South) will find their economies placed even more at the service of Northern interests, and their space for independent policies will be very limited. (Khor 1993, p. 101)

Thus, Khor, and many other critics of trade emphasize the negative political and environmental ramifications of trade.

In this paper, I analyze these claims about the relationship between free trade, economic growth, democracy, and environmental protection. I review modernization perspectives that suggest a positive relationship between development and democracy, and dependency perspectives that indicate a negative relationship. Most such studies, however, have focused on national policies and fail to fully consider the international dimensions of these concerns. As David Held argues,

> [A] theory of democracy (whether focused on empirical or philosophical concerns) requires a theory of the interlocking processes and structures of the global system. (Held 1995, p. 22)

By focusing on the linkage of trade and environmental policy, I address democracy and environmental protection in a global context. I argue that, while there may be some democratic and environmental benefits from it, trade, by and large, is a threat to democratic processes and environmental protection.

Development and Democracy

Many posit a positive relationship between economic development and democracy. Economists argue that competition between goods is best complemented by competition between political leaders (Friedman 1962). In sociology, modernization theorists argue that economic development and political legitimacy are both requisites for democracy (Lipset 1994). The role of the middle class is championed for gaining the right to vote and form political parties (Lipset 1960).[2] Furthermore, many large-scale surveys reveal a relatively strong relationship between economic development and democracy (Inglehart 1990; for a review see Rueschmeyer, Stephens, and Stephens 1992).[3] Even critics of modernization theory indicate the important role of emerging capitalist classes in pressing for democracy; as Barrington Moore concluded, "No bourgeois, no democracy" (Moore 1966, p. 418). Marxists have indicated that unequal development can block the development of an autonomous bourgeoisie in the periphery, thus inhibiting democratic rule (Amin 1976; Sandbrook 1993, p. 98).

These critics force attention to processes of uneven development and dependency on developed nations, showing that authoritarianism often ensures docile workers and increases social inequality (Frank 1967; Wallerstein 1974; Evans 1979, 1985; Sandbrook 1993, p. 99). Casting doubt on modernization theories, some quantitative analyses have found industrialization to be associated with both democratic and authoritarian regimes (Inglehart, Nevitte, and Basañez 1996, p. 22).

Comparative case studies of development indicate a complex dynamic with democracy. While modernization theorists suggest the important role of the middle class, the mechanisms by which democracy follows development are left unspecified (Rueschmeyer et al. 1992, p. 7; Tilly 1995). Pointing to differences in class mobilization, David Held argues that, while capitalists demand civil rights, labor and social activists press for welfare rights (Held 1989, p. 168). Similarly, there are intricate dynamics between length of democracy and economic gains (Muller 1988; Simpson 1990). These interactions suggest the importance of class mobilization for democratic outcomes (Rueschmeyer et al. 1992; Tilly 1995; Simpson 1990).

There are, moreover, many dimensions of social life that need to be understood in the struggle over democracy. As David Held states, citizenship involves more than simply the "inclusion or exclusion of social classes" (Held 1989, p. 173).[4] He suggests the need to move beyond the modernization literature, influenced by T. H. Marshall:

> The post-Marshall debate needs to extend the analysis of citizenship to take account of issues posed by, for instance, feminism, the black movement, ecology (concerned about the moral status of animals and nature) and those who have advocated the rights of children. (Held 1989, p. 173)

In this sense, there are many issues to consider regarding the dynamics of economic and social change.[5]

Free Trade and Environmental Protection

Free trade advocates argue that trade facilitates modernization, which spurs greater efficiency in production and more sound environmental management practices. They argue that the growth of the middle class leads to "postmaterial" values such as environmentalism. Finally, they suggest that democracy increases as citizens gain resources and an increased capacity to lobby for social policy generally, and for environmental protection more specifically.

I argue, however, that trade agreements are created in an undemocratic manner and that, while some gains in efficiency may emerge, economic development increases environmental threats. I further indicate problems in the theory of middle-class formation and postmaterial values, suggesting that increased inequality, heightened competition, and economic pressures limit environmental protection policies.

Creating Free Trade

The process of trade agreement creation has important limitations for democracy and environmental protection, the central problem being that government and industry have the greatest influence in this domain. While some have examined the fractured political interests that limit the implementation of free trade (Schattschneider 1935; Destler 1992), concentrated economic interests have recently been shown to be effective in pressing for freer trade (Davis 1992; Lewis and Ebrahim 1993).

In Mexico, the president does not need permission to enter into trade negotiations, but does need Senate approval for passage. Once passed, treaties are the supreme law of the land. In the NAFTA debates, the strong PRI control of Congress and the centralized decision-making structure of the Mexican polity gave President Salinas few obstacles in passing NAFTA (Cornelius 1996, p. 26). In the United States, the procedures of trade negotiation are highly undemocratic and provide a great deal of discretion to executive branch administrative agencies, notably the U.S. Trade Representatives Office (USTR). After the agreements are negotiated between the countries, the U.S. Congress can only vote up or down, with only a limited period of debate.[6] Defenders of the U.S. policy of fast track negotiating procedures argued that such measures are necessary in order to preempt fracturing public debate (Cotton 1992, p. 550). However, labor, citizen, and environmental groups are left out of the process. In addition, as many political scientists have indicated, foreign policy is the least democratic element of public policy because of constraints in managing foreign nations, citizens, and state interests (see Nincic 1992). While advocates of trade call for expedient processes, they ignore a variety of social, political, and environmental consequences, and fail to consider the manner in which citizens are left out of important debates (Avery, Drake, and Lang 1993).

The international trade agreements and related panels and organizations that are created lack democratic accountability. In GATT and NAFTA negotiations, technical advisors from major corporations like Quaker, Ralston Purina, and Cargill have had a major influence on standard setting (Wiener 1992, p. 549). Similar international harmonization has already occurred in the form of the U.N. *Codex* standards. While there has been some movement to include environmental actors in dispute resolution, trade panels have been run by economic, not environmental, experts (Avery et al. 1993; Goldman and Wiles 1994). Trade agreements lack the legitimacy of domestic laws and have threatened a variety of regulatory measures (Esty 1994).

Production and Efficiency

Many trade advocates suggest that free trade inherently creates more environmentally sound production processes (for a review see Grossman, forthcoming). Defenders of NAFTA assert that the economy-environment relationship is not inherently antagonistic. Jagdish Bhagwati, a leading proponent of free trade, states that environmentalism and trade are ultimately complementary concerns:

> The simultaneous pursuit of the causes of free trade and a protected environment often raises problems to be sure. But none of these conflicts is beyond resolution with goodwill and by imaginative institutional innovation. The aversion to free trade and the GATT that many environmentalists display is unfounded, and it is time for them to shed it. Their admirable moral passion and certain intellectual vigor are better devoted to building bridges between the causes of trade and the environment. (Bhagwati 1998, p. 243)

Many argued that corporations have an inherent interest in environmental protection. USA*NAFTA, the leading corporate group supporting NAFTA, claimed that NAFTA encourages efficient use of natural resources, technologies, and management practices (USA*NAFTA 1995, p. 696). Digital Corporation executive, C. Foster Knight, argued that businesses adopt sustainable practices by reducing raw material use, energy and water use, and waste product disposal (Knight 1993, p. 33). Trade advocates made great use of modernization arguments suggesting the increased convergence between societies to argue that free trade increases competition and results in greater efficiency in production.[7] They point out that larger, more efficient companies are better able to comply with environmental regulations and that older, inefficient, and heavily polluting industries will be driven out of business (Anderson and Leal 1991; see Anderson 1993). They also claim that multinational corporations do not seek out countries with weak environmental standards, but that they use the same standards that they use in developed countries, with strong environmental protection. While many have criticized the *maquila* industry in Mexico, the Mexican government claims that foreign corporations have stronger safety records than domestic firms, suggesting a positive influence on environmental conditions (Barry 1995, p. 66). Furthermore, trade advocates argue that, through the process of industrialization, Mexican businesses will increasingly comply with U.S. standards (Hufbauer and Schott 1992, p. 135). In the NAFTA debates, businesses insisted that the environmental problems on the U.S.-Mexico border would improve, rather than deteriorate.

Businesses also claim that efficient utilization of resources and less environmental impact occurs with increased scales of production, new technology, and management practices. They indicate that clean natural gas and hydroelectric power become important energy sources, and that it is more efficient to use environmentally sound technologies rather than to refit factories to weaker standards (Oil and Gas Journal 1993, p. 44). Representatives doing business in Mexico insist that they carefully follow environmental regulations and sound environmental practices that have met with widespread approval (USA*NAFTA 1995).

Free trade advocates admit that pollution levels may rise initially with development, but they suggest that they ultimately decline. In their study, Gene Grossman and Alan Krueger (1992) find improved environmental conditions with economic development. Similarly, Robert Lucas, David Wheeler, and Hemamala Hettige find a curvilinear relationship between gross domestic product (GDP) and toxic emissions, which suggests that emissions increase at first, but later taper off (Lucas, Wheeler, and Hettige 1992, p. 69). Ultimately, trade advocates assert that trade ensures sustainable development by increasing competition, efficiency, and self-interest in the reduction of environmental impact.

There are some environmental benefits from trade; however, trade advocates dismiss many real environmental concerns. A fundamental point that is frequently ignored is that economic development increases production, transportation, and consumption, which places greater stress upon the environment (Greenpeace 1992; Schnaiberg and Gould 1994).[8] It cannot be expected that new technologies adequately compensate for the increased energy and industrial production associated with trade. For example, while many point to the benefits of hydroelectric power, the environmental costs have been vastly underestimated, and Canadians are effectively subsidizing American energy consumption (Canadian Environmental Law Association n.d., p. 2). Free trade increases access to raw materials, and limits federal and state government controls over resource sectors, which inhibits sustainable resource management (Bunker and Ciccantell 1999, pp. 116, 120; Hudson 1991, p. 53).

Free trade also has negative effects on sustainable agricultural production. While there is some increased efficiency through increased production and economies of scale, free trade discourages sustainable agriculture by hurting small family farms and encouraging large-scale, intensive agricultural production. NAFTA, combined with legal reforms in Mexico, has resulted in a farm crisis in Mexico (Barry 1995). Trade-related shifts in agricultural production also increase the use of pesticides and chemicals, putting farm workers at higher risk of pesticide poisoning (Greenpeace 1992, p. 1; Canadian Environmental Law Association n.d., p. 1). Trade also increases the use of biotechnology and genetically modified food, which can create environmental, health, and safety threats (Sifry 1999). Intensification of agricultural production by large-scale agribusiness threatens small-scale family farmers; it also increases Third World dependency on developed nations (Canadian Environment Law Association n.d., p. 1; Rosset 1999; Margaronis 1999).[9] Increased trade has raised health threats as there are difficulties inspecting the increased imports (Wiener 1992).

Trade has led to many environmental abuses by multinational corporations operating in developed nations. Extensive pollution, unlawful toxic waste dumping, and dangerous workplaces were some of the offenses found along the U.S.-Mexico border (McGaughey 1992, p. 64; Simon 1997). Research suggests that pollution abatement costs affect trade patterns (Robinson 1988), and studies indicate that reduced environmental protection costs have been a factor in industry relocation (U.S. General Accounting Office 1992).[10]

Trade is an important influence on economic development, which in turn affects pollution levels. In their study of economic development, Albert J. Bergesen and Laura Parisi (1999) find rising toxic emissions which then moderate. While trade advocates emphasize the leveling off of emissions, Bergesen and Parisi indicate that the process of development still creates increased environmental pressures. They agree that there may be improvements in efficiency, as well as a shift to a postindustrial service sector, which may be less environmentally threatening. However, there are limits to efficiency gains and, ultimately, development increases the volume of production (Bergesen and Parisi 1999, p. 50–1). Furthermore, Bergesen and Parisi, controlling for GDP per capita, find more toxic emissions with democracy (p. 51), which suggests a further problem in the hypothesized relationship between free trade, democracy, and environmental protection.

Finally, while trade advocates admit that some trade-related environmental problems exist, they continually treat environmental protection as something that can be put off to be dealt with at a later date. While there are frequent calls for "goodwill" and "imaginative institutional innovation" (Bhagwati 1998, p. 243), such arguments consistently assert the importance of trade while downplaying environmental concerns. As a result, there are no assurances that environmental concerns will be dealt with later. There may be some situations in which trade and environmental protection emerge together, but without environmental regulation incentives for green practices they will be quite limited (Marchak 1998).

The Middle Class and "Postmaterial" Values

Trade advocates also claim that free trade encourages the growth of the middle class, which then develops "postmaterial" values such as environmentalism (Inglehart 1990; Anderson 1993). The postmaterialism argument asserts that people want environmental protection in the same way that they want other goods, and suggests that economic development from trade provides more wealth, making people better able to afford environmental protection.[11]

The middle class does play an important role in pressing for environmental protection (Cable and Cable 1995, p. 119). However, environmental protection is not universal and reflects power imbalances in society (Schnaiberg and Gould 1994, p. 156; Cable and Cable 1995, Chapter 8). As environmental justice studies have indicated, toxic waste dumps and heavily polluting industries are disproportionately located in poor communities of color (Bullard 1993). High levels of inequality create uneven abilities to influence political processes and conditions of competition rather than harmonization of interests. Such conflicts exist not only within, but across nations (Athanasiou 1996; Goldman 1998).[12]

Furthermore, some research calls this "postmaterial" view into question. Steve Brechin and Willet Kempton (1994) find that environmentalist values are often as high in developing countries as they are in developed ones. This similarity in attitudes and values suggests that resources and political opportunities are the differences that explain the greater development of environmental policy in developed nations. Modernization theory may be correct in that development may provide the resources for social movement activism and advances in environmental policy. However, economic development through free trade can be associated with high levels of inequality, which often makes environmental protection the privilege of a few (Barry 1995). Much research on environmental justice indicates the uneven ability of individuals to protect themselves from environmental problems (Cable and Cable 1995, p. 107; Bullard 1993).

Mexico, despite having signed on to environmental agreements as part of NAFTA, has consistently maintained that it is a Third World country upon which demands are being placed that it have First World environmental standards. Mexican opposition to environmental provisions in a potential Free Trade Agreement of the Americas indicates that neither freer trade nor development associated with GATT and NAFTA have resulted in a willingness to institutionalize environmental values in binding commitments.

Competition for Capital

Pluralists have emphasized the importance of competing interest groups for democratic governance (Dahl 1970), and some have claimed that competition between states for capital investments and jobs creates a situation in which governments are forced to be responsive to social and economic needs (Friedman 1962). Trade advocates extend this logic in arguing that free trade reduces the burdensome effects of governmental regulation and encourages economic growth (USA*NAFTA 1995, p. 697). At the same time, they suggest that free trade will provide governments with the resources to enact more social and environmental protections. While they admit that governments may feel pressured to construct standards in consideration of industry location, they insist that such considerations are negligible and that industry movement is not really an important concern (Levinson 1996, p. 429). Many trade advocates indicate that corporations are unlikely to move because of high relocation costs, the USTR indicates that polluting industries are often capital-intensive and thus costly to move (U.S. General Accounting Office 1992). Corporations assert further that free trade is pursued in the interest of reaching new markets, not in finding "pollution havens" with weak labor laws and low environmental standards. Some studies suggest that environmental protection costs are not a major factor in industry location (Grossman and Krueger 1992; see also Low 1992).

However, trade advocates present contradictory indications about the gains from trade. On the one hand, trade is expected to bring in greater resources for the state, while on the other hand it limits state involvement in the economy. Free trade also limits state capacity for social and environmental policy because such policies are treated as barriers to trade (Greenpeace 1992).

In addition, the conflict between global trade and national governance is highlighted in that states must compete for capital. This is an observation made by both Karl Marx (1995) and Max Weber (1981 [1927], p. 337). State competition for capital, however, threatens social and environmental policy as states reduce production costs including labor rates, benefits, health care, and environmental protection costs. In his study, David J. Molina (1993) finds lower pollution controls to be a significant influence on industry relocation. As Steven Yearly (1991) argues, even if pollution is not the major reason for industry relocation, environmental dumping still becomes an important cost saving device. It is true that many corporations will not relocate if environmental protection costs constitute only a small percentage of production costs. However, in the case of NAFTA, the large disparity between

U.S. and Mexican environmental protection costs was a significant influence on industry relocation. The growth of the *maquiladora* industry suggests that extraordinary gains can be reaped by corporations that move from one country to the next seeking cheaper and cheaper production costs (Simon 1997). Even corporations that do not move use the threat of moving against their current jurisdiction (Yearly 1991). As Frederick Buttel argues, while states face significant demands for environmental protection, world order constraints from corporations and elites frequently preempt such initiatives (1998, p. 282). Because states seek industrial development, they face pressure to reduce social and environmental protection costs.[13]

National Power and Social Rights

Trade advocates argue that strong economies result in strong states that can pursue a variety of social goals. Former Canadian Prime Minister Brian Mulroney has stated, "(More) trade means more jobs, and a strong economy is the guarantee of a distinctly Canadian program in health care, education, social services and environment" (Macleans 1988, p. 22). Similarly, former Mexican President Salinas, who had previously pushed aside the environmental concerns, made statements proclaiming the importance of NAFTA for environmentally sound development:

> Mexico's commitment to a better environment, however, does not arise just because of the pressures of NAFTA, but because of the very strong social demand that has arisen in recent years in Mexico. There is a new environmental culture that has awakened in Mexico. We are also toughening the enforcement capabilities of the federal government to ensure that new, tougher laws will be implemented. We have closed down factories in Mexico on the spot because they exceed allowable levels of pollution. How often do other countries do that? (Salinas 1994, p. 24)

In the early 1990s, at the time of NAFTA negotiations, Mexico doubled its environmental inspectors from 100 to 200, procured an 84 million dollar loan from the World Bank, and took part in a debt for nature swap around Mexico City in 1991. In response to both domestic and international pressures, Mexico reorganized the environment agency SEDUE into a social development agency called SEDESOL. Budgets were increased, the National Ecology Institute was created to address technical norms, and the Attorney General for the Protection of the Environment gained greater enforcement power (Griffith 1993, p. 194). Accordingly, some environmental improvements have occurred alongside the development of free trade.

However, while restructuring has taken place in Mexican environmental policy, many critics argue that environmental concerns remain subsumed to economic development ones and that funding remained inadequate for the many problems in Mexico. Thus, while President Salinas proclaimed the development of an autonomous environmentalist culture in Mexico, the new environmentalist actions can be seen as surface repairs in order to gain international approval and passage of the NAFTA agreement. The decisions to purse free trade are often made under fiscal constraint and by governments and administrations that limit public influence, extended debate, and political activism (Sandbrook 1993, p. 114). Miguel Centeno's study of economic and political change in Mexico finds, at least initially, economic change with only limited political reforms (Centeno 1994). Peter H. Smith (1992) argues that analysts have failed to explore the many possible political outcomes of free trade on Mexico, and Ester Wilson Hannon suggests that neoliberalism in Mexico has the "paradoxical goal of strengthening a centralized political system" (Wilson Hannon 1994, p. 145).

This also suggests the importance of organizational dynamics and interagency politics in achieving substantive goals, such as environmental protection. Research on both developed and developing countries indicates the importance of bureaucratic politics. Studying the U.S., Richard Tobin (1993) shows that conflicts between agencies have limited the protection of biological diversity. Similarly, Clark Gibson (1999) indicates the centrality of politics in African bureaucracies by showing how bureaucratic design is not simply a technical endeavor but involves the interests, strategies, and power of political actors.[14] As a result, state structures and political dynamics often limit effective environmental protection.

Finally, while theorists of nationalism and state development have argued that individual citizenship develops in conjunction with state power (Giddens 1987, p. 210; see also Calhoun 1997), trade agreements can be seen as constraints on states and citizens. As Anthony Giddens indicates, nationalism helps to define particular areas of interest while blocking off others, "If programmes of reform on the part of subordinate classes (or other groupings) are to succeed, they have normally to be made to appear in the 'national interest'" (Giddens 1987, p. 221). Accordingly, arguments about the power of markets, and "right to work" development strategies, which lower the costs of production, are proclaimed in terms of national interest. While such practices may encourage the national agenda of industrial development, they often leave worker rights and environmental problems unaddressed.

In the same manner that international trading patterns can lead to conditions of inequality that benefit developed countries (Frank 1967), free trade agreements often encourage the transfer of pollution and waste from advanced industrialized nations to less developed ones (Simon 1997).[15] Yet, at the same time, however, developing countries are subject to repeated demands that they join international treaties and make commitments to environmental protection. Both trade agreements and international environmental treaties are often forms of imperialism in which nations become subject to foreign laws.

Environmental Citizenship

I have indicated several limitations to arguments which suggest that trade influences modernization, environmental values, and state capacity for public policy. I want to further argue that free trade alters public culture in such a way as to constrain democratic initiatives and limit avenues for sound environmental policy and practices. Free trade creates conditions under which few feel that they can afford to make the investments needed for environmental protection.

Social theorists have argued that there has been a dual expansion of state sovereignty and citizenship rights (Giddens 1989, p. 268; see also Mann 1993). While modernization theorists view these developments as developing in a pacific manner, such gains are the outcomes of political struggle; greater attention is needed to the political processes by which citizenship, democracy, and social and environmental gains are achieved.

Substantive models of democracy suggest the importance of policy developments in particular issue areas (Mansbridge 1986), and formal models indicate the importance of institutions that allow public access and involvement (Dahl 1970). However, democracy involves more than simply formal institutions and substantive gains:

> Neither the celebration of liberal democracy nor its dismissal as a purely formal mechanism or "empty shell" provides adequate means of assessing its strengths and limitations. Democracy bestows an "aura of legitimacy" on modern political life. Yet, under what conditions political regimes may reasonably be considered legitimate and when one can justifiably claim the mantle of democracy remain unclear. (Held 1996, p. 219)

While formal democratic institutions may flourish, free trade increases economic pressures, constraining civil society and a strong public sphere. Trade can increase income inequality within and across nations, highlighting a tension inherent in the concept of liberal democracy:

> Democracy is associated with the ideal of equality, in particular, formal political equality; liberalism champions liberty, especially the right of individuals to accumulate property. In practice, the power of the dominant classes or elites often obstructs state-directed reformism under the guise of defending liberty and the efficacy of market forces. And market relationships, in the absence of a welfare-oriented state, inevitably favour those individuals, firms, and regions that are already richer and better endowed than

> others, thereby exacerbating inequality. (Sandbrook 1993, p. 120)

Thus, democracy involves more than formal institutions, regular elections, and political parties (Habermas 1989, p. 345; Tilly 1995; Held 1995, 1996). While democracy has developed along with the centralization of authority and the expansion of representation in nation-states (Mann 1993; Tilly 1995), trade weakens these elements of national power by placing power in international trade agreements. The market relations defined by large-scale corporations can act, therefore, as a limiting force upon social movements.

While trade advocates utilize modernization arguments about the growth of the middle class and emerging claims for environmental goods, by pressing against international environmental governance they deny environmentalist claims. Thus, they fail to recognize that democracy has emerged through struggles and by elite concessions. Trade advocates, while indicating trends toward democracy and environmental protection, try to resist those trends.

Democratic citizenship is compromised because state agents are bound to global capital through international trade agreements. Democracy involves a dynamic relationship between citizens and the state. As Charles Tilly describes:

> Democracy combines broad and relatively equal citizenship with (a) binding consultation of citizens in regard to state personnel as well as (b) protection of citizens from arbitrary state action. (Tilly 1995, p. 370)

Trade liberalization involves secretive negotiations, limited public involvement, inequality, and a heightened sense of competition. Democratic rights may develop, but they are often more symbolic than real (see Held 1989, p. 177). The environmental organizations created in association with NAFTA are widely cited as insulated and having no effective sanctions. As a result, free trade agreements may support formal rights rather than actual capacities for social change. The environmental side agreements created in NAFTA are significant institutional developments in terms of international environmental management, but they still lack effective environmental protection mechanisms (Mumme 1993). The bureaucracies created, while under the control of the environmental ministers from the three countries, are not directly under a legislative body subject to public pressure. As Max Weber emphasized, state organizations must be under the control of a strong parliament to ensure effective policies. The risk of bureaucratic autonomy and inefficiency exists even more with international than national governance. The European Union parliament is of questionable power, and the World Trade Organization and the North American Free Trade Agreement lack parliamentary control. As critics have argued, these agreements fail to provide adequate citizen input (Public Citizen 1996; Arden-Clarke 1991). Indicating the importance of social actors, Frederick Buttel states:

> If sustainable societies are to be achieved, they will need to be societies that are embedded in civil society in the most broad-based manner imaginable, societies that reject the notion of a self-regulating market—that is, the market as master rather than servant of society. (Buttel 1998, p. 281)

The political and economic relations created by free trade, however, constrain civil society and sustainable development.

Conclusion

Arguments for free trade center on the possibilities for increased economic growth, democracy, and environmental protection. While some evidence indicates a correlation between free trade and environmental protection, there is also evidence that free trade is an environmental threat. It is difficult to assess whether one type of economic form is necessarily more environmentally sound than another. There are many changing factors that can influence environmental protection. As the National Wildlife Federation has stated:

> While narrow economic protectionism can itself undermine sustainable

> development, unfettered or deregulated global commerce also represents a serious threat to the wise use of natural resources at a local, national and global level. (National Wildlife Federation n.d.)

Scientific knowledge about the environment is incomplete, and it is hard to measure the effects of trade on the environment. However, free trade advocates fail to take a precautionary approach, and fail to fully consider the social and environmental costs of globalized production, finance, and trade.

An economistic definition of development and democracy fails to consider the contested nature of social change, and the qualitative dimensions of democracy. Ultimately, trade advocates ignore the socially constructed nature of these processes. Under the conditions of free trade, competition is heightened and individuals, corporations, and governments find themselves less able to expend resources on environmental protection. In this sense, free trade shapes how decisions are made and alters the social construction of reality. Democracy, as Charles Tilly states, is a social construction; accordingly democracies are always "under construction" (Tilly 1995).

Development involves social, economic, and environmental values, and the cultural conceptions about how to achieve those ends. Thus, free trade, which alters structural conditions, should also be seen as a debate over meaning creation. It cannot be assumed that growth leads to democracy, which leads to environmental protection. Global economic conditions give rise to a culture of competition in which states defend economic national interests at the expense of environmental protection. Strong corporate and state actors resist environmental protection at subnational, national, and international and supranational levels as a threat to economic development. Environmental activists have difficulty overriding these pressures. The remaining problem is that individuals and groups in both developed and developing countries feel constrained by the competitive threats of global capitalism.

Notes

Direct correspondence to Perry Grossman, grossman@mail.soc.nyu.edu. An earlier version of this paper was presented at the 1999 New York University Sociology Graduate Student Conference. Thanks for comments to Richard Sennett, Wolf Heydebrand, Carrie James, and the reviewers of *Sociological Inquiry*.

[1] What Khor refers to as the MTO became the World Trade Organization (WTO), an outgrowth of the General Agreement of Tariffs and Trade (GATT).

[2] T. H. Marshall's "Citizenship and Social Class" (1973 [1952]) is an important influence on modernization theorists. Marshall, using Britain as an example, suggests a three-fold process in the development of citizenship rights. First, he describes the development of civil rights in the legal system during the 18th century and argues that people gain equality under the law as judicial decisions free them from the customary relations of feudal society. In the next stage, during the 19th and 20th centuries, political rights emerge as citizens gain influence over the institutions of parliament and local government. Civil rights, Marshall argues, provided a necessary platform for political rights because only where the individual is an autonomous agent are political rights and responsibilities a possibility. Finally, in the 20th century, social rights emerge in which an organized working class secures economic and welfare rights such as unemployment pay and sickness benefits. David Held argues that modernization theorists have presented an overly evolutionary model of Marshall's work (Held 1989, p. 167 n16; see also Giddens 1989, 1996; Mann 1993).

[3] Edward Muller (1988) finds that high levels of inequality undermine democratic regimes (p. 66). Miles Simpson (1990) also indicates the important relationship between democratic rights, general educational levels, and income inequality (p. 689).

[4] Again, on Marshall (1973 [1952]) see Held (1989).

[5] Debates over identity politics indicate the importance of these many issues [see Calhoun (1995); specifically on the environmental movement and identity see Lichterman (1995)].

[6] Ackerman and Golove (1995) defend the fast-track process of trade policy, but critics suggest that fast-track policy may be a violation of constitutional law (see Tribe 1994). Following the lawsuit *Public Citizen v. USTR*, David T. Gibbons (1994) argues that an environmental impact statement should be requires for NAFTA.

[7] For debates on modernization and industrialization underlying these arguments, see Kerr (1983), Kerr, Dunlop, Harbison, and Myers (1973), Inkeles (1998), Inkeles and Smith (1974) and Gerschenkron (1965).

[8] See Buttel (1998) for an important critique of Schnaiberg and Gould's (1994) conception of the treadmill of production. Buttel is correct to point out the many cases of environmental improvement. However, trade increases economic activity and ultimately increases environmental pressures (Daly 1993).

[9] For a review of issues involving agriculture and sustainability, although not specifically on the issue of free trade, see Buttel, Larson, and Gillespie (1990), also Rudel (1993).

[10] Research also suggests that larger companies, those most likely to succeed under free trade, can better afford to mount legal challenges to environmental suits, and that they may use environmental laws to help drive competitors out of business (see Yeager 1991).

[11] This connects well to arguments that emphasize intermediate groups and associations in democratic society (Putnam 1993). Capitalism, it is argued, helps facilitate civil society through urbanization, improvements in communication, transportation, and literacy (Lipset 1994; see also Calhoun 1992).

[12] It is questionable as well whether free trade leads to a growing middle class or increased polarities of rich and poor. Recent research indicates trends toward rising levels of inequality (Gottschalk and Joyce 1995; Sklair 1991, p. 56–57, 62–65).

[13] James O'Connor (1973) indicates, for example, the tendency toward fiscal crisis as states attempt to mediate between business desires for low costs and social pressures for civic gains. As such, there is a conflict between accumulation and legitimation.

[14] Lyle Scruggs (1999) also indicates the importance of political structures on environmental protection. He suggests that neocorporatist democracies exhibit greater environmental performance than pluralist democracies.

[15] The celebrated note of former World Bank economist Lawrence Summers, which was leaked to the press, suggests something of this logic by arguing that economic theory would posit that precisely this sort of relationship should develop (Sklair 1991).

References

Ackerman, Bruce, and David Golove. 1995. *Is NAFTA Constitutional?* Cambridge, MA: Harvard University Press.

Amin, Samir. 1976. *Unequal Development: An Essay on the Social Formations of Peripheral Capitalism.* New York: Monthly Review Press.

Anderson, Terry L. (ed.). 1993. *NAFTA and the Environment.* San Francisco: Pacific Research Institute for Public Policy.

Anderson, Terry L., and Donald Leal. 1991. *Free Market Environmentalism.* San Francisco: Pacific Research Institute for Policy Studies.

Arden-Clark, Charles. 1991. *The General Agreement on Tariffs and Trade, Environmental Protection and Sustainable Development.* Geneva, Switzerland: World Wildlife Fund.

Athanasiou, Tom. 1996. *Divided Planet: the Ecology of Rich and Poor.* Boston: Little, Brown and Co.

Avery, Natalie, Martine Drake, and Tim Lang. 1993. *Cracking the Codex: An Analysis of Who Sets World Food Standards.* London: National Food Alliance.

Barry, Tom, with Beth Sims. 1995. *The Challenge of Cross-Border Environmentalism: The U.S.-Mexico Case.* Albuquerque, NM: Resource Center Press.

Bergesen, Albert J., and Laura Parisi. 1999, "Ecosociology and Toxic Emissions." Pp. 43–58 in *Ecology and the World-System*, edited by Walter L. Goldfrank, David Goodman, and Andrew Szasz. Westport, CT: Greenwood Press.

Bhagwati, Jagdish. 1998. "Democracy and Development: New Thinking on an Old Question." Pp. 379–408 in *A Stream of Windows: Unsettling Reflections on Trade, Immigration, and Democracy*, edited by Jagdish Bhagwati. Cambridge, MA: MIT Press.

Brechin, Steven R., and Willett Kempton. 1994. "Global Environmentalism: A Challenge to the Postmaterialism Thesis?" *Social Science Quarterly* 75:245–69.

Bullard, Robert D. 1993. *Confronting Environmental Racism: Voices from the Crossroads.* Boston: South End Press.

Bunker, Stephen G., and Paul S. Ciccantell. 1999. "Economic Ascent and the Global Environment: World-Systems Theory and the New Historical Materialism." Pp. 107–122 in *Ecology and the World-System*, edited by Walter L. Goldfrank, David Goodman, and Andrew Szasz. Westport, CT: Greenwood Press.

Buttel, Frederick H. 1998. "Some Observations on States, World Orders, and the Politics of Sustainability." *Organization and Environment* 11:261–86.

Buttel, Frederick, Olaf F. Larson, and Gilbert W. Gillespie Jr. 1990. *The Sociology of Agriculture.* Westport, CT: Greenwood Press.

Cable, Sherry, and Charles Cable. 1995. *Environmental Problems, Grassroots Solutions: The Politics of Grassroots Environmental Conflict*. New York: St. Martin's Press.

Calhoun, Craig J. 1997. *Nationalism.* Minneapolis: University of Minnesota Press.

Calhoun, Craig (ed.). 1995. *Social Theory and the Politics of Identity*. Cambridge, MA: Blackwell.

Calhoun, Craig. 1992. "The Infrastructure of Modernity: Indirect Relationships, Information Technology, and Social Integration." Pp. 205–36 in *Social Change and Modernity*, edited by Hans Haferkamp and Neil J. Smelser. Berkeley: University of California Press.

Canadian Environmental Law Association. n.d. *NAFTA and Agriculture, Democratic Process, Standards, Energy, Resources, and Water*. Toronto, ON: CELA.

Centeno, Miguel Angel. 1994. *Democracy Within Reason: Technocratic Revolution in Mexico.* University Park, PA: Pennsylvania State University Press.

Cornelius, Wayne A. 1996. *Mexican Politics in Transition: The Breakdown of a One-Party Dominant Regime*. La Jolla, CA: Center for US-Mexican Studies, UC San Diego.

Cotton, James. 1992. Testimony on "NAFTA: Environmental Issues." Hearings before the Sub committee on Rules of the House of the Committee on Rules, House of Representatives, One Hundred Second Congress. October 16 in *The North American Free Trade Agreement (NAFTA): Documents and Materials Including a Legislative History of the North American Free Trade Agreement Implementation Act, Public Law 103-182*, Vol. 11, edited by Bernard Reams and Jon S. Schultz. Buffalo, NY: William S. Hein.

Dahl, Robert. 1970. *Modern Political Analysis.* Englewood Cliffs, NJ: Prentice-Hall.

Daly, Herman E. 1993. "From Adjustable to Sustainable Development." Pp. 121–32 in *The Case Against "Free Trade"*. San Francisco: Earth Island Press.

Davis, Diane E. 1992. "Mexico's New Politics: Changing Perspectives on Free Trade." *World Policy Journal* Fall/Winter: 755–72.

Destler, I. M. 1992. *American Trade Politics.* Washington, DC: Institute for International Economics.

Esty, Daniel C. 1994. *Greening the GATT: Trade, Environment, and the Future*. Washington, DC: Institute for International Economics.

Evans, Peter. 1985. "Transnational Linkages and the Economic Role of the State: An Analysis of Developing and Industrialized Nations in the Post-World War II Period." Pp. 192–226 in *Bringing the State Back In*, edited by Peter Evans, Dietrich Reuschmeyer, and Theda Skocpol. Cambridge: Cambridge University Press.

———. 1979. *Dependent Development*. Princeton: Princeton University Press.

Frank, Andre Gunder. 1967. *Capitalism and Underdevelopment in Latin America*. New York: Monthly Review Press.

Friedman, Milton. 1962. *Capitalism and Freedom.* Chicago: University of Chicago Press.

Gerschenkron, Alexander. 1965. *Economic Backwardness in Historical Perspective, a Book of Essays*. New York: Praeger.

Gibbons, David T. 1994. "NAFTA vs. the Environment: The Court's Mandate to Require the Preparation of Environmental Impact Statements." *Hamline Journal of Public Law and Policy* Winter:15.

Gibson, Clark C. 1999. "Bureaucrats and the Environment in Africa: The Politics of Structural Choice in a One Party State." *Comparative Politics* April:273–93.

Giddens, Anthony. 1996. *In Defense of Sociology*. Cambridge, MA: Blackwell Publishers.

———. 1989. "A Reply to My Critics." Pp. 249–301 in *Social Theory of Modern Societies*, edited by D. Held and J. B. Thompson. New York: Cambridge University Press.

———. 1987. *The Nation-State and Violence*. Berkeley: University of California Press.

Goldman, Michael. 1998. *Privatizing Nature: Political Struggles for the Global Commons*. New Brunswick, NJ: Rutgers University Press.

Goldman, Patti, and Richard Wiles. 1994. *Trading Away US Food Safety*. Washington, DC: Public Citizen, Occasional Report. April 12.

Gottschalk, Peter, and Mary Joyce. 1995. The Impact of Technological Change, Deindustrialization, and Internationalization of Trade on Earnings Inequality: An International Perspective Pp. 197–230 in *Poverty, Inequality, and the Future of Social Policy: Western States and the New World Order*, edited by Katherine McFate, Roger Lawson, and

William Julius Wilson. New York: Russell Sage Foundation.

Greenpeace. 1992. *NAFTA Threatens the Environment: Greenpeace Proposals for a New Agreement.* December.

Griffith, Kathleen Ann. 1993. "NAFTA, Sustainable Development, and the Environment: Mexico's Approach." *Journal of Environment and Development* 2:193–203.

Grossman, Gene M., and Alan B. Krueger. 1992. *Environmental Impacts of a North American Free Trade Agreement.* Discussion Paper. Princeton, NJ: Princeton University. February.

Grossman, Perry. 2000. "Corporate Interest and Trade Liberalization: The North American Free Trade Agreement and Environmental Protection." *Organization and Environment* 13:61–85.

Habermas, Jürgen. 1989. *The Theory of Communicative Action: Volume Two, Lifeworld and System: A Critique of Functionalist Reason.* Boston: Beacon Press.

Held, David. 1996. *Models of Democracy.* Stanford, CA: Stanford University Press.

———. 1995. *Democracy and the Global Order: From Modern State to Cosmopolitan Governance.* Cambridge: Polity Press.

———. 1989. "Citizenship and Autonomy." Pp. 162–84 in *Social Theory of Modern Societies*, edited by David Held and John B. Thompson. New York: Cambridge University Press.

Hudson, Stewart. 1991. Testimony on "NAFTA: Environmental Issues." Hearings before the Subcommittee on Rules of the House of the Committee on Rules, House of Representatives, One Hundred Second Congress, October 16. In the *North American Free Trade Agreement (NAFTA): Documents and Materials Including a Legislative History of the North American Free Trade Agreement Implementation Act, Public Law 103-182*, Vol. 11, edited by Bernard Reams and John S. Schultz. Buffalo, NY: William S. Hein.

Hufbauer, Gary C., and Jeffrey J. Schott. 1992. *North American Free Trade: Issues and Recommendations.* Washington, DC: Institute for International Economics.

Inglehart, Ronald. 1990. *Cultural Shift in Advanced Industrial Society.* Princeton, NJ: Princeton University Press.

Inglehart, Ronald, Neil Nevitte, and Miguel Basañez. 1996. *The North American Trajectory: Cultural, Economic, and Political Ties among the United States, Canada, and Mexico.* New York: Aldine De Gruyter.

Inkeles, Alex. 1998. *One World Emerging?: Convergence and Divergence in Industrial Societies.* Boulder, CO: Westview Press.

Inkeles, Alex, and David H. Smith. 1974. *Becoming Modern: Individual Change in Six Developing Countries.* Cambridge, MA: Harvard University Press.

Kerr, Clark. 1983. *The Future of Industrial Societies: Convergence or Continued Diversity?* Cambridge, MA: Harvard University Press.

Kerr, Clark, J. T. Dunlop, F. H. Harbison, and C. A. Myers. 1973. *Industrialism and Industrial Man.* Harmondsworth: Penguin Publishers.

Khor, Martin. 1993. "Free Trade and the Third World." Pp. 97–107 in *The Case Against Free Trade: GATT, NAFTA, and the Globalization of Corporate Power.* San Francisco: Earth Island Press.

Knight, C. Foster. 1993. "Helping the Environment Through Trade." *The Environmental Forum* 10(March/April):33–4.

Levinson, Arik. 1996. "Environmental Regulations and Industry Location: International and Domestic Evidence." Pp. 429–58 in *Fair Trade and Harmonization: Prerequisites for Trade?* Vol. 1, edited by J. Bhagwati and R. Hudec. Cambridge, MA: MIT Press.

Lewis, Charles, and Margaret Ebrahim. 1993. "Can Mexico and Big Business Buy NAFTA?" *The Nation* 256(June 14):826–39.

Lichterman, Paul. 1995. "Piecing Together Multicultural Community: Cultural Differences in Community Building Among Grass-Roots Environmentalists." *Social Problems* 42:513–34.

Lipset, Seymour Martin. 1994. "The Social Requisites of Democracy Revisited." *American Sociological Review* 59:1–22.

———. 1960. *Political Man.* New York: Doubleday.

Low, Patrick (ed.). 1992. *International Trade and the Environment.* Washington, DC: World Bank.

Lucas, Robert E. B., David Wheeler, and Hemamala Hettige. 1992. "Economic Development, Environmental Regulation and International Migration of Toxic Industrial Pollution." Pp. 60–88 in *International Trade and the Environment*, edited by Patrick Low. Washington, DC: World Bank.

Macleans. 1988. "Battle Lines on the Gut Issue: Tablets of Stone from 23 Prominent Spokesmen on the Fundamental Election Issue of Free Trade." *Macleans* November 21:22.

Mann, Michael. 1993. *The Sources of Social Power.* Vol. 2. New York: Cambridge University Press.

Mansbridge, Jane. 1986. *Why We Lost the ERA*. Chicago: University of Chicago Press.

Marchak, M. Patricia. 1998. "Environment and Resource Protection: Does NAFTA Make a Difference?" *Organization and Environment* 11:133–54.

Margaronis, Maria. 1999. "The Politics of Food." *The Nation* December 27:11–6.

Marshall, T. H. 1973. *Class, Citizenship and Social Development*. Westport, CT: Greenwood Press.

Marx, Karl. 1955. *The Communist Manifesto*. Northbrook, IL: AHM Publishing.

McGaughey, William, Jr. 1992. *A U.S.-Mexico-Canada Free Trade Agreement: Do We Just Say No?* Minneapolis: Thistlerose Publications.

Miller, Morris. 1991. *Debt and the Environment: Converging Crises*. New York: United Nations Publications.

Molina, David J. 1993. "A Comment on Whether Maquiladoras Are in Mexico for Low Wages or to Avoid Pollution Abatement Costs." *Journal of Environment and Development* 2(Winter): 221–41.

Moore, Barrington. 1966. *Social Origins of Dictatorship and Democracy*. Boston: Beacon Press.

Muller, Edward. 1988. "Democracy, Economic Development, and Income Inequality." *American Sociological Review* 53:50–68.

Mumme, Stephen P. 1993. "Environmentalists, NAFTA, and North American Environmental Management." *Journal of Environment and Development* 2:205–19.

National Wildlife Federation. n.d. "In Brief: Trade and Environment." http://www.nwf.org/nwf/pubs/positions/fatrade.html.

Nincic, Miroslav. 1992. *Democracy and Foreign Policy: The Fallacy of Political Realism*. New York: Columbia University Press.

O'Connor, James R. 1973. *The Fiscal Crisis of the State*. New York: St. Martin's Press.

Oil and Gas Journal. 1993. "Appeals Court: No Environmental Study for NAFTA." *Oil and Gas Journal* October 4:44.

Public Citizen. 1996. *NAFTA's Environmental Effects* January:1–6.

Putnam, Robert D. 1993. *Making Democracy Work: Civic Traditions in Modern Italy*. Princeton: Princeton University Press.

Robinson, H. David. 1988. "Industrial Pollution Abatement: The Impact on Balance of Trade." *Canadian Journal of Economics* 21:187–99.

Rosset, Peter. 1999. "The Parable of the Golden Snail." *The Nation* December 27:22.

Rudel, Thomas K. with Bruce Horowitz. 1993. *Tropical Deforestation: Small Farmers and Land Clearing in the Ecuadorian Amazon*. New York: Columbia University Press.

Rueschmeyer, Dietrich, Evelyne Huber Stephens, and John D. Stephens. 1992. *Capitalist Development and Democracy*. Chicago: University of Chicago Press.

Salinas de Gortari, Carlos. 1994. "The Painful Road." *HC Supplement to Across the Board* January:32–4.

Sandbrook, Richard. 1993. *The Politics of Africa's Economic Recovery*. New York: Cambridge University Press.

Schattschneider, E. E. 1935. *Politics, Pressures and the Tariff*. New York: Prentice-Hall.

Schnaiberg, Allan, and Kenneth Alan Gould. 1994. *Environment and Society: The Enduring Conflict*. New York: St. Martin's Press.

Scruggs, Lyle A. 1999. "Institutions and Environmental Performance in Seventeen Western Democracies." *British Journal of Political Science* 29:1–31.

Sifry, Micah L. 1999. "Food Money." *The Nation* December 27:20.

Simon, Joel. 1997. *Endangered Mexico: An Environment on the Edge*. San Francisco: Sierra Club Books.

Simpson, Miles. 1990. "Political Rights and Income Inequality." *American Sociological Review* 55:682–93.

Sklair, Leslie. 1991. *Sociology of the Global System*. Baltimore: Johns Hopkins University Press.

Smith, Peter. 1992. "The Political Impact of Free Trade on Mexico." *Journal of InterAmerican Studies and World Affairs* 341(Spring):1–25.

Tilly, Charles. 1995. "Democracy Is a Lake." Pp. 365–87 in *The Social Construction of Democracy, 1870–1990*, edited by George A. Reid and Herrick Chapman. New York: New York University Press.

Tobin, Richard. 1993. *The Expendable Future: U.S. Politics and the Protection of Biological Diversity*. Durham, NC: Duke University Press.

Tribe, Lawrence. 1994. "Statements." *GATT Implementing Legislation: Hearings Before the Senate Committee on Commerce, Science, and Transportation*. 103rd Congress. 2nd Session. 285.

USA*NAFTA. 1995 [1993, March 8]. "Position of USA*NAFTA on the Environmental Side

Agreement to the NAFTA." Pp. 696–713 in *NAFTA and the Environment: Substance and Process*, edited by D. Magraw. Chicago: American Bar Association.

U.S. General Accounting Office. 1992. *US-Mexico Trade: Assessment of Mexico's Environmental Controls for New Companies*. GAO/GGD-92-113. August.

Wallerstein, Immanuel. 1974. *The Modern World System: Capitalist Agriculture and the Origins of the European World Economy in the Sixteenth Century*. New York: Academic Press.

Weber, Max. 1981 [1927]. *General Economic History*. New Brunswick, NJ: Transaction Books.

Wiener, Don. 1992. "Comments at Roundtable Discussion: The North American Free Trade Agreement: In Whose Best Interest?" Held October 17, 1991, at Northwestern University School of Law. *Northwestern Journal of International and Business* 12:546–70.

Wilson Hannon, Esther. 1994. "The Politics of Mexican Free Trade and the North American Free Trade Agreement." Pp. 127–48 in *Economic Development Under Democratic Regimes: Neoliberalism in Latin America*, edited by Lowell S. Gustafson. Westport, CT: Praeger Press.

Yeager, Peter C. 1991. *The Limits of Law: the Public Regulation of Private Pollution*. New York: Cambridge University Press.

Yearly, Stephen. 1991. *The Green Case: A Sociology of Environmental Issues, Arguments and Politics*. London: Harper Collins.

Globalization: The Empire Strikes Back

Douglas H. Constance

The Sociological Imagination is the greatest contribution sociologists have to offer to students and society. Understanding how our lives intersect history enables us to see the barriers and opportunities that people encounter in life better. Similarly, when we learn that peoples' personal problems are often the results of social forces, we can then deal with the causes instead of the symptoms of social pathologies. One person losing their job at the TV factory may well be due to individual psychological problems, but everyone losing their jobs because the transnational corporation (TNC) closed the U.S.-based factory and reopened it in Mexico to avoid high labor costs and strict environmental regulations is a result of global social forces. The rise in poverty, drug abuse, and violence in the abandoned community is linked directly to the globalization of economy and society. Today our lives intersect history in a period referred to as globalization.

The expansion of the capitalist system from city-States, to nation-States, to a world system is well documented. Many scholars note that the current phase of globalization that began in the late 20th century is different than previous phases and deserves special attention from social scientists. One of the differences centers on the changing relationship between the economy and polity whereby the former now transcends the spheres of influence of the latter. While the economy has gone global in the form TNCs, the polity remains geographically bounded in nation-States. This divergence has serious implications regarding the ability of (1) nation-States to effectively plan their national socio-economic agendas and (2) nation-based subordinate groups to advance their interests in the form of social movements.

To illustrate the salient aspects of globalization, it is useful to divide recent history up into three eras and employ several sociological concepts to interpret the changing relationship between the economy, the polity, and social movements. Following a neo-Regulationist approach (see Aglietta 1979; Lipietz 1992), recent history is divided into the "Frontier Era" (mid-1800s to 1929), the "Fordist Era" (1929 to 1973), and the Post-Fordist Era (1973 to present). Regulationists divide history up into stable eras of capital accumulation and social stability divided by crises of instability. Each era is represented by a particular "regime of accumulation" and a "mode of regulation." The regime of accumulation refers to the technological and labor process aspects of economic production such as the relationship between capital and labor (i.e., craft-based or wage labor). The mode of regulation refers to the socio-cultural system that supports the period of economic accumulation and social stability (i.e., interventionist or laissez faire nation-State).

Three other conceptual frames are utilized to interpret the changing relationship between the economy and the polity. First, theories of the nation-State can generally be divided into three camps (see Bonanno and Constance 1996). The "instrumental" camp sees the nation-State as a tool of capitalists whereby the government implements the policies of the capitalist class with little regard to the interests of subordinate groups. The "relative autonomy" view sees the economy/polity relationship as one in which the nation-State, while still having to provide a socio-economic climate conducive to capitalist investment, has some ability to represent the interests of subordinate groups. The "state autonomy" view grants the nation-State full freedom to set its own agenda irrespective of the interest of the capitalist class.

Second, all nation-States must perform at least three broad functions to maintain social stability: accumulation, legitimation, and mediation (Friedland 1991; O'Connor 1974). The "accumulation function" refers to the fact that nation-States must provide a stable business climate to attract capital investment. Without investment, there are no jobs; without jobs, no taxes; and without taxes, no government. The "legitimation function" refers to the fact that while the state must provide a business climate that supports capital accumulation, it must also represent the public interest or lose its legitimacy with its citizenry. If the government provides a business environment that degrades the environment and/or exploits workers to a severe degree, or engages in ill conceived military expeditions, then citizens might declare it "illegitimate" and replace the political elites. Finally, the "mediation function" balances competing class conflicts.

The last conceptual frame deals with political economy. The "Theory of Political Economy" (Smith 1974 [1774]; Ricardo 1996 [1821]) argues that markets, as opposed to states, should be the primary organizers of society. Government regulations should be minimal because a laissez-faire approach to polity/economy relations creates the greatest good for the greatest number of people. As long as there are many buyers and many sellers in anonymous markets, market power is not a problem. The "Critique of Political Economy" (Marx 1906 [1867]) argues that while laissez-faire approaches do generate high levels of accumulation, because in capitalism the firms must "grow or die," this approach is not suitable for sustained societal growth as competitive markets soon give way to oligopoly and monopoly. In this situation, the government must intervene to protect citizens from rampant capitalism.

The Frontier Era

The Frontier Era starts with an agricultural society in the mid-1800s and ends with the industrial revolution and the crash of 1929. Primary production such as farming, mining, fishing, and forestry dominated the economic sector. The craft-based production system was slowly replaced by Taylorist scientific management and Ford's mass production assembly line. The wage relation spread across the country as technological innovations made rural labor redundant resulting in rural to urban migration. By the end of the period the Robber Barons, labor unrest, and the Roaring Twenties epitomized the laissez-faire economic atmosphere of the time. In 1929 the economic crash brought the era to an end.

The Civil War contributed substantially to the growth in the federal government and its increased role in supporting economic accumulation. In 1862 the United States Department of Agriculture was created. In the same year the Morrill Act created the first part of the Land Grand University system that led to a federally coordinated system of agricultural and mechanization universities. Also in the same year the passage of the Homestead Act encouraged people to settle the new lands, break the prairie, and feed the country and the world. The government subdued the native peoples and relegated them to reservations. It provided lucrative land grants to the railroads to get them to link rural consumers to manufactured products and urban consumers to agricultural products. The railroads also first linked the rural breadbaskets, and later the output of the nascent industrial revolution, to growing export markets. Finally, lax immigration policies provided a constant stream of compliant workers for the emerging factory system.

In the late 1800s and early 1900s populist farmers organized in protest of the oligopoly and monopoly power of the railroads, grain companies, banks, and other trusts. The Packers and Stockyard Act and Sherman Anti-Trust Act represented successes of the populist agenda. Similarly, the suffragette movement secured women the right to vote late in the Frontier Era. Unions were still illegal and violence between companies and union organizers was common.

During the Frontier Era, the large national corporations were the dominant coordinators of the socio-economic system. This era was informed by policies based on the theory of political economy supported by an instrumental state that focused on capital accumulation over societal legitimation. For Regulationists, the regime of accumulation was "extensive" as the wage relation was spread across the country. Surplus labor value was extracted by working more people and working them longer hours. The mode of regulation was competitive with mostly absent or supportive state policies. By the end of the period the Robber Barons and trusts had solidified their economic dominance in the U.S. But, social movements such as the populists, suffragettes, and unionists were beginning to successfully question the legitimacy of the system.

By the early 1900s Taylorist production practices had created a new regime of accumulation, the mass production system of intensive labor control. Millions of products could be produced but there was not enough mass consumption to absorb the output. The tendency for capitalists to pay workers the least amount possible precluded the workers from consuming the product of their labor. The resulting crisis of overproduction and underconsumption contributed to the steady decline in economic prosperity resulting in an accumulation crisis and the Crash of 1929. While a new regime of accumulation had emerged, the complementary mode of regulation needed to balance the socio-economic system was absent. Henry Ford warned other industrialists that capitalism was not sustainable if the workers were not paid enough to buy the products they produced. Due to the laissez-faire orientation to polity/economy relations, the state was not able to intervene to match consumption to production and thereby stabilize capitalism.

The Fordist Era

The Fordist Era stretches from the New Deal to the Great Society. The failure of the Frontier Era's laissez faire system of societal coordination opened the door for an expanded governmental role in coordinating economic growth and social stability. The quasi-socialist New Deal emerged to rebuild the country after the Crash of 1929 and the Great Depression. The Agricultural Adjustment Act provided farmers with price protection from glutted markets. The Social Security Administration provided economic security to seniors. The Work Projects Administration put people back to work during the Depression. The Department of Justice and the Federal Trade Commission protected consumers and companies from market power. Food stamps, unemployment insurance, minimum wage provisions, and later welfare programs provided mechanisms that supported increased consumption by the poor and working classes. The National Labor Relations Act gave unions legal rights. The Soil Conservation Service protected the land from exploitative agricultural practices. Civil rights legislation was passed and the Environmental Protection Agency was created. The nation-State strongly intervened with Keynesian economic policies to balance consumption with production and protected the interests of subordinate groups.

Taylorist labor management practices reached their peak in the post-WWII era as the capital-labor accord brought a truce between the corporations and the workers. In this "great compromise" mediated by the government, workers gained the rights to job protections and benefits in return for granting business control of the labor process and purging communist elements from their ranks. Fearing another post-world war global recession, after World War II the United States and Great Britain created the Bretton Woods system of global socio-economic coordination designed to modernize the developing world using the U.S. as the model.

The World Bank, International Monetary Fund (IMF), and General Agreement on Tariffs and Trade were created as tools to regulate the world economic system. The fact that global currencies were tied to the U.S. dollar on the gold standard provided stable currency markets worldwide. The Marshall Plan rebuilt Europe and Japan and secured U.S. export markets to those regions of the world. Similarly, in the Cold War environment, U.S. military power was often used to make sure the U.S.-based multinational corporations secured and maintained access to natural resources in the developing world.

Early in the Fordist Era the unions were the dominant social movement. By the end of the period the Civil Rights and Women's movements secured important gains. At the same time the anti-War movement called into question the Cold War policy of using U.S. troops to challenge communist insurgency around the world. In response to growing ecological concerns, the environmental movement rose to prominence in the late 1960s. Finally, the emergence of OPEC (Organization of Petroleum Exporting Countries) in the early 1970s represented a new form of social movement that challenged the dominance of the First World Countries.

As long as the mixture of technological innovations and Taylorist production efficiencies increased productivity the truce between labor and capital prevailed. The hegemonic power of the U.S. military and U.S. MNCs overseas supported the long period of prosperity at home. In the late 1950s this complementary arrangement began to unravel. Productivity rates began to decline. Competition from Europe and Japan eroded U.S. business dominance. The Civil Rights, anti-War, Women's, Environmental, and resurgent Union Movements called into question the legitimacy of the current system. By the end of this period the U.S. nation-State was in a fiscal crisis due to the high cost of the Vietnam War, other Cold War costs associated with containing communism around the world, and the War on Poverty at home. U.S.-based corporations were experiencing an accumulation crisis due to the combination of decreasing productivity gains, high labor costs, increasing environmental regulations, and rising costs of energy due to OPEC.

During the Fordist Era the interventionist nation-State took over from the national corporations as the dominant coordinator of society. The state operated within a relative autonomy perspective based on "the critique of the theory of political economy" that allowed it to take actions counter to the general interests of capital accumulation and in support of subordinate groups. The corporatist arrangement saw the strong state mediate the conflicting interests of capital and labor and thereby produce a long period of economic accumulation and social stability. This "intensive" regime of accumulation based on working workers more efficiently combined with a "monopoly" mode of regulation centered on the mediating power of the interventionist state came to fruition in the 1950s. By the 1960s, the rigidities associated with the Fordist system of mass production linked to mass consumption coordinated by an interventionist state brought the system to crisis. The nation-State was not providing an attractive business climate and was suffering legitimation crisis on several fronts.

The Post-Fordist Era

The accumulation crisis of capital was resolved through the strategy of globalization comprised of four components. First, using the practice of capital flight, corporations moved their operations overseas to avoid the high costs of production in regulated First World nation-States. Second, corporations decentralized their production away from single large factories susceptible to labor unrest and toward several smaller operations at different locations globally. Third, corporations reduced their reliance on formal labor relations and increased their use of flexible labor markets such as immigrants, women, temporary, and part-time work. Finally, corporations increasingly practiced global sourcing to obtain the lowest costs factors of production and secure access to lucrative global markets.

These actions were facilitated by the "hyper-mobility of capital" (Harvey 1990). In 1973 President Nixon took the U.S. dollar off the gold standard. This action created instability in global currency markets and the rise of new forms of capital markets called transnational finance capital (TFC). Computer-based technologies allowed economic actors to evaluate investment opportunities at the global level and then invest and disinvest frequently and rapidly. Capital moved rapidly around the globe in search of the highest return on investments. TFC created export platforms in special export processing zones to service global markets (McMichael 1996). Often these actions centered on financial speculation instead of productive investments. These factors combined to create a flexible production system based on computer-assisted design that sourced low cost labor and supportive government policies.

In response to the accumulation crises and resulting capital flight, the highly regulated First World nation-States deregulated and privatized their national economies. President Reagan in the U.S. and Prime Minister Thatcher in the U.K. led this movement. Deregulation refers to the decreased government management of the economy. President Reagan's refusal to support the government employees of the Professional Air Traffic Controllers' union in their strike began a long series of setbacks for unions in the U.S. Privatization refers to the tendency to reduce the level of government ownership of industries and services. In the U.S. it manifested as government downsizing, devolution of services from the national to local level, and welfare reform. Similarly during this time, developing countries often encountered debt crises and were forced by the IMF to restructure their economies based on deregulation and privatization.

The hyper-mobility of capital restricted the ability of nation-States to control their domestic economies as global economic actors invested and dis-invested in various countries and special-regulation export processing zones such as the maquiladoras. If nation-States restricted the flow of capital, commodities, and labor across its borders and/or maintained a fiscal and regulatory socio-economic environment that limited capital accumulation, then the "electronic herd" would pull their money out of that country and thereby punish it for not playing the globalization game (see Friedman 2000). Under Post-Fordism, the allegiance that existed between the MNCs and their home countries under Fordism was reduced. In order to survive, MNCs became TNCs and adopted global production strategies that did not necessarily favor the home country. In summary, because of the increased ability of subordinate groups during the Fordist Era to use democratic processes to enhance their well being, the cost of doing business increased to such a level that corporations were forced to abandon their attachments to their home countries to revive accumulation.

In the Post-Fordist Era TFC and the TNCs take over the role from the interventionist nation-States as coordinators of the new global socio-economic system. The Post-Fordist globalization project is an overt strategy on the part of global capitalism to revive accumulation in the face of the successes of democratic action on the part of subordinate groups in the Fordist Era. It is a strategy to avoid the increased costs that democracy entailed for economic actors. The nation-State has returned to a more instrumental role based again on the theory of political economy while at the same time supra-national forms of the state are emerging such as the European Union (EU), North American Free Trade Agreement (NAFTA) and the World Trade Organization (WTO). A flexible regime of accumulation based on the global sourcing of the most lucrative factors of production, as well as profitable consumer markets, has revived economic accumulation at the global level. The flexible regime combines the extension of the wage relation to unprotected labor from the Frontier Era with intensive labor practices from the Fordist Era. Through computer technologies, this arrangement is able to service the flexible demands of global consumers for non-mass produced, good quality products.

For Regulationists, we are back in a similar situation to the end of the Frontier Era. The workers in the export processing zones do not make enough money to buy the product of their labor. The new global system is based on maintaining and increasing levels of consumption in the privileged First World while at the same time servicing the growing middle- and upper-class markets in the global cities. This arrangement manifests as global-local linkages (Giddens 1990) whereby natural resources and low cost labor are sourced in countries (often Third World) with supportive business regulations, and profitable consumer markets are sourced in the First World and the growing middle and upper classes in the global cities. The new "regime" has arrived but the new "mode" needed to provide stability and balance is yet nascent. The WTO is the current attempt to provide a mechanism for global socio-economic regulation similar to that of the Keynesian nation-State of the Fordist Era.

Star Wars

Like the rebellion used the light side of the Force to fight against the Empire, the Populist, Women's, and Labor Movements of the late 1800s and early 1900s fought for their civil rights against unrestrained capitalism. When the Death Star (i.e. Robber Barons) collapsed from a combination of continued attack and its own arrogance and greed, the following era represented the flowering of the light side of the Force. The rebellion extended its vision of democracy and created a Federation (e.g., United Nations) to diffuse the vision throughout the world. Democracy flourished as social movements gained influence and governments intervened to protect the interests of subordinate groups. Farmers, workers, women, blacks, environmentalists, anti-apartheid, and anti-war activists were all successful at securing increased protection from capitalism through legislation and regulations. These movements were so successful at using their democratic prerogatives that the cost of doing business in First World economies was becoming prohibitive for the multi-national and national corporations. Labor costs, environmental regulations, and corporate taxes to support the burgeoning welfare-State all increased production costs at a time of falling profits.

The Empire Strikes Back

The ensuing accumulation crisis of capital was resolved with the globalization project as the Empire struck back to avoid and defeat the successes of the democratic Federation. The Empire moved its wealth-generating operations to countries where democracy (The Federation) was not powerful and threatened the social-democratic First World nation-States with economic abandonment if they did not deregulate and privatize their countries. Democratic protections had to be weakened to attract investment from the TNCs (the dark side of the Force). The Federation was forced to reduce its protections of subordinate groups (e.g., welfare reform) and the environment (e.g., failure to support Kyoto protocol). The Empire created the WTO to serve its interests and open the world to barrier free global capitalism. It employed its older servants (IMF, World Bank) to force developing countries to deregulate their economies, privatize their government-owned enterprises, and create export processing zones.

The Return of the Jedi

The Empire is being resisted. The "Battle in Seattle" and other demonstrations against globalization indicate that rebel resistance is still active. Labor, Environmental, and Third World movements continue to reveal the terrible consequences of the Empire (i.e., global warming and sweatshops). Each sociology student that develops the Sociological Imagination can become a young Jedi knight and part of the rebellion. Professors of sociology need to proudly wear the robes of the Jedi master and teach the young knights the ways of Force. Only then can we fulfill Comte's vision of sociologists as the new priesthood and lead humanity to emancipation and freedom from the dark side of the Force. May the Force be with you.

References

Aglietta, Michael. 1979. *A Theory of Capitalist Regulation*. London: Verso.

Bonanno, Alessandro and Douglas H. Constance. 1996. *Caught in the Net: The Global Tuna Industry, Environmentalism, and the State*. Lawrence: University Press of Kansas.

Friedman, Thomas L. 2000. *The Lexus and the Olive Tree: Understanding Globalization*. New York: Anchor Books.

Friedland, William H. 1991. "The Transnationalization of Agricultural Production: Palimpset of the Transnational State." *International Journal of Sociology of Agriculture and Food* 1:59–70.

Giddens, Anthony. 1990. *The Consequences of Modernity*. Stanford: Stanford University Press.

Harvey, David. 1990. *The Condition of Post-Modernity*. Oxford: Basil Blackwell.

Lipietz, Alain. 1992. *Towards A New Economic Order: Post-Fordism, Ecology, and Democracy*. New York: Oxford University Press.

Marx, Karl. 1906 [1867]. *Capital: A Critique of Political Economy*. New York: The Modern Library.

McMichael, Philip. 1996. *Development and Social Change*. London: Pine Forge Press.

O'Connor, James. 1974. *The Fiscal Crisis of the State*. New York: St. Martin's Press.

Ricardo, David. 1996 [1821]. *On the Principles of Political Economy and Taxation*. Amherst: Prometheus Books.

Smith, Adam. 1974 [1774]. *The Wealth of Nations*. New York: Penguin Books.

References

Adler, William M. 2000. *Mollie's Job: A Story of Life and Work in the Global Assembly Line.* New York: Scribner.

Andrews, David L., Renn Carrington, Zhiginian Mazor, and Steven J. Jackson. 1996. "Jordanscapes: A Preliminary Analysis of the Global Popular." *Social Science Journal.* 13:428–57.

Appelbaum, Richard P. 1989. "The Affordability Gap." *Society* 26(4):6–8.

Astin, Alexander W. 1993. "Diversity and Multiculturalism on the Campus: How Are Students Affected?" *Change* 25:44–49.

Averitt, Robert T. 1968. *The Dual Economy: The Dynamics of American Industrial Structure.* New York: Morton.

Babbie, Earl. 2002. *The Basics of Social Research.* Belmont, CA: Wadsworth / Thomson Learning.

Ball, Mary and Frank Whittington. 1995. *Surviving Dependence: Voices of African American Elders.* Amityville, NY: Baywood.

Banfield, Edward C. 1958. *The Moral Basis of a Backward Society.* New York: Free Press.

Bazerman, Max H., Jared R. Curhan, Don A. Moore, and Kathleen L. Valley. 2000. "Negotiation." *Annual Review of Psychology* 51:279–314.

Becker, Gary S. 1971. *The Economies of Discrimination,* 2nd ed. Chicago, IL: University Press.

Bellas, Marcia L. 1993. "Faculty Salaries: Still a Cost of Being Female." *Social Science Quarterly* 74(1):62–75.

Berg, Bruce L. 1989. *Qualitative Research Methods for Social Sciences.* Boston, MA: Allyn and Bacon.

Berrill, Kevin T. 1992. "Anti-Gay Violence and Victimization in the U.S.: An Overview." Pp. 19–45 in *Hate Crimes: Continuing Violence Against Lesbians and Gay Men,* edited by Gregory M. Herek and Keven T. Berrill. Newbury Park, CA: Sage.

Best, Joel. 2001. *Damned Lies and Statistics: Untangling Numbers from the Media, Politicians, and Activists.* Berkeley, CA: University of California Press.

Best, Raphaela. 1983. *We've Got All the Scars: What Boys and Girls Learn in Elementary School.* Bloomington, IN: Indiana University Press.

Bianchi, Suzanne, Melissa A. Milkie, Liana C. Sayer, and John P. Robinson. 2000. "Is Anyone Doing the Housework? Trends in the Gender Division of Household Labor." *Social Forces* 79:191–228.

Biggart, Nicole Woolsey. 1989. *Charismatic Capitalism: Direct Selling Organizations in America.* Chicago, IL: University of Chicago Press.

Blackwood, D.L. and R.G. Lynch. 1994. "The Measurement of Inequality and Poverty: A Policy Maker's Guide to the Literature." *World Development* 22(4):567–78.

Blankenhorn, David. 1995. *Fatherless America: Our Most Urgent Social Problem.* New York: Harper College.

Block, Jeanne H. 1984. "Psychological Development of Female Children and Adolescents." Pp.126–42 in *Sex Role Identity and Ego Development,* edited by Jeanne H. Block. San Francisco, CA: Jossey-Bass.

Blumer, Herbert. 1990. *Industrialization as an Agent of Social Change: A Critical Analysis.* New York: Aldine de Gruyter.

Boisot, Max and John Child. 1996. "From Fiefs to Clans and Network Capitalism: Explaining China's Economic Order." *Administrative Science Quarterly* 41:600–28.

Borgida, Eugene, John L. Sullivan, Alina Oxendine, Melinda S. Jackson, Eric Riedel, and Amy Gangl. 2002. "Civic Culture Meets the Digital Divide: The Role of Community Electronic Networks." *Journal of Social Issues* 58(1):125–41.

Bradburn, Norman M. and Seymore Sudman. 1988. *Polls and Surveys: Understanding What They Tell Us*. San Francisco: Jossey-Bass.

Brennan, Teresa. 1997. "The Two Forms of Consciousness." *Theory, Culture, and Society* 14:89–96.

Brians, Craig Leonard and Bernard Grofman. 2001. "Election Day Registration's Effect on Voter Turnout." *Social Sciences Quarterly* 82:170–83.

Brody, William. 1997. "Building a New Kind of Academy." *Planning for Higher Education* 25:72–74.

Brown, Phil. 2000. "Environment and Health." Pp. 143–158 in *Handbook of Medical Sociology*, 5th ed., edited by Chloe Bird, Peter Conrad and Allen Fremont. Upper Saddle River, NJ: Prentice Hall.

Brym, Robert J. and John Lie. 2003. *Sociology: Your Compass for a New World*. Belmont, CA: Wadsworth.

Bullard, Robert D. 1994. *Dumping in Dixie: Race, Class, and Environmental Quality*. Boulder, CO: Westview Press.

Bureau of Labor Statistics. 1999. "What Women Earned in 1998." *Issues in Labor Statistics.* Washington, DC: U.S. Government Printing Office.

Burns, John. 1995. "Hospices Play Bigger Role in Care Continuum." *Modern Healthcare* 25:96.

Burt, Ronald S. 1992. *Structural Holes: The Social Structure of Competition*. Cambridge, MA: Harvard University Press.

Bury, Michael. 2000. "On Chronic Illness and Disability." Pp. 173–183 in *Handbook of Medical Sociology*, 5th ed, edited by in Chloe Bird, Peter Conrad, and Allen Fremont. Upper Saddle River, NJ: Prentice Hall.

Caplow, Theodore, Howard M. Babb, Bruce A. Chadwick, Rueben Hill, and Margaret Holmes Williamson. 1982. *Middletown Families*. Minneapolis: University of Minnesota Press.

Carnevale, Peter J. and Tahira M. Probst. 1997. "Conflict on the Internet." Pp. 233–55 in *Culture of the Internet*, edited by Sara Kiesler. Mahwah, NJ: Erlbaum.

Carruthers, Bruce G. and Sarah L. Babb. 2000. *Economy/Society: Markets, Meanings, and Social Structure*. Thousand Oaks, CA: Pine Forge Press.

Catton, William R. and Riley E. Dunlap. 1980. "A New Ecological Paradigm for Post-Exuberant Sociology." *American Behavioral Scientist* 24:15–47.

Cavan, Ruth. 1994. "The Concepts of Tolerance and Contraculture as Applied to Delinquency." *The Sociological Quarterly* 243–258.

Chaskin, Robert J. 1997. "Perspectives on Neighborhood and Community: A Review of the Literature." *Social Service Review* 71(4):521–47.

Cherlin, Andrew J. 1996. *Public and Private Families: An Introduction*. New York: McGraw Hill.

Cherny, Lynn. 1999. *Conversation and Community: Chat in a Virtual World*. Stanford, CA: CSLI Publications.

Chirot, Daniel. 1977. *Social Change in the Twentieth Century*. New York: Harcourt Brace and Jovanovich.

Chumbler, Neal, James W. Grimm, Corneilia Beck, and Rebecca L. Gray. "Family Relationships and Caregiver Burden." Under review by the *International Journal of Psychiatry.*

Clarke, Lee and James F. Short. 1993. "Social Organizations and Risk: Some Current Controversies." *Annual Review of Sociology* 19:375–99.

Clinard, Marshall B. 1968. *Sociology of Deviant Behavior*. New York: Holt, Rinehart, and Winston.

Cockerham, William C. 1997. *This Aging Society*, 2nd ed. Upper Saddle River, NJ: Prentice Hall.

———. 1999. *Health and Social Change in Russia and Eastern Europe.* London, UK: Routledge.

———. 2001. *Medical Sociology*, 8th ed. Upper Saddle River, NJ: Prentice Hall.

Cooley, Charles Horton. [1902] 1964. *Human Nature and the Social Order*. New York: Schocken.

Cowart, Marie and Jill Quadagno. 1995. *Crucial Decisions in Long Term Care*. Tallahasee, FL: Mildred and Claude Pepper Foundation.

Crawford, Colin. 1996. *Uproar at Dancing Rabbit Creek: Battling over Race, Class, and the Environment*. Reading, MA: Addison-Wesley.

Crispell, Diane. 1993. "Grandparents Galore." American Demographics 19:63.

Cummings, Elaine and Henry William. 1961. *Growing old: The Process of Disengagement*. New York: Basic Books.

Davey, Joseph P. 1992. "Homelessness in the United States: The Reagan Legacy." *The Urban League Review* 16(1):23–33.

Degler, Carl N. 1980. *At Odds: Women and the Family in America from the Revolution to the Present*. New York: Oxford University Press.

Demos, John. 1971. *A Little Commonwealth: Family Life in Plymouth Colony*. New York: Oxford University Press.

Department of Labor. 1995. "Good for Business: Making Full Use of the Nation's Capital." Washington, DC: U.S. Government Printing Office and Department of Labor.

DiMaggio, Paul, Eszter Hargittai, W. Russell Neuman, and John P. Robinson. 2001. "Social Implications of the Internet." *Annual Review of Sociology* 27:307–36.

Dreiling, Michael C. 2000. "Corporate Political Action Leadership in the Defense of NAFTA." *Social Problems* 47:21–48.

Duany, Andres, Elizabeth Plater-Zyberk, and Jeff Speck. 2000. *Suburban Nation: The Rise of Sprawl and the Decline of the American Dream*. New York: North Point Press.

Duncan, Cynthia M. 2000. *Worlds Apart: Why Poverty Persists in Rural America*. New Haven, CN: Yale University Press.

Dunlap, Riley E., Frederick H. Buttel, Peter Dickens, and August Gijwijt. 2002. *Sociological Theory and the Environment: Classical Foundations, Contemporary Insights*. New York: Rowman and Littlefield.

Dunlap, Riley E. and William R. Catton. 1979. "Environmental Sociology." *Annual Review of Sociology* 5:243–73.

———. 2002. "Which Function(s) of the Environment Do We Study? A Comparison of Environmental and Natural Resource Sociology." *Society and Natural Resources* 15: 239–49.

Durkheim, Emile. [1895] 1964. *The Rules of Sociological Method*. New York: Free Press.

———. [1897] 1966. *Suicide*. New York: Free Press.

Dweck , Carol. 1975. "The Role of Expectations and Attributions in the Alleviation of Learned Helplessness." *Journal of Personality and Social Psychology* 31:670–85.

Dweck, Carol, Therese Goetz, and Van Strauss. 1980. "Sex Differences in Learned Helplessness IV: An Experimental and Naturalistic Study of Failure Generalization and Its Mediators." *Journal of Personality and Social Psychology* 38:441–52.

Dyk, Patricia H. and Julie N. Zimmerman. 2000. *The Impacts and Outcomes of Welfare Reform across Rural and Urban Places in Kentucky*. Final report for the Policy Outcome Grant submitted to the U.S. Department of Health and Human Services, Assistant Secretary for Planning and Evaluation. http://www.ca.uky.edu/SNARL/Reportfiles/ReportFrontPage.htm

Edelman, Lauren B. 1990. "Legal Environments and Organizational Governance: The Expansion of Due Process in the American Workplace." *American Journal of Sociology* 95:1401–40.

Edin, Kathryn, Kathleen M. Harris, and Gary D. Sandefur. 1998. *Welfare to Work: Opportunities and Pitfalls*. Washington, DC: ASA Publications.

Eitzen, D. Stanley and Kelly Eitzen Smith. 2003. *Experiencing Poverty: Voices from the Bottom*. Belmont, CA: Wadsworth/Thomson Learning.

Elias, N. 1974. "Foreword." In *Sociology of Community: A Collection of Readings*, edited by Colin Bell and Howard Newby. London, UK: Frank Cass.

Ember, Melvin and Carol R. Ember. 1991. *Anthropology*, 6th ed. Englewood Cliffs, NJ: Prentice Hall.

Erikson, Kai. 1995. *A New Species of Trouble: Human Experiences of Modern Disasters*. New York: W.W. Norton.

Falk, William W. and Thomas A. Lyson. 1988. *High Tech, Low Tech, No Tech: Recent Industrial and Occupational Changes in the South*. Albany, NY: State University of New York Press.

Field, Donald R. and William R. Burch. 1988. *Rural Sociology and the Environment*. Middleton, WI: Social Ecology Press.

Field, Donald R., A.E. Luloff, and Richard S. Krannich. 2002. "Revisiting the Origins of and Distinctions Between Natural Resource Sociology and Environmental Sociology." *Society and Natural Resources* 15(3):213–28.

Fitchen, Janet M. 1981. *Poverty in Rural America: A Case Study*. Prospect Heights, IL: Waveland.

———. 1991. *Endangered Spaces, Enduring Places: Change, Identity, and Survival in Rural America*. Boulder, CO: Westview.

Florida, Richard. 2002. *The Rise of the Creative Class and How It's Transforming Work, Leisure, Community and Everyday Life*. New York: Basic Books.

Freudenburg, William R. and Robert E. Jones. 1991. "Criminal Behavior and Rapid Community Growth: Examining the Evidence." *Rural Sociology* 56(4):619–45.

Frey, R. Scott. 1995. "The International Traffic in Pesticides." *Technological Forecasting and Social Change* 50(2):151–169.

———. 2001. "The Hazardous Waste Stream in the World-System." Pp. 106–20 in *The Environment and Society Reader*, edited by R. Scott Frey. Boston: Allyn and Bacon.

Friedman, Joseph. 1985. *Great Housing Experiment: Urban Affairs Annual Review*. Thousand Oaks, CA: Sage.

Fukuyama, Francis. 1999. *The Great Disruption: Human Nature and the Reconstitution of Social Order.* New York: Free Press.

Furlong, Beth and Marlene Wilken. 2001. "Managed Care: The Changing Environment for Consumers and Health Care Providers." Pp 3–20 in *Research in the Sociology of Health Care*, Vol. 19, edited by Jennie Jacobs Kronenfeld. London: Elsevier Science Ltd.

Galpin, Charles J. 1915. *Bulletin 34: The Social Anatomy of an Agricultural Community*. Madison, WI: University of Wisconsin Agricultural Experiment Station.

Gardyn, Rebecca. 2000. "Retirement Redefined." *American Demographics* 22:52–57.

Garrett, Laurie. 1994. *The Coming Plague*. New York: Farrar, Strauss and Giroux.

Gelles, R.J. and M.A. Strauss. 1979. "Determinants of Violence in the Family: Toward a Theoretical Integration." Pp. 549–81 in *Contemporary Theories about the Family*, edited by Wesley R. Burr. New York: Free Press.

Gereffi, Gary. 1994. "The International Economy and Economic Development." Pp. 206–33 in *Handbook of Economic Sociology*, edited by Neil J. Smelser and Richard Swedberg. Princeton, NJ: Princeton University Press.

Giddens, Anthony. 1990. *The Consequences of Modernity*. Cambridge, UK: Polity.

———. 1997. *Introduction to Sociology*, 2nd ed. New York: Norton.

Goffman, Erving. 1963. *Stigma: Notes on the Management of Spoiled Identity*. Englewood Cliffs, NJ: Prentice Hall.

Gold, Dolores, Gail Crombie, and Sally Noble. 1987. "Relations Between Teachers' Judgments of Girls' and Boys' Compliance and Intellectual Competence." *Sex Roles* 16(7/8):351–58.

Goldschmidt, Walter. 1946. "Small Business and the Community: A Study in the Central Valley of California on the Effects of Scale of Farm Operation." Report of the Special Committee to Study Problems of American Small Business, U.S. Senate, 79th Congress, 2nd Session, Committee Print 13. Washington, DC: U.S. Government Printing Office.

———. 1978. *As You Sow: Three Studies in the Social Consequences of Agribusiness*. Montclair, NJ: Allanheld, Osburn.

Gorey, Kevin and John E. Vena. 1994. "The Association of Near Poverty Status with Cancer Incidence among Black and White Adults." *Journal of Community Health* 20(4):359–66.

Gostin, Lawerence O., Chai Feldblum, and David W. Webber. 1999. "Disabled Discrimination on America: HIV/AIDS and other Health Conditions." *Journal of the American Medical Association* 281:745–52.

Gothan, Kevin Fox. 1998. "Race, Mortgage Lending, and Loan Rejections in a U.S. City." *Sociological Focus* 31:391–405.

Govier, Trudy. 1997. *Social Trust and Human Communities*. London: McGill University Press.

Granovetter, Mark S. 1973. "The Strength of Weak Ties." *American Journal of Sociology* 78(6):1360–80.

———. 1974. *Getting a Job: A Study of Contacts and Careers*. Cambridge, MA: Harvard University Press.

Grimm, James W. and Zachary W. Brewster. 2002. "Explaining Health-Related Inequalities with a Social Capital Model." *Research in the Sociology of Healthcare*, Vol. 20 pp3–27.

Grossman, Herbert and Suzanne Grossman. 1994. *Gender Issues in Education*. Boston: Allyn and Bacon.

Guillen, Mauro F. 2001. "Is Globalization Civilizing, Destructive, or Feeble? A Critique of Fire Key Debate in the Social Science Literature." *Annual Review of Sociology* 27:235–60.

Gusfield, Joseph R. 1963. *Symbolic Crusade: Status Politics and the American Temperance Movement*. Urbana, IL: University of Illinois Press.

Hamilton, Gary G. and Nicole Woosley Biggart. 1988. "Market, Culture, and Authority: A Comparative Analysis of Management and Organization in the Far East." *American Journal of Sociology* 94 (Supplement):552–94.

Hamilton, William. 1979. *A Social Experiment in Program Administration*. Cambridge, MA: Abt Associates.

Havighurst, Robert J., Bernice L. Neugarten, and Shelden Tobin. 1968. "Disengagement and Patterns of Aging." Pp. 161–72 in *Middle Age and Aging: A Reader in Social Psychology*, edited by Bernice Neugarten. Chicago, IL: University of Chicago Press.

Hays, Samuel P. 1987. *Beauty, Health, and Permanence: Environmental Politics in the United States, 1955–1985*. New York: Cambridge University Press.

Henslin, James M. 2002. *Essentials of Sociology: A Down to Earth Approach*. Boston, MA: Allyn and Bacon.

Higgins, Paul C. 1992. *Making Disability: Exploring the Social Transformation of Human Variation*. Springfield, IL: Charles C. Thomas.

Hillery, George A. 1955. "Definitions of Community: Areas of Agreement." *Rural Sociology* 20(2):111–23.

Hirschi, Travis. 1969. *Causes of Delinquency.* Berkley: University of California Press.

Hochschild, Arlie. 1975. "Disengagement Theory: A Critique and Proposal." *American Sociological Review* 40:553–69.

———. 1997. *The Time Bind: When Work Becomes Home and Home Becomes Work*. New York: Metropolitan Books.

Hochschild, Arlie and Anne Machung. 1989. *The Second Shift: Working Parents and the Revolution at Home.* New York: Viking.

Hodson, Randy and Teresa A. Sullivan. 2002. *The Social Organization of Work*, 3rd ed. Belmont, CA: Wadsworth/Thomson Learning.

Hout, Michael and Andrew M. Greeley. 1998. "What Church Officials' Reports Don't Show: Another Look at Church Attendance Data." *American Sociological Review* 63:113–19.

Hoyle, Rick H., Monica J. Harris, and Charles M. Judd. 2002. *Research Methods in Social Relations*, 7th ed. Belmont, CA: Wadsworth/Thomson Learning.

Hummert, Mary Lee., Teri Garstka, Jaye Shaner and Sharon Strahm. 1994. "Stereotypes of the Elderly Held by Young, Middle-Aged and Elderly Adults." *Journal of Gerontology* 49:240–49.

Humphrey, Craig R., Tammy L. Lewis, and Frederick H. Buttel. 2001. *Environment, Energy and Society: A New Synthesis*. Belmont, CA: Wadsworth.

Hunter, Lori M., Richard S. Krannich, and Michael D. Smith. 2002. "Rural Migration, Rapid Growth, and Fear of Crime." *Rural Sociology* 67(1):71–91.

Iannaccone, Laurence R. 1994. "Why Strict Churches Are Strong?" *American Journal of Sociology* 99:1180–211.

International Fund for Agricultural Development. 2001. *Rural Poverty Report 2001: The Challenge of Ending Rural Poverty*. New York: Oxford University Press.

Jacobs, Jane. 1961. *The Death and Life of Great American Cities*. New York: Vintage Books.

Jaimes, M. Annette. 1992. "Federal Indian Identification Policy: A Usurpation of Indigenous Sovereignty in North America." Pp. 123–138 in *The State of Native America: Genocide, Colonization, and Resistance*, edited by M. Annette Jaimes. Cambridge, MA: South End Press.

Janowitz, Morris. 1961. *The Community Press in an Urban Setting: The Social Elements of Urbanism*. Chicago, IL: University of Chicago Press.

Jargowsky, Paul A. 1997. *Poverty and Place: Ghettos, Barrios and the American City*. New York: Russell Sage Foundation.

Jasper, James M. 1998. "The Emotions Protest: Affective and Reactive Emotion in and Around Social Movements." *Sociological Forum* 13:397–429.

Jenkins, J. Craig and Michael Wallace. 1996. "The Generalized Action Potential of Protest Movements: The New Class, Social Trends, and Political Exclusion Explanations." *Sociological Forum* 11:183–207.

Kantor, Rosabeth Moss. 1997. *Men and Women of the Corporation.* New York: Basic Books.

Katz, James E., Ronald E. Rice, and Philip Aspden. 2001. "The Internet, 1995–2000: Access, Civic Involvement, and Social Interaction." *American Behavioral Scientist* 45(3):405–19.

Kaufman, Debra R. 1995. "Professional Women: How Real are the Recent Gains?" Pp. 287–305 in *Women: A Feminist Perspective*, edited by Jo Freeman. Mountain View, CA: Mayfield.

Kaufman, Harold F. 1959. "Toward an Interactional Conception of Community." *Social Forces* 38(1):8–17.

Kaufman, Harold, and L. Kaufman. 1946. *Toward the Stabilization and Enrichment of a Forest Community: The Montana Study*. Missoula, MT: University of Montana Press.

Kerbo, Harold R. 1991. *Social Stratification and Inequality: Class Conflict in Historical and Comparative Perspective*. New York: McGraw-Hill.

Krimsky, Sheldon and Alonzo Plough. 1988. *Environmental Hazards: Communicating Risks as a Social Process*. Dover, MA: Auburn House.

Kronenfeld, Jennie Jacobs. 2001. "New Trends in the Doctor-Patient Relationship: Impacts of Managed Care on the Growth of a Consumer Protection Model." *Sociological Spectrum* 21: 293–317.

Krugman, Paul R. and Maurice Obstfeld. 1991. *International Economics: Theory and Policy*, 2nd ed. New York: Harper Collins.

Kuno, Clifford, Donald Palmer, Roger Friedland, and Matthew Zafonte. 1998. "Lost in Space: The Geography of Corporate Interlocking Directorates." *American Journal of Sociology* 103:863–911.

Ladd, Everett Carll. 1999. *The Ladd Report*. New York: Free Press.

Landis, Paul H. 1938. *Three Iron Mining Towns: A Study in Cultural Change*. Middleton, WI: Social Ecology Press.

Lanier, Mark M. and Stuart Henry. 1997. *Essential Criminology*. Boulder, CO: Westview.

Lauer, Robert H. 1991. *Persepectives in Social Change*. Boston, MA: Allyn and Bacon.

Laumann, Edward O., John H. Gagnon, Robert T. Michael and Stuart Michaels. 1994. *The Social Organization of Sexuality: Sex Practices in the United States*. Chicago, IL: University of Chicago Press.

Le Bon, Gustave. [1895] 1960. *The Crowd: A Study of the Popular Mind*. New York: Viking Press.

Lee, Raymond. 1993. *Doing Research on Sensitive Topics*. Newburg Park, CA: Sage.

Lemert, Edwin. 1972. *Human Deviance, Social Problems, and Social Control*, 2nd ed. Englewood Cliffs, NJ: Prentice-Hall.

Lewis-Beck, Michael. 1995. *Data Analysis: An Introduction*. Volume 103 in the Quantitative Application in Social Science Series. Thousand Oaks, CA: Sage.

Lewis, S., C. F. Ross, and J. Mirowosky. 1999. "Establishing a Sense of Personal Control in the Transition to Adulthood." *Social Forces* 77:1573–99.

Lin, Nan, Karen Cook, and Ronald S. Burt Editors. 2001. *Social Capital: Theory and Research*. New York: Aldine De Gruyter.

Lips, Hilary. 1989. "Gender-Role Socialization: Lessons in Femininity." Pp. 128–48 in *Women, A Feminist Perspective*, edited by Jo Freeman. Mountain View, CA: Mayfield.

Lofland, John and Lyn Lofland. 1995. *Analyzing Social Settings*, 3rd ed. Belmont, CA: Wadsworth.

Lofland, Lyn H. 1998. *The Public Realm: Exploring the City's Quintessential Social Territory*. New York: Aldine de Gruyter.

Loveman, Mara. 1995. "Is Race Essential?" *American Sociological Review* 64:890–98.

Lyon, Larry. 1987. *The Community in Urban Society*. Philadelphia, PA: Temple University Press.

Macionis, John J. 2003. *Sociology*, 9th ed. Upper Saddle River: NJ, Prentice Hall.

Maddox, George. 1964. "Disengagement Theory: A Critical Evaluation." *The Gerontologist* 4: 80–82.

———. 1965. "Fact and Artifact: Evidence Bearing on Disengagement Theory from the Duke Geriatrics Projects." *Human Development* 8:117–30.

Maines, David R. 2001. *The Faultline of Consciousness: A View of Interactionism in Sociology*. New York: Aldine de Gruyter.

Malthus, Thomas R. 1803. *An Essay on the Principle of Population*. New York: Cambridge University Press.

Manton, Kenneth, L.S. Corder, and E. Stallard. 1997. "Chronic Disability Trends in Elderly United States Populations 1982–1994." Proceedings of the National Academy of Sciences 94:2593–98.

Marger, M.N. 1994. Race *and Ethnic Relations: American and Global Perspective*. Belmont, CA: Wadsworth.

Marin, Gerardo and Barbara Vamoss Marin. 1991. *Research and Hispanic Population*. Newbury Park, CA: Sage.

Marot, Michael. 1996. "The Social Pattern of Health and Disease." Pp. 42–70 in *Health and Social Organization*, edited by D. Bane, E. Brunner, and R. Williamson. London, UK: Routledge.

Marshal, Nancy L. 2001. "Health and Illness Issues Facing an Aging Workforce in the New Millenium." *Sociological Spectrum* 21:431–39.

Marshall, Catherine and Gretchen B. Rossman. 1995. *Designing Qualitative Research*. Thousand Oaks, CA: Sage.

Marx, Karl. [1867] 1967. *Capital*. New York: International Publishers.

Mason, Andrew. 2000. *Community, Solidarity and Belonging: Levels of Community and Their Normative Significance*. New York: Cambridge University Press.

McAdam, Doug, John D. McCarthy, and Mayer N. Zald (eds.). 1996. *Comparative Perspectives on Social Movements: Political Opportunities, Mobilizing Structure and Culture*. New York: Cambridge University Press.

McPhail, Clark and Ronald T. Wohlstein. 1983. "Individual and Collective Behaviors Within Gatherings, Demonstrations, and Riots." *Annual Review of Sociology* 9:579–600.

Mead, George Herbert. [1934] 1962. *Mind, Self, and Society*. Chicago, IL: University of Chicago Press.

Menard, Scott. 1991. *Longitudinal Research*. Newbury Park, CA: Sage.

Merton, Robert K. 1968. *Social Theory and Social Structure*. New York: Free Press.

Metcalfe, L. 2000. "Europe Integration and Globalization." *International Review of Administrative Sciences* 66:119–24.

Mielants, Eric. 2002. "Mass Migration in the World-System: An Antisystemic Movement in the Long Run?" Pp. 79–102 in *Global Processes, Power Relations, and Antisystemic Movements*, edited by Ramon Grosfoguel and Ana Margarita Cervantes-Rodriguez. London, UK: Praeger.

Mills, C. Wright. 1959. *The Sociological Imagination*. New York: Oxford University Press.

Mills, Kay. 1998. *Something Better for My Children: The History and People of Head Start*. New York: NAL/Dutton.

Mirowsky, John. 1985. "Depression and Marital Power: An Equity Model." *American Journal of Sociology* 91:557–92.

———. 1987. "The Psycho-Economies of feeling Underpaid: Distributive Justice and the Earnings of Husbands and Wives." *American Journal of Sociology* 92:1404–34.

———. 1999. "Subjective Life Expectancy in the U.S. Correspondence to Actual Estimates by Age, Sex, and Race." *Social Science and Medicine* 49:967–79.

Mirowsky, John and Catherine E. Ross. 1998. "Education, Personal Control, Lifestyle, and Health." *Research in Aging* 20:415–50.

National Center for Health Statistics. 1998. "Current Estimates from the National Health Interview Survey, U.S. 1995." *Vital and Health Statistics Series* 10, no. 1999. Hyattsville, MD: U.S. Public Health Service.

Nathan, Richard P. 1988. *Social Science in Government: Uses and Misuses*. New York: Basic Books.

Nelson, Margaret K. and Joan Smith. 1999. *Working Hard and Making Do: Surviving in Small Town America*. Berkeley, CA: University of California Press.

Newton, Rae R. and Kjell Erik Rudestam. 1999. *Your Statistical Consultant: Answers to Your Data Analysis Questions*. Thousand Oaks, CA: Sage.

Nolan, Patrick and Gerhard Lenski. 1999. *Human Societies: An Introduciton to Macrosociology*, 8th ed. New York: McGraw-Hill.

NORC. 2001. *General Social Surveys, 1972–2000. Cumulative Codebook*. Chicago, IL: National Opinion Research Center.

Ohnuki-Tierney, Emiko. 1997. "McDonald's in Japan: Changing Manners and Etiquette." Pp. 161–82 in *Golden Arches East: McDonald's in East Asia*, edited by James L. Watson. Stanford, CA: Stanford University Press.

Orenstein, Peggy. 1997. "Shortchanging girls: Gender Socialization in Schools." Pp. 43–52 in *Workplace/Women's Place: An Anthology*, edited by Dana Dunn. Los Angeles: Roxbury.

Osgood, D. Wayne, Janet K. Wilson Patrick M. O'Malley, Jerald G. Bachman and Lloyd D. Johnston. 1996. "Routine Activities and Individual Deviant Behavior." *American Sociological Review* 61:635–55.

Pakuksi, Jan. 1993. "Mass Social Movements and Social Class." *International Sociology*. 8:131–58.

Constance F. Citro and Robert T. Michael (eds.). 1995. *Measuring Poverty: A New Approach*. Washington, DC: National Academy Press.

Parisi, Domenico, Duane. A. Gill, and Michael Taquino. 2000. *Building Community Step by Step to Shoulder More Responsibility: A Procedure to Identify and Measure Community*. Social Science Research Center. Mississippi State, MS: Mississippi State University.

Park, Robert E. and Ernest W. Burgess. 1925. *The City: Suggestions for Investigations of Human Behavior in the Urban Environment*. Chicago, IL: University of Chicago Press.

Peacock, Mary. 2000. "The Cult of Thinness" http://www.womenswire.com/image/toothin.html June 13, 2000.

Perrow, Charles. 1999. *Normal Accidents: Living with High-Risk Technologies*. Princeton, NJ: Princeton University Press.

Portes, Alejandro. 1998. "Social Capital: Its Origins and Application in Modern Sociology." *Annual Review of Sociology* 24:1–24.

Powell, Gary N. (ed.). 1999. *Handbook of Gender and Work*. Thousand Oaks, CA: Sage.

Putnam, Robert D. 2000. *Bowling Alone: The Collapse and Revival of American Community*. New York: Simon and Schuster.

Quadagno, Jill. 1999. *Aging and the Life Course. An Introduction to Social Gerontology.* Boston, MA: McGraw Hill.

Ragin, Charles C. and Howard S. Becker. 1992. *What is a Case? Exploring the Foundations of Social Inquiry.* Cambridge, UK: Cambridge University Press.

Reskin, Barbara and Irene Padvic. 1994. *Women and Men at Work.* Thousand Oak, CA: Pine Forge Press.

Ritzer, George. 1995. *Expressing America: A Critique of the Global Credit Society.* Thousand Oaks, CA: Pine Forge Press.

———. 1998. *The McDonaldization Thesis: Explorations and Extensions.* Thousand Oaks, CA: Sage.

———. 2000. *Sociological Theory*, 5th ed. New York: McGraw-Hill Higher Education.

Robert, Stephanie A. 1999. "Socioeconomic Position and Health: The Independent Contribution of Community Socioeconomic Context." *Annual Review of Sociology* 25:489–516.

Robertson, Roland. 1992. *Globalization.* Newbury Park, CA: Sage.

Robinson, John P. and Geoffrey Godbey. 1997. *Time for Life: The Surprising Ways Americans Use Their Time.* University Park, PA: Penn State Press.

Robinson, Thomas N., Marta L. Wilde, Lisa C. Navracruz, K. Farish Haydel, and Ann Varady. 2001. "Effects of Reducing Children's Television and Videos Game Use on Aggressive Behavior." *Archives of Pediatric and Adolescent Medicine* 155:17–23.

Rodgers, Harrell R. 2000. *American Poverty in a New Era of Reform.* Armonk, NY: M.E.Sharpe.

Rodin, Mari, Michael Downs, John Petterson, and John Russell. 1997. Pp. 193–205 in *The Exxon Valdez Disaster: Readings on a Modern Social Problem*, edited by J.S. Picou, D.A. Gill and M.J. Cohen. Dubuque, IA: Kendall/Hunt Publishing Company.

Rosenfeld, Rachel A. 1992. "Job Mobility and Career Processes." *Annual Review of Sociology* 18:39–61.

Ross, Catherine E. and John Mirowsky. 2000. "Does Medical Insurance Contribute to Socioeconomic Differentials in Health." *The Milbank Quarterly* 78:291–321.

Ross, Catherine E., John Mirowsky, and John Huber. 1983. "Dividing Work, Sharing Work, and In-Between: Marriage Patterns and Depression." *American Sociological Review* 48:809–23.

Ross, Catherine E. and Chia-Ling Wu. 1995. "The Links Between Education and Health." *American Sociological Review* 60:719–45.

Rossi, Peter H. and Katharine C. Lyall. 1976. *Reforming Public Welfare: A Critique of the Negative Income Tax Experiment.* New York: Russell Sage Foundation.

Rowe, John Wallis. And Robert L Kahn. 1998. *Successful Aging* New York: Pantheon Books.

Rubin, Beth A., James D. Wright, and Joel A. Devine. 1992. "Unhousing the Urban Poor: The Reagan Legacy." *Journal of Sociology and Social Welfare* 19(1):111–47.

Rubin, Jeffrey Z., Frank J. Provenzano and Zella Luria. 1974. "The Eyes of the Beholder: Parents' Views on Sex of Newborns." *American Journal of Orthopsychiatry* 44:512–19.

Rudwick, Elliot M. 1996. *Race Riot At East St. Louis, July 2, 1917.* Cleveland, OH: Meridian Books.

Rural Sociological Society Task Force on Persistent Rural Poverty. 1993. *Persistent Poverty in Rural America.* Boulder, CO: Westview.

Schaefer, Richard T. 2001. *Sociology*, 7th ed. New York: McGraw Hill.

Schnitzer, Martin C. 2000. *Comparative Economic System*, 8th ed. Cincinnati, OH: Southwestern College Publishing.

Schutt, Russell. 1999. *Investigating the Social World.* Thousand Oaks, CA: Sage.

Schwartzman, Kathleen C. 1998. "Globalization and Democracy." *Annual Review of Sociology* 24:159–81.

Sears, David O., Jim Sidanios, and Lawrence Bobo, eds. 2000. *Racial Politics.* Chicago: University of Chicago Press.

Secombe, Karen and Cheryl Amey. 1995. "Playing by the Rules and Losing Health Insurance and the Working Poor." *Journal of Health and Social Behavior* 36:168–81.

Serbin, Lisa and Daniel O'Leary. 1975. "How Nursery Schools Teach Girls to Shut Up." *Psychology Today* 9(7):56–58, 102–03.

Servon, Lisa J. and Marla K. Nelson. 2001. "Community Technology Centers: Narrowing the Digital Divide in Low-Income, Urban Communities." *Journal of Urban Affairs* 23(3–4):279–90.

Shapiro, Joseph D. 1993. *No Pity: People with Disabilities Forging a New Civil Rights Movement.* New York: Random House.

Shepard, Jon M. 2002. *Sociology*, 8th ed. Belmont, CA: Wadsworth-Thomas Learning.

Skocpol, Theda. 1995. *Social Policy in the United States.* Princeton, NJ: Princeton University Press.

Smelser, Neil J. 1962. *Theory of Collective Behavior*. New York: Free Press.

Smith, D. Clayton, James W. Grimm, and Zachary W. Brewster. 2002. "Managed Health Insurance Effects Physical and Emotional Well-Being." Under Review by *Sociological Inquiry*.

Sorokin, Pitirim A. [1937] 1985. *Social and Cultural Dynamics*. New York: Porter Sargent Publishing.

Snizek, William E. and Jospeh J. Kestel. 1999. "Understanding and Preventing the Premature Exodus of Mature Middle Managers from Today's Corporations." *Organization Development Journal* 10:63–71.

Stone, R., G.L. Cafferata and J. Sangl. 1987. "Caregivers of the Frail Elderly: A National Profile." *The Gerontologist* 27:616–26.

Strauss, 1980. "A Sociological Perspective on the Causes of Family Violence." Pp. 7–31 in *Violence and the Family*, edited by Maurice R. Green. Boulder, CO: Westview.

Sutherland, Edwin H. 1990. "White Collar Criminality." *American Sociological Review* 5:1–12.

Sutherland, Edwin H. and Donald R. Cressey. 1992. *Principles of Criminology*, 11th ed. Dix Hills, NY: General Hall.

Suttles, Gerald D. 1972. *The Social Construction of Communities*. Chicago: University of Chicago Press.

Taylor, Marylee C. 1995. "White Backlash to Workshop Affirmative Action: Peril or Myth?" *Social Forces* 73:1385–414.

Tarrow, Sidney. 1994. *Social Movements, Collective Action and Politics*. New York: Cambridge University Press.

Thornborrow, Nancy M. and Marianne B. Sheldon. 1995. "Women in the Labor Force." Pp. 197–219 in *Women: A Feminist Perspective*, edited by Jo Freeman. Mountain View, CA: Mayfield Publishing Co.

Thompson, William E. and Joseph V. Hickey. 2002. *Society in Focus*, 4th ed. Boston, MA: Allyn and Bacon.

Thompson, T.C. and E. Zerbinos. 1995. "Gender Roles in Animated Cartoons: Has the Picture Changed in 20 years?" *Sex Roles* 32:681–73.

Tilly, Chris and Charles Tilly. 1998. *Work Under Capitalism*. Boulder, CO: Westview.

Tinder, Glenn. 1980. *Community: Reflections on a Tragic Ideal*. Baton Rouge, LA: Louisiana State University Press.

Tomaskovic-Devey, Donald. 1993. *Gender and Racial Inequality at Work*. Ithaca, NY: Industrial Relations Review Press.

Trueba, Enrique T. 1999. *Latinos Unidos: From Cultural Diversity to the Politics of Solidarity*. Lanham, MA: Rowman and Littlefield.

Turner, Ralph H. and Lewis M. Killian. 1993. *Collective Behavior*, 4th ed. Englewood Cliffs, NJ: Prentice Hall.

U.S. Congressional Budget Office. 1988. *Older Americans Reports*. Washington DC: April 29, 1988.

U.S. Bureau of the Census. 1993. *Historical Statistics of the United States*. Washington DC: U.S. Government Printing Office.

———. 2001. *Historical Income Tables: People, Table P–10* Online at http://www.census.gov/hhes/income/histinc/.

Voth, Donald E., Molly Sizer, and Frank L. Farmer. 1996. "Patterns of In-Migration and Out-Migration: Human Capital Movements in the Lower Mississippi Delta Region." *Southern Rural Sociology* 12(1):61–91.

Walder, Andrew G. 1995. "Local Government as Industrial Firms: An Organizational Analysis of China's Transitional Economy." *American Journal of Sociology* 101:263–301.

Wallerstein, Immanuel. 1974. *The Modern World-System*. New York: Academic Press.

———. 1979. *The Capitalist World-Economy*. New York: Cambridge University Press.

———. 1984. *The Politics of the World Economy: The State, the Movements, and the Civilizations*. New York: Cambridge University Press.

Walsh, Diana Chopman, Glorian Sorensen and Lori Leonard. 1995. "Gender, Health, and Cigarette Smoking." Pp. 131–171 in *Society and Health*, edited by B. Amick, S. Levine, A. Tarlor, and D. Walsh. New York: Oxford University Press.

Walters, Malcolm. 1995. *Globalization*. New York: Routledge.

Walton, John and Charles Rogin. 1990. "Global and National Sources of Political Protest: Third World Responses to the Draft Crisis." *American Journal of Sociology* 98:1044–93.

Wanner, Richard A. 1986. "Class." Pp. 46–48 in *The Encyclopedic Dictionary of Sociology*, 3rd ed. Guilford, CN: Dushkin.

Weber, Robert Phillip. 1990. *Basic Content Analysis*. Newburg Park, CA: Sage.

Weber, Max. [1904] 1958. *The Protestant Ethic and The Spirit of Capitalism*. New York: Charles Scribner's Sons.

Weber, Max. [1921] 1978. *Economy and Society*. Berkeley, CA: University of California Press.

Weeks, John R. 1999. *Population*, 7th ed. Belmont, CA: Wadsworth.

Weitz, Rose. 2001. *The Sociology of Health Illness and Health Care: A Critical Approach*, 2nd ed. Belmont, CA: Wadsworth / Thomson Learning.

Wellman, Barry and Kenneth A. Frank. 2001. "Network Capital in the Multilevel World: Getting Support from Personal Communities." Pp. 233–37 in *Social Capital: Theory and Reseach*, edited by Nan Lin, Karen Cook and Ronald S. Burt. New York: Aldine De Gruyter.

Wellman, Barry and Barry Leighton. 1979. "Networks, Neighborhoods, and Communities: Approaches to the Study of the Community Question." *Urban Affairs Quarterly* 14(3):363–90.

Western, Bruce. 1997. *Between Class and Market: Postwar Variation in the Capitalists Democracies*. Princeton, NJ: Princeton University Press.

White, Lynn. 1972. *Medieval Technology and Social Change*. New York: Oxford University Press.

Whiting, Larry R. (ed.). 1974. *Communities Left Behind: Alternatives for Development*. Ames: Iowa State University Press.

Wilkinson, Kenneth P. 1991. *The Community in Rural America*. Middleton, WI: Social Ecology Press.

Wilson, William Julius. 1987. *The Truly Disadvantaged: The Inner City, The Underclass, and Public Policy*. Chicago: University of Chicago Press.

———. 1996. *When Work Disappears: The World of the New Urban Poor*. New York: Alfred A Knopf.

Will, Jerrie., Patricia Self and Nancy Datan. 1976. "Maternal Behavior and Perceived Sex of Infant." *American Journal of Orthopsychiatry* 46:135–39.

Wuthnow, Robert. 1998. *Loose Connections: Joining Together in America's Fragmented Communities*. Cambridge, MA: Harvard University Press.

Wynn, Victor T. 2001. *Shifting Class Structures: Assessing the Dynamic Nature of Class and Class Resources as the Postindustrial Economy Evolves*. Unpublished Dissertation. Iowa City, IA: University of Iowa.

Yan, Yunxiang. 1997. "McDonald's in Beijing: The Localization of America." Pp. 39–76 in *Golden Arches East: McDonald's in East Asia*, edited by James L. Watson. Stanford, CA: Stanford University Press.

Young, T.R. 1988. "Class Warfare in the 80s and 90s: Reaganomics and Social Justice." *Wisconsin Sociologist* 25(2–3):68–75.

Zekeri, Andrew A., Kenneth P. Wilkinson, and Craig R. Humphrey. 1994. "Past Activeness, Solidarity, and Local Development Efforts." *Rural Sociology* 59:216–35.

Zimmerman, Julie N., Deb Kershaw, and Lori Garkovich. 2000. *It's Not Just The Numbers: A Monthly Budget Case Study Update*. Social and Economic Education for Development. Lexington, KY: University of Kentucky, College of Agriculture.

Index